Doug Welsh's
Texas Garden Almanac

Doug Welsh's TEXAS GARDEN ALMANAC

Illustrated by Aletha St. Romain

Texas A&M University Press   College Station

The paper used in this book
meets the minimum requirements
of the American National Standard
for Permanence of Paper
for Printed Library Materials,
Z39.48-1984.
Binding materials have been
chosen for durability.

LIBRARY OF CONGRESS
CATALOGING-IN-PUBLICATION DATA

Welsh, Douglas F.
    Doug Welsh's Texas garden almanac / Doug Welsh ; illus-
trated by Aletha St. Romain. —1st ed.
        p. cm.
Includes index.
ISBN-13: 978-1-58544-619-3 (flexbound : alk. paper)
ISBN-10: 1-58544-619-X (flexbound : alk. paper)
1. Gardening—Texas.   2. Almanacs, American—
Texas.   I. Title.
SB453.2.T4W45   2007
635.09764—dc22   2007007634

To my wife,

Laura,

for her loving support,

counsel & encouragement

Contents

Select Plant Lists

Almanac at a Glance

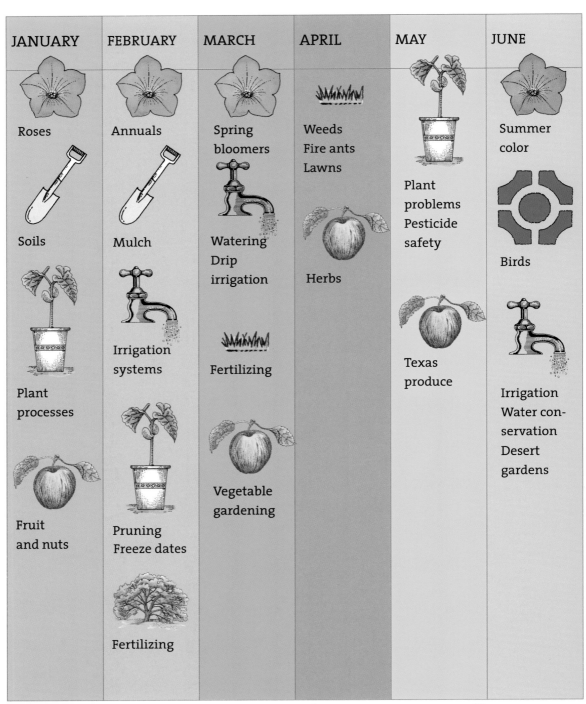

JANUARY	FEBRUARY	MARCH	APRIL	MAY	JUNE
Roses	Annuals	Spring bloomers	Weeds Fire ants Lawns	Plant problems Pesticide safety	Summer color
Soils	Mulch	Watering Drip irrigation	Herbs		Birds
Plant processes	Irrigation systems	Fertilizing		Texas produce	Irrigation Water conservation Desert gardens
Fruit and nuts	Pruning Freeze dates Fertilizing	Vegetable gardening			

KEY: Flowers and pretty plants; Garden design; Soil and mulch; Water; Plant care;

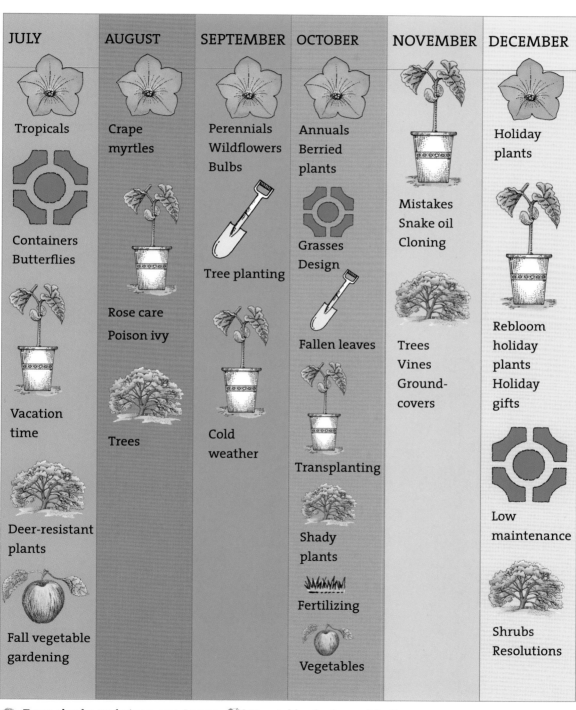

JULY	AUGUST	SEPTEMBER	OCTOBER	NOVEMBER	DECEMBER

JULY
Tropicals
Containers
Butterflies
Vacation time
Deer-resistant plants
Fall vegetable gardening

AUGUST
Crape myrtles
Rose care
Poison ivy
Trees

SEPTEMBER
Perennials
Wildflowers
Bulbs
Tree planting
Cold weather

OCTOBER
Annuals
Berried plants
Grasses
Design
Fallen leaves
Transplanting
Shady plants
Fertilizing
Vegetables

NOVEMBER
Mistakes
Snake oil
Cloning
Trees
Vines
Ground-covers

DECEMBER
Holiday plants
Rebloom holiday plants
Holiday gifts
Low maintenance
Shrubs
Resolutions

Trees, shrubs, and vines; Lawns; Vegetables, herbs, and fruits

Introduction

I AM BLESSED that my vocation and avocation are the same—gardening. For over three decades, I have studied horticulture. I have never gotten tired of it and continue to learn daily. Over the past 28 years as a garden educator in Texas, I have written thousands of gardening fact sheets, publications, and news columns. I have also produced more than a thousand garden segments for television and have fielded tens of thousands of gardening questions in person, on the telephone, and during call-in radio shows. I discovered that if I knew as much as I could about the "Three Ts"— trees, turf, and tomatoes—I was able to answer most questions correctly.

Through the years, I have pursued, researched, or learned by experience the answers to all kinds of gardening questions. If I don't have the answer, I am fortunate to have extension, research, and teaching colleagues at Texas A&M University to call upon to get one that is accurate and thorough. Through them, I not only find out what to do in the garden but also try to understand the hows and whys to help others (and me) do the best possible job in the garden with the best possible outcome.

With this background and philosophy, I wrote this book to put to paper the vast majority of gardening knowledge I have gained and shared over the years, giving us both a handy one-stop reference. After having written, edited, compiled, and resurrected the information to produce the essays, information boxes, lists, charts, and tips in this book, I assure you I will not walk into a radio studio or sit at my desk without the book being close at hand.

If you are a gardener, I hope this almanac provides in-depth answers to all your gardening questions not only by telling you what to do and how to do it but also by explaining why. I hope it gives you information that you need to manage your garden and to help others manage theirs. For you "yardeners" (a term popularized by garden book author Jeff Ball to describe homeowners who simply want to take care of their yards properly with the least amount of time and effort), this almanac is meant to inspire, invoke a call to action, and help you overcome the fear of the unknown in gardening. Follow the advice in the essays to make your gardening experiences easier, more successful, and more fun. Who knows? You may become a gardener!

How to Use This Book

Think of this almanac as a giant garden calendar, packed full of information month by month. Within each month you will find essays, information boxes, plant lists, charts, and questions and answers covering garden topics that com-

monly arise in that month. Each month's essays are arranged in the same order by topic, although every month might not cover every topic.

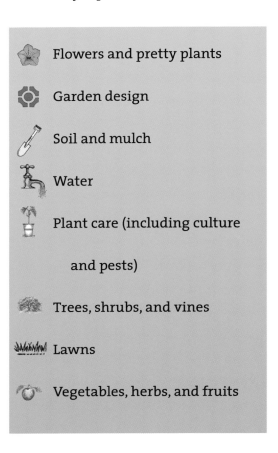

Flowers and pretty plants

Garden design

Soil and mulch

Water

Plant care (including culture

and pests)

Trees, shrubs, and vines

Lawns

Vegetables, herbs, and fruits

At the end of each month are Timely Tips, designed to help you quickly identify what garden activities you should be doing each month.

To help you navigate through the book and find the information you want, you can refer to these sections:

- Table of Contents at the beginning of the book
- "Almanac at a Glance"—a two-page calendar year with topic icons keyed to essay subjects
- First page for each month, which has a "mini" table of contents for that month
- Cross-references within essays directing you to more in-depth, related information
- Index at the end of the book

This is a big book made to be consumed in small bites (or all at once by some of you speed readers). It is intended to be fun, not intimidating. I hope you go back to it repeatedly throughout the year and for years to come as your most reliable gardening reference.

January

'Old Blush' China rose

HEADING TOWARD SPRING

Roses in the Landscape

Roses are the "Queen of Flowers" and have been cultivated for thousands of years. However, the use of roses in the landscape has undergone a tremendous transformation in the past 20 years. Once thought of primarily in terms of the formal rose garden, roses are now incorporated into the landscape, replacing the drab, green "meatball- or meatloaf-shaped" evergreen shrubs (e.g., Burford holly, ligustrum, pittosporum).

Whether you are planting your first rose or want your established roses to perform better, follow these six basic steps to rose gardening:

1. Plant selection
2. Site selection
3. Soil preparation and planting
4. Insect and disease management
5. Pruning
6. Long-term care

Step 1: Plant Selection

When deciding which of the literally thousands of rose varieties to plant, you have more than just a *color* decision; you also have a *type* decision.

The modern hybrid rose is the rose that first comes to mind for most people: a long-stemmed red rose on a stiff, upright bush with lots of thorns. Modern hybrid roses include the following types:

Hybrid tea—romantic, long-stemmed blooms in vibrant colors; formal, upright shrubs; 4 to 5 feet

Floribunda—clusters of small flowers; shrublike growth habit; 3 to 4 feet

Grandiflora—a cross between hybrid tea and floribunda, with flowers similar to the tea rose but smaller and clustered; 5- to 6-foot shrub

Other common rose types, including miniatures, climbers, and tree form

The challenge to growing the vast majority of modern hybrid roses is that they are not adapted to many parts of Texas or even our entire state. You must know whether a variety is adapted to your area. Can it withstand common Texas weather conditions, such as hot summers, cold winters, varying rainfall, or high humidity? Can it adapt to the alkaline soil and water prevalent in much of Central and West Texas? Lack of adaptation kills more roses than does lack of proper care. To find a list of adapted varieties, turn to your local experts, such as local nursery professionals, county extension agents, or Master Gardeners. Visit an area botanical garden. You could even contact the American Rose Society via the Internet for their help in identifying varieties suitable to your area.

The list of modern hybrid roses to follow contains varieties that will increase your success with roses in Texas. (*Note:* I have successfully grown over half of them in my gardens through the years in multiple Texas cities and have observed the rest performing beautifully in botanical gardens and landscapes across the state.)

Start small by growing a few modern hybrid roses in a bed before you head off to build a formal rose garden. You can plant a modern hybrid rose or two into your existing landscape to provide a splash of season-long color.

Old-fashioned roses (often called heritage roses, old garden roses, or antique roses) are rose species or varieties characterized by clusters of softer-colored flowers on robust, well-shaped shrubs. Vibrant, in-your-face colors on rigid plants they are not. These roses are, in general, lower maintenance, longer blooming, hardier, more pest resistant, and more befitting of most Texas landscapes. The renewed interest in old-fashioned roses is fueled by the fact that

'Mr. Lincoln' modern hybrid tea rose, All American Rose Selection 1965

they require less care than modern hybrid roses and are more adapted to our often harsh Texas climate and soil conditions.

For hundreds of years these roses have been passed from generation to generation. Now these varieties are available in quantities. They are truly "living antiques," having been propagated by cuttings from original plants developed over 100 years ago. These living antiques are time-tested for success—they are known for their toughness and ability to withstand adverse growing conditions. Old-fashioned roses have a variety of growth habits and sizes. Most varieties are quite fragrant and bloom generally in clusters in colors varying from red to deep rose to pastels of pink and yellows to white. They are among the most versatile plants for any landscape.

Based on their origin, characteristics, and lineage, old-fashioned roses are categorized into several classes:

- Bourbon
- China
- Hybrid musk
- Hybrid perpetual
- Noisette
- Polyantha
- Rugosa
- Tea

There are thousands of varieties of old-fashioned roses. Confusion over selection can set in quickly, so check with your local experts for variety recommendations. The table on page 10 contains some of the most widely adapted old-fashioned roses for Texas. (*Note:* I have grown all of these in my gardens and can attest to their toughness and beauty.)

Not to confuse you too much, but there are now newer rose varieties that look like old-fashioned roses. David Austin, Griffith Buck, Robert Bayse and David Byrne from Texas A&M University, and other rose breeders have developed varieties to meet the need for durable, beautiful, old-fashioned-style shrub roses for the landscape. In 1988, William Raddler bred a rose variety that hit the market in the late 1990s and is now perhaps the most prolific-selling new, old-style landscape rose ever, the 'Knock Out' rose.

'Old Blush' China rose, living antique from 1752

In recent years, an exciting effort to identify the toughest-of-the-tough roses for Texas landscapes was initiated by extension horticulturists and county extension agents from Texas A&M University. The program tests all types of roses under grueling conditions. The selection criteria identify roses that are widely adapted throughout Texas that need no spraying, minimal watering, and little pruning, yet bloom beautifully on handsome shrubs. Roses that make the cut are designated as Earth-Kind roses and are labeled as such in local nurseries and garden centers.

If your goal is to have roses blooming in your landscape virtually all season for both cut flowers and landscape flowers, you would be wise to plant a combination of modern hybrid roses; old-fashioned roses; and new, old-style roses.

MORE THAN A DOZEN MODERN HYBRID ROSES

Hybrid tea
Double Delight (red and white)
Mr. Lincoln (red, fragrant)
Olympiad (red, not fragrant)
Peace (yellow)
Sterling Silver (lavender)

Floribunda
Betty Prior (pink)
Europeana (red)
Iceberg (white)
Sun Flare (yellow)

Grandiflora
Gold Medal (yellow)
Queen Elizabeth (pink)
Tournament of Roses (pink)

Climbers
Altissimo (red)
Climbing Peace (yellow)
Don Juan (red)
Dortmond (red)

NOTE: New varieties hit the market each year, so check with experts for the plants' adaptability to your area.

Step 2: Site Selection

Site selection requires only a few guidelines, but they are critical:

- Provide roses at least 6 hours of sunlight per day for maximum performance.
- Choose an east-facing site if possible. The morning sun will dry the foliage quickly, which reduces pest problems.
- Select a site that receives gentle breezes, providing air circulation to reduce insect and disease pressure.

Step 3: Soil Preparation and Planting

Expend the money and the effort to prepare the soil for roses. It is dirty work but a critical investment that will pay off.

More Than a Dozen Old-Fashioned Roses

Variety	Date introduced	Flower color	Notes
Belinda's Dream	1992	dark pink	upright shrub; a Bayse rose with characteristics of both a modern hybrid and old-fashioned rose; fragrant
Caldwell Pink	unknown	lilac-pink	a found rose with unknown origin; everblooming compact shrub filled with flower clusters
Carefree Beauty (Katy Road Pink)	1977	deep pink	a Buck rose that looks old-fashioned
Cecile Brunner or The Sweetheart Rose	1881	pink	everblooming compact shrub for border or mass planting; also available in a climbing form
Cramoisi Superieur	1832	red	everblooming medium shrub; excellent for a border hedge or mass planting; also available in a climbing form
Knock Out (Radrazz)	1988	cherry red	everblooming rounded shrub; also available in pink, pink with a yellow center, and double bloom forms
La Marne	1915	pink	everblooming medium shrub; makes a nice hedge
Lady Banksia	1807 (yellow); 1824 (white)	yellow; white	spring blooming; huge climbing rose
Marie Daly	1999	pink	a pink-flowered mutation of 'Marie Pavie'; fragrant
Marie Pavie	1888	white with pink blush	everblooming medium shrub; great as hedge or mass planting; fragrant
Mrs. B. R. Cant	1901	silver rose	fat, full flowers; very large shrub; 6 to 7 feet; steady bloomer; excellent cut flower; fragrant
Mutabilis or Butterfly Rose	1894	multicolored based on age of bloom; yellow through orange to pink to crimson	very large, robust shrub; also available in a climbing form
Old Blush	1752	pink	everblooming large shrub useful as a hedge or an accent plant

- Create a raised bed of well-drained, highly-organic soil, at least 10 inches tall. The bed can be edged with masonry, rock, or timbers or simply crested toward the middle of the bed.
- Prepare the soil using organic matter, such as compost, manure, and/or shredded bark. The goal is to create a soil mixture of half organic matter and half existing or trucked-in topsoil; a soil test can be helpful in creating the perfect soil for your roses.
- Don't plant too deep—dig the hole only as deep as the root system is tall. If soil preparation has been done well, digging the hole can be done with your hands. The top of the root-ball should be at the same level as it was grown in the field or the pot. If there is a graft union (on most modern hybrid roses, the swollen area at the junction of the roots and trunk), it should be 2 inches above ground level in most of Texas, and 2 inches below ground level in far North Texas where soils may freeze.
- Plant roses almost year-round, depending on how they are sold and purchased. Modern hybrid roses are most often sold as "packaged" roses in nurseries during midwinter. The plants are dormant and look lifeless, yet they can be planted in January or February throughout Texas and will bloom by late spring. Old-fashioned and old-style shrub roses are most of-ten grown in nursery containers and can be purchased year-round; however, summertime planting should be avoided if possible. If purchased through mail-order catalogues, the plants would be shipped like packaged roses in midwinter.

Step 4: Insect and Disease Management

Beyond selecting adapted rose varieties, the most important prevention of pest problems is your presence in the garden. Get out in the garden, and look for abnormal leaves, stems, or flowers, which may indicate insect or disease problems.

- Identify the pest problem first before you treat! Get help from the local nursery or county extension office.
- Remember that a few insects or spots on your roses may not pose a big enough problem to warrant spraying a pesticide. Healthy plants, natural predators, and the environment can prevent most pests from becoming a major problem.
- Use the least toxic pesticide that is effective if you use a pesticide.
- Always read the pesticide label, and use caution when using any pesticide (chemical or organic).
- Spray pesticides from the bottom up on the plant, coating the underside of the leaves thoroughly.

- Prevent pests by using proper sanitation. Pick diseased, damaged, and dead leaves and twigs off the plants and off the ground, and throw them away.

INSECT PROBLEMS

Look for tiny insects like thrips, aphids, and spider mites. Use the direct method of inspection—look at the tops and bottoms of the leaves. Also, check for pest presence by shaking leaves over a white sheet of paper, and look closely—thrips are cigar-shaped walking dashes; aphids are globular, fat, and shiny; and mites are tiny reddish dots that move.

Look at the plant also for indications of insect infestations:

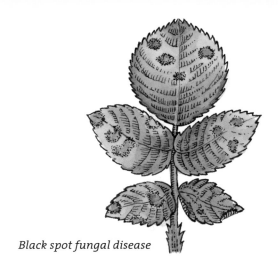

Black spot fungal disease

- If blooms are brown, are deformed, or won't open, break them open and check for thrips.
- If new growth is yellow or covered with shiny honeydew or black sooty mold, check under leaves and on stems for aphids.
- If leaves are puckered or have a bronze sheen or tiny, white spots, check for spider mites underneath the leaves.
- If leaves and blooms are chewed, check for caterpillars and beetles.

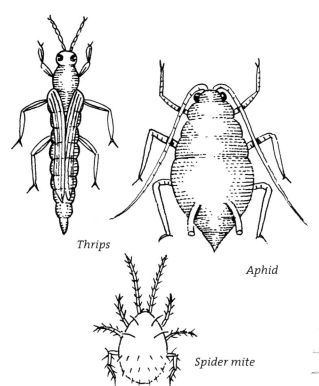

Thrips

Aphid

Spider mite

If an insecticide is warranted, spray with the least toxic insecticide that is effective—common chemical insecticides are acephate, carbaryl, delemethrin, imadichlorprid, malathion, and permethrin; alternative, less-toxic insecticides include insecticidal soaps, neem oil, pyrethrin, and high-pressure water sprays.

DISEASE PROBLEMS

Yellowing leaves with black spots indicate the presence of the fungus black spot. This disease can spread rapidly by water splashing from one leaf to another, usually during irrigation or rain. Try to water the soil without hitting the leaves.

A whitish, powdery covering on leaves, stems, or blooms indicates the presence of the fungus powdery mildew. This disease spreads rapidly when temperatures are above 80°F and humidity is high. Splashing water does not spread this disease.

Commonly used, effective fungicides for roses include Bayleton, captan, Daconil, Dithan, Funginex, and neem oil. Fungicides often require repeated applications if weather and plant conditions are conducive to further spread of the disease.

Powdery mildew fungal disease

Step 5: Pruning

There is no big mystery about how to prune roses. For modern hybrid roses, prune heavily each year 2 to 3 weeks before spring growth begins (about February 14 for much of the state). The goal is to prune each bush back to a height of 18 to 24 inches, having only four to six main stems (canes), each facing outward in a different direction so they form a vase shape. Visualize creating an umbrella turned inside out.

Old-fashioned and old-style shrub roses should simply be pruned to fit the landscape setting, seldom pruning off more than one-third of a plant's height. Use of hedge clippers to prune old-fashioned roses works well.

For spring-blooming climbing roses, prune immediately after they bloom and then only remove dead or damaged canes, plus one or two of the oldest canes to promote new cane growth.

For all types of roses, prune to maintain blooming and health:

- Remove old blooms (deadhead) as they fade to encourage increased flowering.
- Prune off bad parts (damaged, diseased, or dead leaves, twigs, and blooms) to encourage new, healthier growth.
- Pull off heavily infested or damaged leaves resulting from black spot

Deadheading (removing old blooms) is essential to encourage continued blooming.

or insects to curtail current and future disease and insect populations.

Step 6: Long-Term Care

Roses are blooming machines if given the nutrient energy from fertilizers. Fertilizer types include slow-release, granular forms; water-soluble forms (diluted and poured onto the soil); and organic fertilizers, such as blood meal.

At a minimum, fertilize once in the spring and again in the fall. For maximum performance, fertilize every month using predominantly nitrogen fertilizers.

In general, roses require more water than most shrubs but less than most flowers and lawns. Water only when the soil is dry a few inches under the surface of the soil. Use your index finger as your soil moisture meter. If the soil is cool to the touch, there is ample moisture. If it is the same temperature as the air or talcum-powder dry, water. Apply 2 to 3 gallons of water per plant, keeping the water off the leaves and blooms to prevent disease.

For gardens receiving less than 35 inches of rainfall per year, drip irrigation will make watering easier and more efficient. Check with your local nursery professional or irrigation contractor for help in setting up a drip irrigation system. Refer also to the March essay "Saving Water Drip by Drip."

Mulch is a final, but important addition to rose gardening. It provides major benefits, including reducing disease, conserving water, reducing weeds, and keeping soil temperatures cooler in the summer and warmer in the winter. Mulch with organic products, such as pine bark, cypress bark, and compost. Apply a 2- to 3-inch layer of mulch every spring and perhaps again in the fall.

Soils 101 for the Garden

The best gardeners acknowledge that soil is the biggest limiting factor in successful gardening. It can make or break not only your garden but your garden spirit. You MUST know your soil. A good garden soil results in healthy root systems, which result in healthy, beautiful, productive plants. Working the soil is the hardest task in the garden, but soil preparation is imperative and must be done properly.

First, understand that few yards and landscapes have undisturbed native soil in them. Through the homebuilding process, most native soil is disturbed, the topsoil is scraped off, and the underlying poorer-quality subsoil is exposed. Trenching for multiple utility lines (e.g., water, sewer, cable, electric, gas) churns up the subsoil to the surface. Dozens of trucks used to bring building materials to the site also compact the soil. Post-construction, a thin layer of "topsoil" is usually brought in and placed on top of the compacted soil to smooth out the terrain. This becomes the soil you will contend with in your lawn, landscape, and garden.

A second observation worth noting is that the "best" soils in a city are generally in the city center. Think about it: Where would you have built a city over a hundred years ago? The pioneers erected towns on good soils where water was readily available. For example, San Antonio was built on rich, alluvial (river-deposited) soils next to the San Antonio River—same for Houston, Austin, Dallas, and El Paso, and the list goes on. Visit older neighborhoods near the city center of your town, and look at the quality, diversity, and size of the plants in the landscapes. As the town expands, the soils generally become less desirable. Building in the Hill Country on the outskirts of San Antonio, Austin, and Waco may provide natural beauty and spectacular vistas, but the soil is a huge challenge.

Three basic soil characteristics are of primary importance in managing your landscape: soil texture, soil pH, and percent organic matter. There are three ways to find out what these soil characteristics are in your yard:

- Have a soil test done by the Soils, Water, and Forage Testing Laboratory at Texas A&M University (Room 345 Heep Center, Mail Stop 2474, College Station, TX 77843-2474; telephone: 979-845-4816; http://soiltesting.tamu .edu/). Cost is less than $50 and varies depending on analysis. Sample bags can also be obtained from your local county extension office.

- Contact your county extension agent, and simply ask what your soil characteristics are likely to be. The agent has seen dozens of county soil test results and can accurately describe your soil for gardening purposes. Local nursery professionals can also be a source for this information.

- Follow the basic information below to characterize your soil yourself, and understand the impact soil has on your gardening success.

Soil texture (or type) is determined by the relative amounts of different-sized soil particles. These particles range from coarse-textured sand to fine-textured silt to even finer-textured clay. If these particles are mixed naturally in somewhat equal proportions, the result is the preferred soil texture called loam. Forget it; large areas of loam seldom exist naturally in Texas, much less in the disturbed soil environment of your landscape.

Most natural soils in Texas have textures predominated by sand or clay. Some loamy sands or clay loams exist, and occasionally you may find the "Holy Grail," a natural sandy loam that contains sufficient silt and clay particles in the sand to hold moisture yet provide sufficient air space and drainage, which is great for plant growth and health.

The topsoil marketed as "sandy loam" is not a real sandy loam. Rather, it is often more of a sand or sandy clay, quarried from a riverbed or sandpit. It generally drains like a sieve and then sets up a surface crust that is as hard as rock.

With some experience, you can estimate soil texture by grabbing a handful of moist soil and working or squeezing it out of your hand between your thumb and index finger (much like the hand movement of shelling out coins to a clerk or your children). You know the rough, gritty feel of sand. Clay feels like molding clay. Silt feels more like talcum powder, flour, or graphite. By feel you can determine the dominant soil particle in your soil—sand, clay, or silt. If you're really good, you can identify a loam by feel because of its combined textures of sand, clay, and silt.

In general, sandy soils predominate in East Texas and the Gulf Coast, with some oases of sandy soils spread around the state in areas around Bastrop, Mexia, Fredericksburg, and west of Fort Worth.

Sticky, gumbo clay and blackland clay dominate from Houston to Dallas, between IH-45 and IH-35. West of IH-35 and IH-37, you enter the challenging soils of West and South Texas, ranging from pockets of deep sand to heavy clay, to caliche rock and calcareous (calcium-rich, highly alkaline) soils, to sodic soils (salty). However, throughout the many river valleys of Texas exist some of the most wonderful soils—deep, fertile, fine-textured alluvial soils. Remember that these are generalizations; nature is much more random with soil placement.

The measure of the soil's acidity and alkalinity is noted by its pH, a logarithmic scale with 7 being neutral. Less than 7 is acidic, and higher than 7 is alkaline. In Texas, acidic soils are primarily found in the sandy soils of East Texas. The soil from Houston north to Dallas along IH-45 and west to almost IH-35 is neutral (7.0) to mildly alkaline (8.0). Virtually everything west, south, and along IH-35 and IH-37 is alkaline to highly alkaline

(8.0 to 8.5). However, there are pockets of sandy, more acidic soils even in North and West Texas (hope your garden is in one of them).

The soil pH is important because it determines the level of nutrient availability to plants. Nutrients are most readily available to plants in soils with a pH range of 6.0 to 7.0. Individual plant species have varying abilities to absorb nutrients from soils. Some do it easily, and some don't, especially in alkaline soils. This leads to classifying plants as "acid loving" or "alkaline tolerant." For example, azaleas are acid-loving plants and grow successfully in East Texas; however, azaleas don't grow well in Austin because the pH is high (alkaline). The vast majority of Texas soil is alkaline, which is a primary reason why the garden plants of the northeastern and southeastern United States do not grow well here.

It is important to note that the water in your area is likely the same pH as your soil, thus constantly diluting any efforts to change the soil pH.

Organic matter is the magic ingredient of good soil. Microorganisms break down organic matter—first into humus, then humic acid, and finally into basic chemical elements or nutrients. The microorganisms consume the nutrients for energy. These nutrients are then made available to plants as the microorganisms die. In a highly organic soil, billions of microorganisms are present, billions die, and plants pick up the nutrients. This "circle of life" continues as dead microorganisms, dead plant material, and additions of new organic matter maintain a food supply for the microorganisms.

Unfortunately, the percent organic matter in native Texas soil is zero, zip, nada. Texas soils have less than 1 percent organic matter. The primary reason is that it is so HOT here. The hotter the climate, the faster microorganisms consume any and all organic matter in the soil. Texas is not like, say, Michigan, where temperatures are milder, rainfall is more continuous, and organic matter is commonly four times as high in the native soils.

The amount of organic matter in soil can have an immediate effect on a soil's water-holding capacity (ability) and aeration (pore space). These characteristics are extremely important for garden soils, whether sugary sand or sticky clay. The addition of organic matter can almost double the water-holding capacity of sandy soils, reducing the need for and the frequency of watering. Water is held in the sandy soil by the water-absorbing organic matter.

In clay soils, water-holding capacity is not a limiting factor; lack of aeration is. The more pore space the soil has, the more oxygen is present, which increases root and plant health. Organic matter instantly creates pore space in clay soils by physically holding the clay apart, or dispersed.

Soils 201—Knowing Soils 101, What Do You Do?

Soil texture you cannot change, unless you are willing to pay the high price of bringing tons of sandy loam soil into your yard. You most likely have sandy or clayey soil with which to contend. Now you must amend that texture to build a productive garden soil for vegetable gardens, flower beds, and shrub plantings.

With regard to soil pH, you are better off simply living with what you have naturally. Changing the pH is difficult, especially if the soil is alkaline. The best strategy is to choose plants that can thrive and survive in the pH of your soils. For example, if you have acidic soil (low pH), you may choose American holly, azaleas, camellias, dogwood, eastern redbud, gardenias, hostas, loblolly pine, and southern magnolia. If you have alkaline soil (high pH), look to cedar elm, cenizo (Texas sage), desert willow, Mexican plum, Mexican and Texas redbuds, the native sages (autumn, mealy cup, Mexican), Texas mountain laurel, and vitex. There are a great number of plants, however, that are adapted to a wide range of pH levels, including crape myrtle, lantana, live oak, oleander, roses, verbena, water oak, wax myrtle, and yaupon holly.

Sometimes acidic soils can be too acidic (pH of less than 6.0) for many flowers and vegetable plants to grow vigorously. You can increase the pH of acidic soil by adding agricultural lime (calcium carbonate). Recommended application rates vary depending on the amount of increase in pH desired. Generally, rates do not exceed 5 pounds per 100 square feet.

Whatever soil texture or soil pH (and lack of organic matter) you have, adding organic matter when planting flower beds, vegetable gardens, and shrubs is the key component to creating a great garden soil. Focus your efforts on adding organic matter to your garden and landscape plantings.

Soils 301—So, How Do You Create a Great Garden Soil?

If you buy a flat of petunias and plant them in your existing soil with no soil preparation, you are only reinforcing the old nurseryman's motto, "We grow 'em; you kill 'em!"

The soil preparation recommendation that follows is strictly for creating flower beds, vegetable gardens, and shrub plantings. This recommendation is not followed for planting trees (covered in the September essay "Tree Planting Made Easy") or for establishing a lawn.

Creating a garden soil is physical work, and it costs money, but it is an investment that pays back huge dividends. Your landscape and garden will be healthy, productive, and beautiful and will require less maintenance because of the good soil.

The goal is simple: Create a garden soil with a minimum depth of 12 inches; deeper can be better but is more costly and not needed for most plantings. This 12-inch soil should be composed of 50 percent organic matter and 50 percent the soil in your yard, whatever it is.

To create 12 inches of good garden soil, put 6 inches of organic matter on the existing soil. The organic matter can be pine bark mulch, composted manure, composted cotton bur hulls, home compost, fallen leaves, or a combination thereof. Till or spade the 6 inches of organic matter into the top 8 to 10 inches of soil. This creates the 12-inch root zone for the plants. Ideally, the top 3 to 4 inches of the prepared soil will be higher than the existing grade of the soil around it. This adds a little extra drainage to the bed or planting.

If your soil is shallow and sitting on bedrock, you may have to bring in topsoil and add the organic matter to the topsoil to create the 12 inches of garden soil. Be careful buying topsoil. The fear is bringing topsoil in that has nutgrass (nut sedge) in it, which is one of the toughest weeds to eliminate from the

Prepare soils for garden beds by tilling 6 inches of organic matter (e.g., pine bark) into the top 8 to 10 inches of existing soil.

garden. Ask the topsoil supplier for references, and inspect the soil before it is dumped on you. If in doubt, buy topsoil in bags, since bagged soil is usually screened and nutgrass eliminated.

Add organic matter to your soil every time you replant annual and perennial flowers or vegetables or when you rework shrub plantings. You can't add too much organic matter.

Caution: Don't monkey with the soil too much. One gardener's goal was to create loam, the perfect soil. He mixed his heavy clay soil with coarse builder's sand. Then, to emulate the fine silt particles, he added coastal Bermudagrass hay. He tilled it all together, watered it, and three days later had the biggest adobe brick known to humans!

Thinking Like a Plant

Perhaps the greatest ability you can achieve in gardening is to think like a plant. If you can do so, then you can understand a plant's needs, anticipate and respond to them, and most important, avoid problems associated with not meeting the plant's needs. (*Note:* I know plants don't actually think. My botanist colleagues remind me of that all the time. But it is helpful for me to think like a plant—hopefully for you, too.)

Plants carry out three major processes in their physiological growth and development: photosynthesis, respiration, and transpiration. Below are an illustration and a table depicting products and by-products of these processes. Understand these processes, relate them to human processes, and you will think like a plant.

In addition to understanding these plant processes, it is important to understand how plants respond to environmental conditions (e.g., temperature, wind, light intensity, lack of nutrients). Again, these can be related to human responses to environmental conditions, and you will understand plants better.

Plants and people have differences and similarities. The biggest difference is that plants generate their own food through photosynthesis. They can literally turn energy from the sun, water from soil, and carbon dioxide from air into food (carbohydrates). Humans can't. Humans must eat food that is composed of plants or indirectly derived from plants; cattle eat plants and humans eat beef. Additionally, oxygen is a by-product of photosynthesis, and humans need lots of oxygen. Without plants, humans (and all animals) would not exist.

A second difference is that plants are terrestrial. Their roots are anchored in

PLANT PROCESSES: PHOTOSYNTHESIS, RESPIRATION, AND TRANSPIRATION

PLANT PROCESS	ACTION	RESULTS
Photosynthesis	sugar produced	food provided for plant oxygen released
Respiration	sugar broken down	energy produced for plant carbon dioxide released water released
Transpiration	water lost from leaves	plant cooled water and nutrients drawn from the soil into and throughout plant

the soil, and plants don't move around to get food. So everything they need to produce food for themselves must be

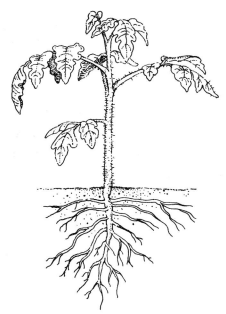

Plant leaves contain chlorophyll and water and absorb sunlight and carbon dioxide to produce sugar (food) through photosynthesis. Water evaporation from leaves, called transpiration, powers plant roots to take in and transport water to the leaves for photosynthesis and cooling. Plant sugars are converted to plant energy through respiration, which occurs in the leaves and roots.

present in their immediate locale. In contrast, humans (and cattle) can move around and find food to eat (e.g., cattle in a pasture or humans from one fast-food restaurant to another).

Both plants and humans can convert food into energy through the process of respiration. This energy is used for growth and development in plants. In humans, it is used for growth and movement (e.g., working, playing, walking, eating). If humans eat more food than can be respired for energy, then humans get fat. Plants are smarter than humans; their food production (photosynthetic) rate and respiration rates are usually balanced. How many obese plants do you see?

Both plants and humans evaporate water from their leaves or skin as a cooling process. Human sweating (perspiration) may seem like a heating process, but as the sweat evaporates from your skin, your body cools. Plants transpiring water from their leaves cools the leaves and allows photosynthesis to continue (since photosynthesis stops at about 90°F). On a 100°F day, a leaf temperature will be about 85°F due to the evaporative cooling of transpiration. The same goes for you as you sweat on a hot day, but the cooling you experience keeps your body from overheating and shutting down (i.e., heatstroke).

Transpiration has an additional role in plants: the movement of water and nutrients into and through the plant. Unlike humans, who have a heart to pump fluid (blood) and nutrients throughout the body, plants don't have a pump.

So, how does water move against gravity to the top of a 100-foot-tall tree? The air surrounding a plant almost always is drier (except during rain) than the 100 percent relative humidity within the leaves. The affinity for water that drier air has literally sucks water from the leaf surface. This suction has tremendous strength. Add to this the ability of water molecules to hold tightly together as well as to the sides of a plant's "blood vessels" (i.e., the vascular tissue of plants, called the xylem). The result is a continuous water column from the leaves, down the stems and trunk, to the roots, where moisture is sucked out of the soil. This is simply amazing—no pump, no expenditure of energy by the plant, but a simple physical movement

of water from the soil to the tips of the leaves.

Plants obtain 90 percent of the nutrients they need from the soil moisture drawn through the roots. Humans ingest nutrients from food and vitamin supplements. The plant does it through the process of transpiration. If the soil is not rich with nutrients, naturally or from fertilizer supplements, then the plant will suffer from nutrient deficiency. This will be seen as slower growth rate (or no growth), yellowing leaves, or unhealthy appearance.

Transpiration is the force that moves water to the tips of a 100-foot-tall sequoia; there is no pump (i.e., heart) in a plant.

Another difference between plants and humans is observed at the cellular level. Plant cells have sturdy cell walls; human cells do not. The cell walls are the "LEGO" pieces that hold the plant upright. Humans have a skeleton of bones to remain upright. (*Note:* This is a simply a fun fact to impress your nongardening friends or your fifth-grader taking biology.)

Environmental conditions can affect both plants and humans in various ways. Temperature is perhaps the most important environmental factor affecting plant health. As temperature rises, so do photosynthesis and respiration. But as mentioned previously, photosynthesis shuts down at approximately 90°F; however, respiration continues at a faster and faster rate as the temperature rises. This can be disastrous for plants. If the plant cannot make enough food through photosynthesis to keep up with respiration, then respiration will begin to steal food from the plant tissues.

Most northern-adapted plants do not do well in Texas gardens because of this imbalance. A typical example is the inability of Kentucky bluegrass to grow anywhere in Texas except the Panhandle. Kentucky bluegrass can withstand 100°F summer days in Kansas, but nighttime temperatures cool off, which allows the plant to rest and respiration to slow. In Texas, summer nighttime temperatures are often in the mid-70s, and photosynthesis has stopped (no sun at night), but respiration continues eating up all the food produced by photosynthesis and then turns to plant tissue as food. The Kentucky bluegrass plant literally eats itself up and dies. Transplanting northern plants to Texas is a gamble. Check with local extension agents or nursery professionals for advice.

In humans, the imbalance of food uptake and respiration is a worldwide problem. People who are starving have their bodies ravaged by continued respiration that consumes body muscle and tissue for food. The horrific results are ever present in the mind's eye. Balancing food supplies and respiration is essential for human health as well.

Like humans, plants can sunburn. Light intensity varies significantly from Michigan to Texas. Think how long you could sunbathe on a Cancún beach versus a South Texas beach versus the waterfront of Lake Michigan: 15 minutes versus 1 hour versus all day. Plants feel the same effect. Again, many northern-adapted plants cannot withstand the light intensity in Texas and simply "sunburn" to death. Adaptation to high light intensity explains why many desert plants have gray foliage or hairy leaves to reflect light and/or small leaves to avoid light. They are Texas tough.

Wind affects plants, but not exactly in the same way it affects humans. Wind increases the cooling effect of transpiration and perspiration. When you step out of a swimming pool on a breezy day, you will be chilled as water evaporates from your skin. For plants, wind can increase transpiration to a point of excess and result in dried-up, dead leaves. This can happen in summer or in winter on evergreen plants (e.g., azalea, photinia). Thus, it is a good idea to irrigate in winter in the absence of adequate rainfall.

Wind chill factor (cold air temperature

plus wind effect) represents another difference between plants and humans. The meteorologist reports a temperature of 35°F and a wind chill factor of 28. The temperature on your skin will feel like 28, but the plant "feels" only 35. Plants are not warm-blooded animals like humans. In the same way that cold-blooded reptiles don't feel wind chill, neither do plants. So rest easy when the wind chill drops below freezing. Just make sure the plants are well watered to avoid desiccation from the wind.

One last environmental factor to address is water: too much or too little. Plants can wilt when overwatered or underwatered. Too much water excludes oxygen in the soil, so the plant can't take up water. Too little water in the soil and the plant can't suck hard enough to get it.

Most plants wilt when water cannot be absorbed by the roots. Some plants have additional drought-avoidance strategies. Ocotillo (*Fouquieria splendens*), a desert plant, will drop all its foliage when water is limited. Many landscape plants will go summer dormant, turning off color and stopping

growth (e.g., azalea, Bermudagrass, Shasta daisy). Some fruit trees at the first sign of drought will pull the rip cord and drop all the fruit to save themselves—for example, figs (this is the reason that fig trees should be mulched heavily and soil moisture monitored carefully).

Recent research on plant response to lack of water indicates that plants can "talk." The study used a stethoscope to measure audible sounds emanating from plants when starved for water. The plants actually made clicking noises as they became more and more stressed from lack of water. Turns out the plants weren't screaming for help, but the clicking was the result of water molecules disconnecting due to increased tension to keep the continuous water column intact (called cavitation, often heard in water wells). So, the next time you walk by your plants, listen carefully.

"Can't you hear me? I need water!"

Growing Fruits and Nuts

Growing fruits and nuts is perhaps the most sophisticated form of home gardening. It is a long-term endeavor with great payoffs in terms of production and pride of accomplishment. Fruit and nut growing can also frustrate you to

the point of torching the orchard and heading to the local farmers' market for something to eat!

Choosing what crop to grow is critical. First decide how much effort you want to put into it. The level of difficulty in growing varies significantly between crops. Here is a list of crops from the least to the most difficult:

Blackberries
Blueberries (in East Texas)
Figs
Citrus
Pears
Pecans
Grapes
Persimmons
Apples
Plums
Peaches

These factors are included in this measurement of difficulty:

- Adaptation to Texas soils
- Winter chilling requirements
- Varieties adapted to Texas climate
- Susceptibility to insects and diseases
- Ease of pest management
- Need for specialized training and pruning techniques

You must have patience; the fruits (literally) of your labors may not be realized for years. The time between planting and bearing fruit for various crops is as follows:

Crop	Time in Years
Blackberries	1–2
Blueberries	1–2
Figs	1–2
Citrus	1–2
Pears	4–6
Pecans	4–6
Grapes	2–3
Persimmons	3–4
Apples	2–5
Plums	3–6
Peaches	2–4

Note also that certain fruit and nut crops bear heavily one year and sparsely the next. This is called "alternate bearing" and happens especially with pecans, apples, and pears.

If this is your first attempt to grow fruits and/or nuts, think small. It is so easy to purchase six different peach trees and plant them. The next thing you know you have six problem children with adolescent attitudes and demands, including required training and pruning and regular pesticide spraying.

Soil Analysis

More fruit and nut plantings in Texas fail because of undesirable soil than from any other single factor. The ideal soils for fruits and nuts are well-drained, including sand, sandy loam, alluvial (river-laid) soil, and some red (oxygen-rich) clay soils. Well-drained soil is particularly critical in growing pecans, peaches, plums, and apples.

Check your soil drainage by digging a hole 12 inches in diameter and 24 inches deep. A posthole digger and a good back are needed. Fill the hole with water, all the way to the top. If the water drains out in 1 hour, you have fantastic soil drainage; 6 hours, good soil; 12 to 24 hours, average soil; over 24 hours—move if you want to grow fruit or nut tree crops.

Unfortunately, not much can be done to correct poor soil. Planting on raised berms or rows is perhaps the only feasible way to add some drainage to clay soils. Large raised beds (10 feet by 10 feet), filled with soil amended with organic matter, can be constructed for crops with limited-size root systems, such as peaches, plums, and apples (dwarf varieties are recommended). Fortunately, blackberries, grapes, pears, and figs are less finicky about the soil type in which they are grown.

Winter Chilling Requirements

Peaches, plums, apples, and pears are fruit tree crops that require a certain amount of cold winter weather, measured in chilling hours, to end their dormancy and to promote proper blooming and spring growth. Chilling hours are the number of hours during which temperatures are below 45°F and above 32°F.

If an apple, pear, plum, or peach variety requires more chilling hours than it actually receives in your garden, the tree may not bloom fully, or at all. Obviously, this is not a good thing. The map indicates the average chilling hours for various regions of Texas.

Pollination

Fruit trees need pollination (male pollen fertilizing the female fruit embryo). Without sufficient pollination, fruit trees may blossom abundantly, but fruit will not develop. Some species of fruit trees have "perfect" flowers. Both anthers (which contain pollen) and pistils (which develop into fruit) are located in the same blossom. Trees that bear fruit through self-pollination (set fruit without the pollen from another tree variety) are called "self-fruitful." There are, however, many types of fruits with perfect flowers that cannot produce fruit from their own pollen. These trees require pollen from another variety and are called "self-unfruitful." They are cross-pollinated by another variety, thus needing a pollinator.

Pecans do not fit conveniently into either category. They have separate male and female flowers on the same plant.

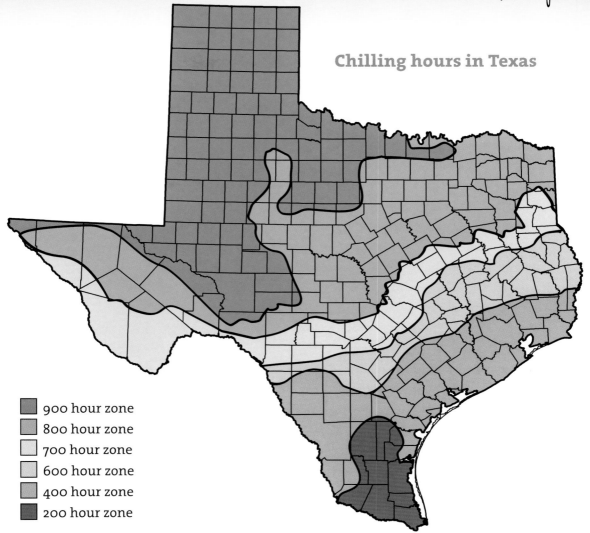

Chilling hours in Texas

- ▉ 900 hour zone
- ▉ 800 hour zone
- ☐ 700 hour zone
- ▉ 600 hour zone
- ▉ 400 hour zone
- ▉ 200 hour zone

In a commercial orchard, variety selection must take into consideration the compatibility of varieties to pollinate one another. For the home landscape, there is no need to worry about this in selecting pecan varieties. Pecan pollen is windblown to female flowers; bees are not involved. There is enough pollen blowing around Texas communities to pollinate your pecan tree(s).

These crops are self-fruitful:

Blackberries
Blueberries
Citrus
Figs
Grapes
Peaches
Persimmons

These crops are self-unfruitful and require cross-pollination by another variety:

> Apples (most varieties)
> Pears
> Plums (some are self-fruitful)

You will need to plant at least two varieties of self-unfruitful crops. This will be noted with varieties mentioned. Also, ask whether the plants are self-fruitful or self-unfruitful when purchasing fruit varieties that are unfamiliar.

Bees and other insects normally pollinate fruit trees. If, by some chance, you don't see bees buzzing in and out of your fruit tree flowers, then you may have to play like a bee and pollinate the flowers. Take a small paintbrush, and dab it in and out of as many flowers as you can, remembering to say "buzz, buzz, buzz" as you go.

Purchasing and Planting Fruit and Nut Crops

Purchasing fruit and nut plants at the nursery or through catalogues generally happens during the winter, for two reasons. First, the fruit and nut plants are dug up out of the nursery fields during winter dormancy and shipped bare-root (no soil). These bare-root plants are dormant and therefore undergo less stress than actively growing plants. Second, when a dormant plant is planted in the winter, the root system has a chance to regrow and establish itself before spring growth begins.

With tree crops, bigger is not always the best buy. Bigger dormant trees have a more difficult time surviving transplant shock. The following sizes are your best investment: pecans—4 to 6 feet tall; apple, peach, persimmon, and plum—3 to 5 feet tall; blackberries, citrus, figs, grapes—1 to 3 feet tall.

Fruit and nut crops need full sun to grow properly and produce well. Dig a hole large enough to accommodate the plant's root system. Don't skimp on the hole width; make sure the root system can spread out fully in the hole. Backfill with the soil that you pulled out of the hole, adding no soil amendments.

Water the plant to settle the soil, and then add a 3-foot-diameter circle of mulch. Mulch helps retain soil moisture, but equally important, mulch prevents weeds. Weeds readily compete for water and nutrients with young transplants, significantly delaying or reducing fruit and nut production.

The long-time recommendation of pruning half the height of the fruit or nut tree at the time of planting is well supported by research. However, it can be excruciating to prune $15 off a $30 plant. A modification to this recommendation is to cut back the central trunk (the tallest branch) 12 inches and any side branches 6 inches. This can still be hard to stomach but is necessary to help the plant survive transplanting. Remember that the tree lost over half of its root system when it was dug from the nursery field.

Fruit & Nut Crops— Comments & Variety Selection

BLACKBERRIES. If you want a lot of fruit each spring with little effort and you have a large yard, plant a blackberry plant. You can plant more than one, but you had better have room. The time-tested varieties 'Brazos' and 'Rosborough' developed by Texas A&M University produce well (a few gallons of berries per plant). These varieties are adapted to the entire state and possess the vicious thorns commonly associated with blackberries.

The University of Arkansas has developed thornless blackberry varieties. 'Arapaho' seems most adapted and productive throughout Texas, followed by 'Navaho.' (*Note:* If you must have raspberries, 'Dorman Red' is the only variety that produces well in Texas, specifically for areas east of IH-35. It is the only raspberry that can take the Texas summer heat.)

BLUEBERRIES. If your soil and water are correct, growing blueberries can be easy. Your soil needs to be an acidic, sandy soil with a pH of 4.5 to 5.5. These soils occur in East and Southeast Texas and occasionally in small areas of North, Central, and South Texas. Blueberries also require high-quality water (low sodium and bicarbonates).

If your soil is not perfect and you want to try to grow blueberries, use one of two techniques. One is to dig a hole at least 36 inches in diameter and 18 inches deep. Mix peat moss with the soil from the hole half and half by volume. Use this mixture to plant the blueberry transplant. You can use even more peat moss if you want. Blueberries will grow wonderfully in 100 percent peat moss. A second way to grow blueberries in areas of Texas that have nonacidic soils is to grow them in large 30-gallon containers. Use a potting soil high in peat moss.

Only Rabbiteye blueberries are adapted to Texas. Choose from the following varieties, and plant at least two varieties. Although blueberries are self-fruitful, production is increased by planting more than one variety. 'Tifblue' is the best blueberry variety for Texas. Others that are available and will produce in Texas include 'Beckyblue,' 'Brightwell,' 'Briteblue,' 'Climax,' 'Delite,' 'Premiere,' 'Sharpblue,' and 'Woodard.'

Mulch plants heavily with organic material, such as pine bark, sawdust, leaves, grass clippings, wood chips, or hay. Mulch aids in moisture conservation and weed control.

Figs. Another crop that will provide lots

of fruit with little effort is figs. They are adapted to most areas of Texas; however, extreme freezing temperatures in North Texas can freeze the plant to the ground and sometimes kill the entire plant. Due to threat of freeze damage, figs are most successfully grown as large shrubs rather than as single-trunk, upright trees.

Varieties recommended for Texas include 'Alma,' a light-colored, large fig with small seeds and fruit that ripens in August (developed by Texas A&M University); and 'Celeste,' a smaller, brown "sugar" fig with sweet pink flesh that bears throughout August.

Figs will drop their unripened fruit at the slightest level of drought stress. Mulch the shrub heavily to moderate fluctuations in soil moisture, and water when needed to keep the soil moisture level high during fruit development.

Citrus. Interest in growing citrus in the home landscape has exploded in recent

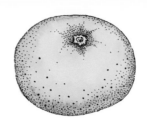

years. The dark, evergreen foliage; fragrant blossoms; and colorful, tasty fruits of citrus are alluring. Commercial nurseries are working hard to produce enough supplies of adapted citrus varieties to meet an ever-growing demand.

Except for those in the Rio Grande Valley of South Texas, most gardeners will grow a limited selection of citrus varieties and grow them in containers. The growing of grapefruit or orange trees in the soil of your backyard is restricted to the Valley and the mildest climates along the Gulf Coast.

Smaller citrus varieties can be successfully grown in 20- to 30-gallon containers. Container-grown citrus will require some form of cold protection to survive freezing temperatures. Moving them indoors during freezes may be the simplest solution. Appropriate container-grown citrus varieties include 'Calamondin' orange; 'Armstrong Early' and 'Owari' satsumas; 'Changsha' tangerine; 'Nagami' kumquat; and 'Meyer' and 'Ponderosa' lemons.

Satsumas are perhaps the highest-quality, most cold-tolerant citrus for Texas. This easy-to-peel, virtually seedless fruit is very sweet and juicy. When temperatures of 26°F or colder are forecast, you must take action to protect these plants from freeze damage.

PEARS. A vacant, old, broken-down, wood-frame home with a couple of pear  trees heavily laden with fruit is a sight often seen across rural Texas. This is a testimony to the adaptability and productivity of pears. With pears, the less you prune and fertilize, the more pears you will get. Generating lots of tree growth through pruning and fertilizing does not equate to loads of fruit.

Pears are self-unfruitful, so two varieties are recommended for good fruit production. Pear varieties that grow well in Texas include 'Ayers,' 'Keiffer,' 'LeCont,' 'Moonglow,' 'Orient,' and 'Warren.' Asian pears are relatively new in Texas and are sometimes called "apple-pears" because of their shape. Varieties include 'Hosui' and 'Twentieth Century.'

PECANS. Native Americans depended heavily on pecans found along rivers  in the land to be named Texas. In 1909, Texas governor James Hogg requested that a pecan (and a walnut) be planted at his grave instead of a headstone and that the nuts from those trees be distributed to the people so that Texas would be a land of trees. In recognition of the pecan's historic contributions and inspired by Governor Hogg's request, the Texas legislature designated the pecan as the state tree in 1919.

This stately tree can be included in most Texas landscapes. The exceptions are those that have highly alkaline, rocky soils west of IH-35. Dozens of improved varieties are available, but a "seedling" pecan tree is perhaps the best choice for a landscape tree. A seedling tree is simply one in which a pecan nut was planted and the seedling arose. The nuts produced by this seedling may or may not be of high quality, but the tree structure will be majestic (compared to that of trees grafted with improved varieties).

If you want improved varieties, a few good selections include 'Caddo,' 'Hopi,' 'Kanza,' 'Nacon,' 'Osage,' 'Pawnee,' and 'Prilop.' For more site-specific recommendations, contact your local county extension office or nursery.

There are more than a dozen insects

GROWN BY TEXANS FOR TEXANS

Since 1937, Womack Nursery Co. has been a wholesale nursery with a retail mail-order catalogue that carries excellent fruit and nut varieties (2551 Hwy 6, De Leon, TX 76444; telephone: 254-893-6497).

and diseases that attack pecans (not to mention the loss of nuts to crows and squirrels!). Unless you are willing to rig up the pesticide sprayer and pull out the shotgun, the philosophy in growing pecans in the home landscape should be "Live and let live." Don't spray; just pray. If you get quality nuts, great! If you

CALLER: *"What can I do about bagworms covering my pecan tree?"*

ANSWER: "Bagworms and pecans go together in Texas like peas and carrots. Most people fear that the annual return of the 'bagworms' (properly called webworms) indicates the arrival of the most devastating and prolific pecan pest. Although detrimental to a tree's beauty, the hungry caterpillars will not kill a tree or prevent a pecan crop. For pecan owners to psychologically cope with webworms, I recommend they simply not look upward while in the landscape between June and September. I consider webworms to be a beneficial insect: eating thousands of leaves, composting them internally, releasing the compost pellets onto the lawn, and significantly reducing the number of leaves to be raked each fall—a win-win for all concerned!"

don't, go buy pecans with all the money you saved by not spraying constantly.

When properly located and given a large space in the landscape, a pecan tree remains a great asset. It can provide shade, offer a habitat for birds and squirrels, and every so often bear hundreds of the most nutritional nuts on the planet.

GRAPES. Texas is a land of grapes. Almost  half of all grape species are native to Texas. Growing native grapes in Texas is easy. Growing high-quality wine grapes is a huge challenge, even for the best commercial vineyard growers. Currently, there are over 100 wineries in Texas.

In the landscape, grapes can provide cover for an arbor or be trained on a fence. For homeowners with small landscapes, the vertical growth habit of grapevines makes them ideal for producing fruit in tight spaces. Remember the saying for grapes (and for most vining plants): "The first year they sleep, the second year they creep, and the third year they leap." Unless you keep them in check with once-every-winter pruning, they will leap over the fence, squeeze and crush your wooden arbor, and engulf slow-moving dogs and cats.

It is a bit odd that Texas has so many native species of grapes, yet there are only a few improved grape varieties adapted to Texas that reliably produce quality fruit for juice, jelly, and/or wine. Several factors limit choices of grape varieties that will grow well in your area, such as freezing temperatures, Pierce's disease (PD), black rot disease, and cotton root rot disease.

Pierce's disease kills vines and is a threat in East, Central, and South Texas. Black rot affects both the foliage and the fruit and must be controlled with fungicide sprays where weather conditions are regularly warm, humid, and/or rainy. Cotton root rot is a soilborne disease that kills plants rapidly. It is prevalent in the alkaline soils of Central and Southwest Texas. Grape varieties differ significantly in resistance to these diseases.

Native to East Texas, muscadine grapes are the most disease-resistant grapes that grow only on acidic soils. The fruit makes wonderful jelly, jam, and juice. Improved varieties of muscadines include 'Regale' (purple fruit) and 'Summit' (bronze).

'Champanel' is the most disease-resistant grape that is widely adapted and requires the least care of any grape for Texas. It has a very vigorous growth habit and produces loads of large, dark purple fruit, great for making red jelly.

'Black Spanish' and 'Blanc duBois' are resistant to Pierce's disease but highly susceptible to black rot. They are best grown away from East Texas and the Gulf Coast because of favorable disease conditions there—humid and rainy. 'Black Spanish' produces large clusters of small black grapes used to produce the wine referred to as LeNoir, plus fine juice and jelly. 'Blanc duBois' is a heavy producer of white grapes for wine and juice.

Vinifera grapes, known to produce the great wines of the world, can be grown in Central, North, and West Texas, but their high susceptibility to Pierce's disease is a continuous concern. For the home gardener, growing vinifera grapes is not fun and seldom productive. Intense management is required, including specialized training and pruning, regular pesticide spraying, and lots of prayer.

PERSIMMONS. Texas has a couple of native persimmons (American persimmon and Texas persimmon), but the Japanese persimmon is preferred by most gardeners because of its large, attractive, "edible" fruit (you have to like persimmons to call them edible).

Different varieties have fruits that differ in size, shape, and color (from orange to red). The fruit stays on these handsome small trees past the first frost and after the leaves fall, making the fruit look like Christmas balls hanging in a tree.

Most varieties are astringent (mouth-puckering, sharp taste) if eaten before they are soft-ripe. Recommended varieties include 'Eureka,' which produces red, extremely high-quality fruit; the tree is self-fruitful. 'Hachiya' has bright orange fruit and is known as much for its beauty as an ornamental small tree as it is for good fruit. Much the same could be said of 'Tane-nashi.' 'Tamopan,' with its orange fruit, is the most vigorous and largest tree of the varieties grown in Texas.

'Fuyu' ('Fuyugaki') is best known for its nonastringent fruit. The tree is self-fruitful with red fruit. 'Fuyu' is more sensitive to freeze damage and is best planted in areas with mild winters.

APPLES. Yes, you can grow apples in Texas. Hard to believe, but with proper variety selection and fair soil, apples can be grown in much of Texas. The more alkaline and rocky the soil, the more difficult it is to grow apples.

Most apple varieties are not self-fruitful and require cross-pollination, so plant two varieties. Choose from these varieties:

- Anna (green with red blush, low chilling requirement, plant with 'Dorsett Golden' for pollination)
- Braeburn (red)
- Dorsett Golden (yellow, low chilling requirement, pollinator for 'Anna')
- Fuji (red)
- Gala (orange-red)
- Granny Smith (green)
- Jersey Mac (red)
- Mollies Delicious (red, a good pollinator)
- Ozark Gold (yellow, good pollinator)
- Pink Lady (pinkish red)
- Starkrimson Red Delicious (red)

Fire blight and cotton root rot can be limiting factors for apples in Texas. In East Texas, incidence of fire blight is increasing. In South, Central, North, and West Texas, cotton root rot is the major cause of apple tree death. Check with the county extension agent or a nursery professional for presence of these diseases in your area.

Apple trees can be purchased in dwarf or semidwarf sizes. Instead of reaching 20 feet or more, apple varieties can be grafted onto rootstocks that reduce the size of the tree in half or more. These grafted trees are not available everywhere. Check your local nursery, Womack Nursery, or the Internet.

Apples usually produce too many fruits per tree and require thinning. Thinning means taking off unripened fruit so that the fruit left will get larger. If you don't thin, you get a bunch of small fruits; if you thin, you get fewer fruits, but they are much larger. Thin to only one fruit (the largest) per cluster of fruits before they reach golf-ball size. Thinning fruits (commonly done on apples, peaches, and plums) is one of the most emotionally difficult tasks in all of gardening.

PLUMS AND PEACHES. Plums and peaches require the highest level of management of any fruit mentioned. Knowing this is all the challenge many of you need to plant your first plum or peach tree. Although plums are much easier to grow than peaches, plums are still difficult to grow because of the plethora of diseases and insects that attack the fruits and tree.

Both plums and peaches need well-drained soil, preferably sand 3 feet deep. Both need regular monitoring for insects and diseases. Both will require you to spray insecticides and fungicides as often as twice a month. Fortunately, there are effective organic insecticides and fungicides now available (e.g., neem oil, spinosad). For pest management information and spray schedules, contact your county extension agent, access AggieHorticulture.tamu.edu via the Internet, or check with your nursery professional.

Variety selection for plums is less rigorous than for peaches. There are very few varieties that are adapted to Texas, and there are simply very few scientists breeding new plum varieties, with the exception of those at the University of Florida (Gulf varieties) and Auburn University (AU varieties).

Variety selection for peaches can be mind-boggling because there are so many. However, the basis of selection is matching the chilling requirements of the variety with the chilling hours expected in your area of Texas. Refer to the "Chilling Hours Map" to determine your area's chilling hours; then choose peach varieties suited for your area. The varieties listed in the table are well adapted to the Texas climate.

Nectarines

Growing nectarines is recommended only for the most ambitious gardeners. Nectarines are fuzzless peaches. The fuzz on the peach skin protects against insects and diseases. Without fuzz, nectarines are a hotel for insects and diseases. If you must try, choose varieties such as 'Armking,' 'Crimson Gold,' 'Redglobe,' and 'Sun Red.'

PLUM VARIETIES FOR TEXAS

VARIETY	FRUIT SIZE	COLOR	HARVEST TIME	POLLINATION AND NOTES
Allred	small	red leaves, skin, and flesh	early June	self-fruitful
Bruce	large	red skin and flesh	mid-May	self-unfruitful; requires pollinator, usually 'Methley'
Gulfgold	small	yellow skin and flesh	May	self-unfruitful; cross-pollinates with 'Gulfruby'; low chilling requirement (for Gulf Coast and South Texas)
Gulfruby	small	red skin and flesh	May	self-unfruitful; cross-pollinates with 'Gulfgold'; low chilling requirement (for Gulf Coast and South Texas)
Methley	medium	purple skin; amber flesh	early June	self-fruitful; excellent pollinator
Morris	large	reddish purple skin; red flesh	mid-June	self-unfruitful; developed at Texas A&M for Texas climate
Ozark Premier	large	red-and-cream–streaked skin; yellow flesh	late June	self-fruitful

PEACH VARIETIES FOR TEXAS
(LISTED IN ORDER OF CHILLING HOURS REQUIRED)

VARIETY	FRUIT SIZE	FREESTONE OR CLING	DATE RIPE	CHILLING HOURS
Yellow flesh				
Flordagrande	medium	semi-cling	early May	100
Flordaprince	small	semi-cling	late April	150
TropicBeauty	medium	semi-cling	late April	150
TropicSweet	medium	freestone	late April	150

EarliGrande	small	cling	mid-April	275
Flordaking	medium	semi-cling	mid-May	350
Flordacrest	small	cling	early May	375
Texstar*	medium	semi-cling	late May	450
La Feliciana	large	freestone	late June	550
TexRoyal*	large	freestone	early June	600
JuneGold	large	semi-cling	late May	650
Juneprince	medium	semi-freestone	mid-May	650
Bicentennial	small	cling	mid-May	750
Dixieland	large	freestone	mid-July	750
Fireprince	large	freestone	late June	750
Harvester	medium	semi-freestone	mid-June	750
Loring	large	freestone	early July	750
Milam	large	freestone	early July	750
Redskin	large	freestone	mid-July	750
Summergold	medium	freestone	late June	750
Bounty	large	freestone	late June	800
Denman	large	freestone	early July	850
Jefferson	large	freestone	mid- to late July	850
Redglobe	large	freestone	late June	850
Sentinel	large	semi-cling	early June	850
Springgold	small	cling	mid-May	850
Ranger	large	freestone	mid- to late June	900
Surecrop	medium	cling	early June	1,000

White flesh

FlordaGlo	medium	cling	mid-May	150
TropicSnow	medium	cling	mid-May	200
Palace	medium	freestone	mid-July	650
White Hale	large	freestone	mid- to late July	750
Melba	medium	freestone	mid-July	800
Belle of Georgia	medium	freestone	mid-July	850
White Star	large	freestone	late July	850

Note: Freestone and cling refer to whether the peach flesh adheres to the pit. Freestones do not adhere to the pit, and clings do.

* Developed at Texas A&M University specifically for the Texas climate.

Proper pruning of plum and peach trees is critical for two reasons. First, pruning keeps the trees short enough for you to pick fruit while standing on the ground or short ladder (otherwise, these trees grow 20 feet tall). Trees should be pruned into a vase-shaped, open-center structure. Envision an umbrella turned inside out—this is how the trunk and major branches of the tree should be arranged.

The second reason to prune is to encourage vigorous growth required for annual fruit production. Each February, you will remove approximately 30 to 40 percent of the small (1-inch diameter and less) branches and twigs. To more fully understand how to prune plum and peach trees, seek information via the Internet or through garden books focused on home fruit production in Texas.

Thinning plums and peaches is important to produce large fruits. If you don't thin, you will end up with bushels of tiny plums or peaches with a thin layer of flesh between the pit and the skin. Pull off unripened fruits by hand about the time they are the diameter of a dime. After thinning, the fruits should hang 3 to 4 inches apart for plums and at least 6 inches apart for peaches.

Timely Tips

Flowers & Pretty Plants

- If you haven't already, plant flowering bulbs (crocus, daffodil or narcissus, Dutch iris, hyacinth, and tulip) now. Hopefully, you purchased the bulbs in the fall and have been chilling them in the refrigerator or garage until now, when soil temperatures are cool enough for these "Yankee" bulbs to root and flower well in Texas.
- Plant or tend already-planted, cool-season annual flowers, such as calendula, cyclamen, dianthus, Johnny-jump-ups, ornamental kale and cabbage, pansies, petunias, snapdragons, stock, sweet alyssum, and violas. Don't forget to add organic matter to the soil before planting; use composted manure, pine bark, and/or composted cotton bur hulls.
- Fertilize established cool-season annuals with a high-nitrogen fertilizer, such as urea, ammonium sulfate, or blood meal. Apply $\frac{1}{4}$ pound of urea, $\frac{1}{2}$ pound of ammonium sulfate, or 1 pound of blood meal per 100 square feet every 4 to 6 weeks.
- Plant bluebonnet transplants into flower beds, or even the lawn. Watch out for pill bugs and sow bugs (doodle bugs); they love eating bluebonnet transplants. Treat with slug and snail baits, if needed.
- Cut off dead portions of perennials killed by freezing weather; if you can tolerate ugly, delay pruning until early spring.

Garden Design

- Take time in midwinter to dream about new additions to the landscape: a butterfly garden, herb garden, flower beds, a birdbath or statuary, or a well-placed tree. Peruse the garden magazines and catalogues for creative ideas for your outdoor living area.

Soil & Mulch

- Add organic matter to open (i.e., plantless) vegetable gardens and flower beds. Bulky organic materials, such as composted or aged manure, fallen leaves and pine straw, and wood chips from tree-trimming companies should be incorporated into the soil now so they have time to break down before spring planting.
- Plan new landscape plantings, and prepare the soil now for future planting. This month's essay "Soils 101 for the Garden" provides guidelines for creating flower and shrub beds.

- Test soil for pH and nutrients through a soil analysis lab only if you suspect major changes in your soil that are affecting plant health. Otherwise, a good estimation of soil type, pH, and nutrient levels can be obtained by calling the county extension office or a local nursery.
- Mulch your flower and shrub beds, vegetable gardens, and young trees. Use organic mulches, such as pine bark, cypress bark, compost, hardwood mulch, or pine straw. Some less attractive but still effective mulches include fallen leaves, straw, hay, and grass clippings.

Water

- Where or when winter is mild, water actively growing vegetables and annual flowers as needed to maintain health of the plants. Use your index finger as your moisture meter.
- Water lawns, landscape plantings, vegetable gardens, and fruit plantings if the ground is dry and frost is predicted. Regardless, water at least once in January in the absence of significant rain. Under dry soil conditions and water stress, plants are more likely to suffer freeze damage and/or desiccation and death of leaves and twigs.

Plant Care

- Most winter damage may already have occurred, but continue protective actions if freezing temperatures prevail for several days. Refer to tips for citrus protection below, or refer to the September essay "Cold Weather Protection for Plants."
- Refrain from pruning off freeze-damaged plant material, because it actually provides some insulation for healthy plant tissue. This pruning is best done in February or March.
- Exception on pruning is for deep South Texas: Prune now just before spring growth begins on perennial flowers, trees, shrubs, roses, citrus, and other fruit trees.
- Pull weeds from flower and shrub beds and vegetable gardens. Herbicides should be a last resort; besides, most are not effective in cool temperatures.
- Remove plant debris (e.g., dead leaves, flowers, and twigs) from planting beds. This debris may harbor plant disease or insect pests, so don't put it in the compost pile. This "sanitation" task reduces future disease and insect infestations.

Trees, Shrubs & Vines

- Plant newly purchased trees following the guidelines in the September essay "Tree Planting Made Easy."
- Choose, purchase, and plant bare-root roses. See this month's essay "Roses in the Landscape" for further details.
- Move living Christmas trees to a shady location outdoors following the holidays. After a week or so of adapting to the outdoors, the tree can be planted into the landscape using the guidelines in "Tree Planting Made Easy."
- Transplant shrubs and trees during the dormant season to significantly increase survival chances. See step-by-step procedures for transplanting established plants in the October essay "Transplanting Shrubs and Trees."

Lawns

- Mow winter weeds. Keep weeds, such as annual ryegrass, clover, and henbit, in check by mowing to reduce their spread and improve the lawn quality when spring arrives.
- Water the lawn thoroughly at least once in January if rainfall does not exceed 2 to 3 inches for the month.

- Fertilize fescue and bluegrass lawns or lawns overseeded with perennial or annual ryegrass. Use a high-nitrogen fertilizer at $\frac{1}{2}$ pound of actual nitrogen per 1,000 square feet.

Vegetables, Herbs & Fruits

- Transplant cool-season crops, such as asparagus, broccoli, brussels sprouts, cabbage, cauliflower, Chinese cabbage, collard and turnip greens, Irish potato, kohlrabi, leaf lettuces, onions, and Swiss chard. Sow seed of beets, carrots, English peas, greens, leaf lettuces, radishes, sugar snap and snow peas, and turnips. Remember to incorporate organic matter every time you plant.
- Transplant cold-tolerant herbs, such as chives, cilantro (coriander), dill, fennel, garlic, oregano, parsley, rosemary, sage, and thyme.
- Fertilize lightly with high-nitrogen products. On young tender seedlings and transplants, water-soluble fertilizers (those you mix with water) are particularly effective and safe (won't burn foliage).
- Choose and purchase bare-root fruit and nut plants at local nurseries or through mail-order catalogues.
- Plant these trees, shrubs, and vines following the recommendations in this month's essay "Growing Fruits and Nuts."

- Protect citrus from freezing weather. If temperatures in the mid-20s or lower are predicted, cover the trees with cardboard boxes or blankets. Supplemental heat from a utility light or Christmas lights may be needed. If the plant is growing in a container, simply move it indoors or, at minimum, into the garage.

Houseplants

- During winter, place house-plants in the brightest light in the house, usually a south-facing win-dow.
- Water when needed, using your index finger to test soil moisture. Dry, warm air inside the house causes houseplants to use more water than you might think.

- Watch for insect infestations. Dry, warm air indoors may rapidly increase populations of aphids, fungal gnats, mealybugs, spider mites, and white flies. Perhaps the best way to control populations is to give your houseplants a shower every couple of weeks to wash insects off the stems and tops and bottoms of the leaves.

Butterflies, Birds & Squirrels

- Provide water for birds and squirrels with birdbaths or other con-tainers. You may attract many birds to your landscape that don't eat seeds, such as mockingbirds.

Notes:

February

*Pansy (*Viola x wittrockiana*)*

HINTS OF SPRING, REMINDERS OF WINTER

Annual Flowers . . . Icing on the Cake!

Annual flowers are literally the icing on the cake for your landscape. The shrubs, trees, and lawn are the foundation of the landscape, but annuals can provide more seasonal variety, color, and pizzazz than any other group of plants.

By definition, annuals complete their life cycles in one season, from seed germination through growth, flowering, seed production, and death. A more practical definition is that annuals are those plants that are planted every year because they die out naturally or die because of summer heat or winter freezes. Some annuals act more like perennials in the mild winters of the southern half of Texas and will live for multiple years. Begonias, dianthus, impatiens, and petunias often survive summer and winter in the Gulf Coast and in South Texas. Some perennial flowers can actually be used as annuals, appropriately named a "perannial" by Jerry Parsons, an extension horticulturist in San Antonio. Blue salvia and groundcover forms of lantana are great examples of perannials.

Some annuals will "reseed" themselves, coming back every year from their own seed. Johnny-jump-up, peri-

Pansy blooms—the "happy faces" in the garden

winkle, poppy, and zinnia are good at reseeding, whether you want them to or not. Note also that not all annuals are grown for their flowers; some are grown for their foliage, such as caladium, coleus, and Joseph's coat (amaranth).

Annual flowers are not the toughest plants in the landscape and need thorough soil preparation, adequate fertilizing, proper sunlight levels, timely planting, and attentive garden care. This is not said to discourage their use. It simply must be your philosophy when you choose to grow annuals.

To have success with annuals, keep in mind that you should not plant more annuals than you can adequately care for. There seems to be an innate impulse in humans to buy annuals by the truckload, only to see them wither and die from lack of care. Start small with your annual plantings. A small spot of beautiful, healthy annuals has a great positive impact on the landscape, but a plethora of poorly tended, sparsely blooming annuals has a huge, negative impact on your landscape.

Annuals can be incorporated into the landscape in multiple ways:

- Solid plantings of one type and/or color of annual to serve as a focal point for your landscape that will stop traffic (e.g., a 100-square-foot planting of red petunias)
- Smaller plantings or "pockets of color" using one type and/or color of annual repeated across the landscape to provide unity and harmony in the landscape (e.g., three separate plantings of white periwinkles)
- Plantings that combine multiple colors of the same type of annual (e.g., purple and yellow pansies)
- Plantings that combine multiple types of annuals based on their flower form (e.g., snapdragons, which have spike-type blooms, and petunias, which have tubular blooms)
- Floral carpet or collage planting of many types and colors of annuals (e.g., dianthus, pansy, petunia, and sweet alyssum)
- Border plantings in front of an existing shrub hedge (e.g., a 2-foot band of periwinkles planted in front of a boxwood hedge)
- Container plantings as an accent with one type and color of annual per pot (e.g., red geraniums in large pots on either side of the front door)
- Dish garden or "living flower arrangement" with a variety of bloom types and colors (e.g., snapdragons, surrounded by dianthus, with petunias and sweet alyssum spilling over the edge of the container)
- Cut-flower garden full of annuals for use in floral arrangements (e.g., bachelor button, cosmos, larkspur, periwinkle, snapdragon, sunflower, zinnia)

The list is endless—use your imagination; envision how Disneyworld uses annuals!

Sun Exposure for Annuals

Where to plant with regard to sun exposure is critical for many annuals. Much of the sun-tolerance information for annuals is based on northern rather than Texas climates. Full sun in Michigan is not full sun in Texas. Think about lying on the beach in the summer on Lake Michigan versus the Gulf Coast. You would burn to a crisp in Texas in less than 3 hours; not so in Michigan. Geraniums will take full sun all summer in Michigan but not in Texas. Refer to the "Select Annuals" lists for sun-exposure guidance.

Fortunately, plant breeders now recognize the sun's intensity in the South and have developed new sun-tolerant varieties for old-time annuals, such as begonia, caladium, coleus, and petunia. If you are concerned about an annual's sun and/or heat tolerance, try planting it in a bed that gets morning sun and afternoon shade. (*Note:* My best flower beds are always in morning sun and afternoon shade.)

When to Plant

Annuals can be divided into cool-season or warm-season annuals. Don't jump the gun either way! Most warm-season annuals should not be planted until after the danger of killing frost has passed. Some warm-season annuals also need warm soil temperatures before they will perform well. Periwinkle and caladium are prime examples of annuals that need soil temperatures above 70°F to grow well and flourish.

Cool-season annuals are best planted in September when days become significantly shorter and nighttime temperatures are reduced. For freeze-tolerant annuals (e.g., bluebonnet, cabbage, dianthus, kale, pansy, petunia, snapdragon, viola), plants set out in fall will provide nice flowering (or foliage) in fall, limp through the dead of winter while developing a large root system, and then burst forth with a profusion of color in spring. When everyone else is just planting these cool-season annuals in the spring, your flower bed will be the best in the neighborhood. This planting schedule works in all but the harshest winter areas of the Panhandle and high altitudes of West Texas.

Annual plantings can be rotated between warm-season and cool-season flowers at least twice in Texas. Sometimes, a third "change out" can be made to keep your landscape full of color and interest. Warm-season annuals can be planted after the last frost and will bloom through early June. A second planting of especially heat-tolerant annuals, such as penta, periwinkle, portulaca, or purslane, can be used from June through the hot summer months. Cool-season annuals, such as dianthus, pansy, and snapdragon, can be planted in late September to October and will last through the winter in all but the coldest areas of Texas. Timing these color change outs is a key technique in keeping annuals healthy and beautiful.

Soil Preparation

Thorough soil preparation is a must. If you buy a flat of petunias and don't buy organic matter to amend the soil, you walk out of the nursery perpetuating the "we grow 'em; you kill 'em" motto described in the January essay "Soils 101 for the Garden." Prepare the soil by adding organic matter every time you plant annuals—the more the better. Without proper soil preparation, your hard-earned money will be lost with every purchase of annuals.

Purchasing & Planting Annuals

Most annuals are best planted as transplants purchased from nurseries and garden centers. Annual transplants can be purchased in less costly "six-packs" (six transplants in individual cells). The transplants should be planted 8 inches apart in the flower bed. Larger transplants are available in "jumbo packs" or 4-inch or 6-inch pots. These cost more, but the impact on the landscape is immediate. Larger transplants should be planted 12 to 14 inches apart. Confirm spacing recommendations from the plant tag or list to follow.

Seed racks are full of annual flowers, but relatively few can be planted from seed directly into the flower bed with great success. Growing from seed can reduce the cost of planting annuals significantly but is best limited to the following annuals:

> Alyssum
> Bachelor button
> Caladium (from bulbs)
> Larkspur
> Marigold
> Periwinkle
> Poppy
> Sweet pea
> Sunflower
> Zinnia

When planting transplants, dig a hole slightly wider than the root-ball, set the plant in place with the transplant soil level at the same level of the garden soil, and press the soil firmly around the roots. Water the newly planted bed immediately; follow-up waterings should be done every other day lightly for the first week. Then use your index finger to test soil moisture, and water when the soil is dry to the touch a couple of inches deep.

When planting seeds, rake the soil level, scatter the seeds, and rake again lightly to create firm contact between the seeds and the soil. Sprinkle water lightly on the seeded area, and repeat sprinkling daily. The goal is to keep the soil moist but not saturated. When sowing seed, remember that seed is cheap, so overplant to guarantee a good stand of seedlings. After the seedlings have grown about an inch, pinch out (thin) crowded seedlings to the recommended spacing on the seed package. This may not be easy on your emotions but is necessary to allow the seedlings to develop into sturdy, vigorously growing plants.

Mulching

Mulching is critical to reduce soilborne diseases, prevent weeds, and maintain more constant soil moisture levels. Add to the planting 2 to 3 inches of mulch, such as composted cotton bur hulls, cypress bark, pine bark, or pine needles. This should be done immediately for transplanted annuals. A very thin layer of mulch can be used over seeded plantings to help conserve soil moisture, and more mulch can be added as the plants grow larger.

Plant Care

Annual flowers are blooming machines. Just as in your Ferrari, you must use a high-octane fuel to maintain high performance. Select fertilizers high in nitrogen (e.g., urea, ammonium sulfate, and blood meal) to increase flower (and foliage) production. Application rates should range from 1 pound of urea per 100 square feet to 4 pounds of blood meal per 100 square feet. Scatter the fertilizer evenly over the planting, and water to drive the fertilizer into the soil. Monthly applications of fertilizer, even in the winter, will provide the energy for continuously blooming annuals.

Once the annuals are established, deep, infrequent watering is generally better than frequent, light watering. Drip irrigation is much preferred over sprinkler irrigation to avoid disease and decay of flowers and foliage.

Many annuals, such as ageratum, alyssum, begonia, impatiens, periwinkle, petunia, and salvia, require little additional care. Their dying flowers fall off the plant and do not need to be removed by hand. Other annuals, such as calendula, dahlia, geranium, marigold, and zinnia, need to have dried-up flowers removed. This is known as "deadheading" and not only keeps plants attractive but also encourages further blooming instead of seed production. Deadheading can be done with pruning shears, with scissors, or by hand.

With proper soil preparation, planting, fertilizing, and watering, annuals experience few insect infestations or diseases. However, these few need to be identified early and controlled if damage is significant.

Soilborne fungal rot of the roots or foliage is sometimes seen, particularly on pansies, periwinkles, and petunias. If you see a plant that is wilted or has decaying foliage and lack of water is not a possibility, then simply remove that plant from the bed. This reduces the chance that the disease will spread. If several plants are infected, either treat with an appropriate fungicide or remove all infected plants and replant.

The most common insects seen infesting annuals are aphids, spider mites, and white flies. These must be identified while populations are low and controlled with a chemical or organic insecticide promptly. Left untreated, your annuals will not perform well and will likely die.

Slugs and snails can do surprisingly heavy damage on annuals, such as marigolds, pansies, petunias, and salvia. These slow-moving pests can be collected by hand and destroyed. For the squeamish, slug and snail baits are very effective. **Use extreme caution with any pesticides, and be sure to read the label and follow label directions.**

Weeds may populate the flower bed, even when mulch is used. Remove weeds by hand or hoe as soon as possible so they do not compete for water and nutrients.

Select Annuals for Texas Landscapes

There are dozens of annuals to choose from and even more varieties for each annual. Selecting which annual and what variety can be overwhelming. Use the lists below for guidance, and consult your nursery professional, county extension agent, or a Master Gardener for the best recommendations for your area of the state.

SELECT ANNUALS FOR TEXAS LANDSCAPES

Cool-season annuals

NAME	SUN EXPOSURE	HEIGHT; WIDTH (INCHES)	NOTES
Alyssum	sun/partial shade	2–6; 6–12	white or purple fragrant flowers; attracts butterflies; excellent border
Calendula	sun/partial shade	8–18; 8–12	orange or yellow blooms; not freeze tolerant in North Texas
Dianthus	sun/partial shade	6–10; 6–12	single carnation flower in red, pink, and white; blooms nearly year-round; must be deadheaded; attracts butterflies; old-fashioned garden pinks, carnations, and sweet William are similar, related annuals
Johnny-jump-up	sun/partial shade	6–12; 6–12	widely adapted and underused; can be seeded easily; miniature pansy flower in purple, yellow, and blue; will reseed itself
Kale/cabbage	sun	12–16; 10–12	ornamental foliage in white, green, purple, and red, edible; many new fancy-leaved varieties
Larkspur	sun	24–36; 6–12	can be seeded easily or transplanted; old-fashioned type flower in pink, purple, blue, and white
Pansy	sun/partial shade	6–10; 6–12	time-tested hardy annual; old-fashioned "happy faces" type with colorful combinations of purple, yellow, maroon, and black; modern single-color varieties of yellow, blue, purple, and maroon
Poppy	sun/partial shade	24–36; 12–18	can be seeded easily or transplanted; cut flower in red, pink, purple, and white; fancy carnation-form flower and simple peony type available; closely related Iceland and California poppies also adapted in Texas
Snapdragon	sun/partial shade	6–24; 6–12	dramatic spike flower in all colors but blue; attracts butterflies and hummingbirds; shorter varieties easier to grow

Stock 🔪	sun/partial shade	12–24; 8–12	dense, spiked bloom; fragrant blooms in soft red, pink, and white
Sweet pea 🔪	sun	24+; 24	mounding or climbing vine; fragrant flowers in all colors; can be planted from seed easily
Viola	sun/partial shade	6-8; 6-12	a smaller version of the pansy and larger than Johnny-jump-up; solid colors of yellow, white, purple, and blue

🔪 Note: Annuals that also serve as cut flowers are noted by a shears icon.

Warm-season annuals

Name	Sun exposure	Height; width (inches)	Notes
Amaranthus/ Joseph's coat	sun	36–48; 12–18	brilliant foliage of reds, yellows, and greens
Bachelor button/ 🔪 gomphrena	sun	12–24; 12–24	purple or red flowers; dried flower
Begonia	shade/sun	6–12; 6–12	sun-tolerant new varieties available; flowers in red, pink, and white; bronze foliage on some varieties
Bluebonnet	sun	12–14; 8–12	available in transplants or seed; blue, white, pink, or maroon flowers
Caladium	shade/sun	18–20; 12–16	sun-tolerant varieties available; bold foliage; varieties of white or red combined with green
Cockscomb 🔪	sun	8–24; 8–12	crested and plume-type flowers in red, pink, orange, yellow, and purple
Coleus	shade/sun	12–24; 12–18	sun-tolerant varieties available; brilliant foliage in wide variety of color combinations of red, purple, yellow, and green
Copper plant	sun	24–36; 24–30	large plant with bold, multicolored foliage of copper, maroon, bronze, green, and cream
Cosmos 🔪	sun	18–36; 12–24	can be seeded or transplanted; wide variety of flower colors in red, pink, orange, yellow, and mixtures

🔪 Note: Annuals that also serve as cut flowers are noted by a shears icon.

NAME	SUN EXPOSURE	HEIGHT; WIDTH (INCHES)	NOTES
Geranium	partial shade	12–18; 12–18	red, pink, or white flowers; needs shade to endure summer; attracts butterflies
Impatiens	partial shade/ shade	12–24; 12–16	brightly colored flowers in red, pink, and white; sensitive to salty irrigation water; best in containers; New Guinea impatiens also available
Marigold	sun/partial shade	12–24; 8–12	simple or pompom flowers of yellow and orange; performs particularly well in late summer to fall; spider mites often a problem
Mexican heather	sun/partial shade	12–24; 10–12	tiny purple blooms and fine-textured green foliage; may be perennial in southern half of Texas
Moon vine	sun/partial shade	36+; 24	fast-growing vine with large, blue tubular flowers
Morning glory	sun	36+; 24	fast-growing vine with large purple, pink, or white tubular blooms
Nicotiana/ flowering tobacco	sun/partial shade	18–30; 6–12	tall annual flower adds height to the garden; star-shaped flowers in white, pink, maroon, lavender, green, red, and yellow; wonderful evening fragrance from flowers; not used as a smoking tobacco because it is reportedly low in nicotine
Petunia	sun/partial shade	6–8; 12	several types based on bloom size; new varieties more adapted (e.g., 'Wave'); old-fashioned, small-blossom type bloom longer and reseed (e.g., 'Laura Bush,' 'VIP')
Portulaca/ moss rose	sun	6–8; 6–12	excellent heat tolerance; prolific bloomer in all colors but blue

Name	Sun exposure	Height; width (inches)	Notes
Purslane	sun	6–8; 6–12	excellent heat tolerance; prolific bloomer in all colors but blue; only problem is it blooms from midmorning until late afternoon (If you work away from the home in these hours, you will never see the blooms.)
Salvia	partial shade/ shade	12–18; 8–12	spike bloom in red, pink, purple, and white; will not tolerate summer heat without shade; not to be confused with native perennial salvias
Sunflower	sun	24–120 (2–10 feet); 18–24	easily grown from seed; new varieties ranging from tall plants with single mammoth flower to shorter plants with masses of flowers; wide range of colors and fancy-form flowers in red, yellow, orange, brown, and multicolor
Verbena	sun	6–12; 8–12	heat-tolerant groundcover; flowers in all colors but blue; annual form is not as tough as native perennial verbenas
Zinnia	sun	12–36; 8–12	easily grown from seed; plant multiple times from spring to late summer; old-fashioned simple and pompom blooms and newer daisy-type blooms; heat tolerant; blooms in all colors but blue; must be deadheaded for continual bloom

Note: Annuals that also serve as cut flowers are noted by a shears icon.

Mulch—Low Tech, High Impact

Mulch is simply a layer of material covering the soil surface around plants. There is nothing glamorous about mulch, but it is by far the lowest-technology, highest-impact gardening practice of all.

My dissertation research at Texas A&M University found that unmulched shrubs may lose up to two-thirds of any water applied through evaporation from the soil and only one-third through plant use (transpiration). Further research at Oakwood Middle School (my son John's science fair project, a.k.a., "our" science fair project) found that container-grown houseplants with a 1-inch layer of mulch used 25 percent less water than plants with no mulch. Wow! There is truly much to mulch—mulch everywhere, including flower beds, shrub plantings, hedgerows, vegetable gardens, fruit plantings, and even containerized plants, indoors and out.

The primary benefit of mulching is water conservation, but it also does the following:

• Reduces soil erosion (especially on slopes) from wind and rain, protecting your soil-preparation investment

Mulch—low tech, high impact

• Moderates soil temperatures by keeping soils warmer in winter and cooler in summer

• Reduces weed populations by keeping weed seed in the dark, smothering weeds, restricting weed growth, or making them easier to pull

• Reduces soilborne plant diseases by preventing rain or irrigation water from splashing soil fungi up onto the stems, foliage, flowers, and fruit

• Provides organic matter to the soil by decomposing into the soil or with tilling into the soil annually

• Creates aesthetically pleasing soil covering (Research at Washington State University has indicated that a newly mulched bed with no plants has nearly the same aesthetic rating as a bed filled with plants. What was not acceptable were weedy beds.)

Mulches can be organic materials, such as shredded bark, compost, recycled paper, pine straw, and wood chips; or inorganic materials, such as chipped granite, lava rock, limestone, woven plastic, river rock, and recycled, chipped tires.

Organic mulches are preferred by most, but rock mulches have a place. Take a hint from the natural environment. Pine straw mulch looks natural in East Texas. Stone and rock mulches are natural in West Texas. Yet a constructed arroyo (streambed) of river rock can be a great landscape addition throughout Texas.

Organic mulches still have the advantage over rock mulches in most situations. Organic mulches decompose and add organic matter to the soil. They also reflect less sunlight, reducing heat loads on plants and surrounding buildings. The disadvantages of organic mulches are they can wash away in "toad-floating" rain events and they do need to be replenished annually.

Mulching has been around for centuries. Farmers know that shallow cultivation of the soil's surface after a rain slows the rate of water loss from the soil. The shallow layer of dry surface soil acts as a mulch. Here are some more guidelines for choosing and using mulches:

CALLER: "Can mulching with sawdust or wood chips rob nitrogen from the soil?"

ANSWER: "If you use sawdust or wood chips as a mulch, they can rob nitrogen from the soil because microorganisms use nitrogen to decompose them. No big problem! Simply add some nitrogen fertilizer to compensate. If you have an inexpensive source of sawdust or wood chips, use it."

- For increased water conservation, mulch in late March following winter rains to trap water in the soil and reduce evaporation.

- When seeding crops in vegetable or flower gardens, mulch after seedlings have emerged, recalling that mulch will restrict seed growth of both weeds and wanted plants.

- Replenish mulch in late summer to trap warmer soil temperature, to retard radiating heat loss, and to later insulate the roots of shrubs, flowers, and vegetable crops from cold winter temperatures.

- Don't mulch too deeply because roots can be smothered by reduction of oxygen and carbon dioxide movement in and out of the soil; never use more than 6 inches of mulch.

- Recommended mulch depth varies with the density of the mulch; fine-textured pine bark requires less depth than coarse-textured nugget chips.

- Recommended mulch depth also varies with the region's average rainfall and heat; 1 inch of a fine-textured mulch is adequate in East Texas, 2 inches in Central and North Texas, and 3 inches in South and West Texas and the Panhandle.

- The frequency of replacement of organic mulches increases in East Texas due to high rainfall and faster decomposition (probably twice a year depending on the mulch).

- Cost of mulches varies primarily based on distance shipped to your nursery or garden center; try to use locally processed mulches—don't select pine straw in West Texas or composted cotton bur hulls in East Texas.

- Cost of mulches varies significantly between mulch in bulk versus bagged; bulk is usually cheaper (about 20 percent less) but not often recommended by the best landscape contractors! Bulk mulch must be moved twice: it must be shoveled, shovelful by shovelful, into a wheelbarrow or cart; pushed, pulled, or dragged to the planting bed; dumped; shoveled around the bed; and spread. Too much work!

- Use bagged mulch if at all possible. It is worth the added expense. Bags save you time and lessen the workload; bags are easy to transport to the planting bed, and mulch is easier to spread from the cut bag.

- For the first 3 years after planting a tree in a lawn, maintain a round mulched area, 3 to 4 feet in diameter, around the tree to reduce weed and turf competition for water and nutrients. There is no benefit from mulching around large, mature trees; it is strictly aesthetic.

- If used in the landscape, plastic weed barriers should be limited to woven materials, which allow air and water to move through; these products are costly. Don't use inexpensive sheet plastic; it traps too much moisture and air, resulting in a stinking swamp below the mulch.

• In the vegetable garden, plastic mulches (called films or row covers) are effectively used on top of rows for weed control and water conservation; black plastics are most common, though some research indicates red plastic helps prevent insect infestations.

Mulch Types by Texture and Recommended Depth for East Texas

Fine textured ($\frac{1}{2}$-inch particles, depth 1 inch)

Compost
Cypress bark
Pea gravel
Pine straw
Recycled paper
Sawdust
Shredded pine bark

Medium textured ($\frac{3}{4}$–1-inch particles, depth 2 inches)

Composted cotton bur hulls
Crumbled rubber from tires
Crushed granite
Hardwood mulch
Wood chips

Coarse textured (1-inch and greater particles, depth 3 inches)

Crushed limestone
Lava rock
Pine bark nuggets

River rock

Note: Recommended depth: For Central and North Texas, add an additional 1 inch; for South and West Texas and the Panhandle, add an additional 2 inches.

CALLER: "How do you calculate how much mulch to buy?"

ANSWER: "To figure out the number of bags or cubic yards of mulch to purchase, multiply the area by the desired depth of mulch expressed in feet; then divide that amount by the number of cubic feet in the bag, or cubic yard (27 cubic feet = 1 cubic yard):

1,000 square feet at a 2-inch ($\frac{2}{12}$ foot) mulch depth:
1,000 x $\frac{2}{12}$ = 167 cubic feet
(*Note:* $\frac{2}{12}$ = 0.167)
167 cubic feet ÷ 2 cubic feet per bag = 83.5 or 84 bags

OR

167 cubic feet ÷ 27 cubic feet per yard = 6.5 cubic yards (rounded up for waste)"

Is Your Irrigation System Ready for Spring?

The average life span of a home landscape irrigation system is 15 years. During that time annual inspections, repairs, and adjustments are needed to maintain the proper performance of the system and to prevent water waste.

Most irrigation systems are turned on automatically by a time clock while you are sound asleep; therefore, you may seldom see your system running. Broken heads shooting "Moby Dick" geysers high into the air may go undetected for

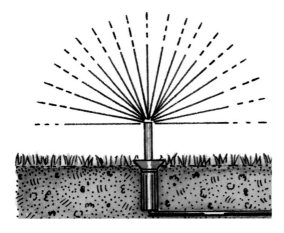

months, wasting thousands of gallons of water (not to mention money) and adversely affecting landscape quality.

Inspect your irrigation system by turning on the time clock (*Note:* It should be O-F-F during the winter) and initiating each station in the system. Look for the following as you progress through each station:

- Did the station turn on? If not, the valve may be stuck, or the solenoid that turns on the valve may be broken.
- Did all the sprinkler heads in the station pop up, spray, and/or rotate properly? If not, grass, soil, or another obstruction may be preventing the head from rising or rotating, or something could be mechanically wrong with the head.
- Did Moby Dick spout a geyser in your lawn? Although fun to look

at, geysers mean the sprinkler head is broken and the nozzle has blown out—replacement time.

- Are the sprinklers aligned properly? If a sprinkler head is spraying water on the driveway, sidewalk, house, or other nonplant areas, adjust the head to eliminate this waste.

- Are any pop-up or riser sprinklerheads misaligned vertically or sunken below ground level? If so, the spray pattern will be directed too high and fall short of the designed pattern, or the spray pattern of a sunken head will be obstructed by grass or soil. These situations often happen when heads are hit by mower wheels or moved by shifts in the soil during winter. Most heads are set on flexible pipe, so simply dig around the head and straighten and/or lift it.

Having performed this inspection, you may be capable of making any needed repairs, or you may call a licensed irrigation contractor to make the repairs. Winter is a great time of year to secure irrigation contractors, in contrast to the springtime rush or the summertime chaos these contractors experience.

Irrigation System Audits

Another more involved, yet extremely beneficial inspection process is called an irrigation system audit. You can do a basic audit for the lawn area, but you probably need an irrigation contractor to conduct a comprehensive audit, resulting in recommendations, repairs, and irrigation scheduling.

Irrigation system audits evaluate the actual performance of your system, not some theoretical performance from a system design book. An audit measures the ability of each station in your system to distribute water evenly across that station. Each station is audited separately.

If the water is not evenly distributed, then one area of a station will receive more water than another area. The portion receiving the least water dictates how long you need to run a station. The result is significant waste of water by overwatering one area to apply enough water to another.

The vast majority of irrigation systems in Texas have poor "distribution uniformity," a measurement of how evenly water is distributed across a lawn (expressed in percentage). The lower the distribution uniformity (percentage), the longer you have to run each station and the more water is wasted. Less than 60 percent distribution uniformity is considered poor and can be improved only by changing or adjusting sprinkler heads and nozzles.

Although it is impossible to get perfectly uniform distribution over 100 percent of a station, you can get close. The true professionals in the irrigation industry strive for high distribution uniformity by "head-to-head" spacing of sprinkler heads; by "matched-precipitation rates"; and by fine-tuning individual heads, nozzles, and spray patterns.

You can perform a basic irrigation audit to tell whether your system needs the help of a qualified irrigation contractor. Follow these steps and calculations to determine the distribution uniformity for two or three stations in your lawn. If the distribution is less than 60 percent uniform, call an irrigation contractor to improve the uniformity.

- Set eight open-top collection cans in the lawn area covered by a station (cans with short sides, such as tuna or cat food cans work best). Number and place the cans in a pattern using these guidelines: a can 3 feet from each head and a can halfway between each head, in this pattern ("O"s are heads and "x"s are cans):

Ox   x   Ox   x   Ox   x   O

- Turn the sprinkler station on for 30 minutes.
- Use a ruler to measure the depth of water in inches caught in each numbered can (e.g., $\frac{1}{4}$, $\frac{1}{3}$, $\frac{1}{2}$, 1), and record the measurements.
- Convert the inch measurements into decimals.

- Calculate the average of the lowest two measurements; divide that number by the average of all the measurements; and then multiply by 100 to determine a distribution uniformity percentage.

EXAMPLE DATA AND CALCULATIONS

Can	Depth (inch)	Decimal equivalent
1	$\frac{1}{2}$	0.50
2	$\frac{1}{2}$	0.50
3	$\frac{3}{4}$	0.75
4	$\frac{1}{4}$	0.25
5	$\frac{1}{3}$	0.33
6	$\frac{3}{4}$	0.75
7	$\frac{3}{4}$	0.75
8	$\frac{1}{2}$	0.50

Average of lowest two measurements:
$(0.25 + 0.33) \div 2 = 0.29$

Average of all measurements:
$0.5 + 0.5 + 0.75 + 0.25 + 0.33 + 0.75 + 0.75 + 0.5 = 4.33 \div 8 = 0.54$

Distribution uniformity percentage:
$(0.29 \div 0.54) \times 100 = 53.7$

RECOMMENDATION. This distribution uniformity is slightly low, and an irrigation contractor should be engaged to improve the system by changing heads or nozzles and/or adjusting the heads. Notice that can numbers 4 and 5 have markedly less water than the others; there may be something mechanically wrong with just one head near these cans.

Are You Ready to Have an Irrigation System Installed?

An irrigation system is the most efficient and effective way to water your landscape and garden, plus it eases your watering chores significantly. If you are ready to have an irrigation system installed (or have an existing system), here are some guidelines for a state-of-the-art system. (*Note:* Unless you understand hydrology and irrigation design well and are capable of piecing it all together, this is not a do-it-yourself project—believe me.)

- Irrigation contractors are licensed by the state of Texas by passing an exam; however, choose your contractor carefully. Get three bids for the job, ask for references, and call them. The lowest bid is not necessarily the right bid.
- The cost for an eight-station irrigation system covering a 5,000–10,000-square-foot landscape may range from $2,000 to $4,000 depending on the complexity of the design and sophistication of the components.
- Although many quality irrigation contractors don't draw an irrigation design on paper, you should ask for one. Once the system is installed and a year has passed, it is tough to

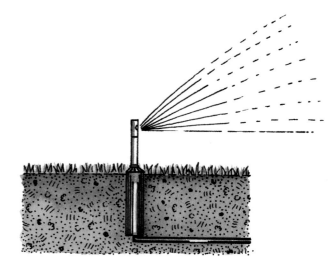

remember where all the valves and stations are unless you have an "as-built" plan (the way the system actually was installed) for reference.

- Time clocks vary significantly in price and complexity; make sure that you can understand and program the time clock to be installed. If you don't understand the time clock, you won't change the time clock. If you don't change the time clock based on the season, rainfall, and plant water requirement, you will waste thousands of gallons of water, particularly in the spring and fall.

- The stations within the system should be "zoned" according to plant type and garden sections. Lawn areas should be zoned separately from shrub plantings and flower beds so that they can be irrigated separately. Vegetable gardens should be zoned separately. A zoned system costs more but is worth it. You will save water and money and have a healthier landscape by not overwatering one group of plants to meet the needs of another.

- Drip irrigation should be included in the system to irrigate shrub plantings, flower beds, and vegetable gardens. Sprinkler heads are still the standard for lawn areas.

- The system should have "head-to-head" spacing between sprinkler heads. This provides complete overlapping of the spray patterns of the heads, resulting in increased uniformity of water delivered to the landscape and lawn. Areas where the sprinkler's spray pattern does not overlap are likely to get insufficient water and develop brown dry spots.

- The system should have "matched-precipitation rate" sprinkler heads. All sprinkler heads in a station should be the same type (e.g., stream rotors, pop-up sprays) and have a matched-precipitation rate (in inches per hour). If heads have differing precipitation rates, applying a uniform amount of water across an area is impossible.

- If you have large existing trees, ask the contractor how he or she intends to avoid damaging the root systems. This is difficult but can be done with careful planning (e.g., trenching and laying distribution pipe on the perimeter of the landscape along the street, driveway, and property lines).

- Ask the contractor to measure the distribution uniformity of the system, that is, how evenly water is distributed across each station. The contractor can conduct an irrigation system audit to determine the "real" distribution uniformity, not one derived from a manufacturer's specification manual.

- Final adjustments to the system should include aligning the spray

heads to avoid spraying your driveway, sidewalks, the house, or fences
and making fine adjustments of
nozzles to match precipitation rates
and optimize spray patterns.

• Additional components worth
considering include a secondary
water meter just for the irrigation system (sewer charges should not apply
to irrigation water—check with your
water utility); a rainfall sensor, which
cuts off the system when it rains; and
soil moisture sensors, which disen-
gage the system if soil moisture is
adequate.

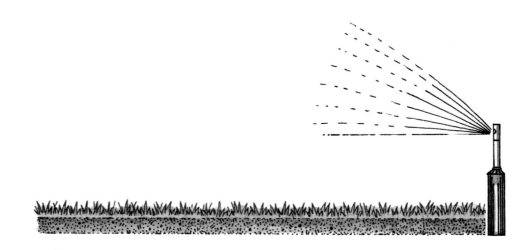

Pruning School

(*Note:* Everett E. Janne served as an extension landscape horticulturist for Texas A&M University until 1984 and wrote dozens of publications for Extension, including "Follow Proper Pruning Techniques" and "Fertilizing Woody Ornamentals." When I was a young extension assistant in the early 1980s, Everett Janne generously shared with me his immense horticultural knowledge. He even let me coauthor his publications as they were revised. I have used information from his original publications for this and the fertilizing trees and shrubs essays, and I have carefully added to them based on my experience and recent research. Everett Janne was a fine horticulturist and gardener who contributed greatly to my knowledge and love of gardening.)

There is nothing like a cool, clear winter day to go outside and drop some wood! (Picking up all the trimmings is not so pleasant.) Pruning can be very therapeutic for the pruner. Results are immediate, and it can be a physical workout and a great way to relieve stress. Remember, though, that overdoing it is not good for the plants. It is tough to glue those branches back on the tree once removed.

There are specific reasons to prune trees and shrubs, for example:

- To train the plant
- To maintain plant health
- To improve the quality of flowers, fruit, foliage, or stems
- To restrict growth

Pruning combines art and science. Proper pruning is a skill that requires both knowledge and experience. A loud chain saw and a pickup truck do not make one a landscape professional nor a "tree surgeon," and certainly not an arborist. Improper pruning ruins or kills more landscape trees and shrubs each year than insects or disease do.

Most pruning can be avoided by simply choosing the right plant for the right space. Plant trees and shrubs based on their mature size (refer to plant nursery tags or lists presented in this almanac). Planting shrubs too close together results in having to prune regularly just to keep them in bounds.

Follow the basic principles, guidelines, and techniques described in this essay to ensure proper pruning of your trees and shrubs.

Pruning Plan

Whether pruning a rosebush, crape myrtle, or shade tree, start with a general pruning plan, in the following order:

1. Remove all dead, broken, or diseased limbs by cutting them at the point of origin (back to a stronger or healthy branch); this may be all the pruning needed.

2. Remove any branch that is rubbing and/or touching another branch; leave the stronger or better-positioned branch.

3. Remove any branch that is growing in the same space or direction as an adjacent branch. Again, leave the stronger or better-positioned branch; the remaining branch will quickly fill the void.

4. Remove any branch that is growing from one side of the plant, through the middle of the plant, and out the other side; it is just taking up space and crossing too many properly placed branches.

5. Remove any "hanger-downers" —branches that are aimed toward the ground and obviously not headed in the right direction.

6. Remove "suckers" and "water sprouts"; suckers are vigorous shoots emanating from the base of the trunk (as on crape myrtles), and water sprouts are fast-growing branches up in the tree that grow straight up parallel to the trunk (as on live oaks, peaches, and pears).

7. Do not remove any branch larger in diameter than a pencil unless there is a good reason. If you find yourself having to remove larger branches, you may need to prune more often or rethink your pruning decisions.

8. Remove any dead blooms (called deadheading), such as on crape myrtles, roses, and vitex.

Now, step back from the plant, and look at the tree or shrub carefully. You may be finished pruning that plant.

Pruning Guidelines

Further decisions about pruning get more involved. Here are some guidelines:

The best time to prune is in winter just before spring growth begins. There are exceptions, which will be pointed out. The least desirable time is immediately after new growth begins in the spring. Limit the amount of pruning done late in summer, as new growth will be encouraged on some plants that are more susceptible to freeze damage. Minor pruning—removing less than 20 percent of the plant—can be done year-round.

Narrow angles are weaker than wide angles. This may seem counterintuitive; however, narrow crotch angles (less than a 45-degree angle between the branch and the connection to its branch of origin) are weak and should be removed. This is often seen on young, fast-growing trees, such as elms, oaks, pears, pecans, and sweet gums. Wide crotch angles (60 to 90 degrees) are much stronger,

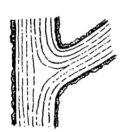 

Branches with wide crotch angles are stronger than those with narrow angles—odd but true.

because more wood fibers connect the two branches. Pecans and pears, which can produce heavy loads of nuts or fruits on a branch, need wide-crotched branches. Also, ice storms can destroy trees by breaking weak, narrow-crotched branches.

The "ideal" tree or shrub structure is critical to long-term health and strength. Visualize a straight central trunk and wide-angled branches, each emanating from the trunk in a different direction. If you looked down on a tree (a bird's-eye view), you would see branches arranged like the spokes on a wheel. This is called radial branch spacing. Some trees and shrubs naturally have multiple trunks (such as crape myrtle, river birch, and yaupon); however, each trunk should have the structure described above with wide-crotched branches circling each trunk.

Maintain the natural shape of the tree or shrub. Take your directions from what nature provides. Butchering trees and shrubs destroys their natural shape and increases the need for regular pruning.

Selective and directional pruning guides plant growth. With a keen eye and careful cuts, you can manipulate how a plant grows. New growth emanates from buds, which can be easily seen on small branches and twigs. Whichever way a bud points indicates the direction that the new shoot will grow. Cutting just above a bud will force the shoot to grow. By selecting which bud to leave just below your cut, you can determine which way the shoot will grow. Do this multiple times throughout the plant, and you can direct the shrub's growth. Using this technique, you can renovate lopsided shrubs, direct growth to fill voids in a tree canopy, or create a hedge shaped like the Alamo (well, maybe not).

Shearing should be minimized. Shearing or cutting back plants regularly with hedge clippers or shears results in a very formal growth habit but destroys the natural shape of the plant. The resulting plant shapes should be referred to as "meatballs" or "meatloaves." How many do you want in your landscape? Limit shearing to hedges, topiary, or formal garden areas.

Pruning results in wounds. Remember that every cut you make wounds the plant, causing a reaction by the plant to heal that wound, plus it exposes the inner wood to insects and disease. Don't make a cut that is not necessary.

Don't leave stubs after a cut. Make pruning cuts smooth, almost flush with the adjacent branch or trunk, using the "Shigo method," to encourage rapid healing of wounds. Stubs hinder scar tissue from covering the wound, and wood decay may result. Alex Shigo, a former USDA Forest Service plant pathologist, determined years ago that large branches (over 1 inch in diameter) should be removed flush to the

"branch collar," not flush with the trunk. The branch collar is an area of tissue containing a plant-generated, chemically protective zone. In response to the wound, the plant directs chemicals and oils to the branch collar. This compartmentalizes (seals off) the wound naturally from wood-decay fungi and insect damage. If the branch collar is removed by cutting the branch flush to the trunk or adjacent branch, the protective zone is removed. Wood decay can then easily infect the trunk.

Remove thick, heavy branches carefully. When cutting branches more than $1\frac{1}{2}$ inches in diameter, use a three-part cut, or "jump cut." First, saw a cut on the bottom side of the branch about 6 to 8 inches out from the trunk or adja-

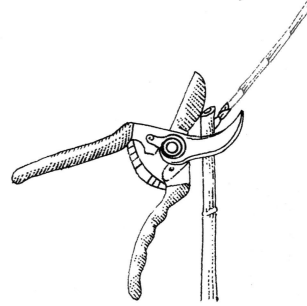

Directional pruning helps train and shape plant growth. When you cut above a bud, it grows in the direction it is pointed.

cent branch, and cut about one-third of the way through the branch. Second, saw from the top of the branch, about 3 inches farther out from the undercut, until the branch falls, or jumps, away. This procedure eliminates any stripping of the bark as the branch falls plus creates a safer, more controlled dropping of the branch. The stub that remains can

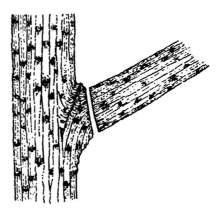

No more flush cuts: Use the Shigo method to remove branches for improved plant health.

CALLER: "Should I use pruning paint?"

ANSWER: "Applying pruning paint (oil-based wound dressings) to wounds resulting from large limb removal has been debated for years. Plant scientists have found that pruning paint is strictly cosmetic and has little to do with preventing insect or disease damage to the wounded area. Pruning paint may, in fact, slow down the healing process. Pruning paint is not recommended, with one exception. On oak trees in areas of Texas where oak wilt disease is prevalent, pruning paint should be used to help prevent bark beetles from spreading this fungal disease through tree wounds caused by pruning."

then be cut back to the branch collar. If there is danger of the cut branch damaging other limbs or objects on the ground, it should be properly tied and supported to carefully lower to the ground.

Topping trees is not recommended. Too often trees are topped ("dehorned") to reduce tree size or to rejuvenate growth. In either case, this "Texas chain saw manicure" is not a recommended practice. Topping is a technique whereby a tree is cut back to a few large branches. After a few months, new growth emerges that is vigorous, bushy, and upright. This new growth is unnatural and seriously affects the tree's structure and appearance. The new growth also has narrow crotch angles, thus is weakly attached and can break off during severe wind- or rainstorms. Topping can even shorten tree life by increasing susceptibility to insects and disease.

Thinning is a better means of reducing tree size or rejuvenating growth. In contrast to topping, thinning removes the tallest unwanted branches by cutting them at their point of origin. Thinning maintains the tree's natural beauty and results in a more open tree, emphasizing the tree's branch structure. Thinning also strengthens the tree by directing growth to the remaining branches that increases their diameter.

Training Young Trees

Young trees can be trained by using pruning techniques that will help promote plant health and long life. After you purchase trees, the first pruning consists of removing broken, crossing, and pest-infested branches.

The main trunk (central leader) of a tree should not be cut back. Trees with

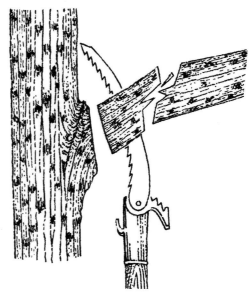

The "three-step jump cut" decreases plant damage and increases safety when removing large branches.

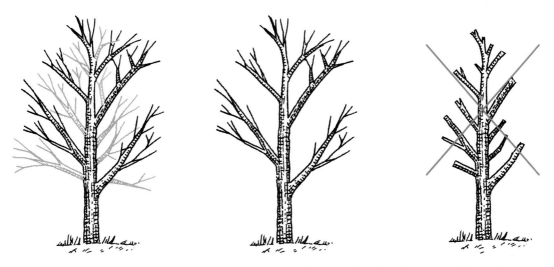

Stop the Texas chain saw manicure. Do not top trees; reduce tree height when needed through proper thinning.

a central leader, such as magnolia, pine, sweet gum, and Texas red oak, may need little or no pruning except to eliminate vigorous branches that are competing with the main trunk (central leader). These competing branches should simply be shortened or removed.

Think twice before removing the lowest branches. One-third of the height of a young shade tree should be in trunk and two-thirds in foliage. Commercial nurseries tend to remove lower limbs too soon, resulting in a "lollipop"-shaped tree. This is not the best way to start a future shade tree. Mature shade trees and street trees may eventually be one-half of the height in foliage and one-half

in trunk. For screening or windbreak trees (e.g., eastern red cedar), the lowest branches may remain only a few inches from the ground.

A "trashy trunk" results in a thicker trunk quicker. Complementary to the guideline above, a trashy trunk refers to leaving all small twigs and branches on the lower trunk. A common mistake in training young trees is stripping the trunk of most small branches on the bottom three-fourths of the tree trunk. This improper training forms a weak "buggy whip" trunk with a small amount of foliage on top. Gradually raise the height of the lowest branches by pruning them

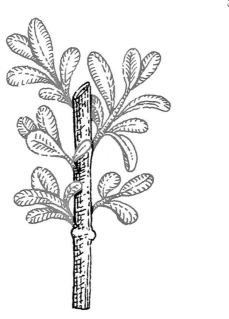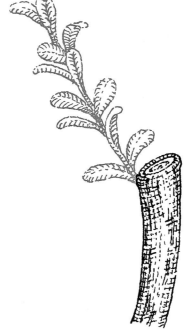

Light cuts and heavy cuts produce different growth responses (denser growth or rapid, single-shoot growth, respectively).

off when they reach 1 inch. This prevents permanent scarring of the trunk caused by removing large limbs.

An important concept in training trees is light versus heavy cuts. The importance of this pruning concept lies in the development of bushy, well-shaped trees (and shrubs) through light pruning or the sometimes-desired, invigorating effect of heavy cuts. The weight of the cut refers to the portion of the branch removed and the desired growth response of that branch. On a young, vigorously growing branch, if the terminal end (far end) is lightly cut back (less than 6 inches), then side branching is induced up and down the branch. If the same branch is heavily cut back (from 6 inches to a few feet), one or two buds located just below the cut will grow vigorously and replace what was just cut off.

Main branches of shade trees should be spaced properly vertically. Branches should be chosen that are at least 8 inches apart vertically, and preferably 20 to 24 inches apart. Closely spaced branches result in long, thin main branches and weak tree structure.

Spacing of main branches around the trunk is also critical. Ideally, this radial branch distribution would equally space five to seven main branches around the tree trunk. No branch would be overshadowed by another branch, reducing competition for light and nutrients. Remove or prune new shoots that are too close or too vigorous in relation to the central trunk and selected main branches.

Pruning Mature Trees

Healthy mature trees should grow about 6 to 12 inches in height annually. If your tree is not achieving this growth, look for reasons why not (drought, lack of nutrients, pests) and/or seek professional help.

On mature trees, pruning low-hanging, nuisance branches is perhaps all that most homeowners should undertake. Leave removing hazardous limbs (overhanging the house), cabling large branches, and overall trimming of large trees to arborists.

Choosing a quality arborist is not easy. Look for affiliations and/or certifications by professional arborist societies or associations. Also, make sure the arborist is "bonded," meaning the arborist has insurance to cover any mishaps while working on your tree. Be an educated consumer—seek referrals and ask lots of questions.

Pruning Shrubs

If the right plant was planted in the right place and the right spacing from other plants, shrub pruning should be minimal each year. If you find yourself pruning a shrub constantly to keep it in bounds, consider replacing it.

Few homeowners today wish to have the formal hedges and tightly manicured shrubs of years gone by. Today, sprawling hedgerows and drifts of shrubs and flowers lend themselves to lower maintenance and informal living. Pruning these shrubs consists of thinning, gradually reducing their size, and rejuvenating deep pruning.

Plants can be maintained at a given height and width for years by thinning. Remove branches or twigs at the point of origin from a branch or the ground. Thin out the oldest and tallest stems first. This technique can cut out significant amounts of the shrub without changing the plant's natural appearance or growth habit. Thinning also results in better air circulation through the shrub, which reduces the incidence of insect infestation and diseases. This method is best done with hand pruning shears or loppers, but not hedge clippers.

Through gradual size reduction, a plant can be shaped to a specific size or grown in a confined space. On an annual basis, cut back the tallest branches. Grab the tallest branch and shake it; follow the movement down to the point of origin, and cut off the branch at that point. Some thinning may be necessary to shorten long branches or maintain a symmetrical shape.

Deep pruning can rejuvenate an old, overgrown shrub. Before new growth begins in spring, remove one-third to one-half of the shrub. Remove the oldest, tallest branches back to another branch or slightly above ground level. Timing is important so that you don't have to stare at an ugly, naked shrub for long before a huge flush of new growth begins.

When a flowering shrub blooms determines when to prune. Spring-flowering shrubs, trees, and vines bloom on last season's growth and should be pruned soon after they bloom. This allows for summertime growth and setting of flower buds for next year's bloom. Following are some examples of spring-flowering trees and shrubs:

- Azalea and rhododendron
- Forsythia
- Fringe tree
- Honeysuckle
- Indian hawthorn
- Japanese quince
- Redbud
- Spirea, or bridal wreath
- Spring-blooming climbing roses and shrub roses
- Texas mountain laurel
- Viburnum species
- Wisteria

Summer-blooming shrubs generally bloom on shoots that grow from spring (same year's or season's growth). These shrubs should be pruned in late winter to promote vigorous shoot growth in the spring that results in more blooms. Following are some examples of summer-blooming shrubs:

- Althea
- Butterfly bush
- Crape myrtle
- Glossy abelia
- Hydrangea
- Roses (most)
- Vitex, or chaste tree

When to prune shrubs with ornamental berries is tricky. Beautyberry, deciduous yaupon, pyracantha, and yaupon holly produce beautiful berries in late summer and fall. They are spring-blooming plants, so how do you prune them? Very carefully. Pruning can be done after the berries have shriveled, dropped, or been eaten by birds and before spring growth begins. Prune them lightly, because whenever you prune, you are removing future flowers and/or berries. Prune only those branches that need to be removed because they are broken, diseased, placed poorly, or rubbing on other branches.

Pruning Hedges

Top-heavy hedges with little foliage near the ground are common in older landscapes. Renovating these unsightly plantings into beautiful, full-foliaged hedges can be done with patience and proper knowledge and techniques.

The primary reason leaves and new shoots do not grow low on a hedge is lack of sunlight. The goal of renovation is simply to get sunlight to strike the lower branches to initiate growth. This technique is best used on broadleaf evergreen or deciduous hedges, such as hollies, ligustrum, old-fashioned roses, oleander, and photinia. (Needle-leaved evergreen hedges, such as arborvitae, junipers, and yew, that are unsightly and overgrown are best replaced.)

Hedges are most often shaped with flat tops and vertical sides, like a rectangle in cross section. This is the basis for the older unsightly hedge, which ends up being a trapezoid in cross section with the top wider than the bottom. The top is shading out the sunlight. Through renovation, the new shape of the hedge will be a trapezoid in cross section, with the bottom wider than the top. Be patient, as this may take two seasons to accomplish.

In late winter before the spring growth begins, cut back the old, misshapen hedge to eliminate the top corners of the trapezoid. This allows sunlight to strike the lower branches. Spring growth will initiate from both the lower branches and the upper branches. Give preference to the lower growth, lightly

Reduced growth and thinning at the bottom of hedges can be eliminated by proper shaping— trapezoid for a formal hedge or rounded for a more natural hedge.

shearing the upper growth throughout spring to ensure that the lower growth continues to get sun. It may take a second season of this type of pruning to get the hedge shaped up and full bodied.

When planting a new hedge, the best shape is a more natural form. Trim the hedge into a rounded or slightly flattened top with sides slanting to a wide base. Or better yet, choose the right plants and space them far enough apart so that at mature size, the plants overlap by a few inches. An example would be dwarf yaupon hollies spaced 3 feet apart, or wax myrtles spaced 6 to 8 feet apart. This will reduce pruning needs significantly.

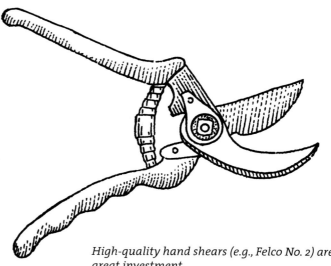

High-quality hand shears (e.g., Felco No. 2) are a great investment.

Pruning Equipment

"You know you are a gardener when your pruning shears cost more than $40."

—Doug Welsh

It's tool time, and there are many types and brands. Foremost, always buy quality. You can waste money and effort using the wrong pruning equipment. Quality of pruning equipment varies significantly, as does price. This is one case where the more you pay for it, the better it is. For example, Felco hand pruning shears are considered by most professional gardeners to be the best. They retail for over $40 (my pair is 25 years old and still great).

Hand pruning shears will cut stems up to $\frac{1}{2}$ to 1 inch in diameter. Two common styles are the scissor action and the anvil cut. In scissor-action shears, a thin, sharp blade slides closely past a thicker sharp blade. These usually cost more but make cleaner, closer cuts. In anvil-cut shears, a sharpened blade cuts against a broad, flat blade.

Lopping shears (loppers) have long handles that are operated by both hands. Loppers can cut branches up to 2 inches in diameter. They also come in scissor action or anvil cut. Some have ratchet or gear-drive action, which allows larger cuts with less effort. Handles for loppers come in wood, steel, and fiberglass or composites.

Hedge shears are used mainly for shearing plants into hedges or formal shapes. They are also handy for deadheading (removing old blooms) of old-fashioned roses and perennials. Manually operated, scissor-action shears are most common; however, electric and gasoline-powered shears are available.

Pruning saws, both rigid and folding, are useful for cutting large branches. Pruning saws usually cut on the pull stroke and have teeth set for a wider cut. This allows the sawdust to kick out and results in less binding in green wood. A less expensive option is a simple bow saw.

Pole pruners usually have a shear on one side and a saw blade on the other. Poles can be made of several materials and have sections that telescope. Use of pole pruners can be dangerous. Material cut overhead can fall on the operator. Eye and head protection is a must.

Gas-powered and electric chain saws come in a variety of horsepower or amps. They can be dangerous, and safety is priority one. Chain saws used up in a tree are best operated by professional arborists.

Last and First Freeze Dates: What They Mean and Why They Are Important

A freeze in the garden ranges from a light frost to a deep freeze. Plants absorb heat from the sun during the day. On a cold night, plants quickly lose this stored heat to the atmosphere. Temperatures within the plants may drop a few degrees colder than the air since leaf temperature cools faster than air (this explains why frost can occur on the lawn and the air temperature still be 38°F). Clouds and wind insulate or protect plants from freeze damage. Cold, clear nights with little wind are perfect for frost and freeze to occur.

As air temperatures drop, moisture in the air condenses into dew, which then freezes on leaves and stems when surface temperatures drop to 32°F. This is called frost, a covering of minute ice crystals on a cold surface. Frost may advance to a freeze when temperatures go below 32°, and ice crystals may form inside plant cells and rupture them, killing plant tissue, if not the entire plant. A "hard freeze" occurs when temperatures dip below 28°, and the duration of the freeze often determines the severity of plant damage. A few hours at below 28° is bad, but 12 to 24 hours can be devastating for many Texas landscapes.

Be aware also that cold air is heavier (denser) than warmer air. Cold air, therefore, sinks, causing lower-lying areas of the landscape or neighborhood to be several degrees colder and more likely to experience a frost. Sloping areas are less prone to frost because the cold air rolls on down to the lowest spot.

The Last Spring Freeze

The average date of the last spring freeze is important in determining when to plant frost-sensitive vegetables and annual flowers and when to move tropical container plants out of the garage.

For example, green beans, peppers, squash, and tomatoes are frost sensitive. A frost will either severely damage their leaves and tender shoots or, at a minimum, retard their growth for weeks. If your frost-sensitive vegetables experience a frost, it is better to jerk them out of the ground and plant new ones than to nurse them along and receive reduced production.

Frost-sensitive annual flowers and tropical plants, including bougainvillea, ficus, marigolds, periwinkles, and zinnias, should be planted or put outdoors after the last spring freeze to ensure plant health.

Texas' Two Growing Seasons

The number of days between the last spring freeze and the first fall freeze determines the "growing season" for your area. This ranges in Texas from over 346 days in Galveston to 193 days in Amarillo. Realistically, Texas has two optimal growing seasons: (1) from the last spring freeze through early summer and (2) from late summer to the first fall freeze.

The objective is to get frost-sensitive plants into the garden and landscape as soon as possible in the spring so that they can be productive (e.g., fruit, flower,

and grow) before the heat of summer. Then the objective becomes to get frost-sensitive plants into the garden early enough in late summer to be productive before the first fall freeze.

For example, green beans take 60 days from planting seeds to harvesting beans. To plant a fall crop of beans, you must count back 60 days from the first fall freeze date:

- Amarillo: plant seed September 1
- Dallas/Fort Worth: plant seed September 16
- Houston: plant seed October 1

Freeze Dates for Texas Cities

The table on page 84 provides dates for the last spring freeze and the first fall freeze for 68 Texas cities. Remember that these dates are averages from decades of climatological data collected by the National Oceanic and Atmospheric Administration. This leads to the statistical truism: "Averages mean you are wrong 100 percent of the time!" So be cautious when using these tables and the maps that follow to determine planting dates for your frost-sensitive vegetables and annual flowers.

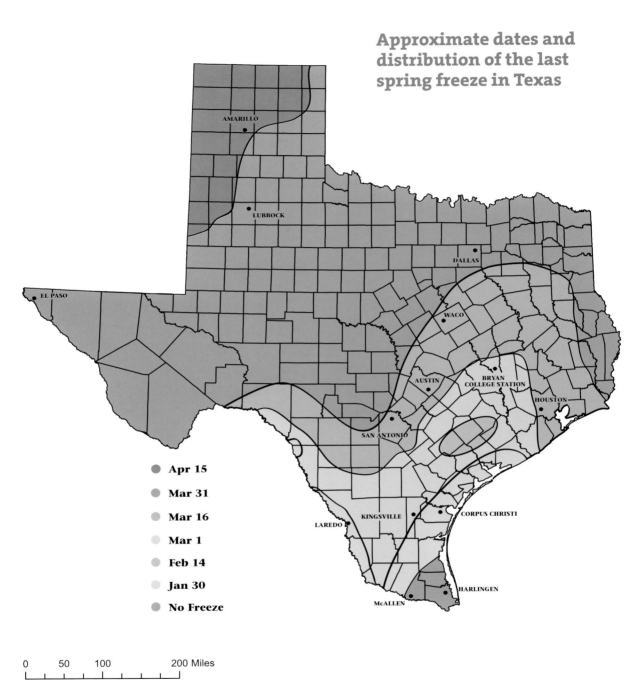

Approximate dates and distribution of the last spring freeze in Texas

- Apr 15
- Mar 31
- Mar 16
- Mar 1
- Feb 14
- Jan 30
- No Freeze

0   50   100   200 Miles

Source: R. J. Hildreth and R. B. Orton, Freeze Probabilities in Texas (MP 657) (College Station: Texas Agricultural Extension Service, 1963).

Approximate dates and distribution of the first fall freeze in Texas

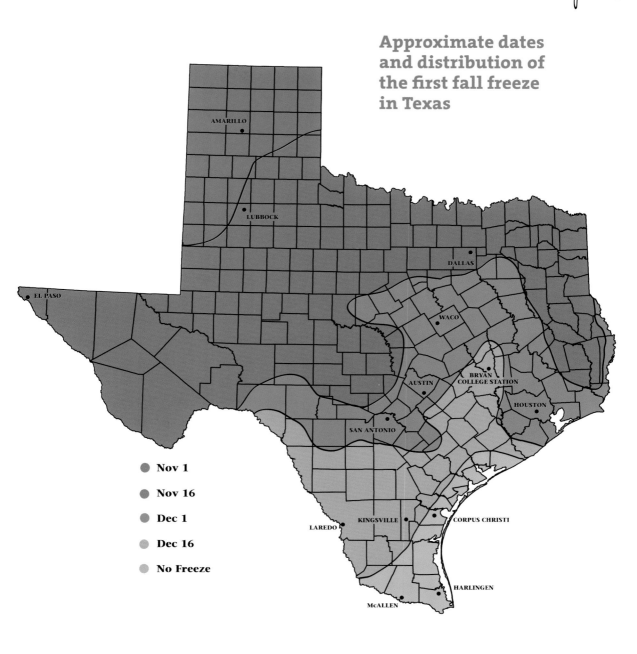

- ● Nov 1
- ● Nov 16
- ● Dec 1
- ● Dec 16
- ● No Freeze

```
0    50   100          200 Miles
```

Source: R. J. Hildreth and R. B Orton, Freeze Probabilities in Texas (MP 657) (College Station: Texas Agricultural Extension Service, 1963).

FREEZE DATES (AVERAGE) FOR TEXAS CITIES			
CITY	LAST SPRING FREEZE	FIRST FALL FREEZE	FREEZE-FREE DAYS
Abilene	03/24	11/11	232
Amarillo	04/14	10/24	193
Austin	02/24	12/05	284
Bastrop	03/09	11/22	258
Beaumont	02/17	12/09	295
Beeville	02/23	12/07	287
Boerne	03/24	11/11	232
Brenham	02/27	12/05	281
Brownsville	02/02	12/31	323
Brownwood	03/24	11/11	232
Cameron	03/08	11/22	259
Childress	03/21	11/20	244
Cleburne	03/28	11/13	235
College Station/ Bryan	03/07	11/28	266
Conroe	03/07	11/27	265
Corpus Christi	02/12	12/20	311
Corsicana	03/13	11/22	254
Dalhart	04/27	10/18	174
Dallas	03/07	11/22	260
Del Rio	02/26	11/29	276
Denison/Sherman	03/17	11/15	243
Denton	03/21	11/13	237
Eagle Pass	02/22	12/03	284
El Paso	03/22	11/10	233
Fort Stockton	03/28	11/10	227
Fort Worth	03/20	11/12	241
Fredericksburg	03/24	11/13	234
Galveston	01/09	01/28	346
Georgetown/Taylor	03/10	11/16	251
Greenville	03/25	11/11	231
Hillsboro	03/21	11/13	237
Houston	02/12	12/12	303
Huntsville	03/06	11/30	269
Kaufman	03/22	11/13	236
Laredo	02/27	12/02	278

City	Last spring freeze	First fall freeze	Freeze-free days
Liberty	02/28	11/25	270
Llano	03/21	11/13	237
Longview/ Marshall	03/25	11/11	231
Lubbock	04/05	11/02	211
Lufkin	03/12	11/11	244
Matagorda	02/12	12/14	305
Midland/Odessa	03/28	11/06	223
Mount Pleasant	03/28	11/04	221
Muleshoe	04/17	10/20	186
Nacogdoches	03/16	11/12	241
New Braunfels	03/07	11/25	263
Palestine	03/14	11/18	249
Poteet	03/04	11/30	271
Presidio	03/08	11/21	258
Raymondville	02/12	12/22	313
Rosenberg	02/28	12/05	280
San Angelo	03/26	11/12	231
San Antonio	03/06	11/28	267
San Marcos	03/12	11/21	254
Sanderson	03/25	11/11	231
Stephenville	03/20	11/15	240
Temple/Killeen	03/11	11/16	250
Texarkana	03/10	11/15	250
Tyler	03/07	11/21	259
Uvalde	03/06	11/17	256
Victoria	02/12	12/11	302
Waco	03/14	11/22	253
Wichita Falls	03/27	11/10	228

Source: Adapted from A. J. Vega, K. D. Robbins, and J. M. Grymes, *Frost/Freeze Analysis in the Southern Climate Region*, Southern Regional Climate Center: Technical Report Number One (Baton Rouge: Southern Regional Climate Center, Department of Geology and Anthropology, Louisiana State University, 1994), http://www.srh.noaa.gov/oun/climate/srcc/srcc1994.pdf.

CALLER: "Can I get a jump on spring by growing giant transplants?"

ANSWER: "Absolutely. To get a jump on spring and produce frost-sensitive vegetables (and annual flowers) before anyone else in the neighborhood, grow giant transplants. Buy frost-sensitive vegetable transplants from the nursery as soon as they are available (you can grow these from seed, too). If you plant transplants immediately into the garden, you are gambling big time. There may not be a frost, but even a temperature of forty degrees Fahrenheit will do damage.

"Instead, put the transplants into one-gallon containers, using good potting soil. Place the plants outdoors in the full sun, watering and fertilizing regularly.

"The advantage is that your giant transplants are mobile. You can move them indoors when temperatures are forecast to be in the low fifties. Keep them inside with you by the fireplace until temperatures warm up to the sixties. Plant your giant transplants into the garden after the last spring frost date for your area."

Get a head start on spring by planting transplants into larger, still-mobile, containers.

USDA Plant Hardiness Zone Map

The USDA Plant Hardiness Zone Map (page 87) indicates what the lowest winter temperature will likely be based on historical records. It is not perfect but does provide a general guide to determine whether a plant will survive the winter in your area. Texas includes more hardiness zones than any other state—ranging from 6a in the Panhandle to 9b in the Rio Grande Valley.

The value of this map seems to increase the farther north you are in Texas and the nation. Winter temperatures are not the limiting factor for plant survival for most of Texas—summer temperatures are. If you have a question about a specific plant's ability to survive an average winter in your area, (1) identify the hardiness zone for your area; and (2) determine the hardiness rating for the plant using landscape plant references, the Internet, or the plant nursery tag.

Be cautious about depending too much on the hardiness zone map. It is based on averages, which are seldom on target in any given year. And your neighborhood or landscape may have microclimatic factors that make it warmer or colder than the average. Perhaps the best way to determine whether a plant is cold hardy to your area is to ask a nursery or landscape professional or county extension agent, and have him

or her direct you to a living specimen of the plant in your community.

HARDINESS ZONE RANGE IN TEXAS

Zone	City	Temperature range (°F)
6a	Dalhart	−10 to −5
6b	Amarillo	−5 to 0
7a	Lubbock	0 to 5
7b	Midland/ Odessa	5 to 10
8a	Waco	10 to 15
8b	Austin	15 to 20
9a	Houston	20 to 25
9b	Brownsville	25 to 30

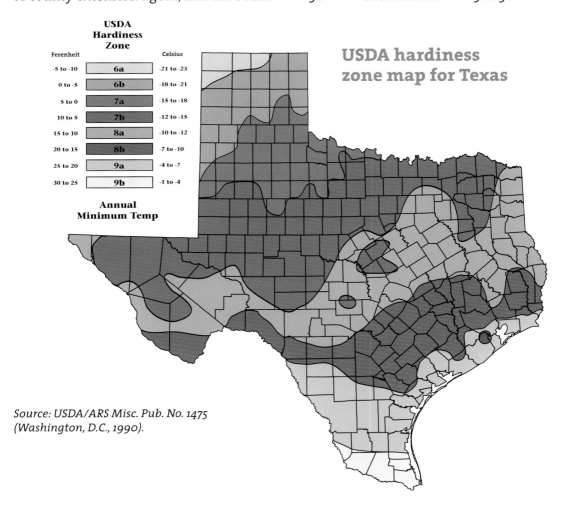

USDA hardiness zone map for Texas

Source: USDA/ARS Misc. Pub. No. 1475 (Washington, D.C., 1990).

Fertilizing Trees and Shrubs

Before fertilizing trees and shrubs, look for plant signs indicating the need for fertilization, including lack of growth, pale green or yellow leaves, or dead or thinning branches.

General tree health and growth can be determined by comparing the length of twig growth during the past 2 to 4 years as depicted in the adjacent illustration. Young trees should have at least 9 to 12 inches of growth from each branch each year. Large, mature trees usually average 6 to 9 inches of growth per year. Shrub growth can be judged in the same way.

To measure tree growth, examine several branches. Look at the tip of the branch (terminal end), and follow the branch back to a point where there are bud scale scars (multiple, small ridges circling the branch). The distance from the terminal end back to the first group of bud scars is the length of growth made this year (current year's growth).

From the first group of bud scars back to the second group of bud scars is last year's growth. You can follow the branch back a few years and determine the annual growth rates. Practice determining annual growth by viewing trees with prominent bud scars, such as crape myrtles, elms, and oaks.

Judge tree health by checking yearly branch growth. Start at the tip bud, and measure back to the whorl of bud scars (where growth began that year); continue back from there to the next set of bud scars to measure the previous year's growth; and so on.

Proper Timing

Proper timing of fertilizer applications has a marked effect on the growth of trees and shrubs. In general, the best time to apply fertilizer is in the late winter before spring growth begins.

Do not apply fertilizers between August 1 and the first freeze. Fertilizing at this time can stimulate new growth, making plants more susceptible to winter injury. In South Texas, where freeze damage is rare, late summer fertilizer applications are beneficial and provide needed nutrients for late fall and winter growth.

A fall application after the first freeze can benefit trees and shrubs that grew very little during the current year by helping them expand their root systems during the winter.

Fertilizer Analysis

Fertilizers are purchased according to their analysis, which is the percentage of the three major plant nutrients—nitrogen, phosphorus, and potassium. The analysis is shown on the bag or container and consists of three numbers (e.g., 12-4-8). The first number indicates the percentage of nitrogen (N); the second gives the percentage of phosphorus as phosphoric acid (P_2O_5); and the third is the percentage of potassium as potash

(K_2O). A 50-pound bag of a 12-4-8 fertilizer contains 6 pounds of N, 2 pounds of P_2O_5, and 4 pounds of K_2O.

Tree growth is stimulated predominantly by nitrogen rather than phosphorus or potassium. For this reason, use straight-nitrogen fertilizers on trees and shrubs (unless a soil test recommends otherwise). Following are examples of straight-nitrogen fertilizers:

- Ammonium sulfate (21-0-0)
- Bat guano (10-0-0)
- Blood meal (14-0-0)
- Urea (45-0-0)

Not all nurseries and garden centers carry large bags of urea and ammonium sulfate, so check area farm and ranch stores. Large bags of blood meal and bat guano may be tough to find as well, so telephone nurseries and garden centers to find a supply.

Fertilizer Recommendation

Young trees and shrubs should be "spoon-fed" fertilizer. Instead of placing large amounts of fertilizer around young trees and shrubs to last several months, mix water-soluble fertilizers into solution and make multiple applications. You can make your own straight-nitrogen, water-soluble fertilizer solution by mixing 1 to 2 teaspoons of ammonium sulfate per gallon of water. Drench 2 to 4 gallons of this nitrogen solution around the edge of the planting hole or at the plant's drip line (tips of the branches and straight down to the ground).

Applications can be made every 2 to 3 weeks for maximum growth. Watch for brown tips developing on the leaves; this may be fertilizer burn, and you would need to reduce the frequency of applications. Oak trees have a reputation for being slow growing, but spoon-feeding fertilizer to these trees will create majestic oaks sooner than you would think.

Mature trees and large shrub plantings are best fertilized with granular fertilizers. The amount of fertilizer to be applied should be based on square footage covered by the tree canopy or planting bed. In late winter, apply 1 to 2 pounds of actual nitrogen per 1,000 square feet of area covered by the tree canopy or shrub planting. A second application in midspring can be made if plant growth is not significant. A third application can be made in early summer, if needed. The table below indicates the amount of nitrogen fertilizers needed to supply 1 to 2 pounds of actual nitrogen per 1,000 square feet.

Calculating the Amount of Fertilizer to Use

To determine the amount of nitrogen-containing fertilizer needed, stake off a square or rectangular area that includes the entire branch spread of the trees or shrubs (refer to example). Calculate the square footage of the area. If roots are restricted by pavement, curb, or a building, subtract the restricted area from the total area computed. Multiply the number of thousands of square feet by the number of pounds of fertilizer needed per 1,000 square feet.

Example: Stake the canopy of a tree to estimate the square footage covered by the canopy (30 feet x 40 feet = 1,200 square feet). For a 1,200-square-foot tree canopy and 2 pounds of actual nitrogen per 1,000 square feet (10 pounds using

AMOUNT OF NITROGEN FERTILIZER NEEDED TO SUPPLY 1 OR 2 POUNDS OF ACTUAL NITROGEN PER 1,000 SQUARE FEET

MATERIAL	1 POUNDS N	2 POUNDS N
Urea (45-0-0)	2	4
Ammonium sulfate (21-0-0)	5	10
Blood meal (14-0-0)	7	14
Bat guano (10-0-0)	10	20

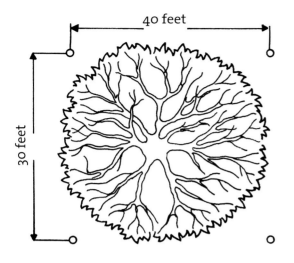

40 feet

30 feet

hand if you're good), and avoid skips and overlapping, which may burn any grass growing beneath the tree. To obtain an even distribution over a large area, divide the fertilizer into two equal lots, and apply one-half lengthwise over the area and the remainder crosswise over the area.

Water the area thoroughly (1-inch irrigation) after fertilizing, soaking the soil to a depth of at least 6 inches, thus driving the nitrogen down into the tree's feeding-root system.

ammonium sulfate), calculate amount of ammonium sulfate to apply as follows:

> 1,200 square feet ÷ 1,000 square feet x 10 pounds of ammonium sulfate = ___ pounds of ammonium sulfate to apply

> 1.2 x 10 pounds = 12 pounds of ammonium sulfate to apply

Application Technique

Research indicates that fertilizing trees and shrubs with surface applications of nitrogen-containing fertilizers is as effective as, and more efficient than, other methods (such as punching holes or deep-root feeding).

Distribute the calculated amount of fertilizer evenly with a spreader (or by

A Final Important Concept in Fertilizing Trees

If you are confident in your ability to fertilize trees, you can target your fertilizer and water applications in a 10-foot-wide area at the drip line of the tree (i.e., the tips of the branches and straight down to the ground); that is, go 5 feet out in both directions from the drip line. The vast majority of a tree's feeding roots are at the tree's drip line. In addition, the majority of the tree's feeding-root system is within the top 18 inches of soil, not deep down at 2 or 3 feet where there is little oxygen for the roots to absorb water and nutrients.

Timely Tips

"Roses in the Landscape" for all you need to know about the flower of love.

Flowers & Pretty Plants

- Cool-season annual flowers can be planted now; but for the southern two-thirds of Texas, the best time to plant these flowers is in the fall.
- Wildflower plantings should be ready to grow and bloom. Pull grassy weeds carefully to avoid disturbing the wildflower plants.
- In established flower beds, replace any winter-damaged or unhealthy plants now. Don't expect unhealthy plants to miraculously recover before spring growth begins.
- Fertilize established cool-season annuals once this month with $\frac{1}{4}$ pound of urea per 100 square feet, $\frac{1}{2}$ pound of ammonium sulfate, or 1 pound of blood meal. Large bags of urea and ammonium sulfate may not be found in nurseries and garden centers but will be available in farm and ranch stores.

Garden Design

- Surprise your loved one by giving him or her an entire rose garden (or maybe just one bush) for Valentine's Day. Read the January essay

Soil & Mulch

- Add organic matter to the soil every time you plant vegetable gardens and flower beds. Materials such as pine bark and/or compost tilled into clay increase the air within the soil, and tilled into sand they increase the soil's water-holding ability. For the rest of the story, refer to the January essay "Soils 101 for the Garden."
- Be wary of products claiming the ability to increase soil microbial activity or other almost magical soil improvement. Ask for research data supporting claims, or test the effectiveness of product yourself. The November essay "Snake Oil in the Garden" addresses this topic in depth.
- Remember to mulch before spring. Mulch will help retain soil moisture built up throughout the winter.

Water

- Realize that winter drought can be devastating to landscape and garden plants, especially combined with windy, freezing weather. Water at least twice this month in the absence of rain—this includes lawns, land-scape plantings, vegetable gardens, and fruit plantings.

- Check your irrigation system for proper performance. Run each station, and look for abnormalities. Call an irrigation contractor to fix problems now. Don't wait until the spring rush. Refer to this month's essay "Is Your Irrigation System Ready for Spring?"

Plant Care

- Recognize that February is pruning month. Prune roses on Valentine's Day (refer to the January essay "Roses in the Landscape"). Prune fruit and nut trees (refer to the January essay "Growing Fruits and Nuts"). Trim off dead and winter-damaged portions of perennial flowers (refer to the September essay "Gardening with Perennial Flowers"). Major pruning, training, and shaping of shade trees, crape myrtles, and other large shrubs are best done this month (refer to this month's essay "Pruning School" and the August essay "Crape Myrtles for Texas").
- Be prepared: February can be the coldest month in Texas. If heavy freezes occur, protect your cold-sensitive plants. Lights under plant coverings might be needed as a heat source. Refer to the September essay

"Cold-Weather Protection for Plants" for more detail.

- Continue to weed and remove old plant debris from flower and shrub plantings and vegetable gardens.
- Apply pre-emergence herbicides now to prevent spring and summer weeds that germinate from seed. Refer to the April essay "Weeds, Weeds, and More Weeds" for safe and proper timing and use of pre-emergence herbicides. Don't apply pre-emergence herbicides in vegetable gardens (because seed is used to start crops).

Trees, Shrubs & Vines

- Fertilize trees, shrubs, and vines this month so that nutrients can be absorbed by the roots in preparation for spring growth. For specifics, read this month's essay "Fertilizing Trees and Shrubs."
- Transplant trees and shrubs around the landscape, if needed, since they are still dormant and a month from heavy spring growth. The November essay "Transplanting Shrubs and Trees" provides step-by-step guidelines.

Lawns

- Start the engines of your mowers and trimmers to make sure they are ready for spring. If a tune-up is needed, get in line fast at small-engine repair stores. They book up quickly in spring.
- Don't fertilize lawns yet unless you are in deep South Texas and have mowed your lawn twice (most likely that will be next month).
- Keep winter weeds in check by mowing and hand pulling; if needed, use a herbicide formulated to work in cool temperatures.
- In the absence of rain, water the lawn thoroughly at least once this month.

Vegetables, Herbs & Fruits

- Transplant cool-season vegetable crops before it's too late, including broccoli, cabbage, cauliflower, Irish potatoes, leaf lettuces, and onions. Sow seed as well of beets, carrots, greens, and leaf lettuces.
- To get a jump on spring vegetable (or flower) gardening, grow giant transplants of cool-sensitive plants in containers. Because they are portable, you can simply move containerized plants indoors if cold temperatures are predicted
- Transplant cold-tolerant herbs, such as chives, cilantro (coriander), dill, fennel, garlic, oregano, parsley, rosemary, sage, and thyme.
- Fertilize vegetable plants lightly with nitrogen products. Fertilizing herbs is not recommended; too much growth results in poor quality. Remember that young seedlings and transplants can be burned by granular fertilizer, so use a water-soluble product to get them started.
- Make last-minute purchases of bare-root fruit and nut plants. For variety selection and planting guidelines, refer to the January essay "Growing Fruits and Nuts."
- Be prepared to protect citrus plants this month in case of a late freeze. Temperatures in the mid-20s can cause severe damage.

Houseplants

- Continue to provide bright light and adequate water, and check for pests.
- Your houseplants are in their last stretch of indoor captivity before they can vacation on the patio from spring to fall.

Butterflies, Birds & Squirrels

- Water is very important to birds and squirrels during late winter. Provide clean water weekly.

Notes:

March

Cardinal on Dogwood (Cornus florida)

SPRING—GET BUSY

Spring Has Sprung When You See These Bloomers

Many landscape plants remain true favorites because they announce spring. To usher in spring to your landscape, choose from these early bloomers. Not all are adapted to your area. Guidance is given in the list, but if in doubt, check with your local nursery professionals, county extension agent, or a Master Gardener. The best time to purchase these plants is when they are already in bloom, as bloom color may vary within species and/or between varieties.

Vines

Carolina jessamine (*Gelsemium sempervirens*)
profusion of fragrant yellow flowers; adapted throughout Texas in acidic or alkaline soils

Clematis (*Clematis* spp.)
multitude of varieties and flower colors; short-lived vine unless grown in ideal conditions of acidic soil in East and Southeast Texas; filtered light a must

Japanese wisteria (*Wisteria floribunda*)
large, deep purple, grapelike clusters of blooms; best adapted to the acidic soils of East Texas, but with good and/or amended soil will perform well in Central Texas

Texas wisteria (*Wisteria frutescens*), Texas native
smaller, lighter purple blooms than Japanese wisteria; best adapted to acidic soils but can be coaxed into growing in amended alkaline soils

Winter honeysuckle (*Lonicera fragrantissima*)

fragrant, creamy white flowers appear prior to leaves; adapted throughout Texas in alkaline and acidic soils

Shrubs

Azalea (*Rhododendron* sp.) thousands of varieties of different sizes; flowering white through rose; best grown in acidic soils of East Texas; however, success possible in isolated pockets of good soil or amended soil west into Dallas, south into Houston, and along IH-45

Flowering quince (*Chaenomeles japonica*) blooms prior to leaves emerging; several flower colors available ranging from red, pink, white, and orange; not well adapted in highly alkaline soils; best adapted to East Texas

Forsythia (*Forsythia* x *intermedia*) yellow flowers in early spring; blooms best in cooler winter temperatures of the northern half of Texas; adapted to acidic and well-drained clay or loamy soils

Italian jasmine (*Jasminum humile*) arching shrub with bright yellow, fragrant flowers in open clusters; adapted throughout Texas

Lady Banksia rose (*Rosa banksiae*) yellow or white cascades of flowers; white is fragrant; huge sprawling climber; highly adapted throughout Texas; amend highly alkaline soils with organic matter

Primrose jasmine (*Jasminum mesnyi*) similar to Italian jasmine, but flowers are single and not fragrant

Pyracantha or scarlet firethorn (*Pyracantha coccinea*) heavy spring bloom of white flowers turning to red-orange fruit in fall; with good soil preparation, adapted to most of Texas

Spirea or bridal wreath (*Spirea* sp.) small white flowers cover the entire plant; also now available in many varieties and colors from pink to rose; adapted to acidic and slightly alkaline soils; seldom successful in Central Texas and west without major soil preparation

Texas mountain laurel (*Sophora secundiflora*), Texas native purple clusters of flowers that smell like grape chewing gum; handsome, evergreen, large shrub; adapted throughout Central, South, and West Texas; surprisingly adapted in heavier, neutral pH soils of College Station and Houston

Trees

American smoke tree (*Cotinus obovatus*), Texas native
medium-sized tree with billowy spring sprays of showy pink to purple-pink flowers that from a distance look like a haze or smoke rising from the tree; highly prized tree; native to the Hill Country and adapted to most alkaline soils

Aristocrat ornamental pear (*Pyrus calleryana* 'Aristocrat')
medium-sized tree with white blooms prior to foliage; adapted throughout Texas; superior to 'Bradford' variety

Chinese fringe tree (*Chionanthus retusus*)
medium-sized handsome tree with thousands of fringy white flowers giving the appearance of white clouds; adapted to the eastern half of Texas

Dogwood (*Cornus florida*), Texas native
graceful, understory tree with white blooms prior to foliage; many varieties available in light pink to rose; best adapted in sandy, acidic soils of East Texas but will appear in pockets of good well-drained sandy loam along IH-45, even into the College Station and Navasota area

Eastern redbud (*Cercis canadensis*), Texas native
small tree with varying shades of purple blooms prior to foliage; best adapted to the eastern half of Texas; unique varieties: 'Forrest Pansy' with burgundy foliage that fades to reddish green as the season progresses; and 'Alba' with its white blossoms

Mexican buckeye (*Ungnadia speciosa*), Texas native
multitrunked tree with pink flowers prior to foliage; adapted to Central and West Texas

Mexican plum (*Prunus mexicana*), Texas native
small tree, single or often in thickets in the wild; beautiful bark and fragrant white blossoms; adapted throughout Texas

Mexican redbud (*Cercis canadensis* var. *mexicana*), Texas native
large, multitrunked shrub with glossy foliage; tremendous variations between plants in leaf size and leaf margins and in bloom color; important to see both bloom and foliage; particularly adapted to rocky, alkaline soils of Central, West, and South Texas

Saucer or tulip magnolia (*Magnolia soulangiana*)
multitrunked, medium-sized tree with large, tuliplike, pink-tinged white blooms prior to foliage; best adapted to acidic, sandy soils of East Texas but have been grown successfully in well-drained heavier soils with near neutral pH from Houston to Dallas

*Texas redbud (*Cercis cadensis *var.* texensis*).*

Texas redbud (*Cercis canadensis* var. *texensis*), Texas native
more treelike than large shrub; flower color can vary between plants; superior variety, 'Oklahoma;' 'Texas White' has white blooms; adapted throughout Texas

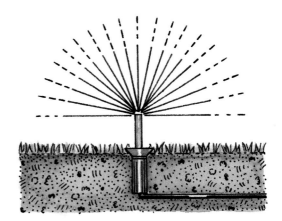

When to Water, and How Long?

The age-old questions of when to water and for how long have challenged even the best of gardeners. The questions apply to lawns, landscape planting, vegetable gardens, flower beds, and even to houseplants.

This essay focuses on lawns, the highest users of irrigation water in the landscape. Additional comments are included to help you adapt these answers, guidelines, and concepts to watering other plants and plantings in your landscape.

WHEN TO WATER? When the lawn needs it, not according to a time clock, calendar, or habit. The best switch on an irrigation system time clock is "O-F-F," off! Keep the system off until the lawn tells you it is time to water. Pay attention to what your lawn is telling you. Lawns readily show you when water is needed. They wilt, show footprints from people who tread on them, or turn dull, gray-

green. St. Augustinegrass will even roll its leaves lengthwise in an effort to reduce water loss from the leaf surface.

For lawns with large trees in them, total water needed combines that used by the trees and the lawn. However, remain focused on the lawn to indicate when to water. Irrigation frequency may be dramatically increased because of the tree's ability to compete for irrigation water.

In a landscape planting, an "indicator" plant can be used, one that will wilt readily and show you that the time to water is at hand. Indicator plants include Asiatic jasmine, crape myrtle, hibiscus, and periwinkle. Look to these plants and others for hints on when to water.

For vegetable gardens and flower beds, when to water is more a predictive decision. If you wait for these plants to show wilt or water stress, you will lose crop or flower production. These garden areas should be drip-irrigated and maintained at a more constant soil moisture level.

If you are having trouble reading the water-stress symptoms of your lawn (or landscape plantings or vegetable garden), then trust the best moisture meter ever invented—your index finger. Stick your finger into the soil 2 to 3 inches deep. During the growing season, if the soil is cool, there is enough moisture present for plant use. If the soil is warm or dry to the touch, it is time to water.

HOW LONG TO WATER? This is a bit more complicated and involves measurements and calculations but is well worth the effort to achieve water conservation and lawn health.

At each watering, you should apply 1 inch of water. One inch of water will penetrate 6 inches deep into a clay soil and 12 inches deep into a sandy soil (or a prepared garden soil using organic matter).

Lawn root systems will grow only 6 inches deep in clay soil and 12 inches deep in sandy soil (the root systems of landscape plants extend 12 inches deep throughout an amended garden soil). This determines the "bank account" of soil moisture to which the lawn has access. Each time you water, you fill up the entire bank account of soil moisture. The lawn "dewaters" the bank account and shows you when it needs watering again. This cycle may be interrupted by rain. Simply wait after a rain until the lawn shows it needs watering.

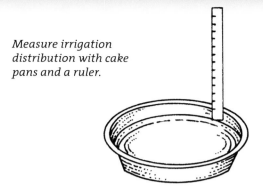

Measure irrigation distribution with cake pans and a ruler.

"How long to water?" is therefore more accurately stated, "How long does it take to deliver one inch of water from my irrigation system or hose-end sprinkler?" The answer is, "It depends." It depends on your irrigation system, water pressure, and/or type of hose-end sprinkler.

You must first measure the actual time it takes for your irrigation system or sprinkler to deliver 1 inch of water to the lawn:

- Steal the cake pans out of the kitchen (two or three pans, or straight-edged containers over 3 inches in diameter will do).
- Throw the pans out on the lawn, spaced randomly, under one station (section) of sprinklers OR surrounding a single hose-end sprinkler.
- Turn the sprinklers on, and note the time on your watch.
- Run the system until approximately 1 inch of water is in each pan; you will get wet running around checking the water depth in the pans (simply place a ruler vertically in the pan to measure depth).

- When 1 inch of water is in most of the pans, turn off the sprinklers and note the elapsed time.

Surprise! See how long it took to get 1 inch of water in the pans, and see how much water has run off down the driveway and gutters. You can run the test until you collect $\frac{1}{2}$ inch in the pans and then just multiply the elapsed time by 2.

Hard to believe it took so long to deliver 1 inch of water on the lawn? Most lawns and landscape plantings are not watered long enough, resulting in much too frequent irrigations. In addition, the plant root systems do not reach the depth of their genetic potential and become "hooked" on light, frequent waterings.

Since each irrigation station can vary significantly in the amount of time it takes to deliver 1 inch of water, you can run the test on each irrigation station for more irrigation accuracy. Test all the sta-

tions if you want, or choose and test one station that is the most representative of the rest.

Precipitation rates of the sprinkler heads dictate how long it takes to deliver 1 inch of water to the lawn. Rates vary significantly between types of sprinkler heads. In general, to irrigate 1 inch of water, follow these guidelines:

- Pop-up spray heads must run 1 hour.
- Stream rotor and impact spray heads must run 2 hours.
- Hose-end sprinklers must run 3 hours.

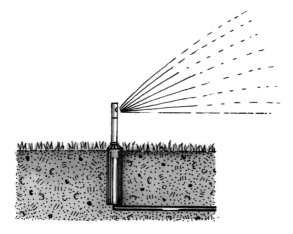

Surprise again! If you run a pop-up spray head for "20 minutes every other day" (the standard time-clock setting), your system is delivering $\frac{1}{3}$ inch of water at each irrigation. One-third inch waters the soil 2 inches deep, and that is where the lawn root system will be, particularly in the summer and year-round in areas with less than 20 inches of rainfall per year.

Recommending such long run times for the irrigation system begs the question, "How can I run an irrigation station for one hour without water running off and wasting water and money?" The answer is "multicycling." Most irrigation time clocks can do this easily. If it takes 1 hour to water 1-inch deep, follow these guidelines:

- Run station number one for 20 minutes, and progress through all the stations for 20 minutes each.
- Come back to station one again for 20 minutes, and go through the rest of the stations again.
- Run station one a third time for 20 minutes, and complete the rest of the stations, thus totaling 1 hour of run time and 1 inch of water.

Multicycling allows the water to percolate into the soil slowly and prevents runoff. Check it out—dig a small hole (6 inches in clay and 12 inches in sand), and see if the irrigation water has reached that depth. If so, you have done the job, so simply irrigate the determined amount of time each time the lawn indicates it needs watering. Multicycling can be done with hose-end sprinklers simply by moving the hose at calculated or predetermined intervals.

Make the commitment today to use the proper irrigation strategy: Water the plants only when they need it, and fill the bank account of moisture each time you irrigate. Your lawn and landscape will be healthier and more beautiful, your water bills will be lower, and you will have helped preserve a precious natural resource.

Advanced Irrigation Concepts—Good to the Last Drip

PLANT WATER USE

Plants are opportunistic. They will use whatever water you provide. They use it in a beneficial process called transpiration, and they use it in a wasteful process called transpiration.

Transpiration cools the plant and is the force that sucks water from the soil to the leaves. Transpiration does not turn off unless the soil moisture level begins to go down significantly. If your watering keeps the soil moisture level near saturation, then the plants will beneficially cool the leaves and simply spew the rest of the high-quality drinking water used for irrigation out into the air with no additional benefit to the plant.

AGRICULTURE IRRIGATION VERSUS LANDSCAPE IRRIGATION

The goal in agriculture irrigation is maximizing production or yield. In contrast, the goal in landscape irrigation is to give the plants as little moisture as possible and still maintain plant health. With the exception of growing vegetable and flower gardens, you are simply maintaining the lawn and landscape. Your goal is not "How many bales of grass clippings can I get per gallon of water?"

IS A "NO-IRRIGATION" LANDSCAPE POSSIBLE IN TEXAS?

"Probably not" is the answer, but you will be surprised how little water is needed by your lawn and landscape when properly irrigated. For areas east of IH-35, irrigation should supplement rainfall. In fact, east of IH-45, you may not even have to irrigate at all if rainfall occurs in June, July, and August. For areas west of IH-35, rainfall may actually be a supplement to irrigation. In this region, your question becomes, "Just how much irrigated lawn and manicured landscape do I need?"

DO IRRIGATION SYSTEMS WASTE WATER?

According to a Texas A&M study, people with irrigation systems use 40 percent more water than people without irrigation systems. People (or the irrigation contractor) set the time clock for the system, which then runs on the same schedule all the time—spring, summer, fall, and even winter. An irrigation system is the most efficient way to water a lawn and landscape, but it must be properly managed by humans. Follow the "when to water and how long" strategy to reduce water consumption by Texas landscapes.

WHICH HOSE-END SPRINKLER IS BEST?

The choices are plentiful, but here is the scoop:

- Impact or pulse sprinklers are best; they make the sound "chew-chew-chew" as they rotate; these sprinklers throw a wide stream of water and large droplets at a low trajectory, which results in less wind drift and less evaporation.
- Traveling or tractor sprinklers are also highly efficient; they distribute water in large droplets low to the ground, which reduces water loss significantly; the only imperative with these is that you must close the garden gate (I forgot one time, and my sprinkler went to Snook!).
- Spinners, sprayers, and whirlybirds all have reduced water use efficiency due to wind drift and evaporation.
- Oscillating sprinklers that throw a wand of water high up in the air and gracefully rotate back and forth are great for children to play in; the water loss from these sprinklers is huge due to wind drift and evaporation; you can lose half of the irrigation water before it hits the ground.

Saving Water Drip by Drip—Drip Irrigation for the Landscape and Garden

Fear of the unknown is the major deterrent to using drip irrigation in vegetable gardens and landscape plantings. With recent advances in drip irrigation products, virtually every vegetable garden and landscape planting should be irrigated with drip.

Initially, the goal of drip irrigation in the landscape and garden was to put an emitter (dripper) by every single plant to be watered. Designing the drip system was difficult; there were hundreds of connectors, fittings, and emitters for a single system; assembly of the system was best done by engineers (or children who like puzzles), and the system costs were high.

Thank goodness, a few extension horticulturists began in the early 1980s to evaluate drip irrigation products and techniques typically used in agriculture for use in the home landscape and garden. Their testing focused on three questions: "Will it work?" "Is it cheap?" and "Can we put it together?" (*Note:* Having been involved with this evaluation, I have found these three questions are good for evaluating most every purchase in my life.)

Voilà, products and techniques were identified that met the criteria. No more reason to fear drip irrigation. If you are *still* anxious, read on to understand how to incorporate drip irrigation in your landscape and garden. If needed, seek help from an irrigation contractor, surf the Internet, or get a book for detailed guidance.

Drip irrigation is a must for garden and landscape plantings.

Benefits of Drip Irrigation

Drip irrigation involves the slow application of water to soil. Under low pressure, water flows through plastic tubing laid along each row or grouping of plants. The water drips out onto the soil through emitters or prepunched holes.

The benefits of drip irrigation are well-documented:

* Increased plant performance, production of vegetables and fruit or flowers, and growth in landscape plantings
* Increased plant health and quality; less disease and decay from splashing irrigation from sprinklers
* Increased ability to manage soil moisture at a more constant level; less "feast-to-famine" cycles experienced by the plants; plants seldom under water stress
* Increased ability to apply precise amounts of water to plants (e.g., 3 gallons every other day in a vegetable garden)
* Increased irrigation efficiency and water conservation; can reduce water loss by up to 60 percent compared to sprinkler irrigation; little, if any, evaporation, wind drift, or runoff experienced with drip irrigation
* Perhaps the most important—decreased difficulty and effort in watering vegetable gardens and landscape planting (A flick of a switch or twist of a handle and the system is on; come back 2 to 3 hours later and turn it off . . . Amazing!)

Two problems sometimes occur with drip irrigation:

* Damage by rodents chewing on the pipes or emitters; can be eliminated by putting out a bowl of water for them, burying the tubing below mulch, or getting a cat that stays outdoors
* Clogging of emitters or holes by sand, algae, or calcium and sodium deposits; can be eliminated with filters and "self-cleaning" emitters

Drip Products

Three types of drip irrigation products are most commonly used in vegetable gardens, fruit plantings, and landscapes; each has its advantages and disadvantages:

* Porous pipe or tubing—water oozes out the entire length of the tube or hose (sort of like Grandma's old canvas "soaker hoses"); products generally inexpensive; no assembly required; precision of water application random at best
* Tapes—plastic film is folded

and molded to create "emitter" holes where water drips out; lowest cost per foot (based on thickness of plastic); can be used for temporary systems to establish landscape plants; precision very good; easily assembled with a few fittings; will last about three to five seasons

- In-line emitter tubing—emitters are "glued" inside durable plastic tubing at fixed intervals (e.g., 12 inches, 24 inches); most sophisticated type; moderate to highest cost for drip, depending on features; self-cleaning emitters available; pressure-compensated emitters available for use on slopes and hilly landscapes; precision excellent; easy to assemble

In addition to drip-type emitters, there are other low-volume, water-efficient devices called "microsprinklers." These miniature sprinklers can be plugged into plastic tubing to deliver water at a slow rate over a larger area. This is particularly advantageous for home fruit plantings and newly planted shade trees.

These drip irrigation products can be purchased through local irrigation supply companies, irrigation contractors, the Internet, and some nurseries. The higher-quality tapes, in-line emitter tubing, and microsprinklers can sometimes be found at home-improvement centers and garden centers.

Drip Cost

The cost of a drip system is relatively low and justified considering the water savings, increased production and beauty, and your reduced watering effort. If you assemble the drip irrigation system, equipment for a 200-square-foot vegetable garden would cost approximately $75 to $100. Drip tapes are less expensive than in-line emitter tubing. Most systems will easily last 3 to 7 years before renovation is necessary.

Design and Installation

You can either design the system yourself or have an irrigation contractor do it for you. You can seek design help from an irrigation supply company or from Internet sites.

The simplest drip irrigation system to set up is one connected to an outdoor water faucet or hose bib on the house. To function properly, the system will need a backflow preventer (antisiphon device), water filter, and pressure regulator. The backflow preventer stops water from flowing back into the hose bib and contaminating your drinking water. The filter helps eliminate particles, such as sand, that might clog emitters. The regulator maintains the proper low-pressure level needed for the system, usually 10 to 25 psi (pounds per square inch). See the

Simple setup for a faucet-connected drip system, including in this order: water faucet, backflow preventer, filter, pressure regulator, and female fitting to plastic tubing or drip line.

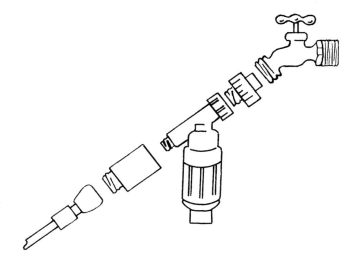

illustration above for details on a faucet-connected drip system.

In addition to this faucet-connection setup, these system components are used:

- Black poly tubing—Use this tubing, which has no holes and is usually ½-inch diameter, to simply deliver water to the emitter tape or drip tubing.
- Drip tape or tubing—Use tape and tubing with 1-gallon-per-hour (gph) emitters spaced 12 inches apart for landscape plantings and 24 inches apart for vegetable gardens.
- Adapters—Use a female adapter to connect tubing to pressure regulator.
- Fittings or connectors and end caps—Use fittings to connect drip tape or tubing to black poly tubing; use end caps to close off the drip tape or tubing.
- "Goof plugs"—Yes, there are even little plastic fittings to plug holes punched by mistake.

A drip system layout (design) for a typical vegetable garden is depicted below.

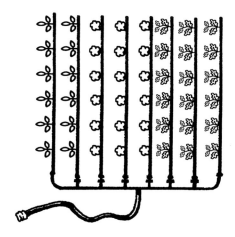

Typical drip system layout for a vegetable garden. Hose or plastic tubing delivers water to the "header" line (tubing running the length of garden), and drip lines are connected to the header line and laid down each garden row.

You can modify this simple design for any landscape plantings, particularly for drip systems using a hose bib for plantings on the side of the house. Drip irrigation stations can also be incorporated into the overall landscape irrigation system. Time clocks can turn the drip stations on and off automatically, just as with the sprinkler stations. Even existing sprinkler irrigation systems can be converted to drip. This takes some expertise, and you should probably consult an irrigation contractor.

Drip irrigation is best suited for vegetable gardens, flower beds, fruit plantings, and landscape plantings. Drip can be successfully installed underground (6 inches deep) to irrigate turfgrass, but the level of design, installation, and maintenance increases significantly. There are hundreds of football fields and golf courses across the arid West using this technology.

Drip Irrigation Schedules

Scheduling drip irrigation depends on what you are watering. With vegetable gardens and flower beds, the objective is to keep the plants from experiencing any water stress so peak production (crop or flower) can be obtained. For shrub plantings, more water stress can be tolerated, and production is not the objective; therefore, scheduling is less critical.

In general, run drip irrigation in vegetable gardens and flower beds during the growing season—every other day for 2 to 3 hours. You will have the best vegetable garden and flower bed ever with much less effort.

With a 1-gallon-per-hour emitter, you are applying 2 to 3 gallons of water in 3 hours. This volume will water a 24- to 36-inch-diameter circle of soil (depending on soil type: 24 for sandy or prepared soil and 36 for heavier, clay soil).

The objective is to water the soil within each vegetable row or the entire flower bed each time you irrigate. This fills the soil with moisture, the plant roots happen upon the water, and they proliferate (plants don't seek out water). The need to put an emitter by every plant is eliminated.

Remember to use your index finger to monitor soil moisture, and increase or decrease the duration (minutes) of the irrigation, not the frequency of irrigation. If it rains, turn the system off until your finger tells you it is time to irrigate. Don't wait until the vegetable or flower plants wilt.

For shrub plantings, drip irrigation schedules should be determined by your index finger. If the soil is cool to the touch, don't irrigate. If the soil is warm and/or dry 2 to 3 inches deep, then irrigate. Turn on the drip system for 3 hours to replenish the soil moisture level of the planting. Then wait until your index finger indicates it is time to water again.

CALLER: "Should I place the drip lines under mulch?"

ANSWER: "Placing mulch over the drip tape or tubing helps reduce evaporation even further, helps prevent sunlight from damaging the tape or tubing, and may hide the tape or tubing from rodents. You can even bury the drip tape or tubing under the soil about two to three inches for the same reasons described for mulch, plus there is added protection against rodents chewing the drip lines.

"If you are one of those people, like me, who have the need to see the drip dripping, then don't cover the drip tape or tubing with either mulch or soil. Either way, it is no big deal."

Drip Maintenance

After about 3 to 5 years, most drip systems will spring a leak or shoot up a miniature geyser. Not to worry; the manufacturers have developed coupler fittings to connect the drip tape or tubing back together.

For northern parts of Texas, you may need to drain the water out of the system to prevent water from freezing and damaging the system components.

If an emitter or line of emitters is clogged or flowing poorly, flushing the system by opening the ends of the drip tapes or tubes may be helpful. Worst case—simply replace the one drip section.

Once you have overcome the fear of the unknown, you will never have a garden or planting that does not incorporate drip irrigation. Increased plant productivity and landscape quality, plus decreased water use and watering effort, spell success for any gardener or yardener.

Lawn Fertilizing Made Simple

In late winter and again in late summer, the television and radio airwaves, garden magazines, and newspapers are jammed with lawn fertilizer advertisements promoting the perfect green lawn as a national standard (the Augusta national golf-course-quality lawn). This perpetuates the neighborhood competition of who has the perfect lawn. Well, phooey on all this hype!

The standard should be to produce an acceptable-quality lawn with the least fertilizer and effort possible. If you agree, read on. If you want to pursue the perfect, golf-course-type lawn, then purchase one or two Texas lawn books written by great turfgrass experts, and follow the guidelines carefully.

Even with all the advertisements, people usually end up guessing how much fertilizer to put out on the lawn every spring and fall. Generally, people buy a 40-pound bag of some highly advertised fertilizer and throw it around the lawn. Sounds simple enough, but there is a better way that is more effective and environmentally sound.

Lawn fertilizers can be a major source of pollution of creeks, streams, and soils. Nitrogen and phosphorus far surpass chemical pesticides as water and soil contaminants. Be careful with lawn fertilizers, and follow these steps to maintain a lawn with less fertilizer and effort and without posing a threat to the environment.

Step 1: Measure Your Lawn

"Pie are square and cake are round," or is it "pie are round and cake are square"? Regardless, get at least an estimate of how many square feet of lawn you have

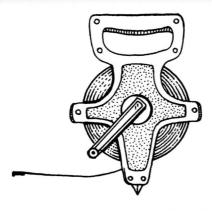

in the landscape. Multiply the length of your lot by the depth, and subtract the square footage of your house, garage, driveway, and landscape plantings. Most folks have a 4,000- to 7,000-square-foot lawn.

Step 2: Choose & Use a Nitrogen Fertilizer

Nitrogen (N), phosphorus (P), and potassium (K) are represented on the three-number analysis on every bag of fertilizer. Each number is the percentage (by weight) of that nutrient in the bag. Example: 15-5-10 has 15 percent N, 5 percent P, and 10 percent K.

For more than 20 years, extension educators (including me) recommended a 3-1-2 ratio of fertilizer for lawns. Thousands of soil tests for lawns have now documented a phosphorus accumulation in lawn soils across Texas. This poses a threat of contaminating creeks and streams as irrigation water runs off lawns. High phosphorous levels also tie up other nutrients and make them less available to plants.

Recommendations have changed to a 1-0-1 ratio of fertilizer, or even 1-0-0 (straight nitrogen). Unless a soil test for your lawn determines the need for other nutrients, consider using only nitrogen when fertilizing your lawn, landscape plantings, trees, vegetable garden, and flower beds. An exception is made for the fall application, when potassium can be added to increase the lawn's tolerance of cold temperatures.

Fertilizer products that are straight nitrogen (1-0-0 ratio) include the following:

- Ammonium sulfate (21-0-0)
- Bat guano (10-0-0)
- Blood meal (14-0-0)
- IBDU (isobutylidene diurea) (32-0-0)
- Sulfur-coated urea (36-0-0)
- Urea (45-0-0)
- Urea formaldehyde (38-0-0)

The nitrogen fertilizers are either quick release or slow release, based on how fast the nitrogen is dissolved into the soil and available for plant use:

- Urea and ammonium sulfate are quick-release fertilizers and generate quick growth and greening, last about 1 month, and are relatively inexpensive; large bags of these products may not be found in your nursery, so check with farm and ranch stores.

- The major advantage of slow-release fertilizers is that they feed the lawn more evenly over a longer period (3 to 4 months).
- Sulfur-coated urea, IBDU, and urea formaldehyde are slow-release fertilizers but are more expensive and not readily available in most nurseries and garden centers unless combined with phosphorus and potassium; farm and ranch stores may have the pure product.
- Blood meal and bat guano are organic fertilizers and are slow release by nature, but their percentage of nitrogen is relatively low, and they are moderately expensive. Make sure you put out enough pounds of fertilizer to get the desired response from the lawn.

Step 3: Determine How Much Nitrogen to Apply Annually

The type of lawn grass you have will dictate how many pounds of nitrogen to apply annually per 1,000 square feet of lawn (refer to the chart below).

The amount of nitrogen per year should be split into single applications of not more than 1 pound of nitrogen per 1,000 square feet.

Grass	Pounds of nitrogen (per 1,000 square feet per year)	Applications per year
Bermudagrass (common)	2–3	2–3
Bermudagrass (hybrid)	3–4	2–4
Bluegrass*	2–3	2–3
Buffalograss	1–2	1–2
Centipedegrass	2–3	2–3
Fescuegrass*	2–3	2–3
St. Augustinegrass	2–3	2–3
Zoysiagrass	2–3	2–3

* Only grown as a permanent lawn successfully in the Texas Panhandle.

Step 4: Apply Lawn Fertilizer at the Proper Time

In spring, apply lawn fertilizer after you have mowed the lawn grass twice. This confirms that the lawn grass is actively growing and ready to use the fertilizer applied.

In fall, apply lawn fertilizer after the grass has stopped growth. Generally, this is after nighttime temperatures are consistently in the 50s. For the Rio Grande Valley and on the Gulf Coast, this may not occur until November; therefore, make the fall application around November 1.

A spring and fall application should be sufficient to maintain a lawn of acceptable quality. However, if you feel your lawn looks unhealthy and needs an additional shot of fertilizer for growth, you can make another application 45 to 60 days after the spring application. For a hybrid Bermudagrass lawn, an additional application may be justified.

Step 5: Determine How Much Lawn Fertilizer to Use in Any Single Application

The fertilizer analysis indicates the percentage of nitrogen (by weight) of the lawn fertilizer product. Refer to the chart below for the pounds of selected lawn fertilizers needed to apply 1 pound of nitrogen per 1,000 square feet of lawn.

(*Important note about organic fertilizers:* Notice that organic fertilizers generally contain less than half the nitrogen of "conventional" or chemical fertilizers. Be sure you perform the calculation provided to make certain you apply enough organic fertilizer to gain the results you expect. Not applying enough organic fertilizer is a common mistake.)

To determine how much lawn fertilizer to purchase, divide the square footage of your lawn by 1,000, and multiply that number by the corresponding pounds of fertilizer you selected from the chart.

FERTILIZER (analysis)	POUNDS OF FERTILIZER (to apply 1 pound nitrogen per 1,000 square feet)
Ammonium sulfate (21-0-0)	4.8
Bat guano (10-0-0)	10.0
Blood meal (14-0-0)	7.1
IBDU (isobutylidene diurea) (32-0-0)	3.1
Sulfur-coated urea (36-0-0)	2.8
Urea (45-0-0)	2.2
Urea formaldehyde (38-0-0)	2.6

Example: Your lawn is 6,500 square feet, and you have chosen to apply ammonium sulfate.

Calculation: 6,500 square feet ÷ 1,000 = 6.5 x 4.8 pounds = 31 pounds ammonium sulfate

To determine the pounds needed for a fertilizer that also contains phosphorus and/or potassium (e.g., 15-5-10), you would still use the percentage of nitrogen to calculate the amount to purchase and apply.

Step 6: Broadcast Your Lawn Fertilizer

The easiest way to broadcast lawn fertilizer is by using a walk-behind spreader on wheels (either a drop spreader or whirlybird [cyclone] spreader is fine). Many nurseries and garden stores will let you borrow (versus purchase) a spreader. The goal is simply to spread the calculated amount of fertilizer evenly across the entire lawn. To do so, follow these guidelines:

- Determine how many sections you have in the lawn that you can easily walk the spreader around without stopping, going across driveways, or through gates.
- Divide the amount of fertilizer

proportionally based on the number and size of sections. For example: Divide the amount in half, if the front yard and backyard are the same size.

- Divide each section's fertilizer amount in half, and pour half into the spreader.
- Cut back the spreader setting to the smallest opening that still lets the fertilizer pellets flow out of the hopper easily. You must be careful not to apply too much fertilizer too fast. The result will be uneven application of the fertilizer and/or fertilizer-burned grass.
- Turn the spreader on, and walk it north to south across the lawn. Try not to overlap the distribution pattern, and keep going back and forth until the spreader is empty.
- Fill the spreader with the other half of the section's fertilizer, and walk the spreader east to west, back and forth, until the spreader is empty.

Walk-behind whirlybird spreader makes spreading lawn fertilizer easy.

- You get the picture—repeat this for various sections of the lawn.
- Sweep any fertilizer pellets back into the grass from the driveway, sidewalks, or patio.
- Water the lawn thoroughly to activate the fertilizer and prevent fertilizer burn on the grass.

Other Lawn Fertilizer Tips

Soil tests can be valuable. Check with your local county extension agent for general results from soil tests in your community. The agent has access to results of local tests run by the Texas A&M University Soils Lab. You might consider having a soil test done for your lawn or garden every 3 years.

In Central Texas and west of IH-35 and IH-37, St. Augustine lawns can be yellow due to lack of iron (iron chlorosis), not lack of nitrogen. Granular iron fertilizers are available to help correct this nutrient deficiency. Iron fertilizers can stain concrete (red), so sweep off any pellets or dust before watering.

Try not to fertilize prior to a predicted heavy rain. Nitrogen, and other fertilizer nutrients, can easily run off in heavy rains into the storm sewers and into creeks and streams. Nitrogen can cause an "algae bloom" that consumes oxygen in the water to the point of killing fish.

Will There Be a Next Generation of Vegetable Gardeners?

My earliest memory in the garden was in Houston. I came home from Bible school with the proverbial bean seedling growing in a cotton-ball-filled cup. My mom helped me plant the bean seedling at the edge of a flower bed; we had no vegetable garden.

I nurtured that plant and learned the desirable characteristic of delayed gratification; "Is it ready yet; is it ready yet?" After fighting off every pestilence and its brother (in Houston), my bean plant finally produced eight beans. My mother lovingly cooked those eight beans. We had five people in my family, so everyone got 1.6 beans. I fed the family!

I was about 5 years old, yet at that early age, I knew I had done something good. My passion for gardening had begun.

Will there be a next generation of vegetable gardeners? A worthy question.

My mom helped me plant that first seed. Who helped you plant that first seed? Or have you not planted that first seed? Read on, because vegetable gardening is for everyone.

Vegetable Gardening Is for Everyone

A major barrier to vegetable gardening is the mental picture of a traditional half-acre garden with row after row of bountiful crops and the stifling reality of how much time and effort it takes to maintain such a garden. Some folks have produced such fabulous vegetable gardens, but most have not.

Some of you have figured out what size garden you can manage and are having success. Some of you have tried vegetable gardening and not been successful. And some of you have not ever tried to grow vegetables. Please try.

You don't even have to have a garden dedicated solely to vegetables. Create an edible landscape:

- Plant a tomato plant or two in a flower or shrub bed.
- Plant a tomato or pepper plant in a whiskey barrel or similar-sized container.

- Plant a row of leaf lettuce as a flower border.
- Plant a pole bean (vine) next to a trellis.
- Plant kale and cabbage in a mass next to petunias.
- Be creative; think outside the vegetable garden!

You might grow your own vegetables for various reasons:

- You want to produce food for the table.
- You want to produce vegetables, knowing what pesticides, if any, were used.
- You want to produce a truly vine-ripened tomato (there is no comparison between tomatoes you grow and those from the grocery store).
- You know that vegetable gardening is rewarding, fun, and good exercise (30 minutes of gardening can burn 200 calories and give your heart a sustained workout).

The idea of saving money on your grocery bill is not realistic as a reason to plant a vegetable garden. Unless you have that half-acre garden, have loads of time, and preserve or can the produce, you will not come close to grocery store prices for your vegetables. (*Note:* My last tomato crop cost probably $10 per tomato, which included the cost of the fuel-injected, turbo rototiller.)

The following vegetable gardening principles will help you plant that first seed or help your vegetable garden be more productive.

Crop Selection

Your first decision is what vegetables to grow. Here are a few guidelines:

- Grow what you and your family like to eat; don't grow eggplant and expect the kids to ask for second helpings.
- Grow what costs the most at the grocery store, including tomatoes, peppers, and broccoli. If saving money is the goal, growing radishes is a waste of time; you can buy a billion for a buck—same with potatoes.
- Choose crops that are relatively easy to grow; green beans are a "if you can't grow them, we can't help you" crop; however, artichokes, brussels sprouts, and iceberg lettuce are not so easy.

Crop selection will also depend on the size of your garden. It is wise to start with a small garden (10' x 10') Small-garden crops can include these vegetables:

Beet
Broccoli
Bush squash
Cabbage

Carrot
Cauliflower
Eggplant
Green bean
Leaf lettuce
Onion
Pepper
Spinach
Tomato

Larger gardens can accommodate crops that vine, grow tall, need lots of plants to produce enough yield, and produce expansive root crops, such as these:

Cantaloupe
Collard
Cucumber
Mustard
Okra
Southern pea
Sweet corn
Potato
Pumpkin
Sweet potato
Watermelon

Grow vertically if space is limited. You can grow vines up a trellis or fence to save space. You can even grow cantaloupes on a trellis if you give the fruit support (using panty hose).

Garden Location

Sunlight is critical to success in growing vegetables. Full sunlight for 6 hours per day is ideal. This is not always possible, but try growing vegetables anyway.

In full sun for 6 hours, tomato plants can produce 20 pounds of fruit per plant. In fewer hours of full sun or filtered sunlight, tomato plants may produce only 10 pounds of fruit. So, plant twice as many plants under less-than-ideal sunlight conditions!

Crops do vary in their sunlight requirement. Most require full sun for peak production; however, crops that will be productive in partial shade include beet, broccoli, cabbage, collards, cauliflower, kale, leaf lettuce, mustard greens, radish, spinach, and turnip.

Here are other garden location guidelines:

- Choose a site with deep, well-drained, fertile soil (not generally available, unless you are in Michigan); good soil preparation will be critical.
- Locate near a water outlet; no dryland vegetable gardening in Texas.

- Keep the garden away from trees and shrubs; the root systems will compete for nutrients and water and reduce production.
- Choose a site with good air circulation (gentle breeze) to reduce disease and insect infestations.

Garden Plan

A little planning up front before the first seed is planted will increase the productivity of the garden and reduce your labor. Follow these planning guidelines:

- Run the garden rows east to west, if possible, to maximize exposure to sunlight (see illustration on next page).
- Space the rows 36 to 48 inches apart to accommodate most vegetable crops.
- Plant crops that take a longer time to yield where they won't interfere with short-term crops—cantaloupe at the far end of garden and bush beans at the near end.
- Plant tall-growing crops where they will not shade or interfere with growth of smaller crops; corn, okra, and tomatoes should be on the north side of the garden.
- Group crops based on their rate of maturity (days to yield); the table to follow provides maturity rates of various crops; as one crop is finished producing, another can be planted.
- Plant an unrelated crop following a previous crop (e.g., follow early bush beans with beets, squash, or peppers); commonly called "crop rotation," it helps reduce diseases and insect populations.
- Plant quick-maturing crops multiple times (e.g., plant each row of bush beans 2 weeks apart); referred to as "succession planting," it stretches out the harvesting period.

Variety Selection

There are dozens of varieties of every vegetable crop. In the seed catalogues, every tomato variety looks great and productive (they don't publish bad pictures in seed catalogues). Choosing the right variety is essential to successful vegetable gardening in Texas. The harsh climate in Texas requires tough, time-tested varieties. Refer to the list of "Vegetable Varieties" as you make selections; but remember that new varieties are developed and some varieties are dropped from production by seed companies. If

"What is the first thing you plant in the garden? Your foot."
—Doug Welsh, told in first grade

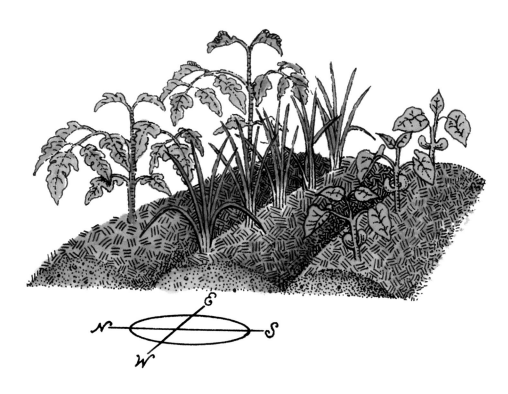

VEGETABLE CROP MATURITY RATES		
QUICK (30–60 DAYS)	MODERATE (60–80 DAYS)	SLOW (OVER 80 DAYS)
beet	broccoli	brussels sprouts
bush bean	cabbage, chinese	cabbage
leaf lettuce	kohlrabi	cantaloupe
mustard	okra	cauliflower
radish	pepper	eggplant
spinach	tomato, cherry	garlic
summer squash		irish potato
turnip		pumpkin
turnip greens		sweet potato
		watermelon

you have any questions about specific varieties and their adaptability or availability in your area, check with your county extension agent, a Master Gardener, or nursery professional.

Soil Preparation

In Texas, very few soils exist that are ideal for vegetable gardening. Amending the soil with organic matter is essential for success with vegetable gardening. As discussed in the January essay "Soils 101 for the Garden," creating a garden soil is physical work and costs money, but it is an investment that pays back huge dividends. Your vegetable garden will be healthier and more productive because of well-prepared soil.

The goal is simple: Create a garden soil with a minimum depth of 12 inches. This 12-inch soil should be composed of 50 percent organic matter and 50 percent the soil in your yard, whatever it is.

You can have a vegetable garden delivered to your backyard. Check with local landscape soil companies in your area. Many will have a "landscape mix" composed of organic matter or compost and sandy clay soil. Go visit and pick up a handful of landscape mix, ask what's in it, and ask who has used it. Call a landscape contractor or nursery professional, and ask for an opinion on the quality of the mix you are considering. Landscape mixes are not cheap, probably $28 to $38 per yard, but using them to create your vegetable garden saves tons of labor and provides instant success.

To create your own 12 inches of good garden soil, put 6 inches of organic matter on the existing soil. The organic matter can be pine bark mulch, composted manure, composted cotton bur hulls, home compost, fallen leaves, or a combination thereof.

Till or spade the 6 inches of organic matter into the top 8 to 10 inches of soil. This creates the 12-inch root zone for the plants. Add organic matter to the garden soil every time you replant. You cannot add too much organic matter.

"Bed up" the garden (prepare the rows and planting beds) with a heavy hoe and/or garden rake (as opposed to a leaf rake). The heavier (more clay) your soil, the taller your planting beds should be to provide added drainage. Sandier soils may need little "bedding up"; they can be "flat landed" (no beds, just rows).

Seeds germinate more readily in well-prepared soil than in coarse, lumpy soil. Use the back side of your garden rake to flatten the top of the soil bed and prepare the soil to a granular texture, rather than powdery fine. Time and effort with the hoe and rake will result in stronger, healthier young plants from seeds or transplants.

When to Plant

Vegetable crops can be divided into two groups: warm-season crops and cool-season crops.

Warm-season crops can tolerate warm to hot temperatures and are injured by cool temperatures below about 50°F. Warm-season crops include cantaloupe, cucumber, eggplant, green bean, okra, onion, pepper, potato, pumpkin, squash (summer), southern pea, sweet corn, sweet potato, tomato, and watermelon.

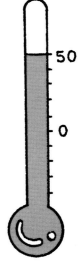

Cool-season crops tolerate cool to cold temperatures, and warm temperatures generally result in bitter-tasting harvests. Cool-season crops include beet, broccoli, brussels sprouts, cabbage, carrot, cauliflower, leaf lettuce, mustard greens, squash (winter), and turnip.

These temperature preferences dictate when to plant vegetables. To determine specific planting dates, first refer to the February essay "Last and First Freeze Dates" (and the chart and maps) to determine the average last and first freeze dates for your area. Then refer to the "Planting Guidelines" table to determine when to plant specific vegetable crops in your garden for either the spring or fall.

Example: If your garden is in Houston and you want to plant green beans, the average last freeze date is February 12; green beans can be planted from seed "on to 4 weeks after" the last freeze date; therefore, plant your green beans from February 12 through March 14. With green beans, stagger your plantings 2 weeks apart to lengthen the harvest time so you don't harvest and eat mountains of green beans all in 1 week.

Transplanting and Seeding

Transplanting vegetable crops provides an earlier and prolonged harvest. Buy transplants (or grow your own) of any crop available. Avoid planting the transplants too deep or too shallow. Plant them so the soil level of the transplant is the same as the garden soil level.

When transplants are not available, use seed planted directly into the garden. To plant seed, cover the seed two to three times its widest measurement. This is especially important for big-seeded crops, such as cantaloupe, cucumber, green bean, sweet corn, and watermelon. For smaller-seeded crops, such as carrot, lettuce, or onion, an average planting depth of $\frac{1}{4}$ to $\frac{1}{2}$ inch is adequate.

The old saying "Seed is cheap" refers to the recommendation of sowing seed fairly thickly to guarantee a good stand of seedlings. You will thin out (pull) the seedlings to the recommended plant spacing (refer to the "Planting Guidelines" or the seed package). While seed is ger-

minating and the seedlings pushing up out of the ground, keep the soil surface moist (not saturated) so that a crust does not form.

Fertilization

Vegetable crops require ample supplies of fertilizer to grow rapidly and produce heavily. During the first couple of years of the vegetable garden, use a complete fertilizer, such as 15-5-10, at a rate of 2 to 3 pounds per 100 square feet of garden. Prior to planting the garden, spread the fertilizer evenly over the area, and lightly water the fertilizer into the soil. Make this fertilizer application prior to each garden season, spring and fall.

In subsequent years (and for older vegetable gardens), use straight-nitrogen fertilizers, such as ammonium sulfate, urea, and blood meal. The recommendation for each garden season is 2 to 3 pounds of ammonium sulfate (21-0-0) per 100 square feet. If needed, additional applications of 1 to 2 pounds of ammonium sulfate per 100 linear feet of row can be made while the crops are growing.

Irrigation

As a general rule, gardens should receive an equivalent of 1 inch of rain (water) per week of the growing season to produce the best crops. The goal in a vegetable garden is to avoid having the vegetable plants experience water stress or drought. If they do, production will be reduced. (This is not the same goal in the landscape.)

If you want a productive and easy-to-water vegetable garden, you must learn to use drip irrigation. You can water using flood irrigation, but you will work yourself to death doing it. You can water using sprinkler irrigation, but you will fight every fungal disease and have to make regular pesticide applications. So take this advice: Use drip. Refer to this month's essay "Saving Water Drip by Drip" to learn more.

With drip irrigation, the system should run approximately every other day for 2 to 3 hours. If it rains, stop the schedule until 2 days after the rain stops. If in doubt, use your index finger (the best soil moisture meter). If the soil is cool to the touch (moist), don't water; if it is dry to the touch, start the schedule. Combining drip irrigation with good garden soil almost guarantees success in vegetable gardening.

Weed Control

Hand pulling of weeds or using a garden hoe is the best way to control weeds in the vegetable garden. Chemical and organic herbicides (weed killers) seldom have a place in the home vegetable garden. If you find yourself spending loads of time fighting weeds, your vegetable garden is probably too big.

Mulch

Mulch is very effective in reducing weed populations. It will also increase crop production by conserving soil moisture, moderating soil temperatures, and reducing soilborne disease. Organic mulches, such as bark, compost, leaves, and straw, are best. Till the organic mulch into the soil at the end of each garden season. As a general rule, 2 to 3 inches of organic mulch applied to the soil surface is adequate.

Pest Management

Diseases and insects can ravage vegetable gardens in Texas. Long growing seasons with relatively mild winters encourage large insect populations.

Employ all strategies for insect control before turning to an organic or chemical insecticide. Hand picking, using high-pressure water spray, and encouraging insect predators are all viable alternatives to insecticides.

If the insect population is too high and damaging the vegetable crop, use the least toxic, effective insecticide. Generally, this will be an organic pesticide, such as *Bacillus thuringiensis* (Bt), neem oil, or spinosad. If these will not control the population, either abandon the crop or choose the least toxic, effective chemical insecticide, such as bifentrin, carbaryl (Sevin), endosulfan (Thiodan), malathion, or methoxychlor.

Disease management is much more a preventive game than an eradication exercise. High humidity, cool temperatures, and splashing water (from rain or irrigation) are all conducive to foliage and fruit diseases. Carefully watch your garden for disease symptoms, such as yellowing leaves, powdery material on the leaves, and brown or black spots. Sanitation (picking diseased leaves off the plant or soil) is important in reducing disease. Eliminating sprinkler irrigation (which spreads diseases) is essential. If warranted, spray an approved fungicide at least two times, 7 days apart. The goal is to cover the new leaves with the fungicide to prevent spread of the disease. Commonly used fungicides labeled for vegetable crops include chlorothalonil

(Daconil), mancozeb, maneb, neem oil, and sulfur.

For photographs and descriptions of disease and insect pests on vegetables, search the Internet and books available in nurseries and bookstores.

Avoid spraying pesticides in the vegetable garden if at all possible. If you do use a pesticide, read the label directions, protect yourself, and be careful. You are dealing with your food and your health.

Vegetable Varieties for Texas

VEGETABLE	VARIETIES
Asparagus	Jersey Gem, Jersey Giant, UC 157, UC 72
Bean	
Flat pod	Calgreen, Greencrop Bush, Roma II
Green (bush)	Benchmark, Blue Lake 274, Contender, Derby, Tendercrop, Topcrop
Green (pole)	Blue Lake Pole, Jade, Kentucky Wonder
Beet	Detroit Dark Red, Early Wonder, Pacemaker, Ruby Queen
Broccoli	Emerald Pride, Green Magic, Lucky, Packman, Patron, Premium Crop
Brussels sprouts	Prince Marvel
Cabbage	
Chinese	Jade Pagoda, Michili
Green	Blue Vantage, Bravo, Rio Verde, Savoy King
Red	Cardinal, Red Jewel, Red Rock, Red Rookie, Rio Grande Red
Cantaloupe	Ambrosia, Magnum 45, Mission, Perlita, TAMUvalde
Carrot	Candy Stix, Danver's 126, Imperator 58, Nantes, Purple/Maroon Dragon
Cauliflower	
Green	Alverde, Green Harmony, Macerata, Spiral Point
White	Guardian, Snow Crown, Snowball Improved, Snowman, White Magic

VEGETABLE	VARIETIES
Chard, Swiss	Lucullus, Ruby Chard, Ruby Red
Collard	Blue Max, Champion, Flash, Georgia Southern, Top Bunch, Vates
Corn, sweet	Honeycomb, Kandy Korn, Merit, Silver Queen, Sweet G-90
Cucumber	
Pickling	Calypso, Carolina
Slicer	Burpless, Dasher II, Poinsett 76, Sweet Slice, Sweet Success
Eggplant	
Large	Black Beauty, Black Bell, Black Magic, Epic
Oriental	Ichibon, Tycoon
Garlic	
Hardneck	German Red, Roja, Valencia
Softneck	California Early, California Late, Creole, Mexican Pink, Texas White
Honeydew melon	Greenflesh, Honeybrew, Megabrew, Morning Ice, TAMU Dew
Lettuce	
Butterhead	Buttercrunch, Summer Bibb
Crisp head	Not recommended
Loose leaf	Grand Rapids, Oakleaf, Red Sails, Red Salad Bowl, Salad Bowl
Romaine	Paris White Island, Valmine
Kale	Blue Armor, Blue Arrow, Blue Knight, Dwarf Scotch, Vates
Mustard greens	Green Wave, Large Smooth Leaf, Southern Giant Curl,Tendergreen
Okra	Cajun Delight, Clemson Spineless, Emerald, Lee

Onion (short day)	
Bunching	Evergreen Bunching
Red	Red Burgundy, Rio, Rio Santiago
White	Krystal, Texas Early White
Yellow	Granex, Grano, TX 1015Y (Texas Supersweet)
Pea	
Blackeye	Arkansas #1, Blackeye #5, Blackeye #46
Cream	Cream 40
Crowder	Brown Sugar, Mississippi Silver, Zipper
Edible pods	Dwarf Gray Sugar, Sugar Ann, Sugar Bon, Sugar Snap
Southern	California #5, Pinkeye, Pinkeye Purple Hull BVR, Purple Hull, Texas Pinkeye
Pepper	
Anaheim	Sonora
Ancho	San Martin
Bell	Bell Tower, Big Bertha, Capistrano, Jupiter, Red Knight, TAMU Rio Grande Gold
Cayenne	Mesilla
Jalapeño	Coyama, Grande, Mitla, TAMU Mild Jalapeño, TAMU Veracruz
Serrano	Fiesta, Hidalgo, Tampico, Tuxtlas
Potato	
Red	Pontiac, Red LaSoda, Viking
Russet	Century Russet, Norgold M, Russet Norkatah
White	Atlantic, Chipeta, Gemchip, Kennebec
Yellow Flesh	Yukon Gold
Pumpkin	
Large	Appalachin, Connecticut Field
Mammoth	Big Mac, Big Max
Mini	Jack-B-Little, Muchkin
Small	Small Sugar, Triple Treat
Radish	Champion, Cherry Belle, Daikon, White Chinese, White Icicle

VEGETABLE	VARIETIES
Spinach	Malabar, New Zealand, Samish
Squash (summer)	
Yellow Crook Neck	Bandit, Dixie, Early Golden, Freedom II, Summer Crook Neck
Yellow Straight Neck	Cougar, Gold Spike, Goldbar, Lemon Drop, Multipik
Zucchini	Black Magic, Commander, Enterprise, Gold Rush
Squash (winter)	Acorn, Butternut, Spaghetti, Sweet Mama
Sweet potato	Beauregard, Lucullus
Tomato	Bingo, Carnival, Celebrity, Florida 47, Porter, Red Cherry, Small Fry, Roma, Sun Pride, Sun Leaper, Sweet 100, Tomato 444
Turnip	
Greens	Alamo, All Top, Seven Top, Topper
Roots	Purple Top White Globe, Royal Globe, Shogoin, York
Watermelon	
Hybrids	Big Stripe, Jamboree, Ole, Royal Flush, Royal Sweet, Sentinel, Star Gazer, Stars-N-Stripes, Tendersweet Yellow
Seedless	Crimson Trio, Dillion, Millennium, Seedless Sweetheart, Sweet Slice, Tri X313, Triple Crown
Standard	Black Diamond, Charleson Gray, Jubilee

Note: Varieties come and go, so check with local nursery professionals or county extension agents for latest recommendations.

Planting Guidelines

Vegetables	Distance between plants (inches)	Spring planting relative to last freeze date	Fall planting relative to first freeze date
Asparagus	18	4–6 weeks before	not recommended
Bean, green bush	3–4	on to 4 weeks after	8–10 weeks before
Bean, green pole	4–6	on to 4 weeks after	14–16 weeks before
Beet	2	4–6 weeks before	8–10 weeks before
Broccoli (plants)	14–24	4–6 weeks before	10–16 weeks before
Brussels sprouts (plants)	14–24	4–6 weeks before	10–14 weeks before
Cabbage (plants)	14–24	4–6 weeks before	10–16 weeks before
Cabbage, Chinese	8–12	4–6 weeks before	12–14 weeks before
Cantaloupe	24–36	on to 6 weeks after	14–16 weeks before
Carrot	2	4–6 weeks before	12–14 weeks before
Cauliflower (plants)	14–24	not recommended	10–16 weeks before
Chard, Swiss	6	2–6 weeks before	12–16 weeks before
Collard (kale)	6–12	2–6 weeks before	8–12 weeks before
Corn, sweet	9–12	on to 6 weeks after	12–14 weeks before
Cucumber	8–12	on to 6 weeks after	10–12 weeks before
Eggplant (plants)	18–24	2–6 weeks after	12–16 weeks before
Garlic (cloves)	2–4	not recommended	4–6 weeks before
Kohlrabi	4–6	2–6 weeks before	12–16 weeks before
Lettuce	2–3	6 weeks before to 2 weeks after	10–14 weeks before
Mustard	6–12	on to 6 weeks after	10–16 weeks before
Okra	12–24	2–6 weeks after	12–16 weeks before
Onion (plants)	2–3	4–10 weeks before	not recommended
Onion (seed)	2–3	6–8 weeks before	8–10 weeks before
Parsley	2–4	on to 6 weeks before	6–16 weeks before
Pea, English	1	2–8 weeks before	2–12 weeks before
Pea, southern	4–6	2–10 weeks after	10–12 weeks before
Pepper (plants)	18–24	on to 8 weeks after	12–16 weeks before
Potato, Irish (seed pieces)	10–15	4–6 weeks before	14–16 weeks before
Potato, sweet (plants)	12–16	2–8 weeks after	not recommended
Pumpkin	36–48	1–4 weeks after	12–14 weeks before
Radish	1	6 weeks before to 4 weeks after	on to 8 weeks before
Spinach	3–4	1–8 weeks before	2–16 weeks before
Squash, summer	18–36	1–4 weeks after	12–15 weeks before
Squash, winter	24–48	1–4 weeks after	12–14 weeks before
Tomato (plants)	36–48	on to 8 weeks after	12–14 weeks before
Turnip, greens	2–3	2–6 weeks before	2–12 weeks before
Turnip, roots	2–3	2–6 weeks before	2–12 weeks before
Watermelon	36–72	on to 6 weeks after	14–16 weeks before

Note: Plant spacing is for seed unless noted as plants.

Gardening with Kids

At age 5 I knew I had done something good. It felt right. I had grown beans and fed the family (see "Will There Be a Next Generation of Vegetable Gardeners?" for the rest of the story). I didn't know why I felt good, but the benefits of participating in gardening by youngsters in school or at home are now well documented by university research. The benefits are significant and include the following:

- Increased self-esteem
- Developed sense of responsibility and accomplishment
- Understanding and acceptance of delayed gratification, success, and failure
- Increased problem-solving and nurturing skills
- Increased academic skills in science, arts, reading, and social studies
- Increased consumption of vegetables (especially when they are home-grown)
- Increased positive relationships fostered within families
- Increased parental involvement in the school

Wow! I just thought I grew a few beans and had FUN doing it. That FUN, and all the benefits, have made me a lifelong gardener. What a great hobby, and I am lucky enough to do it for a living also.

So let's talk FUN! To engage kids in gardening, it had better be fun, hands-on, in relatively short time periods, and successful (at least at first). Here are a couple of ideas for simple garden projects that most kids enjoy.

Plant sunflowers. Choose the mammoth or gigantic varieties that grow 6 to 12 inches per day—ones that will grow to be 12 feet tall with flowers over 12 inches in diameter. Give the kiddo(s) three to five seeds. Plant them after the last freeze date in your area. Plant the seeds in one garden bed, or plant them separately in different beds. The plants must get full sun to reach their full potential. If you (and the kids) want, track and chart the growth measurements of the plants, for example, using these criteria:

- Days to germination
- Daily growth
- Days and height when flower bud forms
- Mature height of the plant
- Diameter of the flowers
- Other dimensions that the kids can measure

Use journaling, drawing, and photographing to help document this experience. Harvest the sunflower, use it for bird and squirrel feed, and save some seed for the next planting. (My two gardeners were simply amazed at how tall the sunflowers were: "taller than Shaquille O'Neal." "Way!?!")

Plant a "living" tepee playhouse. This garden structure, emulating some Native American dwellings, can be constructed by inserting six to eight long poles (material choices include bamboo, plastic pipe, saplings, and wood) into the soil of a garden or flower bed in a circle 6 to 10 feet in diameter. Lean the poles in toward each other, and secure the tops together with wire or rope. Plant rapid-growing vines at each pole of the tepee frame, for example:

- Cardinal vine or cypress vine (fernlike foliage and red, tubular flowers)

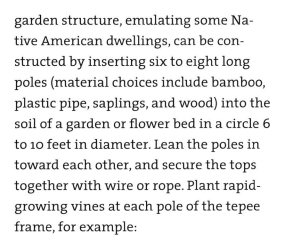

- Confederate or star jasmine (permanent, evergreen vine with fragrant, white flowers in late spring)
- Green beans (Kentucky wonder pole beans or Chinese yardlong beans)
- Mandevilla vine (tropical vine with fragrant, deep pink, funnel-shaped flowers)
- Morning glories (heart-shaped leaves and large, blue, tubular blooms each morning)
- Purple hyacinth bean (beautiful purple vine and flowers, nonedible fruit)
- Scarlet runner beans (ornamental, with red flowers and edible bean

These can be planted in combination for an eclectic display. Some of the vines

will need help climbing the poles by wrapping twine around the vines or tying stems to the poles with twine. (Did you know that some vines climb by wrapping clockwise around the pole and some counterclockwise? Check it out.)

Lay mulch in and around the tepee for a more all-weather surface. Plant some flowers to adorn the new playhouse. The living tepee provides a fun place for kids to play and maybe get a good crop of beans. (Bet they eat the beans before the beans ever get to the kitchen.)

Teaching Texas Children How to Garden

"We wanted to teach children that tomatoes don't come from the back of grocery stores, and we are concerned that there will not be a next generation of gardeners." For almost two decades, these have been the reasons that Texas Master Gardeners have ventured into elementary schools to teach gardening to Texas children.

Seeds for Success with Children

This list includes plants that can be grown easily from seed. A seed contains everything needed to produce a new replica of its parent; just add soil, water, and sunlight. It is a small miracle that will not go unnoticed by a child.

- Annual vines (refer to the "living tepee" project)
- Corn ('Silver Queen' and 'Sweet G90'; not easy to get big ears, but small ones taste good, too)
- Globe amaranth, bachelor's buttons, or gomphrena (annual flower with purple, white, or red flowers; makes great dried flowers)
- Green beans (bush varieties such as 'Contender,' 'Derby,' and 'Tendercrop')
- Periwinkles (annual flower that should be seeded in late spring)
- Pumpkins (plant in early summer; choose small-fruited varieties such as 'Small Sugar' or 'Triple Treat'; if all fruit fails, grow lots of vines, buy pumpkins, and put them among the vines—Happy Halloween!)
- Squash (yellow or zucchini varieties; kids usually will eat what they grow)
- Sunflowers (such an array of varieties: mammoth, dwarfs, new colors, multiflowered; try them all)
- Zinnias (annual flower with many varieties from big to small blooms; great cut flower)

Since the mid-1990s, the school garden movement has flourished in Texas and the nation. Texas Master Gardeners, a corps of 5,000 highly trained volunteer educators from over 115 county extension offices, continue their remarkable efforts to teach children the art, science, and fun of gardening.

The Junior Master Gardener (JMG) program is a youth version of the Master Gardener program that was developed by Texas Cooperative Extension at Texas A&M University. The JMG mission, "To grow good kids by igniting a passion for learning, success, and service through a unique gardening education," has guided the program through a now international network of universities and botanical gardens. Some 250,000 children in Texas alone experience learning and fun through the JMG curriculum. Contact your county extension office, or go to the Web site jmgkids.us to find out more about JMG.

Timely Tips

Flowers & Pretty Plants

- Divide fall-blooming perennials and ornamental grasses, if needed, to allow time for them to reestablish before blooming.
- Plant cool-season annual flowers for immediate color in the landscape, but realize that hot weather is not far away, and these plant will succumb quickly.
- Cut back dead foliage of ornamental grasses only after you have seen new green growth emerging from the plant base.
- Plant spring annuals for a blast of color.
- Fertilize annual and perennial flowers once this month with $\frac{1}{4}$ pound of urea per 100 square feet, $\frac{1}{2}$ pound of ammonium sulfate, or 1 pound of blood meal.

Garden Design

- Implement some of those winter dreams of landscape additions. Draw a blank? For immediate inspiration, read some of this almanac's essays regarding landscape design: "Attracting Birds to the Garden" (June); "Butterfly Gardening Made Simple" (July); "Landscape Design—Concepts, Guidelines, and Fun Ideas" (October); and "Design a Low-Maintenance Landscape" (December).

Soil & Mulch

- Lots of planting takes place this month, so do lots of soil preparation, too.
- Purchase organic matter every time you purchase plants.
- Don't monkey with the soil too much. If you add sand and organic matter to clay soil, you may produce the largest adobe brick known to humanity. Stick to adding just organic matter (e.g., pine bark and compost).
- Remember that there is no need to amend the soil when planting a tree (refer to the September essay "Tree Planting Made Easy").

Water

- Don't be too quick to turn on the irrigation system. Winter rains build up soil moisture levels. In the eastern half of Texas, irrigation systems should probably not be turned on until April. The time to irrigate begins this month with the early spring of the Rio Grande Valley and desertlike conditions of West Texas. Check soil moisture with your finger to determine exactly when to water.

Plant Care

- Be prepared for the onslaught of weeds this month. Mulching, pulling, mowing, trimming, and, as a last resort, spraying are viable strategies in the war on weeds. To arm yourself, read the April essay "Weeds, Weeds, and More Weeds."
- Hopefully, most pruning was done in February. If not, finish up now.
- For severely freeze-damaged perennial flowers and shrubs, it may be best to let new growth begin this month and then prune off all dead wood above the fresh new growth.
- Beware of late freezes. Protect plants if needed using techniques described in the September essay "Cold-Weather Protection for Plants."
- Move cold-sensitive plants back outdoors in March, but be prepared to move them indoors if a late frost is predicted.

Trees, Shrubs & Vines

- Plant trees, shrubs, vines, and groundcovers now while temperatures are cool for the plants and for you—less stress for everybody (everything).
- Plant a spring-flowering tree this season, for example, dogwood and redbud. This month's essay "Spring Has Sprung When You See These Bloomers" provides ample choices for all of Texas.

Lawns

- Mow the warm-season lawn grasses (e.g., St. Augustine and Bermuda) 1 inch lower than the height at which you ended last year. This is not "scalping" the lawn to prevent thatch. This simply removes winter-damaged leaves to clear the way for spring growth.
- Employ weed-prevention strategies quickly, as weeds emerge in March. A properly watered, fertilized, and mowed lawn will win the battle against most weeds.
- Irrigate the lawn only if it shows symptoms of stress due to lack of water—footprinting, leaf rolling, off color of gray-green. To become an expert in lawn watering, read this month's essay "When to Water, and How Long?"
- Don't fertilize the lawn yet. Spring lawn fertilizing occurs in April for Texas, except in deep South Texas, where lawn growth begins early this month.

Vegetables Herbs & Fruits

- If you are a gambler, plant warm-season crops in the first week of March. In the Panhandle you will likely lose due to frost. In the southern half of the state, you might be rewarded with the first tomatoes in the neighborhood.
- If you are less of a gambler, buy transplants and repot them into larger pots that can be moved indoors if temperatures dip into the 50s.
- Warm-season (i.e., cold-sensitive) herbs such as basil and mint can be planted now.
- Fertilize vegetable gardens with high-nitrogen, granular products. Most any lawn fertilizer will do, but you are better off turning to straight-nitrogen sources, including ammonium sulfate, blood meal, and urea.
- Monitor your fruit and nut crops for insect pests and disease. This constant vigil is essential. Control pests if necessary. Refer to the January essay "Growing Fruits and Nuts," or check with county extension agents and nursery professionals for proper control measures.
- Take care of the blooms on your fruit plants; without healthy blooms there will not be any fruit.

Care includes watering when needed, controlling any insect pests damaging the blooms, and keeping the kids' kickball from rattling around the flower-filled branches.

Houseplants

- Let them be free. Move the houseplants (and garaged plants) to vacation on the deck or patio all summer long.
- Trim and shape them, remove dead or damaged branches and leaves, spray-wash the foliage, water the soil thoroughly, fertilize, eliminate any insects, and let your houseplants grow.

Butterflies, Birds & Squirrels

- Plant a few plants that provide the essential needs of urban wildlife: food, shelter, and a place to rear their young. In addition to butterflies, birds, and squirrels, urban wildlife for many Texans includes deer, not the best landscape companion. Refer to the July essay "Deer-Resistant Plants" for help.
- Don't forget to provide water for the birds with birdbaths, bubblers, and fountains.

Notes:

April

*Mexican oregano (*Poliomintha longiflora*)*

GET MOVING—LOTS TO DO

Weeds, Weeds, and More Weeds

Weeds can be a huge challenge, whether in the lawn, vegetable garden, flower bed, or shrub plantings. Those of you who are living in long-established neighborhoods may not agree, but everyone living in new subdivisions, on the outskirts of town, or in rural homesteads agrees with this statement wholeheartedly.

Simply stated, a weed is an unwanted plant. One person's weed is another person's wildflower or native plant. Regardless, if YOU say it is a weed, then it is one.

Weeds can also harbor insect pests and diseases, lower flower or fruit production, and reduce aesthetic quality of the landscape and garden. Weeds can stunt and even kill young plants, shrubs, and trees. Their ability to compete for water and nutrients is unsurpassed. These weeds evolved over eons, and they will probably exist long after humans are gone from this planet. Only cockroaches and weeds will survive Armageddon.

Selecting effective, environmentally sound management strategies and properly identifying the weeds you hope to manage are critical first steps.

Dandelion, a broadleaf weed

Weed Management Strategies

It may sound surprising, but weed-killing chemicals (herbicides) are the last strategy, not the first. Here is a list of strategies and supporting information for the first-to-employ tactics to the last. Several of these done concurrently can result in the establishment of your own weed-free zone!

- Preparing the soil in your planting beds and vegetable gardens is first, believe it or not. Desirable plants grow better and faster in well-prepared soil, therefore competing successfully against weeds. Once the planting bed matures, the shrubs and plants will shade out or retard weed growth.

- Preventing weeds from being brought into your landscape in the first place is critical. The primary way nutgrass (nut sedge) enters landscapes is through trucked-in, contaminated topsoil or poor-quality turfgrass sod. Inspect topsoil loads before they are dumped, and choose sod that has no visible weeds.

- Mowing regularly is the best strategy to keep the weeds in check in your lawn. Few weeds can compete with vigorously growing, dense turfgrasses, such as Bermuda, St. Augustine, and zoysia. Conversely, buffalograss, centipedegrass, and fescuegrass may not have enough vigor and density or form a turf thick enough to ward off many weeds.

- Hand pulling weeds from the lawn, planting beds, and vegetable garden remains a sure way to successfully eliminate weeds. It takes patience, persistence, strong hands, strong back, and tough knees, but it is immediate and gratifying. A glass of chardonnay or bottle of beer in one hand and pulling weeds with the other can be fun. If done with your spouse, it can provide tremendous amounts of quality time and build a stronger marriage (really).

- Getting on the business end of a hoe is also effective in removing even the toughest of weeds. Teach your children, as this can be a character-building experience in immediate and delayed gratification. Persistence is critical.

- Mulching planting beds and gardens will also deter weeds effectively. Applying 2 to 3 inches of mulch will keep the weed seed from sprouting, keep light away from weed seedlings, smother the seedlings, retard weed growth, or make the weeds easier to pull. Mulching works best on weeds that come up from seed (annual weeds).

- Mulching around young trees (shade or fruit) helps keep lawn grasses and weeds from competing for the tree's water and nutrients. This weed-free zone should be maintained for at least 2 years. Mature, established trees compete with grass much better and do not need the mulch.

• Using the right herbicide for the right weed is the final strategy. There are many herbicides that will be discussed later. Most are chemical pesticides and must be used properly. Organic pesticides are also available yet have limited applications and success.

Weed Identification

Know your enemy, and identify (or at least classify) the weeds you are trying to manage. There are two general types of weeds: broadleaf and grassy. Knowing which one you are dealing with will determine the management techniques that will work best, or at all!

Broadleaf weeds have "broad," as opposed to "narrow (grasslike)," leaves. Dandelion is perhaps the best-known example of a broadleaf weed. Broadleaf weeds are "dicots," having two seed leaves (officially now called "eudicots").

Grassy weeds are similar in appearance to lawn or ornamental grasses. They have narrow leaves and are "monocots" (having one seed leaf). Dallisgrass, Johnson grass, nutgrass (nut sedge), and even Bermudagrass are well-known, tenacious grassy weeds.

Beyond this classification of weeds, it is also important to know whether the weed you are trying to manage is an annual weed or a perennial weed.

Annual weeds return each year from seed. Dandelions and annual ryegrass come from seeds each year. Annual weeds are subdivided into summer and winter. Summer annuals germinate in the spring, grow during the summer, usually flower and produce seed, and then die in the fall. Their seeds lie dormant in the soil until the next spring. Summer annual weeds include cocklebur, crabgrass, dandelion, goosegrass, grassbur, morning glory, pigweed, purslane, ragweed, and spotted spurge.

Dallisgrass, a grassy weed

CALLER: "How do I get rid of grassburs in my large lawn?"

ANSWER: "Most complaints about grassburs (field sandburs) come from folks who have large lawns in rural settings or newly developed subdivisions. Eliminating them takes a couple of years using an integrated approach. There is no silver bullet for grassbur control.

"The first step in eliminating grassburs is to have a high-quality lawn. Grassburs do not compete well against dense, manicured lawns of Bermudagrass or St. Augustine. Spring and fall fertilizing, watering when needed, and mowing regularly will create a thicker, high-quality lawn that chokes out most existing weeds and prevents new weed seed from germinating.

"A second step to controlling grassburs is to collect the seeds. Sounds like a painful task, but not really. My brother, Dan, advised me years ago that dragging a burlap bag or blanket behind the walk-behind or riding mower serves as a magnet for prickly grassburs. The less grassburs (seed) you have in the lawn, the less grassburs next year.

"A third step in controlling grassburs is to hoe or pull the grassbur plants. Again, brother Dan could recognize a grassbur plant in the lawn from fifty feet. He recommends a methodical, persistent pulling of these plants that results in a significant reduction in grassbur plant populations and seed production.

"A final step, should you be willing to use a pesticide, is to spread a pre-emergence herbicide or spot-treat with a post-emergence herbicide. Look for pre-emergence granular products labeled for grassbur control, and spread the herbicide in mid-spring. Since grassburs can germinate from late spring through early fall, a second application of a pre-emergence herbicide may be warranted. A post-emergence herbicide, MSMA, can be used ONLY in Bermudagrass lawns to kill individual grassbur plants. As always, read label directions and safety precautions before using any pesticide."

Winter annual weeds grow in cool temperatures. They germinate in late summer, fall, and winter and usually flower and mature their seed in the spring or early summer before dying. Their seeds often lie dormant in the soil during the summer months. Winter weeds include annual ryegrass, burclover, fescuegrass, henbit, sow thistle, and wild mustard.

Perennial weeds have a permanent root system or crown from which shoots emerge each year. Bermudagrass, Dallisgrass, Johnson grass, and nutgrass are grassy, perennial weeds. Creeping, broadleaf, perennial weeds include clover, dichondra, field bindweed, mouse-ear chickweed, wild strawberry, and wood sorrel.

Ideally, you would identify specifically each weed you want to kill. In reality, this may not be necessary to manage the weeds in your lawn, landscape, and garden. If you want the specific identity of the culprit, take a sample to the county extension agent or your local nursery professional, or search through photos on the Internet or in books.

The bottom line is to determine if the weed is broadleaf or grassy; whether it comes back from seed or roots; and when it grows, summer or winter. You will then be armed with the knowledge to annihilate (I mean manage) your weeds.

Herbicides

Do not use herbicides in your landscape, vegetable garden, or home orchard unless you fully understand all aspects of safe handling and application. Read the product labels carefully:

- Look for the weed you are trying to control (grassy or broadleaf, or the specific weed).
- Check to see if the product can be used on edible crops (in your vegetable garden or fruit planting).
- Check to see if the product is not recommended for use on certain species. For example, the herbicide MSMA can be used to kill grassy weeds in Bermudagrass, but not in St. Augustine or centipedegrass.

Herbicide Formulations and Applications

Be careful with any herbicide. Herbicides kill plants, and they can also harm you if not used properly.

Herbicides are available in granular and liquid formulations. Granular materials can be put out with fertilizer spreaders and are quite effective. Liquid formulations are available in ready-to-use (RTU) products and/or concentrates. Use RTUs if at all possible for personal and environmental protection; it is worth the increased cost. Concentrates must be mixed with water. It is during this process when most poisonings or spills into the environment occur.

If you use a concentrate and apply it in solution with a pump-up sprayer, make sure you designate that sprayer as "herbicides only." It is difficult to completely clean an herbicide out of a sprayer, and you do not want to spray an insecticide from a sprayer previously used for an herbicide. You may end up killing both the pest and the patient.

TYPES OF HERBICIDES

Herbicides can be categorized based on their mode of action and/or time of application. Here are descriptions of specific types:

- Growth-regulating or hormonal herbicides control physiological processes of plants, such as cell division and expansion or photosynthesis. The most common example is 2,4-D.
- Soil sterilants are applied to eliminate all plant growth and seldom have a use in landscapes and gardens (maybe for a crushed-rock driveway). These products, often called brush killers, persist in the soil for years. Nothing will grow there for a long, long time.
- Pre-emergence herbicides are designed to kill weed seeds as they germinate in lawns and landscape plantings. They are put out in the early fall to control winter annual weeds and put out in late winter to control summer annuals. Never put a pre-emergence herbicide in a vegetable garden or flower bed where you intend to grow plants from seed. Examples include Amaze, Balan, Dimension, Gallery, Portrait, Preen, Simizine, Surflan, and Team. Corn gluten meal is a patented, organic pre-emergence herbicide developed at Iowa State University and is showing worthy results.
- Post-emergence herbicides kill growing weeds. Most herbicides in the landscape and garden are post-emergent. They kill 'em when you see 'em.
- Selective herbicides are growth-regulating herbicides that kill either broadleaf weeds or grassy weeds. Based on this chemistry, some herbicides kill broadleaf weeds among grasses (dandelions in turfgrass). Examples include 2,4-D, dicamba, Trimec, Weed-B-Gone, and Weed Free Zone. Some herbicides can kill grasses among broadleaf weeds (Bermudagrass in Asiatic jasmine). Examples include Fusilade and Poast. Nutgrass, being a sedge and not a true grass or broadleaf, can be controlled in lawns and planting beds by using Image.
- Nonselective herbicides kill any plant on which they are sprayed. Glyphosate and related formulations

Glyphosate Herbicides— Valuable Weed Management Tools

Few herbicides are needed regularly for managing weeds in the home lawn and garden, yet glyphosate herbicides are a valuable, environmentally safe tool for weed management. (*Note:* This is one I cannot do without.)

Glyphosate (originally packaged only as Roundup) effectively kills the entire weed and can severely damage woody plants (trees, shrubs, and vines). It can be used effectively to edge planting beds to eliminate invasions by Bermudagrass and other weeds. Other uses include edging mulched rings around trees, controlling weeds in driveway and sidewalk cracks, and eliminating weeds or turfgrass at the base of fences. Effective use of glyphosate can reduce the need for flexible-line trimmers and edgers. One or two applications per year can significantly reduce landscape maintenance.

Herbicides containing glyphosate (or closely related formulations) are now available under several brand names. Read the "active ingredients" list on the product, and look for glyphosate. Read the label directions carefully for effective and safe use of this herbicide. Also understand that when using herbicides containing glyphosate and closely related formulas, you may not see visible signs of damage to the targeted weeds for a few days to a week.

Ready-to-use (RTU) products are available, which eliminate the need for mixing concentrated glyphosate with water. These products cost more but are worth using for their safety and convenience.

Glyphosate products are nonselective; they kill, or severely damage, most anything you spray them on, but they do not persist in the soil (like a soil sterilant). Tremendous amounts of research have been conducted on glyphosate products regarding their effectiveness and environmental impact. The definitive research shows that they work, but more important, that microorganisms break down glyphosate rapidly, leaving no residue in the soil.

Glyphosate is absorbed through the leaves of plants, then translocated to the roots, thereby killing the entire plant. Exceptionally tough-to-control weeds, such as morning glory, nutgrass (nut sedge), poison ivy, and smilax, may take multiple applications. Glyphosate can be sprayed on rough bark of mature trees without being absorbed (and damaging the tree).

One caution has arisen from recent research: **Do not spray glyphosate on the trunk of crape myrtles.** The bark of crape myrtle exfoliates (sheds, which is a beautiful characteristic), and thus the trunk will absorb glyphosate and damage the tree.

A final word of caution: When spraying glyphosate, walk backward. Do not walk through sprayed areas, or your shoes will become applicators. Nothing like a polka-dotted lawn to convince you to walk carefully!

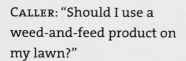

CALLER: "Should I use a weed-and-feed product on my lawn?"

ANSWER: "'Killing two birds with one stone' is a great concept, but combining herbicides and fertilizers in one product may not be. Weed-and-feed products claim to kill weeds and fertilize the lawn at the same time. Weed-and-feed products combine a fertilizer with a pre-emergence herbicide and/or post-emergence herbicide. Sounds good but is seldom recommended by university extension agents and educators.

"For spring lawn fertilization, the concern is that timing for application of fertilizers is not the same as for pre-emergence herbicides. Pre-emergence herbicides for summer weed control should be applied in late winter (February for most of Texas). Spring lawn fertilizer should be put out in midspring (after a couple of lawn mowings). Applying fertilizer in late winter or early spring may cause 'spring root dieback' in turfgrasses—too much shoot growth at the expense of root growth.

"For fall lawn fertilization, application timing conflicts again. Pre-emergence herbicides should be applied to the lawn in late summer or early fall (August or September for most of Texas). The fall application of fertilizer should happen after the first frost and the lawn has stopped growth, usually in mid-October through November.

"If the weed and feed combines fertilizer and a post-emergence herbicide, the concern is for trees, shrubs, and flowers. Post-emergence herbicides cannot tell the difference between a weed and a tree or landscape plant. Labels of weed-and-feed products used on lawns emphasize keeping the weed and feed out from under the canopy of trees and out of shrub and flower beds. This is a must to avoid possible damage to your valued trees and landscape plantings.

"For most lawns receiving moderate levels of management (proper mowing, fertilizing, and watering), weeds are seldom a major problem, and an herbicide application is not justified.

"Weed-and-feed products for use in shrub planting combine a fertilizer and a pre-emergence herbicide. This makes sense and is often recommended. Shrubs should be fertilized before spring growth begins (in late winter), and that, too, is when pre-emergence herbicides should be put out."

are the active ingredients in Com-Pleet, Finale, Kills All, and Roundup. Note that a soil sterilant would also be considered a nonselective herbicide.

- Systemic herbicides are transported throughout the weed, killing both shoots and roots. Glyphosate, and related formulas, is the best example of a systemic, nonselective herbicide.

- Nonsystemic, contact herbicides cause rapid drying of plant tissue. Organic herbicides, such as vinegar, salt solutions, and herbicidal soaps, burn foliage quickly but may not kill the weed roots.

A final comment on weed management: If you do not fully understand safety and application procedures, you should not use any herbicide. A safe rule of thumb is "If in doubt, hoe it out."

Fire Ant Management

*Red imported fire ant (*Solenopsis invicta*)*

Fire ants—the good news and the bad news. Which do you want to hear first? Okay, let's get the bad news over first. Fire ants will never be eradicated in Texas! Let's be clear; this statement refers to the red imported fire ants (*Solenopsis invicta*) that are not native to Texas and are aggressive—stinging you, killing baby quail, and injuring innocent calves and other living things that cross their paths. This species is native to South America and came into the United States over 75 years ago via Mobile, Alabama, in ship ballast and shipped goods. They are not going to get back on ships and go back home anytime soon.

The good news is that extension entomologists at Texas A&M University have developed the strategy and identified the insecticides needed to manage red imported fire ants in your landscape and garden. (*Note:* Research scientists are also working on predators and parasites that will attack the red imported fire ant. Watch the news for developments.)

Extension entomologists developed the "Texas two-step method" for fire ant management. (For those of you new to Texas, "the two-step" is a country-western dance step; pretty cute pun, huh?)

Identification of Fire Ants

"The only good ant is a dead ant" is not a true statement. There are over 260 species of ants native to Texas. Only a few are considered household or garden pests. The rest, including four native species of nonaggressive fire ants, are simply minding their own business, and some are even known competitors of the red imported fire ant.

To identify if an ant mound or colony is that of the red imported fire ant, simply stick a pencil (or twig) into the mound. If the ants sprint to the pencil and rapidly climb it, they are probably the bad guys. For the rest of this essay, they will be referred to simply as fire ants. (*Note:* Please don't use your finger instead of a pencil, as one of Texas' former commissioners of agriculture did on television. Although he did make a dramatic point about how big a problem the fire ant is, this is not a recommended identification technique, for obvious reasons.)

If you don't see mounds, cut hot dogs in cross sections, and impale them to the ground with a wire stake every 20 feet through the landscape (fire ants love hot dogs; the brand doesn't matter). Come back in 20 minutes, and count the number of fire ants on the hot dogs. If there are more than you can count, you have a serious fire ant problem.

Threshold for Application of Insecticides

As with any landscape or garden pest, just because you see one does not justify spreading an insecticide. There is a population threshold that should be observed before treatment is initiated. For fire ants, the threshold is three to five mounds in your landscape or hundreds of fire ants on the hot dogs. If you have young children that play in the yard, then the threshold may approach one mound or a few dozen on the hot dogs.

The Two-Step Method of Management

Fire ants can be managed with persistence, patience, and the right plan. The Texas two-step method provides effective and environmentally safe control of fire ants for home landscapes and gardens. Two-step insecticides, both chemical and organic, can be purchased in most nurseries and garden centers. As always, read the label directions and use insecticides properly, and they will pose little risk to humans, pets, wildlife, or the environment.

The two-step method combines two treatment techniques—use of baits and mound treatments.

Using Baits

Fire ant baits are designed to be broadcast evenly over the treatment area. They contain a food source (usually corn grits or meal) laced with an insecticide. The fire ants ingest the bait and insecticide. Most baits contain either an insect growth regulator that disrupts the life cycle of the ants or a chemical that kills ants immediately.

In recent years a bait containing an organic insecticide, spinosad, was made available (spinosad is also available in a liquid form for mound treatments). Spinosad is an aerobic fermentation product of the soil bacterium *Saccharopolyspora spinosa,* which kills insects when ingested or drenched. Spinosad is an effective nonsynthetic insecticide with well-documented research supporting it.

Baits should be used when fire ants are actively foraging (gathering food for the colony). Baits should be broadcast over the whole landscape (with the exception of a vegetable garden, to be discussed later). The worker ants collect the bait, carry it back to the colony, and share it with the queen and other ants. This technique uses much less insecticide than spraying or spreading a granular insecticide over the entire landscape.

Fire ants are surprisingly adept at finding and picking up baits from the landscape. Fire ants forage when the soil-surface temperature is between 70°F and 90°F (March to September). Fall applications work well to reduce fire ant numbers the following spring. During summer droughts or in winter, fire ants forage little and rarely pick up baits.

Scatter the bait lightly throughout the landscape using a hand-held, whirlybird spreader. The recommended rate for most baits is 1 to $1\frac{1}{2}$ pounds per acre. You can spread the baits by hand (wearing rubber gloves), but you will not distribute it as evenly as with a spreader. Do not use push-type fertilizer spreaders because they put out baits much too heavily and waste bait.

Measure out the recommended rate (refer to the instructions on the bait bag). Set the hand-held spreader on the lowest setting (i.e., smallest opening). Make one pass back and forth over the area to be treated. Make another pass walking perpendicular to the first pass.

Baits do not kill fire ants immediately, so be patient. Baits vary in the time they take to eliminate the fire ant population, ranging from 2 weeks to a couple of months.

Following are additional hints for increasing the effectiveness of baits:

- Check to see if ants are active and foraging by placing a small amount of bait or potato chips next to a mound. If ants begin removing the bait or chips within 30 minutes, bait immediately.
- In summer, apply baits in the evening when ants emerge to collect food.
- Always use fresh bait from unopened containers. Baits in opened containers may last only a few weeks. Unopened containers keep baits fresh for up to 2 years.

- If you question the freshness of the bait, place a teaspoon of the bait next to an active mound. Ants will find and pick up unspoiled bait in about 30 minutes.
- Rain ruins baits, so apply them when rain is not forecast for a few days.

TREATING INDIVIDUAL FIRE ANT MOUNDS

The second step in the two-step method is to treat individual fire ant mounds that pose an immediate danger to humans or pets. Mound treatment is the quickest way to eliminate individual colonies. It is not necessary to treat all fire ant colonies with mound treatments after applying a bait. There are several mound treatment options—some use chemical insecticides; some, organic insecticides; and some, unique noninsecticide techniques.

- Granular products contain an insecticide that releases into the soil, usually when drenched with water. Spread the recommended amount of product around and on top of the mound. Some product labels direct you to apply water to the mound after treatment to drive the insecticide into the mound. Sprinkle the water gently on the mound to avoid disturbing the colony. Stirring up the mound may make you feel good, but it triggers a reaction in the mound for the worker ant to carry the queen deeper down into the mound for safety.
- Liquid drenches are pesticides mixed with water first and then applied directly to the mound. Apply 1 to 2 gallons of the mixed solution per mound. Always wear chemical-resistant gloves to protect your skin when handling liquid concentrates, and follow label directions.

COMMON FIRE ANT BAITS

TRADE NAME	PESTICIDE	SPEED OF CONTROL
Fertilome Come & Get It!, Green Light Fire Ant Killer, Justice, Ortho Fire Ant Killer	spinosad	moderate-slow
Amdro, Combat, ProBait, Siege Pro	hydramethylnon	moderate-slow
Award, Logic	fenoxycarb	moderate
Ascend, Varsity	abamectin	moderate-slow
Chipco, Fire Star	fipronil	moderate-slow
Distance, Spectracide Fire Ant Bait	pyriproxyfen	slow
Extinguish	methoprene	slow

Note: Check for the pesticides listed above as the "active ingredients" in other trade-name baits.

• Acephate (Orthene) is an effective dry dust treatment that does not require added water. Sprinkle lightly and evenly over the entire mound. Avoid disturbing the colony during application. The ants will walk through the dust, which adheres to their bodies and then is tracked throughout the mound by the ants. Although acephate stinks like rotten eggs, it is a convenient and easy-to-apply fire ant control.

• Several "organic" products will control fire ants. Examples include citrus oil (d-limonene), pine oil (turpentine), pyrethrins, rotenone, and spinosad. Liquid formulations should be mixed with water and drenched into the mound.

• Boiling water (about 3 gallons per mound) can eliminate some fire ant colonies; however, this method can be hazardous to the person carrying the hot water. Also, boiling water poured on grass or around plants can damage plants severely.

• Shoveling can be used to remove fire ant mounds from vegetable and herb gardens and compost piles. The captured mounds can be spread on the driveway and the fire ants killed using a chemical or organic insecticide listed above.

CALLER: "Is there an organic two-step method?" ANSWER: "Yes, for a two-step program that uses only organic products, broadcast spinosad bait, and then treat mounds with products containing d-limonene, pyrethrins, rotenone, or spinosad."

Single Application for Season-Long Control

Products have entered the market designed to be broadcast one time over the entire landscape for season-long control of fire ants. The effectiveness of these products has been validated; however, careful consideration should be made before applying any pesticide that has

Common Mound Treatment Insecticides

TRADE NAME	PESTICIDE	SPEED OF CONTROL
Ortho Fire Ant Granules	bifenthrin	fast
Bayer Advanced, Lawn & Garden Multi-Insect Killer	cyfluthrin	fast
Safer Fire Ant Killer	d-limonene	fast
Bengal UltraDust, DeltaDust, Terro Fire Ant Killer	deltamethrin	fast
Conserve, Monterey Garden Insect Spray	spinosad	moderate–slow
Garden Tech Sevin	carbaryl	moderate
Diatec III, Organic Solutions Multipurpose Fireant Killer, Results	pyrethrins	immediate
Orthene, Surrender Fire Ant Killer	acephate	moderate
Eliminator Granules, Real-Kill Fire Ant Killer Granules, Spectracide Bug Stop	permethrin	fast
Bonide Rotenone	rotenone	slow

Note: Check for the pesticides listed above as the "active ingredients" in other trade-name insecticides.

long-term effectiveness (residual) across a large area. These products should be used according to the label directions with adherence to the safety precautions. The two most common products used for season-long control of fire ants are fipronil and indoxacarb:

- Fipronil (Garden Tech's Over 'n Out!) is a granular insecticide to be broadcast over the entire landscape. Its speed of control is moderate yet long-lasting. It controls existing fire ants and prevents new infestation.
- Indoxacarb (Spectracide's Once and Done! Fire Ant Killer) is a bait containing the insecticide. Fire ants pick up the bait and carry it back to the mound, where it is ingested, and ant death results. Indoxacarb's speed of control is fast, usually within 48 hours.

The fire ant detecting technique using hot dogs is a great way to see how fast and effective these products work. Two days after treatment, place new hot dog cross sections out in the landscape, come back in 20 minutes, and see how many fewer fire ants are on the hot dogs.

Lawns 101

The most frequently asked questions via call-in radio shows, e-mails, telephones, and over the fence in neighborhoods throughout the nation are about lawns. This makes sense because virtually every homeowner has a lawn and is in it weekly mowing, blowing, and going. So here is the scoop on establishing and maintaining a beautiful carpet of grass with the lowest level of cost and effort.

Selecting the Right Grass

Whether establishing a new lawn or renovating an existing one, selecting the right species and variety of turfgrass is essential to success. If a proper selection is made, you can determine the level of maintenance (e.g., frequency of mowing) required; avoid chronic disease and insect problems; and wind up with a lawn that meets your, your spouse's, and your neighbors' expectations.

Your choice of turfgrass depends on these factors:

- Geographic location
- Availability of irrigation water
- Amount of shade present
- Amount of time and money willing to expend
- Kind of usage expected (e.g., kickball, crochet, rolling around, simply viewing)

Turfgrasses for lawns are classified as either warm season, which grow predominantly in late spring through early fall, or cool season, which grow predominantly in late fall through early spring.

WARM-SEASON TURFGRASSES

- Bermudagrass
- St. Augustinegrass
- Zoysiagrass
- Buffalograss
- Centipedegrass
- Carpetgrass
- Seashore paspalum

COOL-SEASON TURFGRASSES

- Tall fescue
- Kentucky bluegrass
- 'Reveille' bluegrass
- Ryegrass

Bermudagrass and St. Augustinegrass are the most widely chosen and recommended warm-season grasses for Texas lawns. Relatively new zoysiagrass varieties are available and have great potential for Texas lawns. Also relatively new buffalograss varieties are available for use in much of Texas with the exception of West, East, and Southeast Texas. Centipedegrass and carpetgrass can be successfully grown in East Texas. Seashore paspalum can be grown in South Texas up to about San Antonio.

Cool-season turfgrasses, such as tall fescue and bluegrass, are limited for use as permanent lawns to North Texas and parts of West Texas. The other cool-season grass, ryegrass, is used mostly as a temporary lawn or for overseeding on Bermudagrass.

Each turfgrass species (and sometimes multiple varieties), whether warm or cool season, has various characteristics that should be considered in order to make a proper selection.

Bermudagrass spreads by rhizomes (underground) and stolons (on surface).

St. Augustinegrass spreads just by stolons.

Bermudagrass

Chief advantage: little disease or insect problems, cold tolerant throughout Texas

Major requirement: full sun

Disadvantages: cannot tolerate shade; turns brown after first frost; can be a nuisance invading flower beds and landscape plantings

Bermudagrass (*Cynodon dactylon*) is the most widely used turfgrass in Texas. In addition to lawns, Bermudagrass is used in parks, sports fields, and commercial and public landscapes, for one reason: It is the toughest, least pest riddled, easiest to care for, and most drought tolerant of any turfgrass for Texas. It must be considered first as you choose or renovate your lawn (the only exception is for lawns shaded by large trees).

Bermudagrass is a fine-textured (thin-bladed) grass with two disadvantages: its lack of shade tolerance and its ability to rapidly invade flower beds, vegetable gardens, and landscape plantings via underground runners (rhizomes) if left unchecked. To keep Bermudagrass from becoming a weed pest, you will need to learn to use a glyphosate herbicide (e.g., Roundup and other brand names) a couple of times per year. Organic herbicides can also be effective but will require more frequent applications.

A few varieties of Bermudagrass can be seeded (1 to 2 pounds per 1,000 square feet), which is less costly than purchasing sod to establish a lawn. The highest-quality Bermudagrass varieties are sodded due to sterile seed or to eliminate any genetic variability resulting from seed. Of the dozens of varieties, the ones listed on page 162 are most commonly used for lawns and readily available in nurseries and sod dealers (also noted is whether they can be seeded or sodded and other characteristics).

St. Augustinegrass

Chief advantages: most shade tolerant; remains green but dormant throughout most winters in southern half of Texas

Major requirement: irrigation and disease and insect management required

Disadvantages: lack of cold tolerance north and west of Fort Worth; susceptibility to diseases and insects

St. Augustinegrass (*Stenotaphrum secundatum*) is a wide-bladed, coarse-textured species that forms a dense, thick lawn crowding out most weeds. It is the most shade tolerant of Texas turfgrasses and is easily kept out of flower beds by pulling aboveground runners (stolons). It

Bermudagrass Varieties

VARIETY	SEEDED	LAWN QUALITY	TEX-TURE	GREEN COLOR	MAINTE-NANCE REQUIRE-MENT	NOTES
Common	yes	good	fine	light	lowest	cheapest; lowest quality but acceptable to most people; can also be purchased as sod
Sahara	yes	good	finer	light	low	next-lowest cost; a bit higher quality than 'Common'
Princess 33	yes	better	finer	light	medium	more expensive seeded variety; perhaps highest quality of seeded varieties
Texturf 10	no	better	finer	blue-green	medium	widely used in Dallas area; higher quality than 'Common' but similar care
Baby	no	best	fine	medium dark	high	claims to be less aggressive dwarf variety but still requires frequent and low mowing at $\frac{1}{2}$ to 1 inch
Tifway (419)	no	best	fine	dark	high	highest-quality lawn but requires frequent mowing at 1 to 3 inches and more fertilizing; has been the dominant variety for football and baseball fields in Texas

Note: Varieties listed in order of lawn quality produced.

is not as cold hardy as Bermudagrass and is best grown in areas south of Fort Worth.

St. Augustine is often called "carpet-grass," but it is not. There is a turfgrass species called carpetgrass that will be discussed later. Some Northerners think that St. Augustine looks like crabgrass. To each his own, but in the absence of being able to grow bluegrass, many Northerners have come to tolerate and appreciate St. Augustine.

St. Augustine is a more forgiving grass regarding mowing than Bermudagrass. You can skip a mowing (due to vacation or perhaps laziness). The grass will be tall and tiring to mow, but it will immediately look good. If you do this to Bermudagrass, your lawn will be brown stubbles (leaves grow only at the stem tips on Bermudagrass).

The disadvantages of St. Augustine are significant and cannot be ignored:

- Yellowing due to iron chlorosis is common in alkaline soils of Central and South Texas; leaf blades appear striped with parallel, alternating green and yellow stripes.
- Yellowing due to a viral disease, St. Augustine decline (SAD), is a chronic but not fatal problem with the variety 'Common' St. Augustine (there are resistant varieties thanks to breeders); leaf blades are mottled with polka dots of green and yellow.
- Yellowing and browning can be caused by a fungal disease, brown patch, which is a chronic but not fatal problem in most lawns; brown patch appears most often in spring and fall.
- Death may result from a fungal disease, take-all patch, which is becoming more prevalent.
- Damage or death is often seen due to insects such as chinch bugs and grubworms.
- Damage or death occurs from freezing temperatures north of a line from Dallas to San Angelo to El Paso.
- Severe damage or death will occur during the summer if the lawn is not watered regularly in the absence of rain (Bermudagrass will simply go dormant and turn brown).

There are few varieties to choose from in St. Augustine. 'Common' St. Augustine should seldom be planted due to susceptibility to SAD. All other varieties normally planted are resistant to SAD and include 'Delmar,' 'Floratam,' 'Palmetto,' 'Raleigh,' and 'Seville.' 'Raleigh' is the most commonly used and has become the standard. 'Floratam' has chinch bug resistance but lacks cold tolerance north of San Antonio. No variety stands out as "the best" thus far. New varieties are on their way as breeders look for resistance to disease, insects, and cold. Check with your county extension agent and nursery professionals for any new and improved varieties.

Establish St. Augustine lawn with sod. Seed is sometimes available but cost prohibitive. Laying "solid sod" (i.e., all sod pieces laid side by side) is highly recommended. Laying sod in a "checkerboard" pattern (i.e., lay a sod piece, skip a space, lay a piece) or plugging smaller pieces at 1-foot spacing is not recommended due to the inevitable fight against weeds that will result. If economics is a concern, solid sod only what you can afford, and slowly expand the lawn a section at a time.

Zoysiagrass

- Chief advantage: almost as shade tolerant as St. Augustine; few disease or insect problems
- Major requirement: mow with a high-dollar reel mower (not rotary) or powerful riding lawn mower
- Disadvantages: due to the thickness and density of this turf, mowing will wear you out; earliest turfgrass to turn brown at the first frost and last to green up in spring

Zoysiagrass (*Zoysia* spp. and hybrids) is a viable option for some Texas lawns. It is particularly good for courtyards and small lawns. When properly managed, zoysia is beautiful, wear resistant, and relatively pest free. It is less invasive than Bermudagrass and almost as shade tolerant as St. Augustine. Zoysia will,

however, turn brown at the first frost and stay brown until after Bermudagrass has greened up.

The biggest challenge with zoysia is mowing. There are several new varieties, and none have overcome this challenge for the homeowner. To mow zoysia properly and with some semblance of ease, you will need to have a powerful walk-behind, self-propelled mower or riding tractor or zero-turn mower with sharp rotary blades that are sharpened fre-

CALLER: "Can I encourage one grass over the other in my Bermuda and St. Augustine lawn, or will one win regardless?"

ANSWER: "If your lawn has lots of shade, St. Augustine will win. If your lawn is in full sun, it will be a battle, but you can help determine the winner. If you want St. Augustine to win, mow tall (four inches), and do not let the St. Augustine suffer from lack of water. If you want Bermudagrass to take over, mow short (one and one-half to two inches), fertilize lightly once a month, and water only when the Bermudagrass indicates drought stress. If you are willing, you can even use an herbicide, called MSMA, that kills St. Augustine but not Bermudagrass."

quently. A mower with reel-type blades makes the job much easier, but this type of mower is expensive, and it is difficult to maintain sharp blades (this is the kind used on golf courses).

New varieties of zoysia developed by Texas A&M University include 'Cavalier,' 'Crowne,' and 'Palisades.' 'Cavalier' is a fine-textured zoysia, whereas 'Crowne' and 'Palisades' are coarser-textured varieties. If you want to try one of these zoysias, do so in a relatively small area to get a feel for the mowing requirement and then expand if warranted. Other varieties worth considering are 'El Toro,' 'Emerald,' 'Meyer,' and 'Omni.'

Zoysiagrass is sodded, not seeded. Always solid-sod the area. Do not plug it, or you will fight every weed and its brother trying to get the plugs to fill in the area.

Although advertisements in the Sunday supplements in the newspaper may claim miraculous, no-mow, no-care characteristics for zoysia, do your homework before leaping into zoysia.

Buffalograss

> Chief advantage: natural look of a short grassland prairie; little mowing required (once a month or less)
> Major requirement: geographic location—predominately Central Texas.

> Disadvantages: weed control is perpetually required; you have to like the look of buffalograss

Buffalograss (*Buchloe dactyloides*) is a thin-bladed grass that is native from Central Texas straight north to North Dakota. It creates a natural-looking short grassland prairie in your lawn. You will either like the look of buffalograss or not; there is no fence sitting.

From a distance, most people think it is Bermudagrass. Standing in it, you can see the relatively thin turf that it develops. It is not a grass that compels you to drop and roll around in. It is aptly named, for buffalo, not humans, love to roll in it.

Having said this, there is no other grass that looks more at home and aesthetically pleasing around a limestone house than buffalograss. (*Note:* Regardless of your politics, President George W. and First Lady Laura Bush's home in Crawford is surrounded by the most beautiful buffalograss lawn I've ever seen. The variety is '609.')

Common buffalograss can be seeded (5+ pounds per 1,000 square feet), but newly developed varieties are sodded. Again, solid sodding is a must. Four varieties dominate the marketplace: '609,' 'Density,' 'Prairie,' and 'Stampede.' All are female selections, lacking the unattractive male seed stalks. Most would agree that '609,' 'Density,' and 'Stampede' are superior in color to 'Prairie,' with 'Density' claiming more density (thickness of turf to prevent weeds) than the others.

Centipedegrass

Chief advantage: low maintenance for acre-plus lawns
Major requirement: must be grown in sandy, well-drained soil
Disadvantage: produces a lower-quality lawn

Centipedegrass (*Ermochloa ophiuroides*) has medium-width leaves and produces a lower-quality lawn than Bermudagrass. However, it requires less frequent mowing and less fertilizer and is easy to keep out of landscape plantings. Centipede is more shade tolerant than Bermudagrass and less than St. Augustine. Perhaps the best use of centipede is for large lawns in sandy soils of East, South, and Central Texas. Centipede can be seeded (2+ pounds per 1,000 square feet) or sprigged to establish a lawn.

Carpetgrass

Chief advantage: low maintenance; low-quality lawn for acreage in East Texas
Major requirement: must be grown in East Texas
Disadvantages: frequent, prolonged production of tall seed stalks; frequent mowing required to maintain an attractive lawn

Carpetgrass (*Axonopus affinis*) is a wide-bladed, warm-season grass that can thrive under low maintenance and no fertilizer. Its most objectionable characteristic is its frequent and prolonged production of seed stalks. Frequent mowing is required to maintain a nice-looking carpetgrass lawn. Carpetgrass is best adapted to the moist, sandy soils of Southeast Texas. A carpetgrass lawn is established with seed (4 pounds per 1,000 square feet).

Tall Fescue

Chief advantage: "looks like a real lawn" (looks like bluegrass)
Major requirement: must be grown in North or West Texas under irrigation
Disadvantage: being a cool-season grass, summer browning (dormancy) will occur unless in full shade and irrigated heavily

Tall fescue spreads by tillers (small offshoots).

Tall fescue (*Festuca arundinacea*) is a bluegrass-looking, cool-season permanent lawn grass adapted to the Panhandle and upper elevations of West Texas. Its primary growth period is from fall to spring. Summer heat and drought will cause tall fescue to go dormant and turn brown. Regular, heavy irrigation is needed to prevent this summer dormancy.

Tall fescue has good shade tolerance and is adapted to heavy clay soils. Improved turf-type tall fescue varieties are available that create a higher-quality lawn. Improved varieties also maintain green color throughout the winter months.

Choose turf-type tall fescue varieties, including 'Falcon II,' 'Houndog,' 'Plantation,' 'Rebel Exceda,' 'Rebel III,' and 'Rembrand.' Often you will find these varieties in a product blend of two or three varieties. This is a fine way to improve the success of a tall fescue lawn. Also, sowing additional seed each fall in thin areas of the lawn is a good practice. The seeding rate for tall fescue is 8 to 10 pounds per 1,000 square feet.

Kentucky & 'Reveille' Bluegrass

Chief advantage: it is bluegrass—enough said

Major requirement: must be grown in the Panhandle of Texas and upper elevations of West Texas under irrigation

Disadvantage: will not grow in all Texas lawns

Kentucky bluegrass (*Poa protensis*) is the most popular lawn grass in the United States. All the national fertilizer commercials feature Kentucky bluegrass lawns. In Texas, adaptation is limited to the Panhandle and upper elevations of West Texas where nighttime temperatures cool significantly. Kentucky bluegrass is a cool-season, perennial bunch grass that forms a dense, dark green lawn. It is not shade or drought tolerant, is prone to weed invasions, and suffers from several disease and insect pests.

Kentucky bluegrass can be established from seed or sod. The rate for seeding is 1 to 2 pounds per 1,000 square feet. Varieties adapted to Texas include 'Adelphi,' 'Baron,' 'Bristol,' 'Glade,' 'Vantage,' and 'Victa.' As with tall fescues, products including blends of bluegrass varieties (and often tall fescue and ryegrass) are available and recommended for increased success.

Texas A&M University has bred a bluegrass worth considering called 'Reveille.' This bluegrass is a cross between Texas bluegrass (*P. arachnifera*) and Kentucky bluegrass. It is more heat and shade tolerant than Kentucky bluegrass. Irrigation is still a must, but this variety can create a year-round green lawn for the Panhandle, much of West Texas, and even the northern half of Central Texas. Check with your local county extension agent for adaptability in your area, and ask to see a lawn or two before you invest. 'Reveille' bluegrass is available only in sod.

Ryegrass

Chief advantage: overseeded on Bermudagrass to create green lawn in winter; perennial varieties can be grown as permanent lawn in the Panhandle

Major requirement: mowing and watering all winter; must be in Panhandle to grow as a permanent lawn

Disadvantage: will die due to high nighttime temperatures of summer in most of Texas

Ryegrass (*Lolium* spp.) is sometimes called the "throw and grow" lawn. The seeds can be sown without the hassle of thorough soil preparation and still produce an almost instant lawn cover. Ryegrass is available in two basic types: annual and perennial.

Annual ryegrass is less expensive than perennial ryegrass but survives only 1 year. It is used primarily for a temporary lawn cover from fall through spring. This is especially applicable when new homes or buildings are completed in fall or winter. Annual ryegrass is seeded at 10+ pounds per 1,000 square feet, and the most commonly used variety is 'Gulf.'

Perennial ryegrass is commonly used to overseed permanent Bermudagrass lawns to maintain a green lawn (or sports turf) all winter (at 12 to 15 pounds per 1,000 square feet). However, annual ryegrass varieties recently bred at Texas A&M University are viable alternatives to perennial ryegrass. These varieties, 'Pantera' and 'Axcella 2', establish a green winter lawn quicker in fall and die out in early spring to allow the Bermuda (or St. Augustine) lawn to green up rapidly without competition (a common problem with perennial ryegrass).

In the Panhandle, perennial ryegrass can be used as a permanent lawn seeded at 5 to 10 pounds per 1,000 square feet. Perennial ryegrass varieties are usually available in product blends including such varieties as 'Applaud,' 'Blazer,' 'Buccaneer,' 'Delray,' 'Diplomat,' 'Integra,' 'NK 200,' 'Pennant,' 'Shining Star,' 'Sonata,' 'Vivid,' 'Wind Dance,' and 'Wind Star.' Perennial ryegrass varieties are also blended with tall fescues or bluegrasses to create a green, year-round permanent lawn.

Establishing a New Lawn

Whether you are establishing a new lawn or renovating a poorly performing area of an existing lawn, proper soil preparation and watering are essential. Any fertilizing should be postponed until your new lawn is mowed at least three times.

For a landscape planting, soil preparation includes adding large amounts of organic matter to improve the soil. Bottom line: That would be great for a new lawn, but the cost of such preparation is something most folks cannot afford. For most homeowners, the goal is to have 6 inches of clay-type soil or 12 inches of a sandy soil as the soil base for planting turfgrass seed or sod. If you have to haul in soil to get this soil base, be very careful where you purchase the soil. Nutgrass (nut sedge) seems to come in every dumptruck load of topsoil. It and other weeds can create a weed-control nightmare in your lawn. Ask landscape contractors, nursery professionals, and county extension agents for reputable sources of weed-free topsoil. Beyond this critical step, leveling out the lawn area and contouring it if needed to avoid water collecting in certain spots are all you need to do.

Seed warm-season grasses once the soil has warmed to about 75°F. This is generally in April. Seeding too early is a waste of seed because it will rot before it germinates. Cool-season grasses should be seeded in September.

Seed should be broadcast evenly by using a hand-held whirlybird spreader. One pound of Bermudagrass seed contains over 10,000 seeds, so be careful. The recommended seeding rates for turf-grass species are listed in the accompanying chart; however, check the seed bag for any difference for a specific variety. Set the hand-held spreader on the lowest setting (i.e., smallest opening). Make one pass back and forth over the area to be seeded. Make another pass walking perpendicular to the first pass.

SEEDING RATES FOR TURFGRASS SPECIES

TURFGRASS	POUNDS PER 1,000 SQUARE FEET
Annual ryegrass (for temporary lawn)	10+
Bermudagrass	1–2
Buffalograss	5+
Carpetgrass	4
Centipedegrass	2+
Cool-season turfgrass blends check bag for rates	
Kentucky bluegrass	1–2
Tall fescue	8–10
Annual ryegrass (for temporary lawns)	5–10
Perennial ryegrass (for overseeding)	12–15
Perennial ryegrass (for permanent lawn)	5–10

There are companies that can "hydro-mulch" your new lawn. This is a more costly technique but results in even coverage of the seed over the area and a higher-quality lawn faster. Hydromulch contains a slurry of water, seed, and cellulose fibers that is sprayed onto the lawn area.

Sod is more expensive than seed for those varieties that can be either sodded or seeded (e.g., common Bermudagrass and seeded hybrids, Kentucky bluegrass, and tall fescue). For all other species and varieties, sod is available. A pallet of sod will cover approximately 450 square feet and range in price, depending on the species and variety, from $95 to $200+ per pallet. Generally, 'Raleigh' St. Augustine and 'Common' Bermudagrass are the least expensive, followed by hybrid Bermudagrasses, buffalograss varieties, Kentucky bluegrass, tall fescue, and zoysia varieties.

Lay sod side by side in a staggered pattern to establish a smooth lawn quickly; 6 inches of clay soil below the sod is recommended, and 12 inches for sandy soils.

An important note: Sod is a perishable product and declines and dies quickly if left on a pallet. Sod should be cut and shipped from the sod farm one day, received by the nursery or sod dealer the second day, and placed into your lawn the third day. Schedule this carefully with the nursery or sod company. Do not buy sod that has been sitting for days on a pallet.

Installing sod is relatively easy. Simply lay sod pieces tightly side by side. You can rent a roller (that is filled with water) and pull it over the sod to smooth it and firmly set the sod pieces into the soil.

Watering is the next critical step in establishing a new lawn. With seed, the first watering will set the seed in firm contact with the soil and initiate germination. Water lightly with no runoff. If runoff occurs, your seed will wash and pool in some areas, the result being an uneven distribution of the seedlings across the lawn area. After the first watering, the objective is to keep the soil moist but not saturated, so light, frequent irrigations will be needed for about a week. This may be as frequent as twice daily depending on the weather. After a week, germination should occur. Maintain the soil moisture. Use your index finger to check.

To establish sod, water the lawn heavily immediately after laying the sod to drive moisture through the sod and into the soil below. Making mud underneath the soil is a good thing. This sets the sod in firm contact with the soil. Subsequent irrigations should maintain soil moisture but not create a swamp. Saturated soil over a week's period can slow the establishment of the sod's new root system.

Once the seed has grown 2 inches or the sod has grown an inch, mow. Set the mower at just low enough to remove half the height of the new growth. This will actually stimulate greater and denser growth.

After you have mowed two or three times, a light application of fertilizer (preferably straight nitrogen, such as urea or ammonium sulfate) can be applied. This is not a must, and if fertilizer is overapplied, new seedling and sod growth can be burned. Continue to mow weekly, and water as needed to create a healthy, dense lawn in a short period of time.

Maintaining a Healthy Lawn with Minimal Effort

If you have selected the best grass for your lawn and properly established it, maintaining it is much easier than you might think. This is also true for those of you who have existing lawns. Generally, too much fertilizer, water, and pesticides are used to maintain lawns. The bar-

rage of commercials and advertisements lead you to believe that products are the answer to having a healthy lawn. Explaining how to minimize your time, effort, and applications of fertilizers and pesticides is the objective in the following sections.

Fertilizing your lawn twice a year should be sufficient. For thorough guidelines, refer to the March essay "Lawn Fertilizing Made Simple." Proper watering is critical to maintain lawn health and reduce water waste. Water the lawn only when it shows symptoms of lack of water (e.g., footprints, dull gray-green color, leaf rolling). The March essay "When to Water, and How Long?" provides in-depth answers to these age-old questions.

MOWING. Mowing is perhaps the most critical maintenance practice in lawn care. Proper mowing is your best defense against weeds. An adequately watered, properly mowed lawn will outcompete most weeds.

Lawn mowing must be frequent enough to encourage dense, rapid

growth. The more you mow, the denser the turf will be. Mowing too short or too infrequently damages turfgrass and leads to unhealthy lawns. Always remember that mowing is a wounding process, so there is a balance between enough and too much. The wounding process is minimized by a sharp mower blade—sharpen the blade at least once a year, preferably twice.

How often you should mow is determined by the "mowing height" of the turfgrass in your lawn and the rate at which it is growing. Follow this guideline: When you mow, do not remove more than one-half of the mowing height for your specific turfgrass. For example, for 'Common' Bermudagrass, which can be maintained at 2 inches, never mow more than 1 inch off; and for St. Augustine, which should be maintained at 4 inches, never mow more than 2 inches off.

In general, turfgrasses with lower mowing heights will be mowed more frequently than grasses with taller mowing heights. 'Common' Bermudagrass may be mowed every 5 to 7 days, and St. Augustine mowed every 7 to 10 days. Buffalograss's mature height is about 6 inches; therefore, it may be mowed only once a month or less often.

This may all sound complicated, but follow the guidelines for a few mowings and you will easily recognize when to mow, and the quality of your lawn will be noticeably better.

Proper Mowing Heights for Texas Turfgrasses

Bermudagrass, 'Common'	1–3 inches
Bermudagrass, hybrids (seeded or sodded)	$\frac{3}{4}$–2 inches
Bluegrass	$1\frac{1}{2}$–3 inches
Buffalograss	5–6 inches
Carpetgrass	2–3 inches
Centipedegrass	2–3 inches
Ryegrass	$1\frac{1}{2}$–3 inches
St. Augustinegrass	3–4 inches
Tall fescue	3–4 inches
Zoysiagrass	$1\frac{1}{2}$–2 inches

Following are additional mowing guidelines and concepts:

- There is no need to collect clippings. The Don't Bag It program, developed by Texas Cooperative Extension in the late 1980s, proved to the masses that collecting clippings is a waste of time and landfill space. Mulching mowers are now standard (although some companies are again selling bagging attachments). Mulching mowers slice and dice the grass clippings into small pieces that fall into the lawn and decompose rapidly. These clippings provide valuable nutrients to the lawn and do not lead to thatch (a water-impermeable layer of dead grass stems and debris).

- Thatch is simply not a common problem for most Texas lawns. Too

Don't collect lawn clippings.

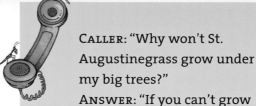

much fertilizing, too much watering, and infrequent mowing can lead to thatch in hybrid Bermudagrass, tall fescue, and Kentucky bluegrass lawns. It is virtually impossible to develop thatch in St. Augustine, 'Common' Bermudagrass, buffalograss, centipede, and carpetgrass lawns.

- During the summer, mow your lawn at the highest recommended height to increase the lawn's ability to withstand heat and drought.

- If the lawn is thinning out due to shade, increase the mowing height to increase the leaf area for receiving limited sunlight.

- Mowing height affects the depth of root growth. Taller grass-mowing heights develop deeper root systems that withstand drought conditions more readily.

AERATION. Aeration is a valuable maintenance practice for lawns suffering in heavy clay soils and/or highly compacted soils from foot traffic. Aeration opens up the soil by pulling plugs of soil, creating avenues for water and air to penetrate for increased root health and thus, lawn health. Core aerators can

CALLER: "Why won't St. Augustinegrass grow under my big trees?"

ANSWER: "If you can't grow St. Augustine, the most shade-tolerant turfgrass, then other actions must be taken. A professional arborist can thin the tree branches and remove lower limbs to let more sunlight hit the lawn. The trees are likely more valuable to you than the lawn, so this pruning must be done properly or not at all. Another option is either establishing a more shade-tolerant groundcover or mulching the area beneath the trees. Shade-tolerant groundcovers include Algerian ivy, English ivy, holly fern, mondo grass, river fern, and vinca major. Combining mulched and planted areas can be quite attractive. Be careful not to damage the root system of the trees by rototilling and preparing the soil for plantings. It is best to create a four- to six-inch raised planting bed filled with a landscape soil mix on top of the existing soil. More than six inches of soil can smother tree roots below."

be rented from equipment rental companies. The soil moisture content must be relatively high for the core aerator to effectively pull plugs of soil. Once plugs are pulled, "top-dressing" (raking in) with a thin layer of compost that falls into the holes will greatly increase the lawn's ability to absorb water and will expand its root system.

WEEDS. Healthy turfgrass is the best control for weeds in the lawn. If you mow regularly, water when needed, and fertilize twice a year, you won't have a weed problem. If weeds are a major problem, refer to this month's essay "Weeds, Weeds, and More Weeds" for control techniques and herbicide usage.

INSECTS. Insects that damage Texas lawns are limited primarily to chinch bugs and grubworms, both of which are predominantly seen in St. Augustine. In the Houston/Southeast Texas area, chinch bugs and St. Augustine are like "peas and carrots." Watch for yellowing in the lawn, particularly in the hottest spots of the lawn and areas next to the street or driveway. If you see lawn yellowing, get down on your hands and knees, look up to the sky, and pray; no, look down deep into the lawn where the soil and stems meet. Adult chinch bugs are $\frac{1}{8}$-inch black insects with white wings; immatures are smaller, with either black or reddish brown bodies and no wings. Any granular lawn insecticide will control them.

White grubworms, the larvae of the June bug (beetle), have C-shaped white bodies with reddish brown heads. They feed on the roots of the lawn and, in high populations, cause a yellowing lawn area. Because of the reduced root system, the infested lawn may pull up like a loose carpet. Carefully dig up a shallow section of questionable lawn area. If you count more than five grubworms in a square-foot area of soil, you have a population worth treating (if less, don't treat). Use a granular lawn insecticide labeled for white grubworm control.

Sod webworms, armyworms, and Bermudagrass mites occasionally cause enough damage in tall fescue, Bermudagrass, and zoysia lawns to warrant spraying. Remember the strategy in insect control is to first identify the insect causing the problem; determine whether enough damage has occurred to justify treatment; purchase the most

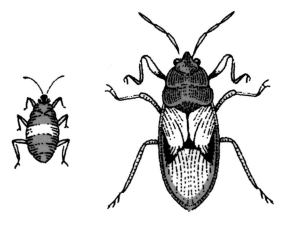

Chinch bugs (immature and adult) can be devastating to St. Augustine lawns.

effective, least toxic insecticide; and apply it, following the label directions.

DISEASES. Lawn diseases in Texas are primarily seen in St. Augustinegrass and Kentucky bluegrass. In St. Augustine, brown patch is a fungal disease that causes a brown patch (who names these diseases?). The brown patch with a yellowing grass perimeter can be the size of a trash can lid to half the front lawn. It is a chronic, not a fatal, problem that occurs in the spring or fall when temperatures are cool and rainfall frequent. A yellowing grass blade can easily be pulled from the stem and has brown rotted tissues at the base of the leaf. Take-all patch is a fungal root rot that kills the lawn in the infected area. All that is left is dried-up St. Augustine stolons (stems); all the roots are gone.

Since brown patch is a chronic problem and not lethal, you may choose not to treat, and the area will regrow as spring temperatures heat up or will go dormant as fall turns to winter. Generally, St. Augustine lawns that are overfertilized and overwatered are more susceptible to brown patch. Backing off on fertilizing and watering is an effective control. If you choose to treat infected areas, properly apply one of several granular fungicides labeled for brown patch.

Take-all patch is fatal to the area it infects. Expansion of the disease may progress throughout your lawn, leaving you nothing but dead stems. This is

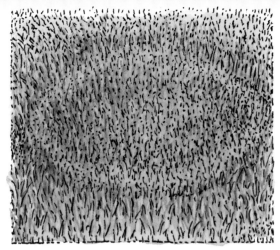

Brown patch is a fungal disease that regularly infects St. Augustine lawns.

an opportunity to decide whether your lawn environment could better support Bermudagrass or zoysia, which are much more disease and insect resistant than St. Augustine. If you stick with St. Augustine, there are a couple of fungicides effective against this disease, and one of them should be applied before new sod is laid. Check with your local county extension agent or nursery professional for the latest fungicides labeled for take-all patch control.

Kentucky bluegrass, although highly prized, could be called a hotel for diseases. Leaf spot, melting-out diseases, necrotic ring spot, and summer brown patches are found regularly in bluegrass lawns. Check with county extension agents and lawn and nursery professionals for accurate diagnosis and management of these fungal diseases.

Another Cause of Yellow & Brown Patches in the Lawn

In addition to the insects and diseases associated with St. Augustine, yellowing and browning of lawn areas can be caused by poor distribution of water by your irrigation system (or hose-end sprinkler). Lay cake pans in the lawn, run the system, and check whether the unhealthy lawn area is receiving adequate moisture. Adjust the sprinkler system as needed.

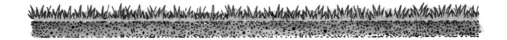

Herb-Growing Hints for Texas

*Mexican oregano (*Poliomintha longiflora*)*

(*Note:* I am not an herb expert, but I know enough to grow some and to help get you started. A reliable herb reference is *Southern Herb Growing* by Madalene Hill and Gwen Barclay with Jean Hardy [Shearer Publishing]. Madalene Hill and Gwen Barclay are a Texas mother-daughter team that brought expertise, enthusiasm, and evangelical leadership to herb gardening throughout the South.)

Many folks think herbs come only from the grocery store in little bottles, as dry flakes or powders, and are sprinkled in spaghetti sauce. If store-bought dried herbs have been your only source for spicing up your food, please try growing some of your own herbs. Once you begin using homegrown fresh herbs in your favorite recipes, you will never go back to using store-bought dried herbs again.

A glance at any herb book or catalogue can quickly overwhelm a gardener with the sheer number of herbs available. The Brooklyn Botanical Garden *Handbook of Herbs* lists 73 different types of herbs. In mail-order catalogues specializing in herbs, you may find 50 or more herbs, including several different types of mints, onion-type herbs, sages, and thymes.

Simplify which herbs to grow by identifying which store-bought dried herbs you use regularly, such as anise, basil, chives, coriander/cilantro, dill, oregano, parsley, rosemary, sage, and thyme. Focus on growing the herbs you use. Most are relatively easy to grow. If you can grow a tomato plant or a petunia, you can grow most herbs.

In Texas gardens, you can substitute the classic oregano and anise species with easier-to-grow and more-ornamental Mexican oregano (pink flowers all season) and Mexican mint marigold (anise-flavored foliage and a profusion of yellow fall blooms).

CALLER: "Are cilantro and coriander from the same plant?"

ANSWER: "Yes, the herbs cilantro and coriander are from the same plant, *Coriandrum sativum*. Cilantro generally refers to the leaves, and coriander refers to the seeds, most often ground. Cilantro is widely used in Mexican food and has a pungent smell and taste. The seeds (coriander) have a much different spicy, lemony aroma and taste. Coriander is widely used in Asian and Middle Eastern cooking."

Having access to fresh herbs at home can be as simple as having a large squatty pot on the patio or even indoors next to the brightest sunlit window in your home. Indoors during the winter, supplemental light may be needed—use "grow lamps" or fluorescent lights. When creating this mini–herb garden, combining both upright and trailing herbs makes an attractive planting, such as creeping thymes and oregano with basil and chives.

Combining herbs in containers or garden plantings that are used in similar recipes provides an added twist to herb gardening. A Mexican food mix might include chives, cilantro, and a jalapeño pepper plant. The Italian planting would include basil, chives, oregano, rosemary, and even bulbing onions.

You can also incorporate herbs into your shrub or flower bed. Many herbs are fine ornamentals and have brightly colored flowers or foliage, such as Mexican oregano's pink flowers, dill's yellow flowers, and basil's range of maroon to green foliage. Some herbs have variegated foliage, such as Cuban oregano, lavender, mint, and variegated thyme. Rosemary and chives contribute unique foliage textures to the landscape.

Herbs can be grown in vegetable gardens. Place annual herb crops, such as anise, basil, coriander, and dill, in rows. Perennial herbs, such as chives, mint, rosemary, and thyme, can be grouped out of the way in the back of the garden.

If you want to get into herb gardening in a "classic" way, plant an herb garden. An 8-foot by 10-foot rectangular garden is plenty of space for all the herbs you will need. Within this area, you can create a beautiful addition to the landscape by planting a traditional herb "knot garden" or parterre garden.

Planting Herbs

Nearly all herbs can be grown from seed, but for a nonexpert (that includes me), transplants purchased from a nursery or garden center work best. If you want to try seeding herbs, start with basil. It can be sown directly into good garden soil or potting soils with great success.

Miniature herb gardens can be grown in containers.

Growing Herbs

Two keys to success in growing herbs are well-drained soil and full sun. A well-drained garden soil cannot be over-emphasized. Many herbs will not thrive, or survive, wet feet (i.e., heavy clay soil). The exceptions to this are mint and parsley, which grow best in soils that retain higher moisture levels.

Thorough soil preparation is critical. Add organic matter to clay soils to add drainage and to sandy soils to increase moisture-holding capacity. In wet climates, such as the upper Gulf Coast and East Texas, soil drainage should be maximized with raised beds and more organic matter. Unfortunately, even with added soil drainage, some herbs may not thrive in your area. Ask for advice from nursery professionals, or be a pioneer and find out by trial and error.

Full sun is considered 6 hours of direct sunlight each day. Most herbs require this bright, heated environment to thrive. A few herbs prefer half-day sun or filtered light (partial shade), such as borage, chives, lemon balm, mints, and parsley.

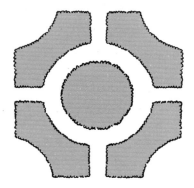 

Parterre gardens and knot gardens are traditional, formal herb garden designs.

In addition to soil preparation and full sun, care for herbs is much like growing vegetables or flowers. Mulch should be used throughout any herb planting or garden. Organic mulches, such as pine bark or pine needles, are good. Rock mulches, such as pea gravel, are especially good for herbs because they radiate heat and maintain a lower humidity around the herb plants. The humidity of Gulf Coast and East Texas areas can be detrimental to health for many herbs, such as oregano and thyme. Humidity can lead to fungal diseases on the leaves and root and crown rots.

Drip irrigation is particularly useful with herbs since irrigation water never touches the leaves, stems, or crowns. Keep the soil moist but not saturated by scheduling irrigations, using your finger as your moisture meter.

Fertilizer should seldom be needed for herbs (except parsley). Overfertilization can lead to rangy or excessive growth that dilutes the herb's natural flavor.

Although not often needed, insect and disease control can be challenging in an herb garden since you would be spraying a pesticide (chemical or organic) onto the plant parts you eat. Fortunately, few diseases affect herbs, and picking off diseased leaves and removing infected branches are perhaps the best disease management techniques. A keen eye and early treatment are best for insect control. Aphids, spider mites, and thrips can be washed off with water or controlled using an organic insecticide such as neem. Caterpillars can be hand-picked or controlled with the organic insecticide *Bacillus thuringiensis* (Bt). By all means, think twice before applying a chemical pesticide. If you do use a chemical, make sure the specific herb is included on the treatment label, and follow the directions carefully.

Harvesting Herbs

Harvesting leaves and stems actually benefits herb plants by ensuring thick, vigorous growth. Pinching back tip growth also promotes branching and denser growth.

Fresh leaves, stems, and flowers may be picked as soon as the plant has enough size and foliage to maintain future growth. Harvesting herb leaves just prior to plant flowering is often recommended for peak flavor, especially on basil, fennel, mint, sage, sweet marjoram, and tarragon. To ensure peak flavor (oil content), also pick leaves or seeds after dew has disappeared in the morning but before the sun becomes too hot.

Drying and Freezing Herbs

If you have a bountiful harvest from your herbs beyond what you can use fresh, you can dry herbs by air-drying or oven-drying them. Refer to *Southern Herb Growing* or the Internet for proper drying and processing of culinary herbs. As you will read, handling and processing are as important to the success of your herb harvest as good growing practices.

A BAKER'S DOZEN OF HERBS
FOR BEGINNERS
Basil
Chives
Cilantro (coriander)
Dill
Mexican mint marigold
Mexican oregano
Mints
Oregano
Parsley
Rosemary
Sage
Sweet bay laurel
Thyme

Cooking with Fresh versus Dried Herbs

When you cook with fresh herbs rather than dried herbs, use this conversion: 1 tablespoon of fresh herbs equals 1 teaspoon of crumbled dry herbs, or $\frac{1}{4}$ to $\frac{1}{2}$ teaspoon of ground herbs. You use a smaller amount of dried herbs because their flavor is more concentrated. If you are cooking something for several hours, avoid cooking out the flavors, and wait until the dish is almost ready before adding either fresh or dried herbs.

Drying basil, and other herbs, upside down is a common preservation technique today, as it was a thousand years ago.

Basics of Drying & Freezing Herbs

Air-drying: Dry plants by hanging them upside down in bunches. In garages or garden sheds, cover the bunches with paper bags to eliminate dust accumulation and to keep bugs out. Tie stems very tightly in small bunches since individual stems will shrink and fall. Hang in a dark, warm (70°F to 80°F), well-ventilated area. Leaves are ready in about 1 to 2 weeks, when they feel dry and crumbly.

Oven-drying: Place leaves or seeds on a cookie sheet or shallow pan not more than 1 inch deep in a partially opened oven at low heat (less than 180°F) for 2 to 4 hours.

Microwave oven–drying: Place the clean leaves on a paper plate or paper towel, and microwave for 1 to 3 minutes, mixing every 30 seconds.

Freezing: Sounds strange, but herbs can be frozen and keep their high quality for months; this works especially well for basil, chives, dill, and mint.

The following herbs are the easiest for beginners to grow. Each description includes the size of the plant and gives information about how to grow the herb.

Basil (*Ocimum basilicum*), 20 to 24 inches tall and 12 inches wide

This annual herb is among the easiest to grow and most attractive. Types with multiple leaf colors, from light green to dark maroon, and bold to frilly leaf shapes are available as seed or transplants through nurseries or catalogues. Basil even produces attractive tiny white flowers, often with a tinge of lavender. Plant in early spring, and basil will grow until the first frost. It grows best in full sun. Pinch off the stem tips to create a bushier, compact plant. The leaves are of highest quality if harvested when blooming begins. Harvest by picking individual leaves or by cutting the whole plant back to 6 inches in height. The leaves can be used fresh or dried, or even frozen to preserve for future use.

Chives (*Allium schoenoprasum*) and **Garlic chives** (*A. tubersum*), 12 to 18 inches tall and 6 inches wide

These perennial herbs have onionlike leaves that provide a unique, attractive border or planting in landscape beds. Planted from bulbs or plantlets (sets) sold in nurseries, chives are cold tolerant and will survive freezing temperatures in all but the toughest Panhandle winters. Plants can be grown in containers or the garden in full sun to partial shade. Starts of chive plants can be shared with neighbors by dividing the plant clump. Harvest by simply clipping off leaves as needed. Chives provide a mild onion taste to eggs, salads, soups, and dips. Garlic chives are a garlic substitute for these uses.

Cilantro (coriander) (*Coriandrum sativum*), 24 inches tall and 18 inches wide

This fast-growing annual can be grown from seed or transplants. Cilantro prefers full sun but will tolerate partial shade. This herb is grown for both its seed and leaves. The leaves can be harvested when the plants are 4 to 6 inches tall. The seeds should be harvested as they turn brown. Cilantro is widely used in many Mexican dishes, salads, and salsas. This is an herb that you either love or dislike because it "tastes like kitty litter smells" (according to a confidential source). Recall that cilantro refers to the leaves, and coriander is the ground seeds. Cilantro and coriander are not interchangeable in recipes.

Dill (*Anethum graveolens*), 24 to 36 inches tall and 12 inches wide

This annual herb is a handsome ornamental as well. Dill is a tall plant with feathery green leaves and open, umbrella-shaped heads of yellow flowers. It can be grown from seed or from transplants, in full sun or partial shade. Harvest the mature browning seed heads before the seeds drop. Seeds and small leaves are obviously used in pickles but also to season fresh green beans, salads, sauces for fish, vinegars, and breads. If you like dill, you can grow and use loads of it. The higher-quality difference in fresh versus dried dill is significant.

Mexican mint marigold (*Tagetes lucida*), 24 inches tall and 18 inches wide

This perennial is an anise substitute, providing licorice-flavored leaves for salads, breads, beverages, and cookies. In addition, this herb is ornamental with a profusion of yellow, daisy-type flowers in fall. This native of Central America is extremely drought and heat tolerant.

Mexican oregano (*Poliomintha longi-flora*), 24 inches tall and 36 inches wide

This substitute for the true oregano is used widely as an herb in Mexico and Texas. It is also a fabulous ornamental with season-long flowering of pink and white tubular blooms. The plant is perennial from Austin southward but may need to be planted annually in the northern half of Texas.

Mints—Peppermint (*Mentha piperita*), **Spearmint** (*M. spicata*), and *Mentha* spp., 12 to 36 inches tall and 12 to 24 inches wide

This very hardy (almost invasive) perennial herb has many different varieties, including peppermint, spearmint, and chocolate, ginger, and orange mints. These are among the easiest-to-grow and most popular herbs. They may be started from seed or cuttings or purchased as transplants. Mints grow best in full sun but will tolerate shade. They prefer more moist soil conditions (i.e., clayey soils) than other herbs. Remove flower stalks to direct the growth into the leaves and stems. In the northern half of Texas, mints may freeze back to the ground in winter but should sprout back from the roots. Mints are harvested for their stems and leaves; the more frequent the harvest, the better the plant grows. They are traditionally used in summer drinks and tea, in pork seasonings, as a garnish, even as a breath freshener for gardeners.

Oregano (*Origanum vulgare*), 24 inches tall and 9 inches wide

A perennial herb, oregano is not the easiest to grow in a landscape planting. It probably is best grown in containers with well-drained potting soil or in a flower bed with well-prepared garden soil. Oregano prefers full sun but may need to be moved to a morning sun–afternoon shade location. This herb produces a broadleaf, shrublike plant with pale pink flowers. Cutting back the flowers will generate more foliage growth. Oregano is grown for its leaves, which can be used at any stage of growth. Cuban oregano is a handsome variegated oregano that will need to be replanted annually in the northern half of Texas.

Parsley (*Petroselinum crispum*), 6 inches tall and 6 inches wide

This herb is worth growing for use as a garnish and ingredient for soups and Italian dishes. But its value as an ornamental is often overlooked. With plain dark to curled, serrated leaves, this herb is available in a variety of forms. It is not the easiest herb to grow from seed, so try to find transplants in nurseries or mail-order catalogues. Harvest the mature leaves as needed, and fertilize every couple of weeks lightly to generate new growth.

Rosemary (*Rosmarinus officinalis*), 36 inches tall and 24 inches wide; and

Prostrate rosemary (*R. officinalis* 'Prostratus'), 36 inches tall and 36+ inches wide

This herb is the toughest of the tough: drought and heat tolerant and adapted to acidic and alkaline soils (as long as they are well drained). This evergreen herb is available in an upright shrub form or a prostrate, trailing form. The prostrate form is less cold tolerant and should be grown south of Waco. Even the upright form will freeze to death if temperatures dip below 10°F for over 12 hours. Rosemary is an excellent ornamental plant with its fine texture, gray-green foliage, and pale blue flowers. Its value as an herb is varied and significant because it is used so widely as a seasoning for poultry and meats; in oils, vinegars, sauces, and dressings; and even on pizza. Dried leaves can be used in sachets to place in drawers or closets. What a versatile plant for any landscape!

Sage (*Salvia officinalis*), 24 inches tall and 24 to 36 inches wide

This shrublike perennial has gray-green leaves and purple flowers. Sage is best planted from purchased transplants. Good soil drainage is critical, as is full sun. Sage plants eventually become woody, and growth slows significantly. The plants should be removed and replaced with new plants every 3 to 4 years. Sage is grown for its leaves and should be harvested before bloom. Sage

> *"What is green and sings? Elvis Parsley." (Told by Doug Welsh in third grade; no one laughed.)*

is difficult to grow in the high-humidity areas of East Texas and the upper Gulf Coast of Texas.

Sweet bay laurel (*Laurus nobilis*), 8 to 15 feet tall and 2 to 4 feet wide

This handsome and useful evergreen shrub is easy to grow in the neutral to acidic soils of the eastern half of Texas. With good soil preparation, this herb can be grown in alkaline soils. Morning sun and afternoon shade are best for this tall shrub. Sweet bay laurels are particularly adapted and attractive in large containers as patio plants. For areas of Texas where winter temperatures regularly dip below 15°F for 12 hours, you must protect outdoor-planted laurels or move containerized plants indoors. The attractive deep green leaves are 2 to 4 inches long and very aromatic. The leaves are used either fresh or dried to season stews and spaghetti sauces. With bay leaves, fresh leaves are stronger flavored than dried, so use very sparingly. One or two fresh leaves should be plenty for most dishes.

Thyme (*Thymus vulgaris*), 8 to 12 inches tall and 12 inches wide

Several types of thyme are available, but common thyme is most often grown in gardens. Thyme is a perennial that produces a shrublike plant with narrow, gray-green leaves and purple flowers. Thyme grows best in well-drained, drier soil in full sun. Constant harvesting of fresh growth prevents the plants from becoming woody, although the plants should be removed and replanted with new ones every 3 to 4 years. Leaves are used in soups, salads, dressings, gravies, breads, and in vegetable and egg dishes.

Timely Tips

Flowers & Pretty Plants

• Remove dead blossoms (dead-head) from annuals, perennials, and roses to perpetuate blooming. Plants will slow or stop blooming if the plant develops seeds after blossoms die.

• Fertilize annual and perennial flowers with a nitrogen fertilizer—no need for additions of phosphorous. Most garden soils have plenty of phosphorous either naturally or due to prior applications.

• Fertilizer rate is monthly: $\frac{1}{4}$ pound of urea per 100 square feet, $\frac{1}{2}$ pound of ammonium sulfate, or 1 pound of blood meal.

Garden Design

• Design and install a new planting(s) during this wonderful time of year. New plantings add interest and quality to the garden and reduce the size of the lawn, the landscape's highest user of irrigation water.

Soil & Mulch

• Keep adding organic matter (e.g., pine bark, compost) every time you plant in shrub and flower beds and the vegetable and herb garden. Texas soils contain less than 1 percent organic matter. High temperatures increase the rate at which micro-organisms consume organic matter. It is virtually impossible to add too much organic matter to Texas soils.

• Mulch around the base of trees in the lawn area to help prevent trunk damage by mowers and trimmers.

Water

• Water when the plant needs it—plants will show when they are stressed by lack of water through wilting and leaf rolling. The best setting on the irrigation time clock is "OFF." Tremendous amounts of water and money are wasted by letting the time clock run on the same schedule spring, summer, and fall.

Plant Care

• Apply baits laced with insecticides to continue the war on fire ants. Fire ants forage in the spring (and fall), picking up the baits and returning to the mound. The queen and colony feed on the bait, and control occurs within 2 to 6 weeks. This technique is part of the "Texas two-step method" of fire ant management. For more information, refer to this month's essay "Fire Ant Management."

• Consider one-time insecticide application techniques to control fire ants. These products contain long-lasting insecticides to effectively control fire ants.

• If you choose to use an herbicide, read the label carefully to make sure the product will not damage the grass in the lawn, the flowers and shrubs in beds, or the vegetables in the garden. Weed growth is in full swing now, so recognize that some herbicides kill grasses only, some kill broad-leaf plants, and some kill both. This month's essay "Weeds, Weeds, and More Weeds" is a must read.

Trees, Shrubs & Vines

• This is a great time to plant palm trees throughout the southern half of Texas. For a list of palms possibly cold tolerant in your area, refer to the July essay "Go Tropical!"

• During spring growth, young trees can be pruned to direct growth and create a strong structure to the trunks and branches. Tree training is discussed in the February essay "Pruning School."

• Prune trees and shrubs that bloom in the spring after they have bloomed, and only if needed.

Lawns

• Apply spring lawn fertilizer for warm-season grasses (e.g., Bermuda and St. Augustine) after the second or third mowing of this season. Consider using a straight-nitrogen fertilizer if you have in years past used complete fertilizers (i.e., containing nitrogen, phosphorus, and potassium). Straight-nitrogen fertilizers include ammonium sulfate, blood meal, and urea. Sulfur-coated urea is a good slow-release form of nitrogen fertilizer for lawns. If nurseries don't have these fertilizers, turn to farm and ranch stores.

• Mow lawns at recommended heights and frequency (see this month's essay "Lawns 101"). The more frequent the mowing, the denser the lawn—a denser lawn has a better appearance and wards off weeds.

• Irrigate the lawn ONLY if it show symptoms of stress due to lack of water—footprinting, leaf rolling, off color of gray-green.

Vegetables, Herbs & Fruits

• Take advantage of warm days and cool nights this month by fertilizing vegetables to generate lots of growth. The more growth and foliage there are, the more energy is produced by the plant for production of a bountiful harvest.

- Lengthen the harvest period of fast-producing crops (e.g., green beans, bush type) by sowing a second and third planting in early and mid-April.
- Mulch the vegetable garden to preserve soil moisture from spring rains and to reduce disease-causing fungi splashing from the soil to the plant and/or fruit.
- Remember that the best pest management strategy is your presence in the garden.
- Thin fruits from overburdened branches of fruit trees. This is the toughest job in growing quality apples, peaches, pears, and plums. Immature fruits are pulled off the tree to allow the remaining fruits to obtain maximum size. For comforting information, turn to the January essay "Growing Fruits and Nuts."
- Continue checking for insect pests and diseases on your fruit and nut plants. Insect control is "kill them once you see them." In contrast, disease control is much more preventive, so applications are often made before the disease is actually seen.

Houseplants

- As sun intensifies for your houseplants vacationing outdoors, check for sunscald (burn) on the foliage. Move plants to conditions of morning sun and afternoon shade or daylong filtered sunlight. Many houseplants are tropical and naturally accustomed to filtered light in the jungle (that is why they tolerate low light levels indoors).
- Fertilize the houseplants now while they are outdoors in bright light and can generate growth. Any water-soluble or time-release fertilizer will do.

Butterflies, Birds & Squirrels

- Admit it: Bird lovers either love or hate squirrels. If loved, feed them corn, peanuts, and sunflower seed. If not, than find a truly squirrel-proof bird feeder, such as the Yankee Flipper.
- Enjoy butterflies as mobile artwork; however, their babies (caterpillars) are eating machines. If you attract butterflies to the garden, be prepared emotionally to allow some of your prized plants to be devoured by caterpillars. Access butterfly references to distinguish butterfly-generating caterpillars from moth caterpillars (usually, the bad guys).

May

Bougainvillea (Bougainvillea spectabilis)

FULL STEAM AHEAD

What's Wrong with My Plant?

In May, telephone calls to radio garden shows, nurseries, and county extension offices invariably focus on "What's wrong with my _____ (plant)?" Spring has passed, bugs and diseases are in full force, plants begin to experience stress, and symptoms indicating unhealthy plants show up. Responders to these calls are tested to properly diagnose plant problems and prescribe effective, environmentally friendly solutions.

Undoubtedly the biggest challenge for home gardeners and yardeners is diagnosing plant problems. Armed with a keen eye and knowledge, you can make a correct diagnosis that will lead to proper action to manage the problem. Accurate identification of "the enemy" causing the plant problem is critical. The enemy can be placed in three categories:

- Insects (including mites and other insectlike pests)

- Infectious plant diseases
- Cultural or environmental causes

Believe it or not, the vast majority (75 percent or more) of problems result from improper cultural practices or the environment; however, the easiest to

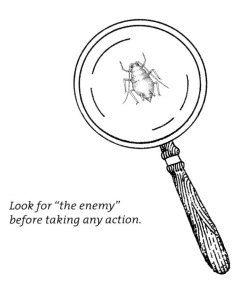

Look for "the enemy" before taking any action.

CALLER: "Why won't my
_____ plant bloom?"
ANSWER: "No, don't fill in
the blank with an exple-
tive. Fill it in with a plant
name—bougainvillea, crape
myrtle, lantana, rose, wisteria,
or most any flowering plant.
This question is among the most
common on call-in radio shows
regarding 'what is wrong with
my plant?' Invariably, the answer
is lack of sunlight. People try
fertilizing with high-phospho-
rous fertilizers, watering more,
stressing the plant by watering
less, cutting the roots, playing
music, cajoling, and threatening
to cut the plant down. None of
these work. These plants must
have full sunlight at least six
hours a day to bloom properly. If
the plant is in a container, move
it to sun. If it is in the ground,
either transplant it or simply
enjoy the foliage. Once the plant
is in the full sun, fertilize with a
water-soluble fertilizer every two
to three weeks. Water when the
soil is dry two inches deep. Step
back and enjoy the blooms."

*Bougainvillea (*Bougainvillea
spectabilis*)*

diagnose are insect and disease problems. Diagnosing plant problems is a
process of elimination. Look first for insects and related pests and their damage
to the plant. If not this, then consider
plant damage caused by diseases. If not
disease, then improper cultural practices
or stressful environmental conditions
will be the cause of poor plant health.

Insect Pests

Plant damage due to insects or related
pests is the most obvious, easiest-to-
recognize plant problem. Follow this
process for identifying the insect pest (or
eliminating insects as the enemy):

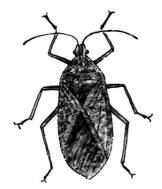

Squash bug

• Look for the presence of insects or related pests. The most common insect pests include aphids, beetles, caterpillars, grasshoppers, grubworms, leaf-cutting ants, mealybugs, scale, and true bugs (e.g., squash bugs). Related pests that are not classified as insects but commonly cause plant damage are pill bugs/doodle bugs/sow bugs (crustaceans, like lobsters and shrimp), snails and slugs (mollusks, like clams), and spider mites (arachnids, like spiders and ticks, with eight legs; insects have six). If you see insects on your plants, identify them using field guides, other books, or the Internet, or collect some and take them to a nursery professional or county extension agent.

• Not all bugs are bad guys. There are a 1,000 times as many good bugs or "do-nothing" bugs as there are insect pests. Just because insects are on or around your plants does not mean they are causing damage.

• Look for insect damage on the plant, whether insects are present or not. Insect damage can be described in four primary categories:

1. Injury by chewing leaves, flowers, and stems (e.g., beetles, caterpillars, doodle bugs, grasshoppers, snails)
2. Injury by piercing and sucking plant juices (e.g., aphids, leafhoppers/sharpshooters, mealybugs, mites, scale)
3. Injury by boring and feeding inside the plant (e.g., squash vine borers)
4. Injury by feeding on the roots (e.g., grubworms)

The above categories represent 95 percent of insect damage on plants, but there are other minor categories:

1. Injury by laying eggs on plant parts that fall to the ground (e.g., cicadas)
2. Injury by gathering plant leaves for food production (e.g., leaf-cutting ants)
3. Injury by disseminating and vectoring plant disease (e.g., beetles spreading oak wilt; honeybees spreading fire blight)

Ladybugs, more correctly called lady beetles, are predatory insects.

Good Bugs

"The only good bug is a dead bug" is NOT a good motto. Imperative is the understanding that most insects are harmless to humans and animals, and many insects provide great benefit to the natural environment and the home landscape and garden. Insects benefit the landscape and garden in several ways:

- They pollinate flowers of many fruit and vegetable crops, as well as ornamental flowers.
- They destroy various weeds in the same way they may injure desired plants.
- They consume decaying dead animals and plants.
- They improve soil conditions by tilling and burrowing through the soil while consuming organic matter and debris; dead insects and insect droppings also serve as fertilizer.
- Perhaps most important, they serve as predators and parasites of insect pests.

Predatory insects capture and eat thousands of insect pests. For example, lady beetles (ladybugs) and lacewings and their larvae eat aphids, and praying mantids eat young grasshoppers. Parasitic insects lay eggs in insects, the eggs hatch, and the larvae eat the host insect (reminds me of the 1979 movie *Alien* with Sigourney Weaver). Parasitic wasps lay eggs in aphid and armyworm caterpillars.

So think twice before you squash or spray an insect. It may be your new best friend.

Plant Diseases

Most plant pathogens (i.e., organisms that cause disease) are microscopic; therefore, looking for the enemy is not possible for most gardeners. Looking for symptoms of disease is the appropriate technique.

The initial step in looking for disease symptoms is the ability to recognize the appearance of a healthy, "normal" plant. Whether it be an apple tree, tomato plant, or petunia, having the experience and vision of what the plant is supposed to look like is key. Look around the neighborhood, check out garden books,

CALLER: "What is the black stuff on my crape myrtle leaves?"

ANSWER: "This question is heard repeatedly, not only about crape myrtles but hollies, roses, and houseplants. The answer is 'black sooty mold.' This is not a disease; it is a secondary result of an insect infestation. The possible culprits are aphids, leafhoppers, mealybugs, scale, or sharpshooters. These sap-sucking insects use their hypodermic-like mouthparts to puncture and extract the sweet, sugary juices of the plant. The insects absorb what they need and excrete the rest. The excretion is still a sweet, sugary substance that lands on the leaf and stem surfaces. (It also feels like light rain on your head if you are under the tree.)

Black sooty mold on crape myrtle leaf— aphid are the cause.

"Black sooty mold, a fungus, happily grows on the sugary substance. The mold takes no nutrients from the plant and does not cause disease; it is a saprophyte. It is simply unsightly and an indicator that you may need to control the insect population using a high-pressure water spray, organic insecticide (for example, neem oil), or a targeted systemic insecticide (for example, acephate—Orthene) that kills only bugs that suck sap from the plant."

search the Internet, ask experts—determine what your plant should normally look like. Deviations from the norm are the symptoms of disease for which you are looking.

Following are symptoms of plant disease:

- Blight—a general term used to describe a rapid and general killing of leaves, flowers, or stems, for example, fire blight, aerial phytopthora on periwinkles, and cotton root rot on rose species
- Dieback—a progressive dying back of stems, shoots, and roots from the tips, for example, repeated defoliation on roses by black spot and phomopsis twig blight (fungus) on ficus/weeping fig
- Mildew—a whitish, powdery coating on leaves, flowers, or stems,

Fungal blight (aerial phytothora) on periwinkle

for example, powdery mildew (fungus) on roses or crape myrtles and downy mildew on squash (underside of leaves)

- Lesion or spot—localized spot of diseased tissue surrounded by living tissue, most often on leaves, for example, entomosporium leaf spot (fungus) on Indian hawthorn and photinia
- Chlorosis—yellowing of the leaves due to loss of chlorophyll, for example, downy mildew (fungus) on squash, which also causes chlorosis symptoms
- Rot—decaying of plant tissue of leaves, stems, or roots, for example, fungal root rot on vegetable crops and take-all patch (fungus) on St. Augustinegrass
- Canker—a dead area on a stem surrounded by living tissue; often sap oozes from the canker, for example, bacterial canker on peach branches or trunk

- Damping-off—sudden dying of individual seedlings, for example, pythium, the soilborne fungal disease of flower and vegetable seedlings
- Gall—a pronounced localized swelling on roots, stems, or branches, for example, root-knot nematode on tomatoes or figs and crown gall (fungus) on roses
- Mosaic—mottled, alternating light and dark tissue on leaves, for example, St. Augustine decline (virus) on St. Augustinegrass

The Disease Triangle

Disease in plants and animals develops when three conditions exist at the same time. Without one of the conditions, disease will not occur. The disease triangle depicts the three conditions: a susceptible host, a pathogen (disease-causing organism), and a favorable environment.

Cultural & Environmental Disorders

If you have eliminated the potential enemies of insects and diseases as the cause of your plant problem, next consider cultural or environmental disorders. Remember that improper cultural practices and environmental stress (often called physiological stress) cause nearly 75 percent of plant health problems. Note also that these disorders can have the same symptoms as plant diseases—blights, rots, chlorosis, and dieback.

During investigation of cultural and environmental disorders, many questions must be asked:

Cultural or environmental stresses (e.g., sunburn and heat stress on caladiums) cause 75 percent of plant health problems in the garden.

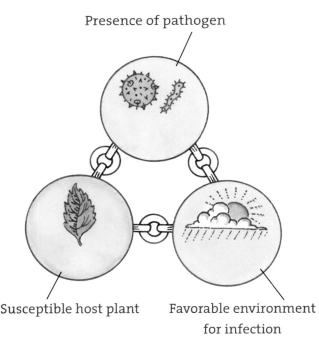

Presence of pathogen

Susceptible host plant

Favorable environment for infection

The disease triangle

* Is the plant truly adapted to the climatic conditions of your area? Does it grow well in other people's gardens?

* Can the plant take the summer heat of Texas? Just because a plant is "heat tolerant" in Poughkeepsie (New York) doesn't mean it is heat tolerant in Texas. Texas nighttime temperatures in the summer are particularly hard on northern-adapted plants.

* Did you prepare the soil properly, or not at all? Many plants simply can't grow in Texas soils.

* Does the plant need acidic or alkaline soil? Alkaline soil causes chlorosis and dieback in many non-adapted plants.

* Have you underwatered or over-

watered the plant? As many plants are killed by overwatering as under-watering. Not adequately watering newly transplanted trees, shrubs, flowers, and vegetables can cause a collapse of the root system and plant death.

• Has an herbicide, including weed-and-feed product, been used around the plant? Many herbicides can't tell the difference between a tree and a weed.

• Has any other pesticide been used? If so, was it used properly? Over-use or improper use of insecticides can burn foliage and flowers.

• Has fertilizer been applied? If so, was it applied properly? Too much fer-tilizer will burn plant roots and cause dieback symptoms.

• What are the sunlight condi-tions? If the plant needs but does not receive full sun, it will not grow properly, usually exhibiting a leggy, elongated type of growth. Lack of sunlight is the primary reason plants won't bloom (e.g., bougainvilleas, crape myrtles, roses). If the plant needs partial shade to deep shade, the intense sun will cause leaf burn that looks similar to a fungal blight.

• Has there been any physical damage done to the plant? Flexible-line trimmers can wound plant trunks and stems and disrupt the normal flow of water in the plant, resulting in leaf burn or dieback. "Mower blight" is another common disorder on trees, caused by running into the trunk.

• Does your irrigation water have high salts (e.g., sodium) that have burned the foliage?

• Have weather conditions changed dramatically? Is there a drought? Drying winds in winter and summer can cause leaf scorch. Hail can physically tear plants apart.

The list of questions can be endless. This is why telephone calls to experts can be lengthy. Know that you can be the best detective. You are in the garden. You can find the enemy that is causing your plant problems—be it insect, disease, or cultural or environmental stress.

Now that you know the enemy, read this month's "Managing Plant Problems" for the rest of the story.

Fungi Cause Most Plant Diseases

Note that most plant diseases are caused by fungi, although, bacteria, viruses, and nematodes are also plant pathogens. This is in contrast to dis-ease and illness in humans, which are more commonly caused by bacteria and viruses (e.g., the common cold—virus; sinus infections—bacteria; and staph—bacteria).

Top Five Insect Pests to Watch For in the Garden

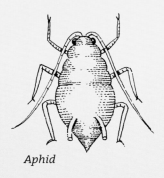

Aphid

Aphids—small, soft bodied, and plump; colors from clear to white to yellow; usually in herds, bunches; suck plant juices and excrete "honeydew," a clear, sticky, sugary substance. They multiply more rapidly than rabbits; females can be born pregnant. Seldom is there a need to control aphids, but if needed, high-pressure water spray, neem oil, or other organic control will work.

Spider mite

Spider mites—almost microscopic relative to ticks and spiders that congregate on the bottom of the leaves and suck plant juices; can cause a whitening to shiny bronzing effect on the top of the leaves. The best way to check for their presence is to take a white sheet of paper, shake the plant leaves over the paper, and look for reddish brown specks that move. In high populations, a fine webbing can be seen where the leaf connects to the stem—particularly a problem on houseplants, lantana, marigolds, and tomatoes. Spider mites are not easily controlled in high populations without the use of a systemic insecticide; low populations can be managed with repeated high-pressure water sprays or organic insecticide.

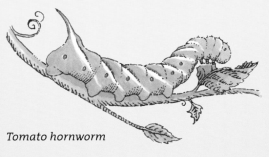

Tomato hornworm

Caterpillars—come in many shapes, sizes, and colors. In general, fuzzy, muted-colored caterpillars are the larvae of moths; and bright-colored, fancy caterpillars are the larvae of butterflies—both can be pests. Caterpillars are eating machines and can cause damage fast; if damage is not acceptable, control is relatively easy by handpicking or using the biological caterpillar killer, Bt.

Thrips

Thrips—small ($\frac{1}{8}$-inch), cigar-shaped insect; color from clear to white to tan; mouthpart rasps leaf and flower tissue and feeds on juices. Thrips are common on roses and vegetable crops; if rose blooms do not open properly, break open the bloom and look for dozens of thrips running around. Light-colored rose flowers are more susceptible. Control is not easy—start with neem, but you may need to progress to a systemic chemical insecticide.

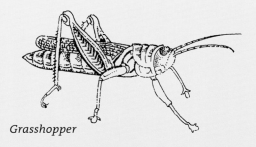

Grasshopper

Grasshoppers—from $\frac{1}{2}$ to 3 inches in length; eating machines; eat most any landscape and garden plant. Grasshoppers are migratory and will come into your landscape from surrounding fields. Start control measures with labeled insecticides when the grasshoppers are small; when they are large, the best control is two bricks!

Top Five Plant Diseases to Watch For in the Garden

Leaf spot—usually fungal, some bacterial; examples: black spot, cercospora, entomospo-

Fungal leaf spot (entomosporium leaf spot on Indian hawthorn)

rium; circular spots range from $\frac{1}{4}$ to $\frac{1}{2}$ inch in diameter; colors from gray with red halo to black with yellow borders; often causes leaves to drop. Control starts by picking off infected leaves and progresses to approved fungicides if warranted; the strategy with sprays is to protect uninfected leaves and new leaves—two to three weekly applications may be needed.

Fungal mildew (powdery mildew on rose)

Mildew—grayish to whitish fine powder covering on leaves, new shoots, and unopened blooms; a chronic problem, usually not severely damaging. Mildew is common on roses, nonhybrid crape myrtles, and some vegetable crops—generally a spring and fall problem. If warranted, you can effectively manage mildew with natural fungicides.

Blight—fungal; often a killer of annual flowers, such as periwinkle and dianthus. The disease is often exhibited as twig blight on shrubs, which kills one twig at a time and progresses through the shrub (e.g., twig blight on Italian cypress, junipers, pittosporum). The most effective control is to remove plants

Fungal blight (aerial phytothora on periwinkle)

killed by the fungus or prune twigs that are dead; sterilize pruning shears (Clorox and water solution) between cuts, or you will spread the fungus.

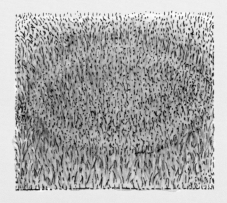

Fungal rot (brown patch on St. Augustine)

Rot—soilborne fungal disease that attacks plant roots or plant tissue close to the soil. Cotton root rot occurs in alkaline soil and causes rapid death of the entire plant in many landscape species.

Take-all patch of St. Augustine kills the roots and thus the infected lawn area. Brown patch of St. Augustine lawn is a rot that attacks where the leaf blade connects to the stem; brown patches appear in the lawn in spring and fall— a chronic, cool-season disease that is seldom lethal. Granular fungicides and fungicides drenched into the soil are effective in controlling some rots—check with your nursery professional or county extension agent.

Viral mosaic (St. Augustine decline, SAD, on St. Augustine)

Mosaic—caused by viruses; classic symptom is mottling of leaves (green and yellow polka-dotted appearance). St. Augustine decline is a weakening disease of St. Augustinegrass, not a fatal disease—resistant varieties, such as 'Raleigh,' are available and should be planted. Vegetable crops often contract viruses from sap-sucking insects that spread the disease— cucumber, pea, squash, and tomato plants are particularly susceptible. There is no pesticide that combats viruses— simply pull out and throw away plants showing mosaic symptoms.

Managing Plant Problems

The best defense is a good offense—an effective strategy in sports and in garden pest management. As discussed in "What's Wrong with My Plant?" you must know your plant's enemy. But wouldn't it be great to avoid the problem altogether? Such is the philosophy behind integrated pest management (IPM), a concept espoused by every major agricultural university in this nation. If your desire is an organic approach to gardening, you will be comforted by the similarities between IPM and organic gardening. The only difference is that organic gardeners strive to eliminate all chemical pest control measures. In IPM, the use of a chemical pesticide is the very last option in pest control.

Integrated Pest Management

The effectiveness of IPM in managing plant pest problems is remarkable.

Rather than make routine applications of pesticides, IPM followers make treatments only when and where pest populations exceed an acceptable level. This threshold varies depending on the garden crop or landscape plant experiencing the problem.

For example, acceptable population levels of aphids on lettuce are low, and control is warranted because damage quickly reduces the quality of the edible portion of the plant. In contrast, aphid populations are acceptable at higher levels on tomatoes because their damage to the fruit is minimal.

In a landscape setting, acceptable levels of plant pests are much, much higher. Aphids on your crape myrtles, photinias, and roses will occur every spring. Insect

predators (e.g., ladybugs and lacewings) and summer heat will reduce the populations naturally, and a pesticide application is seldom warranted.

The objective of IPM is not to totally eliminate pests but rather to keep pest populations below the level at which they cause unacceptable damage.

IPM Strategies for the Garden & Landscape

Here are four basic strategies, plus recommendations, for IPM:

1. Cultural practices

- Thoroughly prepare the soil in gardens and landscape plantings by tilling and adding organic matter. Spend the time, effort, and expense to create a healthy soil. Your plants will then grow healthy root systems. A healthy root system is imperative to overall plant health!

Soil preparation is critical.

Aggie Connection to IPM

Over 35 years ago, Perry Adkisson at Texas A&M University and Ray Smith at the University of California were among the first to deduce that most plant diseases, weeds, insects, and other pests in agriculture could be controlled by employing good crop management practices and maximizing the many controls already existing in nature. Working together, they developed a holistic strategy to managing harmful plant pests of agricultural crops. This new approach, termed "integrated pest management," quickly became a viable alternative to the rampant overuse of chemical pesticides occurring at the time. The "spray-and-pray" philosophy had led to overuse of pesticides, which was killing pests but also killing natural enemies of pests and upsetting nature's system to keep pests in check. IPM employs thoughtful, systematic strategies to manage plant problems through various techniques, including soil improvement; introduction of beneficial organisms; use of resistant crops and crop management techniques; and only when needed, application of the least toxic organic or chemical pesticide. Today, IPM's approach to solving pest problems is employed in agricultural fields and crops, home and commercial landscapes, and even school yards. IPM has truly made a difference by reducing pesticide use throughout the nation.

• Use resistant and adapted plants. Choose disease-resistant varieties when available; examples include tomato varieties (look for "VFN"—verticillium, fusarium, and nematode resistant) and hybrid crape myrtle varieties resistant to powdery mildew (e.g., 'Basham Party Pink,' 'Muskogee,' 'Natchez'). Do not use plants that are "hotels for insects and diseases," such as golden euonymus. Choose plants that are adapted to your soil; don't use southern magnolia in alkaline soil because iron chlorosis will develop. Choose plants that can take the Texas heat. High nighttime temperatures of Texas summers do not allow many northern "heat-tolerant" plants to rest, resulting in slow demise of the nonadapted plant. Choose plants that are adapted to the sunlight conditions present (e.g., full sun, partial sun, shade). Plant the right plant in the right place!

• Time plantings of vegetable and flower crops. Plant prior to summer buildup of insect populations, such as mites and grasshoppers. Plant periwinkles as soil temperatures heat up in May to avoid aerial phytopthora fungus, which devastates periwinkles in spring.

• Prune and pick off disease- or insect-infested plant parts. Pruning and picking pest-riddled plant parts reduce the potential for the spread of the disease or insect. Cut off juniper and pittosporum branches infected by twig blight and branches of hollies that are highly infested by scale. Pick off leaves of Indian hawthorn and photinia infected by entomosporium leaf spot and leaves of roses infected by black spot.

• Employ sanitation to also reduce the potential spread of the disease or insect. Rake and collect dead, disease-laden leaves and twigs from shrub and flower beds and vegetable gardens. Many insects also lay eggs or overwinter in plant debris and spring forth to infest plants.

• Properly water and fertilize plants to increase overall plant health. A healthy plant is naturally more pest resistant.

2. MECHANICAL CONTROL METHODS

• Handpick insects, weeds, and diseased plant parts. It may be gross, but picking and killing caterpillars (unless you are raising butterflies), snails, and grasshoppers can reduce populations before they get out of control and an insecticide is needed. Hoeing and pulling weeds can be boring, but it provides immediate gratification and avoids the need for an herbicide. Weeds can also harbor insect pests and plant diseases. Removing diseased plants may be difficult emo-

Hoe weeds as a mechanical, non-pesticide control.

tionally but may prevent the spread of the disease to healthy plants of the same species.

• Use high-pressure water spraying to dislodge aphids, thrips, and mites from infested plants. A conventional trigger sprayer on the end of the hose will do some good, but the true high-pressure water sprayers incorporate an agricultural spray nozzle attached to a metal tube. For sources, search local nurseries and the Internet. Research documents that an aphid sprayed off a plant and landing a few feet from the plant cannot find its way back to the plant. (How did they do that research—very tiny tracking collars?)

• Use physical barriers to effectively exclude pests. Crop covers and nettings on vegetables, fruits, and prized roses exclude insects (e.g., grasshoppers), birds, and squirrels.

Crop covers on tomato plants are the only effective way to prevent thrips from spreading the lethal disease tomato spotted wilt virus. Sticky barriers on the soil reduce creepy-crawly insects, such as caterpillars, doodle bugs, and snails.

• Use traps and trap crops. Traps for flying insects, such as coddling moths and fruit flies, can be highly effective. Elbon cereal ryegrass planted in the vegetable garden is an effective trap crop for nematodes. Similar in strategy to roach and ant traps, nematodes enter the roots of Elbon cereal ryegrass and can't get out.

3. BIOLOGICAL AND NATURAL CONTROL METHODS

• Protect natural predators and parasites in the garden and landscape. Do so by using a pesticide, chemical or organic, only when truly needed. Birds, lacewings, ladybugs (lady beetles), parasitic wasps, and praying mantids exist in nature to help control insect pests.

• Enhance natural predators and parasites by purchasing and releasing them in the garden and landscape. Lacewings, ladybugs, praying mantids, and trichogramma wasps are available in nurseries and via the Internet. The key to using these biological controls is to have an exist-

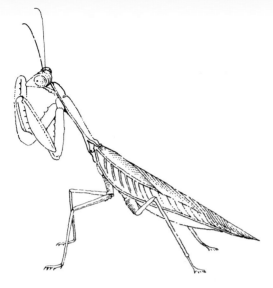

Praying mantid, a natural predator, can be purchased and introduced into your garden.

ing population of their prey in your garden before you let them loose. If there is no prey, they will happily leave your landscape and go to your neighbor's yard in search of prey.

- Use the biological, caterpillar-killing insecticide *Bacillus thuringiensis* (Bt). This bacterium is generally available in a powdered form that is dusted on a plant or mixed with water and sprayed. Bt acts as a stomach poison for caterpillars. It releases toxins in the stomach, which causes the caterpillars to stop eating and starve. Bt's greatest advantage is that it kills only caterpillars and is harmless to humans, pets, birds, and bees. Its disadvantages are that it is slow acting, so the insect may not completely stop eating and die for several

days; it breaks down quickly in the environment (also an advantage); it kills "good" butterfly caterpillars; and it can be a skin irritant.

- Use the least toxic, effective natural insecticide. Natural insecticides have been used for thousands of years. Research is now documenting the effectiveness, and sometimes ineffectiveness, of many products sold as natural insecticides. Here are a few well-known natural insecticides you might consider:

1. Insecticidal soaps—sodium or potassium salts combined with fatty acids. Insecticidal soap must come in direct contact with the insect and is no longer effective once it has dried. The fatty acids in the soap penetrate the insect's "skin" and cause cells to collapse. The pros of insecticidal soaps are that they are one of the safest pesticides; are nontoxic to animals; leave no residue; and can be used on vegetables right up to harvest. The cons are that they can burn or stress plants; they are not recommended for use in full sun or high temperatures; and specific plants may be sensitive to insecticidal soap (check the label).

2. Pyrethrum and pyrethrins—derived from *Chrysanthemum cinerariifolium.* Available in

powder form to be dusted on leaves, wettable powder to be mixed with water and sprayed, and in aerosol sprays. These are contact killers with a rapid "knockdown" effect, causing a quick death. They have a low toxicity to animals and degrade in the environment within a day. The disadvantage is that these insecticides kill most any insect, good or bad, including honeybees. Use cautiously and only when there is a major problem with hard-to-kill insects. Aerosol products can burn plant foliage.

3. Nicotine—one of the earliest known insecticides (eighteenth century) derived from leaves of *Nicotiana* (tobacco) and available as nicotine sulfate. This highly toxic natural chemical is not often recommended for home garden and landscape use. It poses a threat to any animal that inhales or touches it. Some Web sites and publications suggest the use of "tobacco teas," but brewing these concoctions is best avoided. Nicotine is 200 times as toxic as aspirin.

4. Sabadilla—ground seeds of the sabadilla lily. Available in a fine powder to be mixed with water and sprayed. Very effective against true bugs (e.g., leaf-footed bug, stinkbug), it acts as a stomach poison once ingested by the insect. It is highly toxic to bees and irritating to the mucous membranes (nose) of mammals. Use as a final choice and with great caution.

5. Rotenone—derived from the roots of tropical legumes; available as a powder to be dusted on the plant; breaks down quickly in sunlight and leaves a low residue. It kills pests and beneficial insects alike and has a moderate to high toxicity level for humans and pets.

• Consider using three of the newest, well-documented natural/biological insecticides that have very low toxicity to humans and low environmental impact. These natural/biological insecticides represent the greatest advancement in the past 50 years for insect pest management in the landscape and garden:

1. Neem oil and extracts—derived from the seed kernels of the neem tree fruit, which contain a complex mixture of biologically active compounds. The neem tree (*Azadirachta indica*) is a tropical native to Southeast Asia and grows in many countries throughout the world. It is a close relative of the common Chinaberry tree.

Neem oil and extracts act both as an insecticide and fungicide (Wow!). Neem products sprayed onto plant leaves kill a wide range of insects pests. They work especially well on soft-bodied insects, such as aphids, caterpillars, mites, thrips, and whiteflies. Neem is not a quick "knockdown" insecticide; it breaks down quickly in sunlight and washes away with irrigation or rain. It is harmless to humans, but pets should be kept away from the treated area until the leaves dry.

As a fungicide, neem is used as a preventive or applied when disease is just beginning to appear. It is effective against blight, leaf spot, mildew, rot, rust, and scab.

2. Spinosad—derived through fermentation of the naturally occurring soil bacterium *Saccharopolyspora spinosa*. Spinosad kills foliage- and flower-feeding insect pests, including beetles, caterpillars, fruit flies, leaf miners, sawflies, and thrips. Death is rapid due to disruption of the insect nervous system. Spinosad must be ingested by the insect; therefore, it has little effect on sucking insect pests (e.g., aphids and leafhoppers) or beneficial insects (e.g., lacewings and ladybugs). Spinosad provides lower toxicity than conventional chemical insecticides and persists longer in the environment than many other natural insecticides. Spinosad is toxic to bees exposed to

direct spray and should be sprayed in late evening or early morning. It is also available in a bait for fire ant control.

3. Orange oil or d-limonene—extracted from orange peels. Available in liquid products to be sprayed or drenched. Controls a wide variety of insects, both good and bad. It is a well-documented control for fire ants and fleas. Use with care according to label directions. Some pets (especially cats) are sensitive to citrus oil products.

• Try corn gluten meal as a pre-emergence herbicide when appropriate. Corn gluten meal, developed by Iowa State University, has had varying research results reported for controlling weeds in flower and shrub beds and lawns. Corn gluten also contains 10 percent nitrogen and should be considered in your fertilizer schedule for the lawn and garden.

• Try natural fungicides. The oldest recorded fungicide is sulfur. It was used over 2,000 years ago by the Greeks as a control for wheat rust. Sulfur can be used as a preventive fungicide against powdery mildew, rose black spot, rusts, and other diseases in the garden and landscape. Potassium bicarbonate (Remedy) is a more recently identified natural fungicide for powdery mildew on roses, flowers, and vegetable crops. Bordeaux mixture has been successfully used for over 150 years on fruits, vegetables, and ornamentals. Bordeaux mixture combines both a fungicide (copper sulfate) and a bactericide (lime, calcium hydroxide). Although fungicides individually have a low toxicity for humans and animals, they are still chemicals and can harm plants and animals if not used properly. Read and follow the directions.

4. CHEMICAL CONTROLS

• Use chemical pesticides as a last resort. No spraying and praying! Make sure the presence and population of the insect, disease, or weed has caused enough damage, or potential damage, to the plants to justify a pesticide application.

• Use the right pesticide after you have correctly identified the pest. Remember that an insecticide kills insects and does not control diseases. Fungicides control diseases and not insects. Sounds like common sense, but make sure you and your neighbors know this.

• Choose the least-toxic pesticide that is effective in managing the pest. Pesticides are labeled based on toxicity as "Caution," "Warning," and "Danger." Seldom, if ever, should you use a pesticide labeled with "Warning"

"Organic" Cautions

• Just because an insecticide is natural or "organic" does not mean it is harmless to humans and other animals. Nature makes some of the most potent toxic substances on Earth. Nicotine and rotenone are highly toxic, whereas neem and spinosad have low toxicity. Treat all pesticides, chemical or natural, with great caution, and use as directed.

• If a product is not labeled as an insecticide (e.g., garlic, Tabasco sauce), don't recommend it to friends and neighbors. The federal government labels and regulates all insecticides. Recommending nonlabeled products as insecticides can get you into trouble.

• There is interest by some gardeners in making concoctions to control insects, but be careful that the cure doesn't kill the patient. The phytotoxicity (a fancy word for plant-damaging characteristics) of these concoctions can be high.

• Try any product or garden practice that is new to you on a small portion of the plant or garden. Watch for the desired results. If seen, then use it further. Testing is a responsibility for everyone.

or "Danger" in the home garden or landscape.

- Consult a nursery professional, county extension agent, or university Web site for the latest chemical pesticides recommended for use in the home landscape and garden. Tremendous change has marked recent years in the landscape and garden pesticide world. Many products have been taken off the market, for good reason. Many new pesticides have come to the market. Change will continue as

CALLER: "This spring, I have aphids on my roses. What do I do?"

ANSWER: "Following IPM strategies, first understand that seeing aphids on roses in spring is not unusual. Doing nothing may be the best course of action. Natural predators and summer heat will control most of the aphid population."

CALLER: "But these are my favorite roses, and I will be showing them in a garden club show and don't want any damage on the foliage or blooms."

ANSWER: "Then consider using a high-pressure water spray to blast the aphids off the bush. Consider releasing aphid predators, such as ladybugs. If foliage or flower damage is occurring rapidly, consider using the least toxic natural insecticide, such as neem. It should control the vast majority of the aphids. If you must control all the aphids, then use a fast-acting, targeted, systemic insecticide such as acephate (Orthene). Because the insecticide is systemic, only insects that chew or suck on the plant will consume the insecticide and be killed. Acephate is toxic to honeybees; therefore, spray in early morning or later afternoon to avoid harming honeybees. The final decision is yours."

companies compete to develop natural and chemical pesticides that are research-proven to be effective and environmentally safe.

• Protect honeybees. Spray natural or chemical insecticides in the early morning or late in the afternoon to avoid the time when bees are active.

• Use protective clothing, read and follow the label directions, and dispose of pesticides properly. If you have pesticides in your garage or shed that are old and you question their effectiveness, the best way to dispose of them is during a "hazardous waste collection" event in your community (check with your solid waste disposal department).

• For more information and terminology for pesticide safety, refer to this month's essay "Pesticide Safety."

Pesticide Safety

Pesticide safety may sound like an oxymoron, but discussion of the topic is a must. The amount of use, and abuse, of pesticides by gardeners and yardeners is staggering. The vast majority need never be applied. Make sure you need to use a pesticide. If you do, here is the rest of the story on how to effectively and safely apply a pesticide to manage your plant pest problems. This discussion applies to natural ("organic") pesticides and chemical pesticides alike.

The most important component of the safe use of pesticides is understanding the terminology associated with them. The label directions then become much more understandable, and the chances of endangering yourself, others, and the environment are greatly diminished.

Pesticide Terminology & Overview

FORMULATIONS

- Concentrated liquids—to be diluted with water prior to application
- Ready-to-use (RTU) liquids—premixed with water for immediate application (This is perhaps the biggest advance in pesticide safety. Most contaminations of the environment and poisonings of humans occur during the mixing of concentrates with water. RTUs cost more but are well worth the expense.)
- Wettable and soluble powders—

in powder form to be mixed with water prior to application

- Aerosols—premixed with a propellant and ready for application
- Dusts—combined with a talcum-powder substance for spreading on plants
- Granules—combined with an inert material, such as clay particles, to create a coarse particle product for application
- Baits—edible substances (e.g., corn grits) laced with an insecticide to be spread and eaten by insects (e.g., ants, grasshoppers, snails)
- Oils—botanical or petroleum-based oils that smother insect pests and can reduce disease

Pesticide Types and Function

- Insecticide—controls insects
- Fungicide—controls fungi
- Bactericide—controls bacteria
- Miticide—controls mites
- Herbicide—controls weeds

How Pesticides Work

- Contact poison—kills when the pesticide contacts the pest
- Stomach poison—kills when the pesticide is swallowed by the pest
- Systemic poison—kills by being taken into the plant tissue that is then fed upon by the pest
- Translocated herbicide—absorbed by the plant and then moved throughout the plant tissue to kill the entire plant
- Selective pesticide—kills only certain insects (as with an insecticide) or weeds (as with an herbicide)
- Nonselective pesticide—kills any insect (as with an insecticide) or weed (as with an herbicide)

How Pesticides Are Applied

- Spray—directly applying to the plant or plant part
- Broadcast—uniform scattering of pesticide over an area
- Drench—saturating the soil with a pesticide
- Spot-treat—applying a pesticide to a small area

The Pesticide Label

Labels contain the following information:

- Brand name
- Formulation—various formulations available
- Active ingredient—common and chemical name of the pesticide
- Inactive ingredient—inert material included in the pesticide product
- Signal words of toxicity—three categories:

GET THE HECK OUTTA MY GARDEN!

READY-TO-USE INSECTICIDE

FOR USE ON ORNAMENTALS, VEGETABLES, AND FRUIT CROPS.
ACTIVE INGREDIENTS: 2-U, IL-KILL-YA-IFYA-EATIT......... 0.001%
INERT INGREDIENT.. 99.999%

CAUTION! (SEE BACK LABEL FOR ADDITIONAL PRECAUTIONARY STATEMENTS)

Sample pesticide label

1. "Danger" and skull and crossbones—a taste to a teaspoon can kill a human; highly toxic

2. "Warning"—a teaspoon to a tablespoon can kill a human; moderately toxic

3. "Caution"—an ounce to more than a pint can kill a human; relatively low toxicity to nontoxic

- Use of the pesticide—lists the LEGAL uses for the pesticide
- Precautionary statement—describes the hazards to humans and domestic animals
- Environmental hazards—statement to avoid environmental damage
- Statement of practical treatment—lists first aid for the applicator if swallowed or inhaled or comes in contact with the skin
- Application-to-harvest periods—how long after application fruits or vegetables may be harvested and consumed

APPLICATION EQUIPMENT

- Hose-end sprayers—proportionally mixes a pesticide concentrate with water as the water is sprayed through the hose
- Pump-up sprayer—concentrate of pesticide mixed with water and poured into the spray tank; compression by a pump then forces the mix-

ture through a short hose and hand-held spray nozzle

- Walk-behind spreader—used to broadcast granular pesticides over a large area
- Hand-held spreader—whirlybird action broadcasts granular pesticide over a smaller area

Pesticide Safety Tips

- Read the "Precautionary State-ments" on the pesticide label.
- Use ready-to-use (RTU) products if available (e.g., acephate, glyphosate, neem, pyrethrins).
- Use granular insecticides and fungicides for lawn pests.
- Purchase a high-pressure, hose-end water wand to spray small insect pests (e.g., aphids, mites, thrips) off your plants (check the Internet or a nursery for availability).
- Purchase and use protective clothing (e.g., rubber gloves, goggles, mask, jacket, boots).
- Shower thoroughly after apply-ing pesticides.
- Try any insecticide that is new to you on a small portion of the plant or garden. Watch for the desired results. If seen, then use it further.
- Use only a pesticide that has the specific crop on the label when treat-ing edible crops.
- Use insecticides for insects,

fungicides for fungal diseases, and herbicides for weeds.

- Make sure the specific pest you are targeting is on the pesticide label.
- Use the least toxic pesticide that is effective for the pest.
- Use a separate pump-up sprayer for herbicides and a separate one for insecticides and fungicides. It is dif-ficult to thoroughly clean herbicide residue from a sprayer.
- Use hose-end sprayers (propor-tioners) when applicable. Be very careful spraying up into a large shrub or tree—wind drift of the pesticide may occur.
- Always walk backward when ap-plying herbicides, such as glyphosate, to the lawn. Your feet become applica-tors if you walk through the sprayed lawn, and you will have a polka-dot-ted lawn.
- Seek expert advice for questions about pest management.
- Dispose of excess pesticides according to the label direction or at community hazardous waste dis-posal events (check with the city solid waste management department).
- **Read and follow the label directions.**

PESTICIDE POISONING AND SYMPTOMS

- Improper use of pesticides can lead to poisoning of humans.
- Poisoning can occur when a pesticide comes in contact with skin or eyes; when fumes are inhaled through mouth or nose; and if swallowed.
- Mild poisoning or early symptoms of acute poisoning include fatigue, headache, dizziness, blurred vision, excessive sweating and salivation, nausea and vomiting, stomach cramps, and diarrhea.
- Moderate poisoning or early symptoms of acute poisoning include inability to walk, weakness, chest discomfort, muscle twitches, constriction of pupils, and earlier symptoms that become severe.
- Severe or acute poisoning symptoms include unconsciousness, severe constriction of pupils, muscle twitches, convulsions, secretions from mouth and nose, and breathing difficulties.
- Symptoms generally start within the first 12 hours of exposure.
- As with any potentially dangerous activity, notify a family member or friend that you are going to apply a pesticide.

FIRST AID FOR PESTICIDE POISONING

- Read the "Statement of Practical Treatment" on the pesticide label.
- Shower thoroughly after applying pesticides.
- If a pesticide gets on the skin, wash it off immediately.
- If a pesticide gets on clothing, remove the clothing immediately. Detergents remove pesticides better than soaps.
- If pesticide fumes are inhaled, move immediately to fresh air.
- If poisoning symptoms appear, call your physician and/or go to the emergency room.
- Obtain the pesticide information, and take the pesticide container with you to the physician.

EMERGENCY POISON CONTROL TELEPHONE NUMBERS
Post these telephone numbers in the garage and/or garden shed and add to your telephone book:
Nationwide Poison Control Network: 800-222-1222
National Pesticide Information Center: 800-858-7378

Texas Produce: When to Purchase?

Frustration abounds in the produce sections of most grocery stores as people search for high-quality fruits and vegetables for their families. Everyone has probably purchased a beautiful-looking apple, grapefruit, or peach, only to find on first bite a fruit that is either rock hard when it should be soft and juicy, or mealy and mushy when it should be tart and crisp.

With the rise of a global economy, grocery stores are full of "fresh" fruits and vegetables of all kinds year-round. But just how fresh are they? Some apple varieties, for example, can be picked and stored for 6 months before they appear in the grocery stores. Eating a tasteless, pithy apple is a common experience for too many people. Some of these apples and other fruits are old enough to vote. Similarly, tomatoes can be harvested green (immature) in faraway places, turned red during storage and shipping, and stocked in stores for purchase weeks later. The result is a tomato with a bland and mushy taste.

One of the best strategies to avoid using your hard-earned money to purchase and consume low-quality fruits and vegetables is to buy these crops when they are harvested in Texas.

Texas ranks behind California and Florida as the largest producer of fruits and vegetables in the nation. Due to the north-south extent of Texas, fresh fruits and vegetables are harvested throughout most of the year. Texas is known to produce some of the best crops in the world of blueberries, cantaloupes, grapefruit, onions, peaches, pecans, peppers, potatoes, pumpkins, spinach, sweet corn, sweet potatoes, tomatoes, and watermelons.

Use the chart below to determine when Texas produce is available. Find a grocery store, produce market, or vegetable stand in your area that carries these crops. Buy them while they last. For the rest of the year, develop a relationship with the local produce manager, and learn how and when to select high-quality produce from other areas of the world.

Texas Produce Calendar

CROP	JAN	FEB	MAR	APR	MAY	JUN	JUL	AUG	SEP	OCT	NOV	DEC
Vegetables												
Bean, green				X	X	X	X	X	X	X		
Broccoli	X	X	X	X							X	X
Cabbage	X	X	X	X	X	X				X	X	X
Cantaloupe					X	X	X	X	X			
Carrot	X	X	X	X					X	X	X	X
Cauliflower	X	X	X							X	X	X
Corn, sweet					X	X	X					
Cucumber					X	X	X	X	X			
Greens	X	X	X	X	X				X	X	X	X
Honeydew melon					X	X	X					
Lettuce	X	X	X						X	X	X	X
Okra						X	X	X	X			
Onion (1015Y)				X	X	X						
Pea, southern					X	X	X	X	X			
Pepper					X	X	X	X	X	X	X	
Potato					X	X	X	X	X	X		
Spinach	X	X	X						X	X	X	X
Sweet potato								X	X	X	X	X
Tomato					X	X	X	X	X	X		
Watermelon					X	X	X	X	X	X	X	
Fruits												
Apple						X	X	X	X	X		
Blackberry					X	X						
Blueberry					X	X	X					
Grapefruit	X	X	X	X							X	X
Orange	X	X	X	X						X	X	X
Peach				X	X	X	X	X				
Pecan								X	X	X	X	
Plum					X	X						
Strawberry				X	X							

Note: During the months indicated by "X," Texas-grown fruits and vegetables are harvested and available in local produce markets.

Timely Tips

Flowers & Pretty Plants

• Time to change out unproductive cool-season annuals with warm-season annuals, such as marigold, penta, periwinkle, portulaca, purslane, salvia, and scaevola. Turn to the February essay "Annual Flowers . . . Icing on the Cake!" for a more extensive list of warm-season annuals.

• Deadhead perennial flowers to encourage continuous bloom.

• Apply nitrogen fertilizer monthly at a rate of $\frac{1}{4}$ pound of urea per 100 square feet, $\frac{1}{2}$ pound of ammonium sulfate, or 1 pound of blood meal.

• Drip-irrigate annual and perennial flowers (and vegetable gardens) for peak performance. The March essay "Saving Water Drip by Drip" will help uncover the mystery of drip irrigation.

Garden Design

• Summer is around the corner, so consider planting a Texas-tough flower bed. Visit botanical gardens, demonstration gardens, nurseries, or the local extension office to determine the toughest flowering plants for your area.

Soil & Mulch

• Realize that soil preparation is perhaps the biggest contributor to plant health in Texas. Without adequate soil preparation in flower and shrub beds and vegetable gardens, plant root systems have a difficult time developing properly. A healthy root system results in a healthy, productive plant. Spend the time, money, and effort to prepare soils prior to planting. The January essay "Soils 101 for the Garden" describes how to prepare a garden soil.

• Choose any type of organic mulch you prefer; it doesn't matter. Big-nugget pine bark chips to fine-textured cypress bark to hardwood mulch—all conserve water, prevent weeds, and cool soil temperature. Never let your landscape plantings and vegetable garden be without at least a 2-inch layer of mulch.

Water

• Irrigation starts in earnest this month. Remain focused on letting the plant tell you when to water.

• Water thoroughly every time you water. Apply 1 inch of water to soak 6 inches deep in clay soils and 12 inches in a sand or prepared garden soil. Make multiple short applications of water to reach 1 inch without having water runoff down the street.

Plant Care

• Use glyphosate herbicides to save time in controlling weeds. Glyphosate is environmentally safe when used properly. It kills any plant it is sprayed on but does not persist in the soil. Learn more by reading "Glyphosate Herbicides—Valuable Weed Management Tools" among April's essays.

• Insect populations peak in late spring. Remember that not all insects are bad guys; the vast majority are just innocently living their lives, having fun, and producing the next generation.

• Keep a watchful eye, because a group of insect pests that attack the lawn and garden can reproduce quickly, including aphids, chinch bugs, spider mites, and thrips. If damaging populations explode, take control measures immediately. Always use the least toxic, environmentally safe measures first. This month's essay "Managing Plant Problems" will help guide your insect control decisions.

• Read the "Top Five Insect Pests" and "Top Five Plant Diseases" (among this month's essays), and check daily for these problems in your lawn and garden.

• If you have had grasshopper problems in the past, take control measures as soon as you see small $\frac{1}{2}$-inch babies. Now is the time to control them, not after they mature into 3-inch swarming monsters. Two bricks clapped together quickly become the only control for these plant-eating monsters.

Trees, Shrubs & Vines

• Crape myrtles are blooming. Don't forget to prune off the dead bloom spikes to keep the plant blooming throughout the rest of the growing season.

• Black spot, powdery mildew, thrips, and aphids may wreak havoc on your rosebushes. Spend lots of time and effort trying to control these destructive diseases and pests, or better yet, choose rose varieties based on their resistance to these problems. Old-fashioned roses and some newly developed rose varieties are much more resistant to these diseases and pests. Check with your local nursery, botanical garden professional, county extension agent, or Master Gardener for recommended varieties.

Lawns

• Note symptoms of water stress in lawns, including dull, gray-green color; leaf blades rolled lengthwise; and footprints left after walking on the lawn. When you see these, you have 24 hours to water before severe water stress occurs.

• Don't wait for grass to grow back into thin unhealthy areas in the lawn;

purchase and lay sod to immediately increase the quality of your lawn.

- Know that brown or yellow patches in the lawn can be caused by a few different problems. Refer to the April essay "Lawns 101" for specifics in determining the cause and correcting it.
- Sharpen mower blades at least once a year. Cutting grass is a wounding process, and a dull blade increases the damage significantly. Look closely at the cut blades of grass. If the cut is not clean (i.e., the blades are frayed), sharpen the blade yourself; take it to a small-engine repair shop; or perhaps most economical and effective, simply purchase a new blade, and put it on yourself.

Vegetables, Herbs & Fruits

- Protect your harvest. If birds or squirrels are eating your tomatoes, peppers, and other crops, use plastic netting to exclude these opportunistic feeders. Make sure you drape the netting all the way to the ground and cover the ends with soil. Overlap the netting (or sew the edges together) to totally eliminate entry.
- Believe it—doodle bugs (pill bugs), snails, and slugs can inflict major damage on vegetable crops and herbs. Control can be achieved with slug and snail baits. Control techniques using saucers of beer and 2-inch-wide bands of calcite clay ("kitty litter") have shown some success.

- Learn to recognize stinkbugs and leaf-footed bugs, which can severely damage young tomato and pepper fruits. Control measures should be taken immediately if these "piercing-sucking" insect pests appear. Hand collection can work, but large populations will require a pesticide. Again, use the least toxic, effective pesticide labeled for the job.
- Learn to recognize early blight on tomato leaves. This fungal disease may appear this month and is characterized by dead and dying leaves at the bottom of the plant. Pick off diseased leaves to slow the disease's progress. Treating with a fungicide may be warranted to salvage healthy foliage so that the unharvested tomatoes will mature.
- Water fruit trees heavily now. Water trees with an irrigation system using microsprinklers. Or simply lay a slowly running hose on the ground at the drip line (tips of the branches) of the tree. Move the hose every 15 to 20 minutes around the tree drip line.

Butterflies, Birds & Squirrels

- Provide water for the birds with birdbaths, fountains, or bubblers. Squirrels need water, too, and will visit the birdbath.
- Plant heat-tolerant, butterfly-attracting plants, such as buddleia, butterfly weed, lantana, penta, salvia, and verbena.

June

Esperanza or yellow bells (Tecoma stans)

WELCOME TO TEXAS HEAT

Sizzling Summer Color for Texas Gardens

If it can't take the heat, don't plant it in Texas. Heat tolerance has a whole new meaning during Texas summers. Summer nighttime temperature in Texas, not daytime heat, is the major challenge for most plants grown in gardens north of the Red River. When temperatures are still 80°F at 10:00 P.M., plants don't get a chance to rest (reduce respiration).

Without a rest period, respiration continues to consume plant sugars produced during daytime photosynthesis. Without rest, the plant consumes more than it produces and deteriorates. For example, Kentucky bluegrass can take 100°F days in Kansas, because the nights cool off and the plants rest. In all but the Panhandle, Kentucky bluegrass simply eats itself up in Texas and dies of a plant version of consumption.

Fortunately, there are native and adapted plants that thrive in Texas heat.

Texas nursery and landscape professionals and home gardeners have focused in recent years on using Texas-tough plants. Extension horticulturists and

*Esperanza or yellow bells (*Tecoma stans*)*

county extension agents from Texas A&M University developed a landscape plant-testing program to identify such plants, which are appropriately identified as Texas Superstars.

Below is a list of time-tested colorful plants that are especially chosen for heat tolerance and adaptation to the entire state. Prepare a good garden soil, plant them in full sun, give them some water, step back, and enjoy the profusion of summer color in your garden.

ANNUALS

Caladium—sun-tolerant varieties: those with narrow, strap-shaped foliage

Coleus—sun-tolerant varieties: 'Burgundy Sun' and 'Plum Parfait'

Marigold—can plant large mum-type varieties in midsummer (and watch how great they do in fall)

Periwinkle—many new varieties (Don't plant until May to avoid soilborne disease in spring.)

Portulaca or moss rose—succulent-like foliage and vivid flowers in single or double forms

Purslane—any large-flowered variety; Texas tough (Ask any farmer who fights the native weed species.)

Scaevola or fan flower—new varieties, such as 'New Wonder'

Variegated tapioca (*Manihot esculenta* 'Variegata')—large tropical with green and yellow foliage

Zinnia—many flower forms, colors, and plant heights

PERENNIALS

Firebush (*Hamelia patens*)—perennial south of IH-20; used as annual north of IH-20

Gold star esperanza or yellow bells (*Tecoma stans*)—root-hardy perennial north of IH-20

Hardy hibiscus—varieties such as 'Flare' (red, pink, or peppermint), 'Lord Baltimore,' and 'Moy Grande'

Lantana—trailing varieties, such as 'New Gold,' and *Lantana montevidensis* (purple, lavender, or white) (*Note:* Trailing varieties are best used as annuals north of IH-20.)

Lantana—upright varieties, such as 'Confetti,' 'Dallas Red,' 'Irene,' and 'Radiation'

Petunia—smaller-flowered types (less hybridized): 'Laura Bush,' 'VIP,' and 'Tidal wave'

Phlox—garden, perennial types, such as 'John Fanick' and 'Victoria'

Plumbago—any blue variety; don't forget the white-flowered form

Salvias—several perennial, native sages, including

Autumn sage (*Salvia greggii*)—red, hot pink, salmon, or white flowers

Indigo spires (*S.* hybrid)

Mexican bush sage (*S. leucan tha*)—primarily a late summer and fall bloomer

Purple rain (*S. verticillata*)

Superba (*S. superba* 'May Night')

Victoria blue salvia (*S. farinacea* 'Victoria')

Verbena—perennial species and hybrids, including 'Apple Blossom,' 'Blue Princess,' 'Homestead Purple,' 'Taylortown Red,' and 'Texas Rose'

Attracting Birds to the Garden

Gardeners and bird lovers are often the same people. The presence of birds singing, playing, and feeding in the garden seems natural and is a source of great enjoyment. Birds truly add an auditory dimension to the garden.

To attract birds, you can put up bird feeders and entice a few species. If you want a plethora of feathered species, you must provide a habitat that meets their needs:

- Food
- Water
- Shelter
- Places for rearing young

There are numbers of books and resources to fine-tune your landscape into a bird paradise. The guidelines below will get you started, and you can progress further if you like.

*Dogwood (*Cornus florida*) flowers are beautiful, and the late summer fruit is eaten by cardinals and more than 30 other bird species.*

Food

- Not all birds eat sunflowers, so provide as many different food sources as possible. In addition to seeds, birds eat insects, earthworms, nectar, fruits, berries, and nuts.

- Avoid using insecticides if at all possible. If needed, focus any insecticide treatment solely on the pest—no spraying with broad-spectrum pesticides.

- Plant flowers, shrubs, and trees that bear fruits, seeds, berries, or nuts. These include American beautyberry, American holly, Burford holly, coralberry, deciduous holly, elms, figs, native persimmons, oaks (acorns), pecans, pyracantha, sunflowers, tomatoes, and yaupon holly.

- Yes, birds can be a pest in the fruit and vegetable garden, too. If you don't want the birds eating your blackberries, figs, tomatoes, and other crops, you need to use bird netting to cover the plants (all the way to the ground). Other techniques have been tried, and testimonials abound, including red Christmas tree balls hung in tomato plants. The rationale is that the mockingbird pecks at the red "tomato" ball and decides this plant is not worth visiting anymore (no research has documented this, but it sounds fun). Rubber snakes, blow-up owls, and scarecrows are all sold and used with varying reports of success and failure. A specific hint on tomatoes: As soon as the bottom (blossom end) of the tomato turns from green to white with a tinge of red, it is fully mature and will ripen indoors away from the birds. A keen eye and daily visits to the tomato patch will save most of your fruit from the birds.

- Place bird feeders of different types filled with various types of seeds, suet, and fruits. The "typical" bird feeder attracts the "typical" birds: blue jays, cardinals, and sparrows. A platform feeder (wooden frame with screen wire on four legs or hanging from strings) attract these, as well as doves. Column or tube feeders will attract black-capped chickadees, finch-

Platform bird feeders provide ample landing space for mourning doves, which normally feed on the ground.

es, and tufted titmice. Feeders are best placed on poles, shepherd's hooks, or other upright structures. Hanging feeders in trees is asking for squirrels and cats to disrupt your birds.

- Birds also like a "staging" tree near the bird feeders. They land in the tree, check for safety, and then fly down to the feeder. Place your feeders near staging trees but not so close that a cat can use them as a "bird blind" (like, deer blind) or a squirrel can use them as a trampoline to bounce onto the feeder.

- Bird feed varies in composition and quality. Black oil sunflower (versus gray-striped sunflower) seed is perhaps the most universal food for seed-eating birds—cardinals, doves, finches, jays, and sparrows all love it. However, also use seed mixes containing a variety of seed to attract a variety of birds. In general, millet is used as a filler and lowers the quality and price of the feed. Most birds will

"You get what you pay for" can be said about bird seed—buy quality.

CALLER: "Can I prevent my bird seed from creating a weed problem in the landscape?"

ANSWER: "The area beneath the bird feeder can quickly become a weed patch as seeds fall to the ground and germinate. Managing this miniature forest of sunflowers, millet, and corn requires persistent weed pulling or use of an herbicide. Several pre-emergence herbicides are available that can safely eliminate seed germination without harming the birds, pets, or landscape plants. Check with your local nursery and pet store for suggestions. Another option (that is a pain) is to microwave the bird seed to kill the seed embryo but have it remain palatable for the birds."

simply "bill-sweep" the millet out of the feeder to get to the "good stuff." Check with bird experts at local garden and pet stores to expand the smorgasbord of bird feed you can provide to attract the birds you want to see.

• In addition, provide a small area of sand, tiny gravel, or even crushed eggshells. You have seen birds seemingly feeding on a gravel road. They are actually ingesting small gravel and sand into their gizzards to assist in grinding and digesting the seeds they eat.

Water

You can significantly expand the variety of birds visiting your garden by simply providing a water source. Insect-eating birds, such as robins and mockingbirds, will not come to your bird feeder, but they will sure come to a clean, regularly available water source.

Birdbaths and ponds immediately come to mind, but check with suppliers for water misters and drippers especially designed for birds. Don't forget to provide water in the winter months for birds. This is a tough time of year for the birds, and a water source is essential.

Shelter

Birds need cover from predators (the neighborhood cats especially), and they need shelter from rain, summer heat, and winter cold. Dense foliage of trees, shrubs, and vines provides this shelter most often. Species such as blackberry, cherry laurel, deciduous holly, eastern red cedar, juniper, wax myrtle, and yaupon holly provide great shelter. Focus on native plants for use in the garden. They often provide shelter and food for the native birds.

Incorporate areas of native grasses in the garden if possible. Ground-dwelling birds, such as killdeers, meadowlarks, and quail, enjoy the shelter and safety provided by the grasses.

In general, the more trees, shrubs, and other plant shelter you have, the more protection and security are provided for the birds. Open lawn areas, however, play a role in feeding several species of birds, such as flickers, mockingbirds, and robins, because of the insects and worms they find there. In addition, nighthawks and purple martins need open air space to fly and capture insects. They won't venture into wooded areas.

They are not exactly shelter (perhaps environment), but small, open areas of dry, dusty soil are great for birds to use as "dust baths." Like cats and dogs, many birds love to roll in the dust. This activity helps birds eliminate parasites.

Places for Rearing Young

Some birds build nests in trees and shrubs, some build on the ground, some build on ledges and in chimneys, and some will not build except in a birdhouse or tree cavity. Provide as many of these nesting spots as possible in your garden to complete the circle of life for your feathered friends. Like the swallows of Capistrano, many species of birds return to the same spot year after year to raise their young. Give them a family home once, and they will be back for years to come.

Help the birds build nests by not being such a neatnik in the garden. Leave twigs, leaves, pieces of string, feathers, and other small debris that can be used by the birds to build their nests.

When it comes to birdhouses (or nesting boxes), there are building specifications that the "bird zoning commission" requires, or so it seems. Bluebirds

Squirrels—Love 'em or Hate 'em

There seems to be no in between: You either enjoy squirrels coexisting with your feathered friends, or you despise them as selfish pigs in fur coats. You have few options; some may require psychotherapy:

- Enjoy the acrobatic and tenacious attempts, and success, by squirrels to eat food from virtually any bird feeder.
- Appreciate that squirrels need food, too, so feed them specifically the things they love: peanuts, peanut butter, corn, and sunflower seeds.
- TRY to exclude the squirrels from your bird feeders by spraying Pam or WD-40 on the feeder pole (doesn't work for long); mounting an inverted cone-shaped collar around the feeder pole below the feeder; or mounting the collar above the feeder on the support line.
- Purchase one of the Yankee Flipper brands of bird feeders—they truly work. Check out their Web site for a fun video of how this effective invention works (www.yankeeflipper.com).

require a different-sized entry hole to a nesting box than required by purple martins or woodpeckers. Refer to bird books and resources for nesting box specifications for the birds you are trying to attract.

Keep an eye on outdoor cats. They kill thousands of songbirds every year. Flightless baby birds are easy prey for cats. There is not a politically correct answer to this situation, but if you want birds in the garden, keep the cats away.

"Hummers" love blue plumbago.

Hummingbirds

Hummingbirds are migratory, and depending on the season, you may have hummers in your garden from April to October. Hummingbirds are nectar feeders and require a constant supply. You can provide this supply with hummingbird feeders or a diverse variety of flowers on which hummers feed.

Plant these Texas garden plants in full sun to attract hummingbirds to your landscape: anisacanthus, columbine, four-o'clock, foxglove, honeysuckle, lantana, larkspur, petunia, plumbago, all salvias, and verbena.

Irrigation Season Starts in Earnest

This month ushers in the height of the landscape irrigation season, which so often in Texas coincides with drought conditions. The essays this month focus on our role as gardeners and yardeners in protecting the precious natural resource . . . water!

As a county extension horticulturist in San Antonio during the early 1980s, I was fortunate to help bring the Xeriscape concept from Denver to Texas. For over 25 years I have preached the "gospel" of the good news of landscape water conservation. Through the 1980s and 1990s, I crisscrossed the nation, depending on where drought had raised its ugly head. In 1992, I was proud to co-author the first comprehensive book on Xeriscape gardening for the nation, *Xeriscape Gardening: Water Conservation for the American Landscape.*

Landscape water conservation is a widely accepted practice by landscape professionals and homeowners. The strange term "Xeriscape" has been replaced in some locales with other terms, such as "WaterWise," "SmartScape," and "WaterSmart." Regardless of the name, the concepts proclaimed truly remain the same.

Drinking Water and Texas Landscapes

Texas has a finite amount of water resources. As the state's population continues to grow rapidly, the question has been raised: "Will there be enough water in Texas to support its citizens?" This seems to be a pretty heavy question for a gardening book, but it isn't really.

At issue is the use of drinking water in the lawn and garden. Landscape wa-ter use can account for 25 percent of all water used in a Texas city. The percentage increases dramatically to 60 percent for the summer months. For example, the average water use for a residence in Bryan is 6,000 gallons in January; in July it is 16,000 gallons. The difference is primarily landscape and garden irrigation.

Landscape irrigation causes the peak water demand in Texas cities. The "blue industry," composed of municipal water utilities, water districts, and state water agencies, knows this. Their goal is to reduce the peak water demand to preserve current resources for future demand. The blue industry is now asking the question, "Will Texas meet this future demand through education or regulation?" (education is my preference).

Remember the words attributed to Mark Twain, "Whiskey is for drinking and water is for fighting." Emotions boil when Texans discuss property water rights, water ordinances, regulations, and laws. Be aware and be prepared; gardeners and yardeners will be in the fight.

For decades, every Texas schoolchild has learned a worthy scientific concept, "the hydrologic cycle." It states that water is never created or lost; there is the same amount of water on Earth today as there was a billion years ago when the dinosaurs roamed. This is a false assurance. Only 3 percent of the Earth's water is fresh water, and half of that is in glaciers and polar caps.

In the future, desalinization of ocean water will become a freshwater source, but only for those cities, states, countries, and individuals that can afford it.

Building huge new water reservoirs (10,000 to 30,000 acres) is now being discussed and cussed. The "NIMBY" concept ("not-in-my-back-yard") is voiced along with a host of contentious issues regarding any new reservoir: environmental impact, lengthy construction timelines (10 to 15 years), funding concerns, and who owns and gets to use the water.

For the immediate future, the best way to preserve freshwater resources is through conservation. Texas water uses range from flushing toilets to drinking water, fire safety, manufacturing and business, recreation, supporting endangered species, and keeping a green lawn and landscape. When water shortages occur due to drought or if long-term shortages are projected due to population growth, allocation of water is discussed. Allocation is regulation and seeks to rank the importance of water use from most important to least.

Lawn and garden water use is the lowest priority. Keeping a green lawn simply does not compare to human consumption of water. This knowledge heaps a social responsibility on each gardener and yardener to reduce the amount of drinking water used in the landscape and garden.

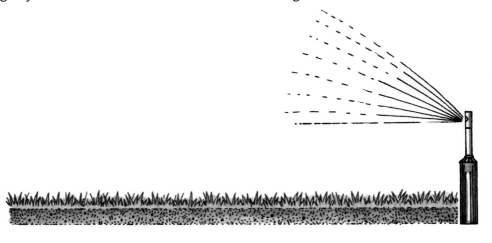

You have now read the "blue" side of the equation; now read the much more fun "green" side presented in the following essays.

(*Note:* I realize I get a bit preachy about landscape water use. I have a selfish reason to be so passionate—my children. As many philosophers have exclaimed, "We don't use resources from years past; we borrow from the future." I want my children, and yours, to have the quality of life that ample water resources bring. I also recognize that many of you are already converted and strive to be water wise. I want to inspire and arm you to become disciples of the "good news." Do I hear an Amen!?!)

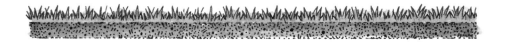

Water Conservation for Texas Landscapes

Whatever catchy name it is called, landscape water conservation makes good sense. Immediate results include reduced irrigation, lower water bills, less maintenance, and a higher-quality landscape. Whether Xeriscape, WaterSmart, WaterWise, or SmartScape, landscape water conservation is quality landscaping that conserves water and protects the environment. Water-wise landscapes are not bleak, rock-filled landscapes accented by wagon wheels and dead cattle skulls. Xeriscapes are not "zeroscapes"!

Water-efficient landscapes incorporate seven principles to produce beautiful landscapes that can reduce landscape water use by half:

1. Planning and design
2. Soil analysis and improvement
3. Appropriate plant selection
4. Practical lawn areas
5. Efficient irrigation
6. Use of mulches
7. Appropriate maintenance

Planning and Design

The norm in home landscaping is a limited foundation planting and 5,000+ square feet of lawn. Changing this norm is a huge challenge for proponents of landscape water conservation.

Try to envision the landscapes in *Southern Living* magazine, *Better Homes and Gardens,* and *Sunset* magazine. The landscapes within these magazines are high-quality landscapes. There are no "lawnscapes" showcased in these magazines. The quality landscapes are balanced landscapes. There is a proportional balance between the lawn area,

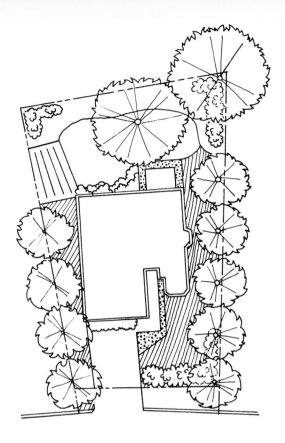

planting beds, and the "hardscape" (e.g., decks, patios, walkways, and driveways).

As you strive to develop a quality landscape, remember that Xeriscape (and other terms) is not a style of landscaping; it is a philosophy. There are Southwest-style Xeriscapes, Mediterranean-style Xeriscapes, and Asian-style Xeriscapes. You can determine the style landscape you want and incorporate water-efficient plantings and practices.

Regardless of the style, water-efficient landscapes should always be in tune with the environment that surrounds them. It is as inappropriate to have cactus in Beaumont as it is to have azaleas in El Paso.

The first step to understanding your landscape environment is determining the average annual rainfall your community receives, using local resources or, for an estimate, the adjacent map (remember, however, that averages mean you're wrong 100 percent of the time). Texas is known for its feast-or-famine rainfall cycles. In Texas, you are always 7 days from a drought!

Texas rainfall averages range from 58 inches in Beaumont to 9 inches in El Paso. The ultimate water-efficient landscape would require no supplemental irrigation. This is nearly possible in Beaumont and impossible in El Paso. What is possible in your landscape will be determined by natural rainfall, soil type, plant selection, landscape maintenance practices, and the landscape design.

Every house has a design, and so should every landscape. Landscape design professionals, computer programs, demonstration gardens, and/or your creativity can develop a design for your water-efficient landscape. With a design in hand, you can install a landscape immediately or over a series of years to reduce large expenditures. Some Texas cities (e.g., Austin, El Paso, Houston, San Antonio) offer water rebate programs and assistance in developing water-efficient landscapes. Check with your local water utility for such programs.

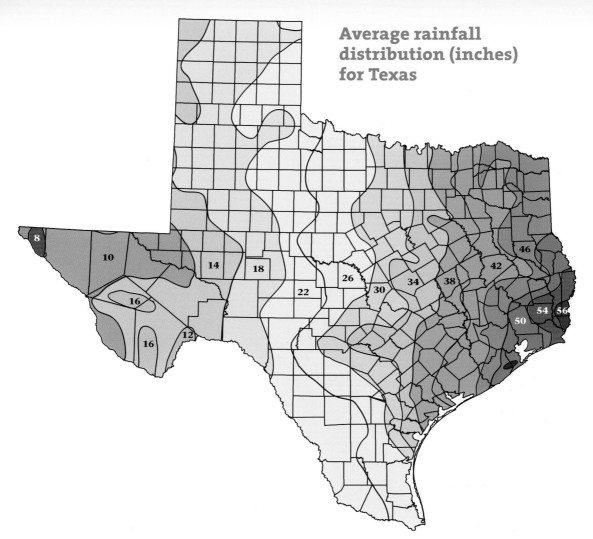

Average rainfall distribution (inches) for Texas

Cool, green landscapes full of beautiful plants that are maintained with water-efficient practices are possible throughout Texas.

matter to the soil for landscape plantings and gardens is paramount in Texas. Thorough soil preparation increases the soil's ability to absorb and store water in a form available to the plants. For trees,

Soil Analysis & Improvement

Creating and preserving a healthy soil are essential to maintain plant health and conserve water. Adding organic

incorporating organic matter is not practical or necessary. For large lawn areas, soil preparation using organic matter is generally not economically feasible. Focus your soil preparation efforts on larger landscape and garden plantings.

Appropriate Plant Selection

Select trees, shrubs, and groundcovers that are adapted to your region's soil and climate. Texas is blessed with beautiful native plants that are naturally adapted to various regions. Most native plants will have lower irrigation requirements and fewer pest problems than many nonadapted, exotic plants. Remember, though, that just because a plant is native to Texas does not mean it is adapted to your location. Whether the plants are native or exotic, the key is to use plants adapted to your area. For guidance, refer to landscape plant lists within this book, consult local nursery professionals and experts, and visit botanical gardens and demonstration gardens.

When you are striving to reduce landscape irrigation requirements, it is critical to understand that lawns are the highest user of irrigation water in the landscape. Large trees may use 250 gallons of water per day, but irrigating with 250 gallons of drinking water daily is not required. Trees have a huge root system mining water from a huge volume of soil. Trees have a big "bank account" of water that is filled by natural rainfall. Lawns have a very small bank account that requires frequent deposits (sounds like my bank account). You cannot wait for natural rainfall to make the next deposit, and high-quality drinking water must be used to maintain a green lawn.

Carefully select the best turfgrass according to its intended use, water requirement, sunlight conditions, and maintenance needs. From Bermudagrass to St. Augustine to buffalograss, each has its advantages and disadvantages. Refer to the April essay "Lawns 101" to aid in selecting the best grass for your landscape.

*Cenizo or Texas sage (*Leucophyllum frutescens)

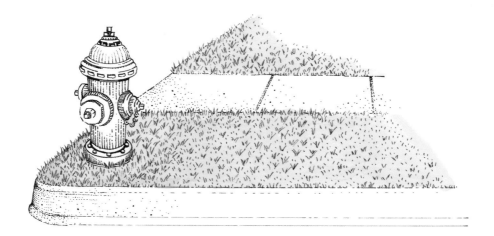

Practical Lawn Areas

The easiest way to define practical lawn areas is to define "impractical" lawn areas: long, narrow strips of turf between the sidewalk and the street and between houses, and small, odd-shaped areas filled with turf. When designing or evaluating lawn size in the landscape, consider more blocky, square, and rectangular lawn areas that require less irrigation and maintenance. Narrow and odd-shaped lawn areas are difficult for any irrigation system to water efficiently.

A significant reduction in irrigation and maintenance can also be achieved by reducing the lawn size through the use of patios, decks, and landscape plantings. Lawns have become the default in the landscape due to the low cost of establishment.

Are you tired of watering, mowing, trimming, and caring for a vast lawn area? Consider the goal of removing 200 square feet of lawn from your landscape each year. Look for lawn areas that are not used for recreation or other functions. No one is suggesting the kids play football games on lava rock, but wall-to-wall turf is not necessary. Increase landscape quality by replacing areas with groundcovers, shrub plantings, decks or patios, or vegetable gardens. A manageable size to establish new plantings, and a functional and economical size for decks and patios, is 200 square feet.

Efficient Irrigation

Irrigating plants only when they need it is the most important concept in landscape water conservation. Of the tremendous amounts of water applied to lawns and gardens, much of it is never absorbed by the plants and put to use.

Some water is lost to runoff by being applied too rapidly, and some water evaporates from exposed, unmulched soil; but the greatest waste of water is applying too much too often.

Most lawns receive twice as much water as they require for a healthy appearance. The key to watering lawns is to apply water only when necessary and wet the soil thoroughly. This creates a deep, well-rooted lawn that efficiently uses water stored in the soil.

To know when to water the lawn, simply observe the grass. Wilting and discoloration are signs of water stress. At the first sign of wilting, you have 24 to 48 hours to water before serious injury occurs. Apply 1 inch of water to the lawn as rapidly as possible without runoff. This will fill up the soil bank account of moisture whether in clay or sand.

Trees and shrubs need more frequent watering from planting time until they have established a larger root system, which may take months. Once established, plants can then be weaned to tolerate less frequent irrigation, or no irrigation, depending on natural rainfall.

To complete a water-wise landscape, drip-irrigate all flower and shrub beds

CALLER: "How do I water my huge live oak tree?"
ANSWER: "Tree watering is misunderstood. Laying a hose at the trunk of a large tree and letting it run for hours does not water a tree. You may have watered China but not the tree. To irrigate trees and large shrubs, apply water just inside and a little beyond the 'drip line,' not at the trunk. The drip line is the area directly below the outermost reaches of the branches. This is where the feeding root system of a tree or shrub is located. Simply lay a slowly running hose on the ground, and move it around the drip line as each area becomes saturated to a depth of eight to ten inches. For large trees, this watering technique may take several hours."

and vegetable gardens. Fear of the unknown is no longer an excuse. Landscape and irrigation contractors stand ready to assist you with a new drip system or to convert your spray system to drip. To learn more about drip irrigation, read the March essay "Saving Water Drip by Drip."

Use of Mulches

Use a mulch wherever possible—in flower beds, shrub plantings, and vegetable gardens and around young fruit and shade trees. Mulch conserves water by significantly reducing moisture evaporation from the soil surface. Mulch also reduces weed populations, prevents soil compaction, and keeps soil temperatures more moderate. Simply put: mulch, mulch, mulch!

Appropriate Maintenance

Proper maintenance reduces irrigation requirements. Maintenance practices, such as replenishing mulch, mowing, weeding, and fertilizing, impact the water efficiency of any landscape, as well as the landscape's ability to survive a drought.

- Organic mulches will decompose and sometimes wash away, so check regularly and replenish when necessary.
- Remove weeds from the lawn, landscape plantings, and vegetable gardens. Weeds aggressively compete against desired plants for water.
- Raise the mowing height to help lawns survive dry conditions. For example, raise the mowing height on St. Augustinegrass to 4 inches or more during drought.

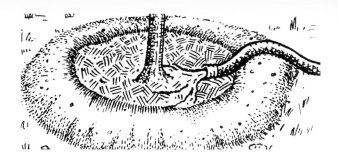

- Do not overfertilize the lawn. Too much fertilizer generates excess growth that requires more irrigation and mowing.
- Check the irrigation system for proper performance, and adjust if needed. Make sure sprinkler heads are not wasting water by spraying sidewalks, driveways, fences, or plantings that don't need irrigation.
- Watch for insect pests and plant diseases. Eliminating pest problems helps your plants be more water efficient.

Landscape water conservation is an essential component in preserving water resources for future generations. Make a commitment today to implement these principles, and reap the many benefits of landscape water conservation.

CALLER: "I have been watering, but my plant's leaves are wilted and yellowing, and some are brown. What is the cause?"

ANSWER: "You have probably watered too much or too little. Sounds like a nonsense answer, but both can cause these symptoms in plants. General yellowing (chlorosis) that progresses to brown (necrosis) can be disease related but is more often water related.

"To determine which is the cause, over- or underwatering, feel the leaves: If the brown leaves are crispy, then underwatering is probably the answer; if the brown leaves are pliable (flexible), then overwatering is most likely.

"Overwatering can also cause a plant to wilt, just like underwatering. Overwatering saturates the soil and drives oxygen out of the soil. Without this oxygen, the plant's ability to absorb water is reduced; thus, wilting occurs. If this situation continues, the root system begins to rot and the plant health diminishes, thus the yellow and brown leaves.

"Use that moisture meter of yours (your index finger) to touch the soil and determine when to water. Cool to the touch indicates adequate moisture in the soil. Warm, drier soil means it is time to water.

"Most plants, both outdoor and indoor, prefer a wet-dry cycle. Water the plant thoroughly, let the soil moisture level dry adequately, and then water again. The health of your plants will increase significantly."

All Plants Welcome in Water-Efficient Landscapes

Perhaps the biggest resistance to water-efficient landscaping is the false notion that only certain plants should be used. All plants are welcome. As long as a plant can be grown successfully in your area, then the decision simply becomes where to put it.

Zoning the plants based on water need drives the decision of where to place plants and allows the use of all adapted plants in a water-efficient landscape. The situation in most Texas landscapes is that the irrigation system must overwater one group of plants to meet the needs of others. The lawn, which requires the most irrigation water to keep it green, often dictates the schedule; thus, landscape plantings are overwatered. Significant water waste occurs because shrub and groundcover plantings do not need as frequent irrigation as the lawn.

Look at the landscape of any bank in town. The FDIC requires that banks plant Asiatic jasmine as a groundcover (just fooling, but it seems that way). The lawn and the jasmine are watered using the same schedule. Asiatic jasmine should seldom, if ever, be irrigated in areas east of IH-35 in Texas, believe it or not!

As you renovate your existing landscape or establish a new one, follow these guidelines to zone your plants according to irrigation need. Existing irrigation systems will need to be renovated or new systems designed to irrigate the zones separately.

Three different plant zones should be incorporated in a water-efficient landscape. Each should be watered as noted once the plants are well established, which may take a few months:

- Plants in the "regular watering zone" require water once a week or more in the absence of rain.
- Plants in the "occasional watering zone" require watering once a month or so, in the absence of rain.
- Plants in the "natural rainfall zone" require only natural rainfall.

Every region in Texas has a palette of plants from which to choose that are adapted to the soil, temperature extremes, and pest problems of the area. The challenge is to categorize the plants based on expected water requirements. By using the categories of regular watering, occasional watering, and natural rainfall, most gardeners and yardeners can place the plants from their region into these water-use zones.

For example, regions of Texas that average 30+ inches of rainfall per year would use the following categorization:

- Regular watering zone—lawns and annual flowers
- Occasional watering zone—perennial flowers and water-sensitive woody shrubs and vines (e.g., azalea, camellia, gardenia)
- Natural watering zone—all trees, plus drought-resistant woody shrubs and vines

As average annual rainfall dwindles in West and South Texas, the regular watering zone would expand to include perennial flowers; the occasional watering zone would include the toughest perennials and more tender shrubs and vines; and the natural rainfall zone would include only the toughest native shrubs and groundcovers and all trees.

All plants do have a place in a water-efficient landscape. If you need help in zoning your landscape, ask a nursery or landscape professional, Master Gardener, or county extension agent. You will be well on your way to reduced water bills and creation of a beautiful landscape that requires much less frequent irrigation.

Desert Gardening: Plants for West Texas

Desert gardens showcase the natural beauty of West Texas–tough plants and should be a landscaping norm in low rainfall areas, not lawnscapes or "zero-scapes." Too often, people want to live in the desert and bring with them their landscape styles and plants from higher-rainfall areas of the country. The result is either very high water bills or very low-quality landscapes.

For areas of Texas receiving annual rainfall of 15 inches or less, the number of plants that thrive under natural rainfall with occasional irrigation is far fewer than that of higher-rainfall areas. However, as the list below indicates, there are plenty of West Texas–tough plants, both native and adapted, to create wonderful desert gardens filled with flowers, fine and bold textures, and unique plant shapes.

The plants on the list are considered "low-water-use plants" and are adapted to El Paso, which has the lowest annual rainfall of any large Texas city. Daphne Richards, county extension horticulturist in El Paso, contributed significantly to this list and defines "low-water-use" the following way:

Low-water-use plants require very little supplemental irrigation. Once established in the landscape, these plants need to be watered at least once per week during the hottest months of the summer and once or twice per month in the winter. It takes approximately 3 to 5 years to establish a tree, 2 to 3 years to establish a shrub, and 1 to 2 years to establish vines, groundcovers, and flowers.

People often ask Daphne, "Why do I need to water these desert plants? They live on natural rainfall in the desert." Reality sets in as you look at the plants in the desert during low-rainfall times of year. Plants have strategies to survive no rainfall: they drop their foliage, sacrifice a branch or two, or turn brown. Bottom line: Most desert plant species look pretty ugly when they are in a survival mode. In a desert garden, a little supplemental irrigation allows these plants to shine virtually year-round, showing off their true natural splendor.

Cold tolerance is a characteristic that must also be considered in desert gardening. El Paso and the higher elevations of West Texas are colder in winter than Midland, Odessa, San Angelo, and Abilene. Some plants may suffer freeze damage to leaves and shoots in Midland but be frozen to death, roots and all, in El Paso (e.g., esperanza/yellow bells). The plants listed below are cold hardy in El Paso with a few noted exceptions (to be used in milder climates). Turn to local nursery professionals, county extension agents, or Master Gardeners for advice on cold hardiness of specific plants for your area, and ask to see a surviving specimen before planting.

Here are a few dozen West Texas–tough plants to consider for desert gardening. It is notable that several of these tough, low-water-use plants can also be grown successfully in Texas landscapes with higher rainfall (e.g., desert willow, esperanza, red yucca, rosemary, salvias, Texas sage). Supplemental irrigation will seldom be needed for such plants once they are established in higher-rainfall landscapes. If you choose to grow these plants, spend extra time and effort preparing the soil to ensure good drainage (e.g., adding pine bark, and perhaps pea gravel, to existing soil). Cross-check this plant list with other "Select" plant lists in this book to choose plants adapted to your area, or check with local plant experts for advice.

Select Plants for Desert Gardening

TREES

Argentina saguaro (*Trichocereus terscheckii*) (not cold hardy in El Paso)

Arizona cypress (*Cupressus arizonica*)

'Desert Museum' palo verde (*Parkinsonia* hybrid)

Desert willow (*Chilopsis linearis*)

Honey mesquite (*Prosopis glandulosa*)

Italian stone pine (*Pinus pinea*)

Sweet acacia (*Acacia farnesiana* var. 'Smallii')

*Autumn sage (*Salvia greggii*)*

SHRUBS AND DESERT ACCENT PLANTS

Agaves
  Century plant (*Agave americana*)
  Chisos agave (*A. havardiana*)
  Mescal (*A. neomexicana*)
  Many other *Agave* species
Desert bird of paradise (*Caesalpinia gilliesii*)
Mexican bird of paradise (*Caesalpinia mexicana*)
Native fairy duster (*Calliandra eriophylla*)
Nolinas
  Bear grass (*Nolina bigelovii*)
  Mexican grass tree (*N. longifolia*)

Saw grass (*N. microcarpa*)
Many other *Nolina* species and varieties
Prairie flame sumac (*Rhus trilobata*)
Prickly pears or opuntias (*Opuntia* spp., includes spineless)
Red bird of paradise or pride of Barbados (*Caesalpinia pulcherrima*) (not completely cold hardy in El Paso)
Sotol (*Dasylirion wheeleri*)
Texas mountain laurel (*Sophora secundiflora*)
Texas sage, cenizo, or Texas Ranger (*Leucophyllum frutescens*, other species and varieties)
Wooly butterfly bush (*Buddleia marrubiifolia*)
Yuccas
  Red yucca (*Hesperaloe parviflora*)
  Soft leaf yucca (*Yucca recurvifolia*)
  Many other yucca species

FLOWERS AND GROUNDCOVERS

Blackfoot daisy (*Melampodium leucanthum*)
Dalea, trailing (*Dalea greggii*)
Esperanza or yellow bells (*Tecoma stans*, various varieties, 'Angustata') (not cold hardy in El Paso but worth using as annual)
Firebush (*Hamelia patens*) (not cold hardy but worth using as annual)
Mexican rain lily (*Zephyranthes citrine*)
Penstemon (*Penstemon* spp.)

Red Indian blanket (*Gaillardia
amblyodon*)
Rosemary, prostrate and upright
(*Rosmarinus officinalis*)
Salvias
Autumn sage (*Salvia greggii*)
Cleveland salvia (*S. clevelandii*)
Many other *Salvia* species

(*Note:* Creation of this list required generous assistance from plant experts: John Begnaud, county extension agent, San Angelo; Cynthia Mueller, extension colleague, College Station; Daphne Richards, county extension agent, El Paso; and Wade Roitsch, Yucca Do Nursery, Hempstead.)

Lawns Don't Waste Water; People Do!

Throughout the past decade, zealous water utilities have launched campaigns to regulate the use of lawns in landscapes, either by restricting the lawn size or eliminating certain turfgrass varieties (e.g., St. Augustine). Since lawns are the highest user of irrigation water in the landscape, focus on the lawns is warranted. The disconnect arises when regulation targets an object lacking intelligence, a lawn. The actions of people are the problem in this situation. Lawns don't waste water; people do! Major universities have spent decades breeding turfgrasses for lawn use. Not a single one has bred a turfgrass that can reach up and turn on the water faucet.

Heated debate continues surrounding the water requirement of lawns. Misinformation and hidden agendas have fueled this controversy; however, there are some well-documented facts about the lawn:

- The lawn is an integral component of the landscape.
- It is the best recreational surface for children and athletes.
- It has a tremendous mitigating effect on the environment by reducing heat loads and noise in the concrete-laden cities and preventing water and air pollution.
- It is second only to a virgin forest in the ability to harvest water and recharge soil moisture and groundwater resources.
- As a design component, it provides landscape unity and simplicity while inviting participation in the landscape.

The lawn has become a focus in reducing landscape water use because of the tremendous overuse of irrigation water in an effort to maintain an expansive green lawn.

Within the traditional landscape, the lawn composes the major portion of the total landscaped area and thus receives the majority of landscape irrigation. Lawn irrigation can be reduced while the homeowner continues to derive the many benefits of turfgrass.

Following are specific strategies to reduce lawn irrigation:

- Irrigate properly based on when the lawn actually needs watering; turn the irrigation time clock off, and let the lawn show you when to irrigate.
- Increase mowing heights during summer to decrease lawn water use and increase drought tolerance.
- Decrease fertilizer rates, and properly schedule fertilizations.
- Let irrigated lawns turn brown where appropriate, or establish non-irrigated turfgrass areas (e.g., homes with acreage, in between irrigated sports turf in parks, in the rough on golf courses, and highway rights-of-way).
- Place lawn areas in landscape irrigation zones based on water requirements so that lawns can be watered separately from other landscape plantings.

- Select adapted, lower-water-demand turfgrass species and varieties (e.g., buffalograss requires 25 percent less irrigation to maintain a green lawn than other species but is not adapted to West, East, and Southeast Texas).
- Reduce irrigated lawn areas to only those that provide function (e.g., recreational, aesthetic, foot traffic, dust and noise abatement, glare reduction, temperature mitigation); look for lawn areas that can be replaced with groundcovers, landscape plantings, or decks and patios (e.g., Why is there lawn between houses; between the sidewalk and the street; or in a long, narrow median?).

By implementing these strategies, homeowners can reduce lawn irrigation requirements and still reap the many benefits of a cool, green lawn.

"Our lawns have a drinking problem, and we are the cause!"

Timely Tips

Flowers & Pretty Plants

• Recognize that Texas summer heat is not the same as in New Jersey, "the Garden State." Flowers tough enough to flourish in Texas heat would laugh at the heat in New Jersey (of course, Texas flowers would freeze their buds off in New Jersey winters). For a list of the most heat-tolerant annuals and perennials, refer to this month's essay "Sizzling Summer Color for Texas Gardens."

• Keep on deadheading, fertilizing, and watering your flower beds to maintain your "yard-of-the-month" status.

Garden Design

• Consider designing and installing a truly water-wise landscape, one in tune with the environment in which you live. In Texas, it is as inappropriate to put cactus in Beaumont as it is azaleas in El Paso. Water-wise landscapes (often called Xeriscape landscapes) are high-quality landscapes that conserve water and protect the environment. If you need design help, turn to garden designers and landscape architects.

Soil & Mulch

• Mulch, mulch, mulch. It is the highest-impact, lowest-tech water-conserving practice.

• Use rock mulches only when they blend aesthetically with the natural environment. White crushed limestone just simply looks out of place in East Texas.

Water

• Expect your water bills to double during the summer due to lawn and garden irrigation. Implement water-conserving garden practices described in this month's essay "Water Conservation for Texas Landscapes."

• Water the lawn and garden between sundown and sunrise, when the wind and temperatures are lower.

• Irrigate at the first sign of moisture stress in the lawn, landscape plants, or vegetable garden.

• If you don't use drip irrigation, make a commitment to set up at least one flower bed this summer. Drip reduces water use significantly and should be the standard for all landscape and garden plantings. Licensed irrigators can be a real help in designing and installing your first drip system.

Plant Care

- Eliminate water-guzzling weeds from flower and shrub beds, vegetable gardens, and lawns. Pulling, hoeing, mowing, tilling, mulching, and, if warranted, spraying are among the arsenal for killing weeds.
- Know that neem oil and extracts are the biggest advance in organic pesticides in decades. Research documents the effectiveness of neem oil and extracts in controlling both insects and diseases. This organic pesticide is derived from the neem tree of India and can be used on ornamental plants and vegetable and fruit crops.

Trees, Shrubs & Vines

- Believe it or not, most adapted shrubs and all trees can survive without any supplemental irrigation in the eastern half of the state. Shrubs are opportunistic and will use any water you give them, but do they need it? Test your shrubs this summer, and see how little water you can give them and still keep them healthy and attractive.
- Understand, however, that in the western half of the state, supplemental irrigation is a must for most shrubs and trees to survive and thrive. Still, the challenge is how little water must

be applied to maintain plant health. Watch the plants for signs of extreme water stress, such as browning of the leaf edges, leaf yellowing or wilting, and dropping foliage.

Lawns

- To help the lawn withstand summer heat, raise the mower height to the maximum level recommended: Bermuda—2 inches; St. Augustine— 4 inches; and buffalo—6 inches.
- Watch for drought stress in the lawn—dull, gray-green color, leaf blade rolling, or footprints left on the lawn after you walk across it. Irrigate as soon as possible.
- Apply 1 inch of water during any irrigation so that you water 6 inches deep in clay soil and 12 inches deep in a sandy soil (or prepared garden soil). Avoid runoff by multicycling: water one station (area), then another and another, and back through the stations (areas) again.
- Watch for chinch bug damage in St. Augustine lawns. Generally, damage occurs first in the hottest area of the lawn along driveways and streets. If you see yellowing patches, step to the edge of the patch where the grass is greener; get on your hands and knees; use your fingers to separate the grass; and look at the soil level for tiny

($\frac{1}{8}$-inch) black insects with white wings or for immature red bugs with a white waistband. These are chinch bugs. Control is relatively easy using an organic or chemical insecticide.

- Don't jump to conclusions. Yellowing or browning patches similar in appearance to chinch bug damage can occur because of a weakness in the irrigation system. The system may not be evenly distributing the water across the lawn. Check for this by throwing the cake pans from the kitchen out into the lawn. The same amount of water should fall in each pan. Check the pan in the yellowing patch—any water in the pan? If not, adjusting the sprinkler head should eliminate the discoloration.

Vegetables, Herbs & Fruits

- With the occurrence of summer heat, strive to mature fruit from the spring garden. The goal is to provide enough care to get the crops to harvest. There is little need for heavy fertilizer or pesticide applications. Just water, monitor pests, and harvest vegetables when ripe.

- With outdoor heat building, garden indoors by planting an herb dish garden. Fill a shallow but wide container with good potting soil, and plant a combination of herb trans-

plants, such as basil, chives, oregano, and rosemary. Place in a sunny window, and enjoy gardening in air-conditioned comfort.

- In areas of the vegetable garden vacated by harvested crops, pull weeds and turn in organic matter to prepare for the fall garden (planting will start next month!).

- Texas-grown vegetables and fruits are pouring into grocery stores and produce stands this month. Black-eyed peas, green beans, onions, peaches, peppers, squash, sweet corn, tomatoes, and watermelons grown locally and shipped short distances help guarantee freshness and quality. With a "global" produce market, it is often tough to know when vegetables were harvested, how far they were shipped, and how long they have been in storage. Use the table in the May essay "Texas Produce: When to Purchase?" as your shopping guide for quality vegetables (and fruit).

- Control Bermudagrass and other lawn or pasture grasses that compete heavily with fruit and nut trees for water and nutrients. Managers of the best orchards combat this competition by eliminating grass and weeds under the tree's canopy with mulch or herbicides. In the home orchard, adding mulch can effectively manage the grass and reduce evaporation of soil moisture.

Butterflies, Birds & Squirrels

- Pull out the binoculars. Bird activity is at a peak in June as adults get away from the nests and the juveniles spread their wings and fly!

- Try different bird feeders and feed to see how many different bird species you can attract into your garden.

Notes:

July

*Monarch butterfly and caterpillar on
butterfly weed (Asclepias tuberosa)*

DOG DAYS OF SUMMER

Go Tropical!

'Pink Flare' hardy hibiscus (Hibiscus x 'Pink Flare')

Whether in Amarillo or Brownsville, you can bring a tropical flare to your garden through landscape plantings and container gardens. Tropical plants feature flowers of vivid warm-season colors (i.e., red, yellow, and orange) and/or bold foliage. These characteristics can infuse a festive feel to the garden. Or the swaying foliage of palms can steal you away to a tropical paradise where you lounge and sip from your favorite beverage (sounds like a beer commercial, *verdad?*).

For purposes of this essay, a tropical plant is defined as any plant that looks "tropical" and annually suffers freeze damage ranging from leaf burn to death of the entire plant.

If you live north of San Antonio, don't immediately discount your ability to grow tropical plants. Many tropicals planted in the ground will serve as annuals for you because of low winter temperatures. Remember, too, that most tropicals can be grown in mobile containers that can be moved to the garage during freezing temperatures.

There are thousands of tropical plants from which to choose. Robert Lee Riffle's book *The Tropical Look: An Encyclopedia of Dramatic Landscape Plants* is a great tropical gardening reference (Timber Press, 1999; American Horticulture Society book award). His most recent book, *An Encyclopedia of Cultivated Palms*, was coauthored with Paul Craft (Timber Press, 2003).

To get you started, here are some tropical favorites:

TROPICAL VINES

Allamanda (*Allamanda cathartica*)—scented, 3-inch tubular, yellow blooms; hardy to 30°F

Blue sky flower (*Thunbergia*

Dog Days of Summer

Many folks think the "dog days of summer" refers to that time of year when it is so hot that the hound dogs of the South are found lounging daily under the porch or shade tree to retreat from the heat. Actually, the phrase has an ancient astrological origin. The Romans noted that the brightest star (Sirius) in the Big Dog constellation (Canis Major) was lined up with the sun during the hottest time of the year. This conjunction of Sirius and the sun was believed to cause the peak heat of summer. The "dog days of summer" occurred 20 days before and 20 days after the conjunction, July 3 to August 11.

grandiflora)—ropelike vine, large leaves, and large tubular blue flowers; hardy to 25°F to 30°F

Bougainvillea (*Bougainvillea* spp.)—classic rosy red flowers (bracts), now dozens of colors; shrubby vine; can be sheared into hedge in South Texas; hardy to 20°F to 25°F

Coral vine or queen's wreath (*Antigonon leptopus*)—hanging clusters of pink flowers; hardy to 15°F to 20°F

Hyacinth bean (*Dolichos lablab* or *Lablab purpureus*)—cluster of purple flowers with purple pods, white and red varieties available; generally grown from seed, so check mail-order catalogues; hardy to 32°F

Mandevilla (*Mandevilla* spp.)—large, scented, tubular, pink or white blooms with yellow centers; hardy to 35°F

Rangoon creeper (*Quisqualis indica*)—truly a tropical vine that freezes back to the ground at 30°F and will grow back from the roots in areas south of College Station to San Antonio; can be used as an annual in the rest of Texas; flowers open white, darken to pink and finally to red; flowers have a wonderful tropical fragrance; can be invasive in areas with very mild winters

Groundcovers

Lantana (*Lantana* spp.)—trailing varieties in yellow, purple, lavender, or white; hardy to 20°F

Purple heart or wandering Jew (*Setcreasea pallida*)—purple, succulent-like vine with occasional pink flowers at ends; foliage hardy to 25°F, roots hardy to 15°F (sprouts back from roots)

Verbena (*Verbena* spp. or *Abronia* spp.)—Texas native with flowers of blue, purple, red, pink, or rose; hardy to 20°F

TROPICALS WITH BOLD, UNIQUE
FOLIAGE AND/OR SHOWY FLOWERS

Bananas (*Musa* spp.)—tremendous number of sizes and foliage colors; search around and try what you can find; don't expect banana fruit unless the main trunk achieves an age of 18 months without freezing back; root hardy to 20°F

Bird-of-paradise (*Strelitzia reginae*)—bold, straplike foliage with unique blooms; best grown in containers except in South Texas and along the Gulf Coast; hardy to 32°F

Butterfly iris or African iris (*Moraea* or *Dietes iridioides*)—fine, swordlike foliage with unique three-lobed white iris blooms; root hardy to 20°F

Cannas (*Canna* spp.)—broad, straplike foliage and striking blooms; dozens of foliage and bloom colors; foliage hardy to 32°F, root hardy to 10°F

Citrus—bold, glossy green foliage, scented flowers, plus fruit (sometimes); hardiness varies but generally must have freeze protection

Elephant ears and taro (*Colocasia* spp. and *Alocasia* spp.)—huge elephant-ear or arrow-shaped foliage in many sizes and color variations; planted from bulbs; hardy to 32°F

Esperanza or yellow bells (*Tecoma stans*)—5-foot-tall or taller shrub with masses of tubular yellow flowers; foliage hardy to 20°F, root hardy to 10°F

Gingers, variegated shell ginger (*Alpinia zerumbet* 'Variegated')—popular ginger known for foliage, not flowers; broad, variegated green and yellow leaves; one of only many potential tropical plants in the ginger family, Zingiberaceae; foliage hardy to 25°F, root hardy to 20°F

Hibiscus (*Hibiscus* spp.)—hundreds of varieties known for their huge blooms of red, pink, yellow, and combinations; two major types: Chinese hibiscus—glossy green foliage, not freeze tolerant, best used in containers; and hardy hibiscus—can be planted in containers or the garden, root hardy to 10°F once established all season

Lantana (*Lantana* spp.)—upright varieties with flowers of red, pink, orange, yellow, white, and combinations; root hardy to 10°F

Louisiana iris (*Iris* spp.)—tall, swordlike foliage with tremendous variety of bloom colors of yellow, purple, maroon, and multicolored; foliage hardy to 20°F, root hardy to 15°F

Mexican bird of paradise (*Caesalpinia mexicana*)—large shrub with medium-textured foliage and gaudy bloom spikes of sulfur yellow; foliage hardy to 20°F, root hardy to 10°F

Mexican oleander (*Asclepias curassavica*)—oleander-like foliage with pincushion flowers of yellow, red, and orange; foliage hardy to 25°F, root hardy to 20°F

Oleander (*Nerium oleander*)—small to large shrub with wide variety of colorful summertime blooms; colors range from hot pink, red, light pink, yellow, white, and cream; varieties range in hardiness, with the most hardy being foliage hardy to 20°F, root hardy to 10°F or lower (For more information, refer to the Web site of the International Oleander Society, Galveston.)

Pride of Barbados (*Caesalpinia pulcherrima*)—large shrub with fine, mimosa-like foliage and extremely gaudy spikes of yellow and red blooms; foliage hardy to 30°F, root hardy to 10°F

Thryallis, golden thryallis (*Galphimia gracilis*)—handsome shrub with a profusion of dainty five-petaled yellow flowers; fine-textured, glossy green foliage; butterfly plant; foliage hardy to 32°F, root hardy to 20°F

Tricolor hibiscus (*Hibiscus tiliaceus*) —medium-sized shrub with flowers of no importance; the variegated leaves of white, green, and dark red are all the show; foliage hardy to 32°F, root hardy to 25°F

Tropical giant spider lily (*Hymenocallis* spp. 'Tropical Giant')— enjoyed primarily for its luxuriant kelly green, straplike foliage; produces white blooms in midsummer; foliage hardy to 32°F, root hardy to 20°F

Variegated tapioca or cassava (*Manihot esculenta*)—deeply lobed green leaves accented with radiating yellow stripes; red stems contrast with the foliage; shrub grows to 6 feet; foliage hardy to 32°F, root hardy to 25°F

Cold-Hardy Palms (from Most to Least; °F)	
Needle palm	−10
Windmill palm	5
Mediterranean fan palm	5–10
California fan palm	10
Dwarf palmetto palm	10
Pindo palm	10
Sago palm	10
Cabbage palmetto	10–15
Canary Island date palm	10–15
Mexican fan palm	10–15
Texas sabal palm	10–15
Pygmy date palm	25

Note: Obviously, this is not an exact science, so check with local experts to identify surviving specimens in your community. Also, palms get hardier with age.

Palms

Mediterranean fan palm (Chamaerops humilis)

Canary Island date palm (Phoenix xanariensis)

to medium texture.Cold-hardy palms canbe grown in Texas, especially south of a concave arching line from Nacogdoches to Austin to Uvalde to the Big

No group of plants evokes a more tropical illusion than palms. The sway of the graceful, feathery leaves or the rustling sound of the broad fan leaves can make your mind's eye envision tropical beaches and relaxation.

Palms are divided into two types based on leaf shape: fan palms and feather palms. Fan palms have broad, hand-shaped (palmate) leaves and, depending on the species, provide a bold dramatic or fine calming texture to the landscape. Feather palms have feather-shaped (pinnate), graceful leaves (fronds) that range from a very fine

Bend (refer to the list on page 265). A few more-cold-tolerant species can be grown north of this line to another arching line from Texarkana to Dallas–Fort Worth to San Angelo to El Paso. North of this line, you're on your own. Not really; regardless of where you live, ask local nursery professionals or county extension agents to show you surviving and thriving examples of palm species in your community that you are considering for your landscape.

Microclimates that provide milder winter temperatures (e.g., a courtyard) will extend the northward reach for palms. In addition, the older a palm is, the more cold hardy it gets, so buy bigger, older plants. Finally, hardiness to low temperatures depends on the duration of the low temperature. A few-hour deep freeze is much less harsh than 24 to 48 hours of deep freeze.

One point of caution about tall palms (i.e., 40 to 100 feet): Maintaining these palms involves removing dead leaves annually to ensure a tidy appearance. This maintenance is best left to tree professionals; thus, this annual expense must be considered. Too many people plant a small, cute, inexpensive Mexican fan palm; watch it quickly grow to 30 feet; and then wonder what to do—"Prune the leaves way up there by myself, call a professional, or cut it down (and with whose chain saw)?"

Listed below are a dozen palms that can help turn your landscape into a tropical paradise.

Cabbage palmetto (*Sabal palmetto*)—quick-growing, single-trunked fan palm reaching 60 feet; large palmate leaves in a 10-foot canopy; slender trunk; state tree of Florida; cold hardy to 10°F to 15°F

California fan palm (*Washingtonia filifera*)—huge, fast-growing, single-trunked fan palm reaching 60 feet with a 25-foot canopy and 18- to 24-inch trunk diameter; hardy to 10°F (more cold hardy than Mexican fan palm)

Canary Island date palm (*Phoenix xanariensis*)—huge, single-trunked feather palm reaching 60 feet tall with long, arching fronds; considered the most beautiful tall palm; cold hardy to 10°F

Dwarf palmetto palm (*Sabal minor*)—native to eastern Texas from Houston to Dallas; trunkless, blue-green fan palm reaching 3 feet tall and 5 feet wide; widely adapted; one of the most cold-hardy palms, surviving temperatures of 10°F

Mediterranean fan palm (*Chamaerops humilis*)—clump-forming fan palm that develops multiple trunks reaching 15 feet tall and a canopy of 15 to 20 feet wide; beautiful multitrunked specimen plant; easy maintenance; very cold hardy, from 5°F to 10°F

Mexican fan palm (*Washingtonia robusta*)—huge, rapid-growing fan palm that can reach 100 feet tall with a 12-inch trunk diameter; hardy to 10°F to 15°F

Needle palm (*Rhapidophyllum hystrix*)—slow-growing, shrubby, trunkless fan palm reaching 5 feet tall and 8 feet wide; named for its vicious needles at the base of each leaf; the most cold-hardy palm, reported hardy to −10°F; can be grown anywhere in Texas

Pindo palm (*Butia capitata*)—slow-growing, single-trunked feather palm reaching 10 to 15 feet tall with long, arching, blue-green fronds (5 to 10 feet) and a 12- to 18-inch trunk diameter; cold hardy to 10°F

Pygmy date palm (*Phoenix roebelenii*)—slow-growing feather palm reaching a height of 10 feet on a single, 12-inch trunk; often planted in groups of three or as single specimen; low maintenance; hardy to 25°F

Sago palm (*Cycas revoluta*)—called a palm because of its feathery leaves connected to a single trunk but is a cycad related to conifers (cone-bearing plants); slow growers to the extreme, growing only a few inches taller each year; plan for a plant size of 3 to 5 feet tall with a 6- to 8-foot spread; hardy to 10°F (but will drop all foliage) (Cycads have changed very little from their origin over 200 million years ago in the Mesozoic era. Sago palms are referred to as living fossils and were enjoyed by the dinosaurs in their gardens long ago.)

Texas sabal palm or Texas palmetto (*Sabal texana* or *S. mexicana*)—native to the lower Rio Grande Valley; a stocky, single-trunked fan palm reaching 25 to 35 feet tall with a 20-foot canopy and 18- to 24-inch trunk diameter; hardy to 10°F to 15°F

Windmill palm (*Trachycarpus fortunei*)—slow-growing, single-trunked fan palm that reaches 20 to 30 feet tall with an 8- to 10-foot canopy and a narrow 8- to 10-inch trunk diameter with thin hairy, fibrous bark; one of the most cold hardy, to 5°F, thus adapted north to Dallas–Fort Worth, San Angelo, and El Paso

Expand Gardening to Containers

Container-grown plants expand your garden to the patio, deck, balcony, and even indoors. In addition, growing in containers can expand the types of plants you can grow in your garden. The native soil and climatic conditions of your region may not be conducive to growing many plants. In a container, you can manipulate the soil environment and, to an extent, the climate. As a result, container gardening is quite rewarding and will increase the beauty of your landscape significantly. Here are some basic design concepts, plant combinations, and growing guidelines to ensure success:

• Dish gardens are "living flower arrangements" composed of multiple plant species. They are a perfect gift for loved ones that can be "handmade" by children or adults. Like a cut-flower arrangement, the design concept most important to dish gardens is combining flowering plants with different bloom types: spike type, daisy type, pincushion type, and tubular. The second consideration is flower color. Annual and perennial flowering plants can be combined to achieve the perfect living flower arrangement. Refer to the "Container Garden Combos" list on page 271.

• Create your own combinations. In the nursery, choose a 14- to 16-inch container that is tall or squatty. Pull together flowering plants with different bloom types. Arrange them in the container (while still in their nursery pots). Trust yourself. Your dish garden will look great. If you want particular colors, then make substitutions, but remember that bloom type is most important.

Dish garden of flowers, container of mesclun (leaf lettuce), and pot of ryegrass just for fun

- Aesthetically pleasing placement of container plants next to each other is an art form. There are only a couple of guidelines; the rest is art and creativity. Use containers in odd-numbered groupings (e.g., three or five). Use containers of varying sizes to create a proportional balance to the grouping. Generally, there should be one large container (16+ inches in diameter) as a focal point, a second container (14 inches in diameter), and then another one to three that are 10 to 12 inches.

- The type of container does not matter, and beauty is in the eye of the purchaser. The only guideline is for the container to have a drain hole in the bottom (or you'll have to drill one). Lack of drainage kills most container plantings. As for combining containers made of different materials (e.g. terracotta, glazed, metal, concrete), whatever you like, just do it. You can use all the same type of containers to provide unity in the container garden, or you can use different materials to create variety. This is art, so have some fun.

CONTAINER GARDEN COMBOS

COMBO	SPIKE TYPE	DAISY TYPE	PINCUSHION TYPE	TUBULAR
Spring	blue salvia	coreopsis	verbena	impatiens
Spring	larkspur	dianthus	geranium	lobelia
Winter	snapdragon	pansy	alyssum	petunia
Summer	autumn sage	zinnia	lantana	purslane

- Plant permanent shrubs and other perennial plants in decorative containers. Not all of your container plantings should be annuals that need to be changed out every season. About one-third of all the containers should be planted with dwarf shrubs, palms, and other perennial plants that provide the permanent backdrop for the container garden. Choose plants such as asparagus fern, aspidistra or cast-iron plant, canna lily, cherry laurel, dwarf Wheeler's pittosporum, holly leaf fern, Mediterranean fan palm, nandina, plumbago, soft leaf yucca, and variegated ginger.

- Plant one species of flowering annual in a container. This is the yang to the yin of dish gardens. Consider these containers full of color as the accents of the container garden. A large pot of geraniums on either side of the front door is classic. White caladiums with green veins in a container provide beauty through bold foliage. Impatiens are tough to grow in most Texas gardens, but you can have great success in containers. If a flower species is tough to grow in your area, try it in a container (e.g., bird-of-paradise).

- Plant annual ryegrass in a container. This is a trendy, yet beautiful, way to complement other container plantings. You'll have a miniature lawn to mow. This will even work indoors, and children love it. Give them some scissors, and let them mow the lawn. Be careful; some unique lawn haircuts may result.

- Plant herbs and leafy vegetable crops (e.g., mesclun—selection of leaf lettuces) in containers, and enjoy their beauty and culinary production.

- Plant dish gardens for indoor use. These miniature gardens for inside the home can be enjoyed year-round. Select plants that can thrive in the lower light and lower humidity of the home. Beyond African violets, cyclamen, and New Guinea impatiens, the majority of plants you can use for indoor dish gardens are foliage plants. The good news is that foliage plants provide beauty through texture instead of flower color. Combine bold-textured and fine-textured foliage plants in the dish garden, plus a flowering plant for a dramatic effect. Bold-textured plants include crotons, English ivy, pothos ivy, and spathiphyllum. Fine-textured plants include asparagus fern, dracaena marginata, dwarf schefflera, false aralia, needlepoint ivy, and Swedish ivy.

• Potting soil quality varies significantly. Anything can be put in a bag and called potting soil. Unlike fertilizers, potting soils are not regulated. The standard in potting soil is one-third each of peat moss, perlite, and vermiculite. Pine bark is often substituted for peat moss in potting soils and is great for shrubs and permanent plantings. In general, the lowest-priced potting soil is not the best. Choose at least a moderately priced potting soil, preferably from a recognized horticultural company. NEVER use native soil for container gardening or combine it with a potting soil. Native soils in a container can make it too heavy to lift, restrict water drainage, and cause soilborne diseases.

• Try incorporating "hydrogels" to reduce the frequency of watering your containers (seldom justified for landscape plantings). These water-holding polymers are available in nurseries. Follow the label directions. Don't use too much, or you will have a slow-motion volcanic eruption of potting soil from your container. Think about it. (I speak from experience.)

• Fertilize with a water-soluble or a time-released product. Once-a-month fertilizing is a maximum.

• Leach your containers at least every 2 months to dissolve and flush away soluble salts that build up in the soil. These can result from fertilizers or city water and cause damage by burning the roots. Simply water each container with enough water to cause a significant flow of water out of the container drain hole.

• Seldom is there a need to have a saucer sit below the container. Excess water needs to flow freely out of the container (not be trapped by a saucer) to prevent salt accumulation in the potting soil. A plastic saucer may be needed to prevent staining of patio or deck surfaces from the container material or the water flowing through dark potting soil.

• Mulch your containers to reduce watering needs. Mulch significantly reduces evaporation of water from the soil surface. Any type of mulch will work, preferably an organic mulch rather than rock.

Butterfly Gardening Made Simple

Butterflies flitting and fluttering are a wonderful addition to any garden—mobile art for the garden. The basics of butterfly gardening are simple:

- Put flowering plants in your landscape that butterflies like both for nectar and forage for their caterpillars.
- Don't kill the butterfly caterpillars even though they are destroying some of your plants.
- Try to eliminate the use of insecticides in your garden.

There are several great books on this subject written specifically for Texas, and you can spend a lifetime fine-tuning your landscape and creating the perfect butterfly garden. This essay does not provide the detailed knowledge needed to renovate your backyard into the equivalent of the Cockrell Butterfly

Monarch butterfly and caterpillar on butterfly weed (Asclepias tuberosa)

Center (at the Houston Museum of Natural Science), where a dozen species and hundreds of butterflies romp around the thousands of visitors. However, follow these few dos and don'ts, use the plant list to guide purchases, and you will have butterflies visiting your landscape regularly.

(*Note:* Your odds of successful butterfly gardening are enhanced by the fact that Texas is blessed with more butterfly species than any other state—over 440 species. Texas is also on the migratory path of the monarch butterflies as millions fly south each fall to breed in the tropics.)

*Tiger swallowtail butterfly and caterpillar on Texas ash (*Fraxinus texensis)

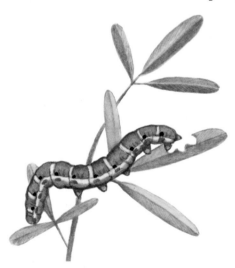

Dos and Don'ts

DO plant flowering plants known to provide nectar for butterflies. Nectar is a potent energy source for butterflies. The plant list to follow provides an array of flowering plants that blend nicely into any landscape.

DO provide plants known as food sources for butterfly caterpillars. Most of the plants eaten by caterpillars will be in the natural environment, but by providing some food sources in your landscape, you may create the circle of life for some butterfly families.

DO create feeding stations to increase the number of species drawn to your landscape. Feeding stations consist of a saucer filled with rotting fruit (e.g., apple, banana, mango). You can make a "smoothie" for butterflies by blending bananas, brown sugar, and a shot of beer or dash of yeast. Place the bait stations up off the ground away from ants and away from the house, because they may also be bee feeding stations.

DO provide a mud puddle (underneath a dripping water spigot) or other moist soil area (or edge of a pond) where butterflies can do their "mud puddling" to consume sodium and nitrogen.

DO create a garden habitat that butterflies enjoy: a sunny garden surrounded by dense shrubbery. Sun warms these cold-blooded insects, and dense foliage provides protection from predators, shelter, and a place to sleep. A few flat rocks can be added for sunbathing (for the butterflies).

DO plant groups of the same species of flowering plants to be a highly visible beacon to the color-attracted butterflies. Plant species that achieve different heights, such as tall sunflowers and groundcover verbena. Some butterflies are high fliers and some are low.

DO encourage flowering plants to continue blooming by pinching off dead flowers (deadheading).

DO accept that some of your beautiful flowering plants will be devoured by caterpillars. They are eating machines. This is tough but comes with the territory. You can nurture your plants back to health after the caterpillars spin a cocoon.

DO your homework to identify caterpillars that turn into beautiful butterflies and moths. Yes, there are pretty moths that will frequent your butterfly garden also. Generally, these are seen in the late afternoon and evening. Refer to butterfly and moth field guides for help identifying caterpillars and their parents.

DON'T spray insecticides in the garden, chemical or organic. Butterflies and their caterpillars are very sensitive to insecticide.

DON'T use the biological caterpillar killer, *Bacillus thurengiensis* (Bt). It kills any caterpillar, good or bad.

DON'T let fire ants go unchecked in the garden. They are vicious predators of the slow-moving caterpillars.

DON'T incorporate a birdbath in the butterfly garden. This will attract birds, not only the seed-eating species but also the caterpillar-eating ones.

DON'T spray-irrigate your flower garden. Overhead irrigation will wash off or dilute the flower nectar. Another great reason to use drip irrigation.

DON'T be a neat freak. Leaf litter in flower beds and gardens provides a home for various overwintering stages of the butterflies: egg, caterpillar, or pupa or chrysalis.

Butterfly garden planting of butterfly weed, butterfly bush, yellow lantana, and purple coneflower

DON'T worry whether you can butterfly garden. You can start by just planting a few butterfly plants in your landscape. If you like it, you can advance to creating a small butterfly garden within your larger landscape. The butterflies will find your plants or your garden.

Garden Plants That Provide Nectar for Butterflies

- Aniscanthus or hummingbird bush
- Aster (*Frikarti aster*/autumn aster/Michaelmas daisy)
- Blue mistflower or eupatorium
- Butterfly bush or buddleia
- Butterfly weed or asclepias (also native milkweed species)
- Coral honeysuckle
- Gayfeather
- Indian blanket flower or gaillardia
- Lantana
- Mexican mint marigold
- Passionflower vine (also native maypop vine)
- Purple coneflower
- Salvias (autumn sage, blue sage, indigo spires, Mexican bush sage, scarlet sage)
- Turk's cap
- Verbena (perennial trailing types)
- Zinnia

GARDEN PLANTS THAT PROVIDE
FORAGE FOR SPECIFIC BUTTERFLY
CATERPILLARS

Butterfly weed—monarch
Canna—Brazilian skipper
Citrus species—giant swallowtail
Cottonwood—mourning cloak
Dill herb—black swallowtail
Fennel—black swallowtail
Hackberry—American snout and
    mourning cloak
Parsley—black swallowtail
Passionflower vine—gulf fritillary
Texas ash—tiger swallowtail
Weeping and globe willow—
    viceroy and mourning cloak
"Your favorite, prized" plant
    (Butterfly caterpillars do not
    read lists and are not limited to
    eating only the plants listed.)

Gulf fritillary butterfly and caterpillar on
*passionflower vine (*Passiflora incarnata*)*

Vacation Time—What about the Plants?

Summer vacations require planning. What to do with the pets comes to mind first, but don't forget the plants. A week or two without care in the summer can take a heavy toll on your plants, both indoors and out. Below is a checklist of activities to do for the sake of your garden plants and houseplants prior to your much-deserved vacation.

Landscape & Garden Activities

- *Water*. Irrigate the landscape and garden thoroughly; maybe overdo it a little. If you have an automated system, set it to come on while you are gone every third day for approximately 20 to 30 minutes per station. This is a survival level for lawn and landscape watering in the absence of rain. If you have a vegetable garden,

irrigation is more critical, so you need a neighbor to water as needed. If you have containerized plants, they will need watering at least every third day to survive summertime heat. You will need a neighbor's help again. Group the containers together in easy reach of the hose.

- *Mow*. Mow and trim your lawn the day before you leave. Don't lower the mower blade thinking you will get a few more days until the next mowing is needed. What you will end up with is a very stressed and damaged lawn from heat and sunscald. The lawn will need to be mowed a week later, so either be home then or make arrangements for weekly mowing.

- *Weed*. Today's weed seedlings are tomorrow's monsters. Pull, spray, or mulch over existing weeds in the garden and landscape plantings. Coming home to a weed-riddled garden is no fun.

- *Prune.* Check roses, perennials, and annual flowers to determine if they need deadheading (removing dead blooms). By deadheading before you go on vacation, you avoid looking at ugly flowerless plants and are welcomed home by beautiful blooming plants.

- *Mulch.* Mulching preserves water in the soil, reduces soil temperatures, reduces weed populations, and gives a fresh look to the garden. For gardeners, the look is likened to coming home to a freshly vacuumed carpet.

- *Do a pest check.* Check for insects and diseases. Take action to control populations of insect pests that are present, or they will enjoy you being on vacation and proliferate. This is especially true for summer insect pests, such as chinch bugs and spider mites. Diseases are less prevalent in summer, but check particularly for black spot on roses, blight and root rot in annual flower beds, and take-all patch in the lawn. Manage these fungal diseases now, not later.

- *Harvest.* In the vegetable garden, harvest all ripe and nearly ripe fruit. Call a neighbor to come harvest for you if you are going to be gone for more than a week. Rotten tomatoes are a waste.

Houseplant Activities

- *Move out.* Move the houseplants outdoors, if they can be placed in a shady spot of the landscape where an automated irrigation system can water them. If not, then leave them in the house.

- *Water.* Put your houseplants in the bathtub or shower, and water them heavily, two to three times the amount you normally use. This excess water thoroughly wets the soil, dissolves soluble salts that have built up in the soil, and lets the salty water drain out of the container.

- *Congregate.* Gather the houseplants together, preferably in the bathtub or shower in a bright, sunlit bathroom. The group of plants raises the surrounding humidity level, thus reducing water use by the plants. The plants will need watering only once per week. If they are in a bathtub, you can even plug the drain and fill the tub with 1 or 2 inches of water that can be absorbed by the plant over a 2-week period as needed through the container drain hole.

- *Get help.* If needed, ask a neighbor to water the houseplants. In a group, the plants are easier to water (instead of the neighbor having to look all over the house). There is also less chance of water damage from spills or overflowing pots or saucers.

Deer-Resistant Plants

Bambi's mother consuming 'Belinda's Dream' rose.

Deer are beautiful, graceful creatures but can be the biggest plant pest for many rural, suburban, and even some urban gardeners. If you have deer wandering regularly through your landscape, you know their relentless pursuit and voracious appetite for your garden plants.

Add a desire by some neighbors to attract these "lovely" animals to their landscape by feeding them, and you have conflict in many neighborhoods. Feeding deer tends to increase the population and reduce any fear the deer have of humans. Some urban townships and neighborhoods are striving to restrict deer feeding and even reduce deer populations through trapping and "harvesting" deer.

As gardeners and yardeners, the first line of defense against deer is choosing plants that deer don't eat or at least prefer less than other plants. You can also employ other techniques to protect your landscape and garden, such as excluding deer with high fences, caging young trees until they are too tall for the deer

CALLER: "Will a scarecrow deter deer from visiting my landscape?"

ANSWER: "No, deer will quickly figure out the scarecrow is not human and eat the straw stuffing and leave the clothes. There are, however, two products on the market that work: ScareCrow (Contech Electronics, Inc.) and Havahart Spray Away ScareCrow. These have a motion sensor connected to an impact sprinkler. Hook the device to the hose with the faucet turned on. When a deer approaches, the sprinkler sprays for about ten seconds and runs the deer off. Place one or more devices in the garden, and watch the fun. They also work to scat cats from bird feeders and raccoons from vegetable gardens and water gardens. What a great invention. Visit the Internet for more details and dealers."

by a disclaimer. Know that many plant species are not attractive to deer when other preferred food is plentiful, but when that food is in short supply, the unattractive species are consumed readily (e.g., dwarf yaupon, vinca). Reduced food supply occurs naturally during droughts and also as deer populations increase. It also seems that newly planted deer-resistant plants are sometimes eaten by deer until the plant matures, if it survives to maturity (e.g., autumn sage, rosemary, standard yaupon). Fawns are often seen eating deer-resistant plants as they learn what is tasty and what is not.

When choosing plants for landscapes frequented by deer, consider the following:

- With the following list in hand, check out the neighborhood and see what plants are thriving, not simply surviving the deer pressure.
- Seek advice from local nursery and landscape professionals, Master Gardeners, and county extension agents for locally recommended plants.
- Test any questionable plant in your landscape by planting only a couple of plants. Confirm that it is deer resistant before planting more.

to reach, persistent spraying with deer repellents, or adopting a more natural landscape and tolerating some collateral damage to the garden from deer.

A truly deer-proof plant list would be awfully short. A deer-resistant list is more practical but must be accompanied

Deer-Resistant Landscape Plants

Key to comments:
P—rarely eaten/deer proof
N—Texas natives

LARGE TREES

Deer eat all young tree species, so the trees should be protected by cages until they are tall enough to hold the leaves higher than the deer can reach. Planting larger, older trees can be helpful. Protecting the trunk with fencing or hardware cloth against rutting bucks (rubbing antlers on the trunk) is essential.

SMALL TREES OR LARGE SHRUBS

Desert willow (*Chilopsis linearis*), N
Eastern red cedar (*Juniperus virginiana*), N
Fig (*Ficus* spp.)
Flameleaf sumac (*Rhus lanceolata*), N
Japanese yew (*Podocarpus macrophyllus*)
Roughleaf dogwood (*Cornus drummondii*), N
Texas buckeye (*Aesculus arguta*), N
Texas mountain laurel (*Sophora secundiflora*), P, N

Texas persimmon (*Diospyros texana*), N

SHRUBS

Abelia (*Abelia* spp.)
Agarita (*Berberis trifoliolata*), N
Autumn sage (*Salvia greggii*), N
Boxwood (*Buxus microphylla*), P
Cast-iron plant (*Aspidistra lurida*)
Cenizo/Texas sage (*Leucophyllum* spp.), P, N
Dwarf Chinese holly (*Ilex cornuta*) (not Burford holly)
Dwarf yaupon (*Ilex vomitoria*), N
Elaeagnus (*Elaeagnus* spp.)
Evergreen sumac (*Rhus virens*), N
Grayleaf cotoneaster (*Cotoneaster glaucophylla*)
Juniper (*Juniperus* spp.)
Lantana (*Lantana horrida*) (natives resistant; hybrids not), N
Mexican buckeye (*Ungnadia speciosa*), N
Nandina (*Nandina* spp.)
Oleander (*Nerium oleander*)
Pineapple guava (*Feijoa sellowiana*)
Pomegranate (*Punica granatum*)
Pyracantha (*Pyracantha coccinea*)
Red-leaf or Japanese barberry (*Berberis thunbergii*)
Split-leaf philodendron (*Philodendron selloum*)
Viburnum (*Viburnum* spp.)
Vitex (*Vitex agnus castus*)
Wax myrtle (*Myrica cerifera*), N

PERENNIAL SUCCULENTS, LILIES, AND ORNAMENTAL GRASSES

Bear grass/nolina (*Nolina* spp.), N
Cactus (*Opuntia* spp.) (any with spines), P, N
Gulf muhly (*Muhlenbergia capillaries*), N
Lily of the Nile (*Agapanthus africanus*)
Lindheimer's muhly grass (*Muhlenbergia lindheimeri*), N
Maiden grass (*Miscanthus sinensis*)
Pampas grass (*Cortaderia selloana*)
Red yucca (*Hesperalae parvifloria*) (flowers eaten), N
Sotol (*Dasylirion wheeleri*), N
Yucca (*Yucca* spp.), N

VINES, GROUNDCOVERS, AND FERNS

Ajuga (*Ajuga reptans*)
Asiatic jasmine (*Trachelospermum asiaticum*)
Bermudagrass (*Cynodon dactylon*)
Carolina jessamine (*Gelsemium sempervirens*), P
Holly fern (*Cyrtomium falicatum*)
Monkey grass (*Ophiopogon japonica*)
Santolina (*Santolina* spp.), P
Star jasmine (*Trachelospermum jasminoides*)
Vinca (*Vinca major*)
Wood fern (*Dryopteris* spp.), N
Zoysiagrass (*Zoysia* spp.)

FLOWERS AND HERBS

Ageratum (*Ageratum houstonianum*)
Artemisia 'Powis Castle' (*Artemisia* x 'Powis Castle')
Begonia (*Begonia* spp.)
Black-eyed Susan (*Rudbeckia hirta*), N
Blackfoot daisy (*Melampodium leucanthum*), N
Bluebonnet (*Lupinus texensis*), N
Copper Canyon daisy/mountain marigold (*Tagetes lemmonii*), N
Coreopsis (*Coreopsis* spp.), N
Cosmos (*Cosmos bipinnatus*)
Damianita daisy (*Chrysactinia mexicana*), N
Dusty miller (*Senecio cineraria*), P
Esperanza/yellow bells (*Tecoma stans*), N
Firebush (*Hamelia patens*)
Foxglove (*Digitalis purpurea*)
Hummingbird bush (*Anisacanthus wrightii*), N
Indigo spires (*Salvia* sp. hybrid)
Iris (*Iris* spp.)
Larkspur (*Consolida ambigua*)
Mealy cup/blue sage (*Salvia farinacea*), P, N
Mexican bush sage (*Salvia leucanthia*), N
Mexican mint marigold (*Tagetes lucida*), P, N
Mexican oregano (*Poliomintha longifolia*)

Periwinkle (*Vinca rosea*), P

Plumbago (*Plumbago auriculata*)

Purple coneflower (*Echinacea angustifolia*), N

Rock rose (*Pavonia lasiopetala*), N

Rosemary, upright and prostrate (*Rosmarinus officinalis*), P

Skullcap (*Scutellaris suffrutescens*), N

Society garlic (*Tulbaghia violacea*)

Spearmint (*Menta spicata*)

Thyme (*Thymus* spp.)

Turk's cap (*Malvaviscus arboreus*), N

Verbena (*Verbena* spp. or *Abronia* spp.), N

Yarrow (*Achillea filipendulina*), N

Zexmenia (*Zexmenia hispida*), N

Zinnia (*Zinnia* spp.)

Note: Most herbs are deer resistant; try them all.

Fall Vegetable Gardening Starts Now!

"Better late than never" may be an appropriate cliché for some garden tasks but not for fall gardening. You must plant in midsummer to ensure fresh homegrown vegetables for your Thanksgiving feast. Fall vegetable gardening is very productive and has distinct advantages over spring vegetable gardening:

- Vegetable crops are maturing as the days are getting shorter and cooler; the quality of crops, such as broccoli, cauliflower, and lettuce, is much higher (less chance of bitter taste developing).
- Rainfall is generally more frequent in the fall; thus, watering chores are reduced.
- Insect pest populations are on the decline, not increasing as in spring.
- The weather is more pleasant for you, the gardener.

Vegetable crops require a growing period between planting and harvesting. This period can be shortened almost a month by using transplants rather than seeds to establish the crops, but not all crops are available as transplants in the nurseries.

The growing period to harvest must be considered for each crop in fall gardening. The following crops require at least 2 months from seed to the beginning of harvest ("W" denotes warm-season vegetable, and "C" denotes cool-season vegetable):

Beet, C
Broccoli, C
Cauliflower, C
Collard greens, C
Cucumber, W
Green bean (bush), W
Kohlrabi, C
Lettuce, C

Mustard greens, C
Spinach, C
Squash (yellow and zucchini), W
Swiss chard, C
Turnip (bulb and greens), C

The following crops require at least 3 months from seed to beginning of harvest (same notation as above):

Black-eyed pea, W
Brussels sprouts, C
Cabbage, C
Cantaloupe, W
Carrot, C
Corn, W
Eggplant, W
Okra, W
Onion, C
Pepper, W
Potato, W
Pumpkin, W
Squash (acorn, butternut), C
Tomato, W
Watermelon, W

The warm-season crops listed will be damaged or killed by the first fall frost. The first frost date for Amarillo is October 24; Austin, December 5; Dallas, November 22; El Paso, November 11; Fort Worth, November 12; Houston, December 12; Lubbock, November 2; San Antonio, November 28; Waco, November 10.

Two months from July is September, and three months is October. Depending on where you garden in Texas, you can determine the level of urgency to plant the warm-season crops.

There are few gardening situations more frustrating than having a tomato plant loaded with green, tennis ball–sized fruit and hearing that the first heavy frost is predicted. Your options are to cover the plants and provide supplemental heat (e.g., Christmas lights) or harvest the green fruit and learn to prepare and enjoy fried green tomatoes or chow-chow.

Establishing Vegetable Transplants in Summer Heat

To ensure a crop of warm-season vegetables before the first frost, grow from transplants, not seed. Transplants of eggplant, pepper, squash, and tomato are generally available at local nurseries in multiple-plant packs or small 4-inch pots. If you can find larger transplants, buy them. It is worth the extra money to shorten the time until harvest.

Quick establishment of transplants in the garden is critical to success. Even with the hot, dry weather of late summer, these transplants will survive as long as you provide adequate watering to each and every transplant.

It will take about 2 weeks for the transplants to establish a large enough root system to begin fast growth of the stems and leaves. During this 2 weeks, you will need to provide light waterings daily to the transplants. Any stress from lack of water will result in stunted plants and delayed fruit and, in the case of tomatoes, more fried green tomatoes and chow-chow. Drip irrigation makes this watering task easy. If you don't have drip, then make small pint-size basins around each plant. This makes it easier to apply a pint of water daily to each plant. Now, don't overwater the plants either, or the root system will begin to rot, not grow.

You may even provide some heat relief from the late afternoon sun by providing shade to the transplants—use a short board placed on the west side of the plants.

After a week of establishment, start fertilizing using a water-soluble or slow-release fertilizer. The more growth you can generate, the better your chances are to have loads of vegetables.

Fall Vegetable Gardening— Do the Math

If you live in Lubbock and want to grow fall tomatoes from transplants, when should you plant?

> Data:
> Average first frost date: November 2
> Days from transplant to beginning of harvest: 90
> Days from transplant to completion of harvest: 120
> Calculation: November 2 minus 120 days equals July 2 to 10
> Solution: Start NOW!

The cool-season crops can be delayed a few weeks before planting because they can tolerate a few light frosts. But don't wait too long, especially in North and West Texas.

Fear not though; with correct timing you can have a bountiful crop of vegetables this fall. The "Planting Guidelines" among the March essays will help you determine when to plant your fall vegetable crops.

Timely Tips

Flowers & Pretty Plants

• Check out the neighborhood landscapes, and determine which flowering plants are performing well in the midst of summer. Be a copycat (I am), and plant those plants in your garden.

• Keep on deadheading, fertilizing, and watering your flower beds.

Garden Design

• Consider planting flowers in containers to add a new element to the garden. Texas soils, heat, and drought challenge the best of gardeners. Growing flowers in containers is one way to control these elements. Use good potting soil, pick from the plethora of decorative containers, and plant a living flower arrangement.

Soil & Mulch

• Mulch container-grown plants as well as the planting beds. Mulch reduces water needs of container-grown plants by 25 percent or more. Place mulch in your potted plants, and you will water less frequently.

Water

• Run drip irrigation for much longer periods of time than sprinkler irrigation. Drip often applies 1 gallon of water per hour, so watering 2 to 3 hours to thoroughly water a flower bed or vegetable garden is often required.

• Monitor water needs of the lawn and landscape carefully. This is the peak water-use month for plants. Infrequent irrigation may in fact be every other day. Watch the plants; they will tell you.

Plant Care

• Be a plant health detective. In the midst of summer, plants respond in various ways to heat and drought stress: yellowing leaves, brown spots on leaves, gray coloration of the leaves, dead or dying stems, drying blooms, and plant death. Many of these symptoms are misdiagnosed as insect or disease damage. Don't turn to a pesticide before correctly diagnosing the source of the problem. About 75 percent of the plant problems occurring in the summer are due to heat and drought stress.

Trees, Shrubs & Vines

• Evaluate the ability of your trees, shrubs, and vines to withstand heat stress. Not only should you evaluate this ability between different types of plants but you should also evaluate their location in the landscape. Is a plant in full sun, full shade, filtered light, morning sun only, or the worst afternoon sun only? Maybe the plant's problem is its location in the landscape. Heat sinks cause extreme stress on plants (e.g., courtyards, west exposures against brick walls, reflective heat from concrete drives and patios). If you have a plant or group of plants that cannot take the heat, then move them or get them out of your landscape. Find a more adapted plant or variety.

Lawns

• Control fire ants in your lawn during the summer with mound treatments, as opposed to baits (the ants are foraging much less now). Mound treatment is the second part of the "Texas two-step" fire ant management program. Organic and chemical insecticides can be sprinkled on the mound or drenched into the mound. Spinosad and pyrethrin are both effective organic insecticides for mound treatments.

• Continue watching for drought stress in the lawn—dull, gray-green color; leaf blade rolling; or footprints left on the lawn after you walk across it. Irrigate as soon as possible.

• Apply 1 inch of water with any irrigation. Avoid runoff by multicycling.

• Be aware that grubworms in the lawn can be devastating. Although not often a pest worth control, large populations cause dead patches of lawn where sod can be pulled up like a loose carpet. In suspect lawn areas, dig up a few separate square-foot areas of soil in the damaged lawn. If there are five or more grubworms per square-foot sample, then your lawn has a grubworm problem and should be treated. Granular insecticides for grubworm control are readily available and effective.

• Know that in Central, South, and West Texas, yellowing of St. Augustine lawns in summer can be caused by iron chlorosis (the inability of the grass to take up iron due to highly alkaline soil). Hold a yellow leaf blade toward sunlight. Alternating yellow and green stripes up and down the leaves indicate iron chlorosis. Apply an iron fertilizer in a granular or liquid form; however, be careful, because iron will stain concrete red.

Vegetables, Herbs & Fruits

- Believe it or not, fall vegetable gardening starts in July. Cold-sensitive vegetable crops (e.g., pepper, squash, tomato) must be given time to mature and fruit before the first frost. This month's "Fall Vegetable Gardening Starts Now!" helps you do the math.
- Continue purchasing Texas-grown vegetables and fruits at grocery stores and produce stands this month. The peak of many crops will end this month.
- Providing water, water, and more water is the key activity this month on fruit trees. Whether the fruit is already harvested or not, irrigating regularly is important. Maintaining healthy foliage on the trees helps ensure next year's fruit crop.

Butterflies, Birds & Squirrels

- Provide water in the heat of summer for the birds and squirrels with birdbaths, fountains, or bubblers.
- Prevent bird seed from becoming weeds in the lawn by using a pre-emergence herbicide underneath the bird feeders.

Notes:

August

'Little Gem' dwarf magnolia (Magnolia grandiflora 'Little Gem')

HOT, HOT, HOT, AND DRY TOO!

Crape Myrtles—a Love Affair

(*Note:* My love affair with crape myrtles began when I was a 1978 summer intern at the Houston Arboretum. I was a junior at Texas A&M, and landing this summer job changed my horticultural life.

Bill Basham, a brilliant horticulturist and wonderful human being, was director of the Houston Arboretum. He mentored me that summer and gently but firmly helped me transfer my book knowledge into practical expertise.

Bill's compadres included the renowned plantsman Lynn Lowery and county extension horticulturist extraordinaire Bill Adams. I remember traveling around the city with Bill and Bill in the front seat and me in the back. I was a wide-eyed young man absorbing the knowledge, fun, and passion these men had for horticulture. At the time, I thought I wanted to be a commercial greenhouse manager growing plants for nurseries. After one trip with these men, I knew I wanted to be like them, a horticultural educator.

Bill Basham's love for crape myrtles was contagious, and I caught it. Bill had obtained and planted in his garden a rare Japanese crape myrtle, *Lagerstroemia fauriei* [white blooms, cinnamon-colored trunk, and known powdery mildew resistance]. His neighbor had the common watermelon red Chinese crape myrtle, *L. indica.* As Bill put it, "the plants got promiscuous one night" and crossbred naturally. In 1963, a crape myrtle seedling emerged in Bill's garden that grew fast, really fast [4 to 6 feet per year], had pink blooms, and never got powdery mildew, a common ailment of *L. indica.* This was the first documented natural hybrid between these species, and Bill recognized its potential. The new seedling had gained the powdery mildew resistance from *L. fauriei,* the bloom color was a blend from both parents, and the seedling had the hybrid vigor [fast growth rate] expected from hybrids both in plants and animals.

Bill named the new hybrid 'Basham's Party Pink'; he said that "the blooms are pink and everyone loves a party." Lynn Lowrey introduced the new variety to the commercial nursery trade in 1965.

Crape myrtle hybridizing using the *L. fauriei* expanded rapidly through the tireless work of Donald Egoff at the National Arboretum, Washington, D.C. His variety releases generally bear names of Native American peoples [e.g., 'Muskogee,' 'Natchez,' 'Tuscarora']. On a sunny summer day in 1992, I stood in reverence in Donald Egoff's research plots at the National Arboretum and in awe of the diverse sizes, growth habits, and colors developed by this prolific landscape plant breeder. He passed away in 1990, but I still felt his presence that day.

Back in the summer of 1978, Bill Basham took me to his former home garden to show me the original 'Basham's Party Pink.' It was almost a religious experience standing by the man and the natural hybrid. The seedling was now 15 years old and stood 40 feet tall and 40 feet wide with a 36-inch-diameter single trunk. The huge tree was in full bloom, thousands of pink blooms. When the gentle breeze blew, delicate pink blossoms rained down. Bill knelt and patted the massive, sculptural trunk and said, "That, my friend, is sensual." My immediate thought was, "A single-trunked tree that grows 6 feet per year, reaches over 30 feet tall, and blooms all summer; what the heck else do you want in life?" I was in love.)

The American love affair with crape myrtles is traced back to colonial America, but the route is not well documented. Most credit André Michaux, who was sent by the French government to collect North American plants for dissemination into France, with introducing the first Chinese crape myrtle (*L. indica*) to America in the area of Charleston, South Carolina, around 1786.

Since then, literally thousands of cultivated varieties have been developed in the United States using crosses within

L. indica, followed by species crosses with *L. fauriei* and others. Crape myrtles adorn gardens from Washington, D.C., west to Tennessee, Arkansas, and Oklahoma, throughout the deep South and southwest to Texas, New Mexico, Arizona, and California. Some especially cold-tolerant varieties can be found in Massachusetts, Oregon, and Washington. Such wide adaptation by a nonnative species is phenomenal. The landscape value of this plant rivals even that of roses.

Often described as the "100-day bloomer," crape myrtles have a place in virtually all Texas landscapes. In fact, the Chinese crape myrtle was officially named the "State of Texas—State Shrub" in 1997.

Many excellent varieties are now available that are resistant to powdery mildew. These varieties should be the mainstay selection over nonresistant varieties, especially in East and Southeast Texas where disease pressure is intense due to high rainfall and humidity.

The first characteristic that comes to mind in choosing crape myrtles is bloom color; however, choose first the size that you want. It is so disheartening to see a crape myrtle slapped up next to a house and watch the plant attempt to grow to its natural size, only to be chopped back annually to keep it in bounds. It is critical to choose the crape myrtle variety that can grow to its natural mature size in the space you provide.

There are several sizes of crape myrtle:

- Miniature (2–3 feet)
- Dwarf (3–6 feet)
- Semidwarf (5–12 feet)
- Large shrub/small tree (10–20 feet)
- Tree (20+ feet)

Keep in mind these guidelines that affect the mature size of the crape myrtle you choose to grow:

- Under the categories "large shrub/small tree" and "tree," the fewer trunks a specimen has, the taller it will be. A multitrunked 'Basham's Party Pink' with three trunks will be taller than one with five trunks. A single-trunked specimen will be the tallest (see illustration). At the nursery, you should sift through the plants to find the specimen with the number of trunks you want. Ideally, each trunk would head in a different direction radiating from the base of the plant. Single-trunked specimens may need to be special ordered but are available in commercial nurseries in Texas.
- Crape myrtle mature size is dependent on the environment, specifically the amount of natural rainfall for your area. A single-trunked "Basham's Party Pink" will become a 40-foot tree in Houston, reach 30 feet

The number of trunks a crape myrtle has affects the ultimate size of the plant: the fewer trunks, the taller the plant.

in College Station, and 25 feet in San Antonio. Crape myrtles will generally be taller in East and Southeast Texas than in the rest of the state. (*Note:* This is true for most trees; look at the size of the forest in East Texas versus that in the Hill Country.)

Landscape Uses

Crape myrtles have such versatility in the landscape and can be used in these ways:

- Specimen or accent plant—a focal point of a landscape planting surrounded by lower shrubs and flowering plants such as blue plumbago, boxwood, nandina, yaupon holly, and/or blooming lantana or verbena

- "Bookend" plants—matching specimens planted at either end of the house providing unity, scale, and beauty to the front landscape
- Groundcover—flowering plantings of miniatures in large groups to replace the mundane green groundcovers, such as Asiatic jasmine
- Drifts—groupings of three to five dwarf varieties that add vibrant color in the summer
- Hedge or alley—straight or sweeping flowering hedge of semi-dwarf or large shrub varieties to provide screening or planted on either side of the drive to form a blooming alley
- Flowering shade tree—use of large varieties as a flowering shade tree should be much more common

(One homeowner, not knowing he had a 'Basham's Party Pink,' called the large single-trunked tree his "mutant" crape myrtle due to its growth rate and size.)

• Massive planting of various varieties—perhaps the most under-utilized strength of crape myrtles (Picture a huge planting, similar to the way azalea plantings are created in East Texas, where a variety of sizes from miniatures to semidwarf varieties of complementary colors are planted in a mass; imagine 100 days of summer blooms from such a planting: beautiful!)

Crape Myrtle Culture

To grow and bloom properly, crape myrtles must be grown in full sun. Only one thing will cause crape myrtles to not bloom: a lack of sun. They can take the heat and intensity of the Texas sun. Just look at the interstate highways throughout much of Texas, and marvel how these plants perform with no irrigation and minimal care.

Crape myrtles are adapted to a wide variety of soils from sand to clay, from acidic to alkaline. For planting in flower and shrub beds, amend the soil with organic matter—the more the better. For planting single plants in hedges, in alleys, or as shade trees, no soil preparation is recommended. Now be careful; if your soil is highly alkaline and rocky or caliche filled, check with local nursery professionals, extension agents, or Master Gardeners to determine what varieties will tolerate the native soil in your area.

Fertilizer can speed growth rates of your crape myrtles, particularly nitrogen fertilizers. Adding copious quantities of phosphorous fertilizer will not make crape myrtles (or any other plant) bloom more. In fact, phosphorous buildup in landscape soils can be a serious detriment to your plants and the environment.

Supplemental irrigation will be needed to establish newly planted crape myrtles. This may take a few months to a year. Use your index finger to monitor when the soil is dry, or watch the plant for timing irrigation. Crape myrtles will wilt readily when water is lacking.

Once established, crape myrtles will thrive on only natural rainfall for all areas east of IH-45 and throughout most areas between IH-35 and IH-45. Again, look at the highways; no irrigation is provided to these crape myrtles.

Monthly to weekly waterings will be sufficient for areas west of IH-35. However, if your irrigation water has a high salt content, prevalent in much of West Texas, crape myrtle growth and health will be compromised. You can still grow crape myrtles but will need to water excessively once a month to dissolve, dilute, and displace (called leaching) the salt buildup in the soil. Growing in raised beds with lots of organic matter increases plant health and helps you manage irrigating with poor-quality water.

Pest management on crape myrtles is minimal compared to many flowering plants. Powdery mildew is the most common disease. The best way to avoid this disease is to plant only mildew-resistant varieties. Many are now available in a variety of sizes and colors (refer to the crape myrtle variety list to follow). Plant varieties that are susceptible to mildew in full sun with good air circulation to significantly reduce infection. If you plant a susceptible variety in a fenced backyard or courtyard with little breeze to move the air, your crape myrtles will fight mildew, especially in East and Southeast Texas. Fungicides for powdery mildew are available and, if needed, require three consecutive weekly sprays. Fungicides include neem oil, triadimefon (Bayleton), and triforine (Funginex).

Crape myrtle aphids can be a significant pest problem. Good air circulation is critical to avoiding this pest. Crape myrtle aphids are tiny ($\frac{1}{8}$ inch), pale, yellowish green in color with black spots on the abdomen. Females give birth to live young, and since it takes only 10 days for the next generation to give birth, populations can explode before you know it.

Aphids suck plant sap for the high sugar content. When they feed, the aphids excrete excess amounts of a sugary liquid called "honeydew." With a large aphid population, the honeydew can coat leaves and stems. It also explains why you might feel like it is misting on you when you stand by your large crape myrtle. That is aphid excretion; gross!

The honeydew also explains why black sooty mold grows on the leaves and stems of aphid-infested crape myrtles. The mold is simply growing in the sugary honeydew and is not harmful to the plant, but it is unsightly and an indicator of aphid problems. Control the aphids, and you control the sooty mold. Although not necessary, you can wash sooty mold off plants by spraying it with a detergent and water solution (4 ounces per gallon of water), waiting a few minutes, and then washing with a strong stream of water. Some control of these aphids can be achieved by planting somewhat resistant hybrid varieties (refer to the crape myrtle variety list).

Ladybugs (ladybird beetles) are an excellent predator for managing aphid populations. Repeated high-pressure water sprays can be used to reduce aphid populations to acceptable levels. Due to aphids' rapid reproductive rate, managing aphids with insecticides takes repeated applications. Plus, insecticides are harmful to beneficial predators. If

application of an insecticide is warranted, organic and chemical products
include insecticidal soap, neem oil, pyrethrins, acephate (Orthene), cyfluthrin,
malathion, or permethrin (first three are
organic).

See a Crape Myrtle You Like? Make Another

Crape myrtles can be easily propagated
from dormant cuttings. In other words,
if you want more of a crape myrtle you
like (one of yours or your neighbor's),
you can have more by taking cuttings
during the winter and rooting them before spring growth begins. Here's how:

1. Take cuttings the diameter and
length of a pencil from portions of
the top branches; this is the youngest
growth that is brownish in color (not
green, tender growth).

2. Immediately cut
the bottom of the
cutting at an angle;
this increases the area
for new roots to form,
plus it tells you which
end to stick in the soil
(you'd be surprised

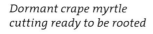

*Dormant crape myrtle
cutting ready to be rooted*

Pruning Crape Myrtles

Pruning crape myrtles seems to have
become "crape murder" across much
of Texas. Here are a few guidelines to
follow:

- Choose and plant crape myrtles
based on their mature size and the
space you want them to fill; plant
the right variety for the space, or you
will be regularly pruning to keep the
plant in bounds; refer to the crape
myrtle list.
- Prune off "suckers" (tender
shoots arising from the trunk at
soil level); suckering seems to be
increased if the trunk(s) is damaged
by mowers or flexible-line trimmers,
so mulch around the plants in the
lawn area to reduce the incidence of
damage.

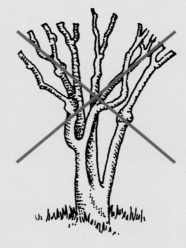

Stop "crape murder"!

• Deadhead the plants (remove old blooms) to prevent setting of seed and to extend the blooming period; through deadheading your crape myrtles will easily bloom 100 days.

• Don't top crape myrtles—it ruins the natural structure of the plant. Specifically, do not cut branches over $\frac{1}{2}$ inch in diameter; occasionally you might need to remove a larger branch, but cut it back to where it originates. As many seasoned gardeners know, topping crape myrtles will result in bigger blooms but fewer of them; this still does not justify the crape murder so often seen in Texas.

• Annual pruning of crape myrtles in the late winter is a good thing, as long as you can reach the top of the tree without endangering your life; for young plants and small enough large shrubs or trees, follow these steps:

1. Remove old blooms to clear the path for the new season's growth; these cuts should be on branches with a diameter smaller than a pencil.

2. Remove any dead, dying, or damaged branches.

3. Remove any branch that is originating from one side of the plant, growing through the middle of the plant, and heading out the other side; these branches just cause congestion by reducing air circulation and sunlight penetration.

4. Remove competing branches; often one branch will be growing directly beneath another branch. Choose the stronger, better-placed branch, and remove the other; the remaining branch will quickly fill the void left by the removed branch.

5. Step well back from the plant, and take an overall look at it; your goal is to create a vase-shaped plant. Envision an umbrella turned inside out with the frame of the umbrella being the major branches of the plant; off these branches arise smaller, medium-sized branches, and off of these come even smaller branches. This all leads to more branch tips, which is where new growth and blooms appear; the more small branches (pencil-size diameter and less) the plant has, the more blooms you will get.

6. Stop pruning, put up your shears, and wait until early summer for a huge display of traffic-stopping color.

how difficult it is to tell up from down on a leafless, dormant cutting).

3. Dip the angled cut in a rooting hormone (available from nurseries); don't pile it on; just a light covering will do.

4. Choose a location in the garden with good, well-drained soil; or fill 1- to 3-gallon garden containers with good potting soil, and place them in a bright garden location where rainfall can reach them (the advantage of pots is you can protect them from deep freezes by moving them indoors).

5. Take a pencil, and poke holes in the soil 3 inches deep and about 6 inches apart; this allows you to place the cuttings in the holes without rubbing off the rooting hormone. Place cuttings in each hole, and firm the soil around each cutting.

6. Water the soil gently to moisten the area; depending on rainfall, you may need to water lightly throughout the winter.

7. Sit back and wait; the objective is for the dormant cuttings to establish roots in the cool soil before warm spring weather causes leaf growth to begin. Realistically, perhaps half of the cuttings will root before spring growth, so the more cuttings you take, the better chances of success.

8. In late February, start checking the cuttings for root development. Use your fingers to gently dig beside a cutting down 3 inches and then begin lifting the soil and cutting; it is sort of like fishing—when you feel a bite, you'll know it. If roots are present, you will feel resistance to lifting the cutting; keep lifting, and try to keep the soil from falling away from the small roots. Place rooted cuttings into individual 1-gallon containers filled with potting soil, firm the soil around the cutting, and water lightly.

9. Rooted cuttings will continue developing more roots and, with warmer weather, begin budding out with leaves.

10. It is not quite time to celebrate; by late March or early April the successful cutting will be growing rapidly. Then you can add some water-soluble fertilizer, and keep the container-grown plants watered.

11. Transplant your new plants into the garden in April and May, or share some with your neighbors and friends; lots of pride and enjoyment come from passing along a special plant that you propagated.

Crape Myrtle Varieties

The number of crape myrtle varieties has exploded over the past decade. It is not as mind-boggling as the number of rose varieties but may seem that way. Choose crape myrtle varieties first by the size you want, then by color, and then find the most powdery mildew–resistant variety that matches the size and color you want (especially for the eastern half of Texas). The following list is arranged by size, with notations of color and mildew resistance. Note some varieties even show some resistance to crape myrtle aphid. New varieties are coming out annually, so check for the latest and greatest through local nursery professionals, county extension agents, and the Internet.

Crape Myrtle Variety List

Variety	Color	Mildew Resistance
Miniature (2–3 feet)		
Baton Rouge	deep red	fair
Bourbon Street	watermelon red	fair
Delta Blush	pink	fair
New Orleans Weeping	purple	fair
Pink Blush	light pink	fair
Pocomoke	rose-red	very good
Rosy Carpet (groundcover)	rose	good
Sacramento	rose-red	good
Velma's Royal Delight	purple, magenta	very good
Weeping Alamo Fire	red	fair
World's Fair Weeping	watermelon red	fair
Dwarf (3–6 feet)		
Chica Pink	bright pink	fair
Chica Red	rose-red	fair
Chickasaw	lavender-pink	good
Dwarf Low Flame	red	good
Dwarf Pink Ruffles	pink	good
Dwarf Royalty	royal purple	good
Dwarf Snow	white	fair
Dwarf White	white	fair

Variety	Color	Mildew resistance
McFadden's Pinkie Myrtlette	light pink	high
Okmulgee	dark red	fair
Petite Ember	rose-red	fair
Petite Orchid	lavender	fair
Petite Pinkie	clear pink	fair
Petite Red Improved	crimson red	fair
Petite Snow	white	fair
Razzle Dazzle series	white, red, pink, rose	good
Tightwad Red	light red	high
Victor	deep red	good
Semidwarf (5–12 feet)		
Acoma**	white	high
Burgundy Cotton	white/ maroon	fair (new growth is red)
Caddo**	bright pink	high
Centennial Spirit	electric red	good
Cheyenne	bright red	high
Christiana	dark red	fair
Firebird	watermelon red	fair
Hopi**	medium pink	high
Mandi	dark red	fair
Pecos**	medium pink	high
Peppermint Lace	pink/white edges	fair
Pink Lace	clear pink	fair

Variety	Color	Mildew resistance
Prairie Lace	pink/white edges	good
Tonto**	red	high
Zuni**	medium lavender	high
Large Shrub/Small Tree (10–20 feet)*		
Byer's White	white	good
Catawba	violet-purple	good
Comanche**	coral-pink	high
Conestoga	pale lavender	good
Glendora White	white (cinnamon bark)	good
Lipan**	medium lavender	high
Near East	light pink	good
Osage**	clear pink	high
Pink Velour	rose-pink	fair
Raspberry Sundae	red-pink/ white edges	good
Seminole	medium pink	good
Sioux**	bright pink	high
Tuskegee**	dark pink	high
Twilight	purple	poor
Yuma**	medium lavender	high
Yvonne	pink- lavender	good
Tree (20+ feet)*		
Apalachee**	light lavender	high
Arapaho	red	high
Basham's Party Pink	lavender- pink	very good

Biloxi**	pale pink	high
Carolina Beauty	deep red	poor
Choctaw**	bright pink	high
Dallas Red	violet-red	very good
Dynamite	red	very good
Fantasy**	white	high
Kiowa	white	high
Miami**	dark pink	high
Muskogee**	light lavender	high
Natchez**	white (cinnamon bark)	high

Potomac	clear pink	high
Red Rocket	cherry red	high
Sarah's Favorite	white	high
Special Red	coral-red	fair
Tuscarora**	dark coral-pink	high
Wichita**	lavender	high

* Remember: The farther east in Texas, the taller the mature size; and the fewer the number of trunks, the taller the mature size.
** Research indicates some crape myrtle aphid resistance.

Summer Rose Care: Preparations for Fall Bloom

As in humans, Texas summer heat causes lethargy in roses. Roses languish as summer progresses, throwing fewer blooms with less vivid color and restricting growth to fend off drought stress. In general, roses look pretty lousy by late summer. Let preparations begin in mid-August to produce a lovely profusion of fall rose blooms.

Prune roses back, not as heavily as in late winter, but pruning will generate new growth, and new growth means more blooms. You will likely cut off some blooms in the process, so be tough. For modern hybrid and old-fashioned roses, prune the bushes back about 25 percent. This can be achieved by using hand shears to prune back each major cane or simply by grabbing the hedge clippers and giving the bush a good ol' 25 percent butch haircut (e.g., a 4-foot bush becomes a 3-foot bush). You might make some additional cuts to shape the bushes; modern hybrid roses should be more vase shaped, and old-ashioned roses more rounded and shrublike.

Make sure your pruning has removed all old blooms, and continue to use this practice of deadheading once the roses begin blooming again to extend the bloom season until the first heavy freeze. Also, make sure your pruning removes diseased rose leaves. Leaving black spot–infected leaves on the bush will result in more black spot during fall's cooler temperatures and splashing rains.

Fertilize the rosebushes with straight-nitrogen products (e.g., urea, ammonium sulfate, blood meal). Apply about $\frac{1}{2}$ pound of urea, 1 pound of ammonium sulfate, or 4 pounds of blood meal to each plant in mid-August. Distribute the fertilizer in a circle at the "drip line" around each bush (i.e., tips of the branches and straight down to the ground). The result should be luxuriant new growth. If new growth is not seen by the first week of September, then make a second application. A third application may produce more growth and blooms, especially for the southern half of the state, where winter comes slowly.

Water the soil thoroughly after you prune and fertilize. In the absence of rain, irrigations should be frequent enough to keep the soil moist but not saturated. Use your index finger to test soil moisture. Avoid wetting the rose foliage and blossoms when irrigating. As with all landscape plantings, the best way to water roses is with drip irrigation.

Add 2 to 4 inches of mulch to the soil surface to reduce loss of soil moisture, to moderate soil temperatures, to reduce weed populations, and to provide a "fresh" look to the bed as the roses grow and bloom.

Keep an eye out for insect pests and diseases. If warranted, use the least toxic, effective pesticide to maintain plant health. For more details on rose pest control, refer to the January essay "Roses in the Landscape."

When preparations are finished, sit back and enjoy a spectacular fall bloom from your roses. Look how much more vivid the rose colors are in the cooling temperatures of fall. Take time and smell those fall roses to help you leap through another short Texas winter.

Poison Ivy, Poison Oak, and Poison Sumac

Poison ivy
(Toxicodendron
radicans)

Most botanists agree that the first European to write about and name poison ivy was Captain John Smith in 1609. Poison ivy and its close relatives, poison oak and poison sumac, all contain a nonvolatile phenolic compound called urushiol (pronounced "oo-ROO-shee-ohl"). This very stable and persistent toxin is found in all parts of the plant, including roots, stems, and fruit. It is toxic whether the plant parts are actively growing or dormant in winter and whether the parts are alive or dead (for a year or more). People highly sensitive to urushiol may even react to small amounts of urushiol present in smoke, dust, tools, contaminated clothing, and pet hair.

Approximately 75 percent of the population is sensitive to urushiol; however, sensitivity varies from an isolated skin rash to massive, whole-body breakouts (dermatitis) to lung inflammation from inhaling toxin-laden smoke or dust.

Medical literature states that urushiol causes cells to produce an "antisubstance" in susceptible people. The antisubstance can transfer from cell to cell in the body and is long-lived. As a result, once a person has developed a single rash from urushiol, the individual's entire body becomes more susceptible to inflammation. This explains why the older you get, the more sensitive you are to poison ivy.

When urushiol comes in contact with the "antisubstance" in the skin, the reaction produces a rash with small watery blisters accompanied by the familiar intense itching. About 15 percent of the population is so sensitive to urushiol that rashes may become severe and widespread in 4 to 12 hours (versus the normal 24 to 48). Swelling and erupting blisters may follow. This becomes an emergency that requires immediate medical attention.

The good news is that any person who touches the actual rash or the fluid in the blisters cannot contract poison ivy. Only through contact with urushiol can you possibly develop a reaction.

Treatment after Exposure

Quick action is needed if you come in contact with urushiol-containing poison ivy, poison oak, or poison sumac. Ten minutes seems to be the time period in which you have a chance to stop a reaction to urushiol. Even if a rash begins developing, cleansing the area and the rest of your body can help prevent further spread.

According to health officials of the Texas Workers' Compensation Commission, follow these steps if you have been exposed:

1. Clean exposed skin first with generous amounts of isopropyl (rubbing) alcohol. (Don't return to the woods or landscape the same day. Alcohol removes your skin's protection along with the urushiol, and any new contact will cause the urushiol to penetrate twice as fast.)

2. Wash exposed skin with cold water. (Warm water opens the skin pores.)

3. Take a shower with soap and warm water. Do not use soap before this point because soap tends to pick up some of the urushiol and move it around your body.

4. Wipe clothes, shoes, tools, and anything else that may have been in contact with the urushiol with alcohol and water. (Wearing disposable rubber gloves during this process is advisable.)

Treatment of the Rash

For minor rash development, over-the-counter lotion or cream may ease the itching and dry up the blisters with some success. Oatmeal or cornstarch baths and cold compresses are soothing. An over-the-counter antihistamine or anti-inflammatory can lessen the discomfort. Total healing may take a week or two.

Again, quick and severe reactions to urushiol require a doctor's attention. Watch for fever, headache, widespread rashes, and swelling or signs of secondary infection. A doctor may prescribe oral, topical, or injected steroids for serious cases. If administered within a few hours of exposure, prescription steroids have been shown to halt progression of the reaction. If people have experienced severe reactions before, they should consult a doctor right after a known exposure to poison ivy, oak, or sumac.

There is now some hope for preventing reaction to urushiol, not by vaccines or desensitization but by a barrier cream. The Food and Drug Administration approved bentoquatam 5%, which is available without a prescription. It provides a protection barrier when applied at least 15 minutes before exposure and reapplied every 4 hours. Bentoquatam 5% is contained in a lotion and available under the trade name Ivy Block.

Identification of the Culprit

Poison ivy is the most widely present *Toxicodendron* (genus name) in Texas. The old saying "Leaves of three, let it be" does provide an accurate guideline for poison ivy. This woody plant tends to be a vine growing up trees and fences but often is found as short, upright tufts of leaves in wooded areas that may grow to almost shrublike in appearance. A single leaf of poison ivy has three leaflets, thus the "leaves of three" saying. Leaflet shapes may vary somewhat but are generally triangular with some smooth to undulating (lobes) on the leaf edges (margins). The leaflets may be glossy or dull green, with some having fine hairs on the underside of the leaflets.

Spring growth can be reddish but is usually bright green, which darkens as summer approaches. Fall leaf color of red and yellow is common, although this fall color is not a tourist attraction.

Perhaps the most unique characteristic of a poison ivy vine growing up a tree or structure is the "hairy" or "fuzzy" appearance of the ropelike vine. Hundreds of brown aerial rootlets extend from the vines to hold them upright as they climb.

Poison oak grows as a low shrub and has leaves similar to those of poison ivy with three leaflets per leaf; however, the leaflets look more "oaklike" in that they have deeply lobed margins. Poison sumac grows as a rangy shrub up to 15 feet tall, and the leaves are much different from those of poison ivy, having seven or more leaflets that look similar to a sumac or pecan leaf.

Refer to the illustration below to assist in identifying which poisonous plant is which.

How to Kill Poison Ivy & Its Relatives

The only nonchemical treatment to control poison ivy, poison oak, and poison sumac is constant mowing or clipping. This takes years and repeated exposure. Like trying to manage Bermudagrass in your flower beds, digging and pulling are generally a waste of time and effort.

Quick ID

Unfortunately, poison ivy, oak, and sumac are not labeled in the wild or your yard. Get a knowledgeable person to point out these plants to you, and memorize what they look like. (I have taught each one of my children how to identify poison ivy.)

Here is a quick reference with guidelines for identifying these toxic plants in hope of avoiding their itchy consequences.

Poison Ivy

- Woody, ropelike vine; a trailing shrub or groundcover; or a free-standing shrub
- Normally three leaflets (per leaf emanating from branches or the larger main stem)
- Green leaves in the summer and red to yellow in the fall
- Yellow or green flowers and white berries

Poison Sumac

- Grows in boggy areas, especially in Southeast Texas
- Rangy shrub up to 15 feet tall
- Smooth-edged leaflets, usually 7 to 13
- Glossy pale yellow or cream-colored berries

Poison Oak

- Eastern half of Texas
- Grows usually as a low shrub
- Oaklike leaves, leaflets of three per leaf
- Clusters of yellow berries

Poison ivy leaf (left), poison sumac leaf (center), and poison oak leaf (right)

CALLER: "I see a couple of other vines similar to poison ivy in the woods. Are they poisonous?"

ANSWER: "Probably not. Although somewhat similar in appearance to poison ivy, they are most likely Virginia creeper (*Parthenocissus quinquefolia*) and pepper vine (*Ampelopsis arborea*). Virginia creeper and pepper vine are common in the eastern half of Texas. You may find Virginia creeper growing up a tree right next to poison ivy. Virginia creeper also produces brown aerial rootlets extending from big vines, but the rootlets are thicker and flattened, not cylindrical like poison ivy's rootlets. The primary difference in appearance between these vines is the number and shape of the leaflets on a leaf—Virginia creeper has five leaflets per leaf, and pepper vine has five leaflets with each leaflet having three more leaflets (a double compound leaf)."

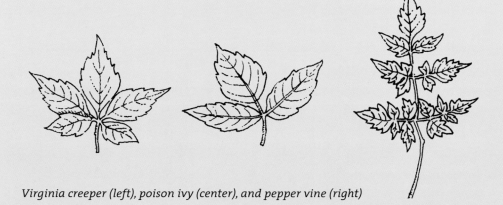

Virginia creeper (left), poison ivy (center), and pepper vine (right)

Unless you get all the roots, the plants will sprout back. Burning live or dead plants is not recommended because heat vaporizes the urushiol, which is then carried in the smoke, inhaled into the lungs, and may cause reactions in sensitive people.

This leaves herbicides. Generally, nonselective glyphosate and related herbicides are best. Don't use a "brush killer" herbicide that persists and sterilizes the soil unless you want to prevent growth or kill every plant growing in the area. Read and carefully follow the label directions of any herbicide you use.

Small, groundcover forms of poison ivy can be spot-treated with glyphosate. Remember that glyphosate kills most anything you spray it on, so it may kill a small spot of lawn or nearby plant. Larger shrublike masses of poison ivy, oak, and sumac can be sprayed with glyphosate, which will provide a "good kill," especially on tender spring growth. Expect these masses to regrow, and you will spray again, and perhaps again.

Where poison ivy has grown into large trees, cut the vines 6 inches above the soil. Let the vines resprout and create a lush mass of leaves. Spray with glyphosate. Don't worry about the tree being damaged by glyphosate. Thick bark prevents the tree from absorbing glyphosate. If you have any concerns, wrap aluminum foil around the tree trunk for protection.

Expect the vines to resprout again, and spray again. New sprouts may also arise from roots surrounding the vines; spot-treat them. Repeat this process over and over until the darned thing is deader than a doornail. Anger management sessions may be required during this season-long process. (*Note:* I have found it helpful to sing or hum the song "Poison Ivy." Jerry Leiber and Mike Stoller wrote this rock-and-roll hit, which was performed by the Coasters and then the Rolling Stones. I thought it was a great gardening song until I researched the song for this almanac. They are not talking about poison ivy. Poison ivy refers to a woman!)

Learn to identify poison ivy, oak, and sumac, and teach your children, too. With proper control measures and persistence, you will rid your landscape of these highly toxic weeds.

Looking for Shade? Think Texas Trees

Live oak (Quercus virginiana)

Waylon Jennings's lyric "Looking for love in all the wrong places" can be modified to describe poor shade tree selection. "Looking for shade in all the wrong places" is the charge for planting only "fast-growing" trees that are synonymous with "short-lived, pest-riddled,

low-quality" trees, such as Arizona trash (sorry, ash), cottonwood, poplar, and silver maple.

These trees, and other "quick-shade" trees, may have a place in your landscape. They can provide a short-term solution for shading, screening, and greening the landscape. But don't build your landscape around them. Choose higher-quality, longer-lived trees that provide shade to outdoor living areas, enhance the aesthetics of your house, and increase the value of it as well.

Planting trees is important to the Texas environment. Thousands of trees are lost each year to commercial development or adverse conditions in the urban landscape. Consider planting a tree this year and in years to come. Having trees of differing ages in your landscape protects against simultaneous loss or decline of your trees due to old age or urban stress. Planting different species of trees protects against loss of all trees from a disease or insect infestation (e.g., oak wilt on live oak or pine bark beetle on pine).

Plant a tree to commemorate a child's birthday or an anniversary, to memorialize a loved one, or to simply provide a future shady spot for someone to escape the heat of a summer day. Everyone can participate in replenishing and preserving our urban and natural forests. Get involved with community tree-planting programs sponsored by the Texas Forest Service or local Keep America Beautiful affiliates, or organize one in your neighborhood.

Tree Selection & Placement

The following will help you choose the right tree for your landscape and where to plant it to adorn and shade your home.

"What tree to plant?" is a big and important question. There are many native and adapted trees from which to choose for Texas landscapes. There is, however, no perfect tree, each possessing positive and negative characteristics. As you already sense, there are generally two kinds of trees: high quality and low quality. Here are a few general characteristics of each (there are exceptions):

HIGH-QUALITY TREES	LOW-QUALITY TREES
Slow/moderate growth rate (1–3 feet annually)	fast growth rate (3–6 feet annually)
Long-lived (lifetime of 30+ years)	short-lived (declining after 15+ years)
Hard, strong wood	soft, brittle wood (thus broken branches)
Few disease and insect problems	numerous pests

The best example to illustrate the difference between a high-quality tree and a low-quality tree is to compare live oak to Arizona ash. A 15-year-old, 35-foot-tall Arizona ash tree in one neighbor's landscape will be discussed and cussed because of springtime diseased leaf drop, blind wood (interior branches with no foliage), and the "cut it down or not" decision (takedown cost $650). Meanwhile, another neighbor's 15-year-old, 25-foot live oak tree is just beginning to mature and will continue growing at 1 foot a year, provide shade for decades to come, and increase the home's value significantly.

For home landscapes void of large existing trees, tree placement and size are an integral part of creating a beautiful landscape. Trees make these contributions to the overall landscape design:

- Provide a green frame for the front of the home

- Broaden (enlarge) the width of the home by masking the ends of the house
- Provide often-needed mass to counterbalance a large garage on the opposite side of the house
- Soften the straight or harsh angles of the home's architecture
- Provide a green backdrop, rising above the back of the home and upward to the blue sky

Trees can also contribute to proper scale in the home landscape. As a general rule, single-story homes should have front yard trees no larger than 35 feet tall. A huge 50-foot-tall pine tree may dwarf a single-story home and make the home appear smaller than it is. The backyard trees should reach upward to 50 feet to provide a green backdrop for the one-story home.

Two-story homes can handle much larger trees and remain in scale. Fifty footers in the front landscape are fine, and even larger in the backyard.

Trees can contribute greatly to the home landscape by providing balance, scale, enframement, and a green backdrop.

Another factor that frequently dictates the size of trees used in the home landscape is the lot or property size. A live oak tree can attain a mature size of over 40 feet tall and 40 feet wide. With smaller lot sizes in many new subdivisions, one live oak tree would overwhelm the whole lot. A better choice would be a medium-sized tree (e.g., Chinese pistache) or a tree with a more upright growth habit (e.g., cedar elm).

Tree choice can also help conserve energy by cooling your home. Evaporative cooling of your landscape occurs as trees transpire water from the leaves. In addition, the tree canopy can shade the home, particularly the windows. Most of the heat load on the house comes through the windows, not through the roof and well-insulated attics. Deciduous trees (e.g., bald cypress and Texas red oak) provide summer shade and let the winter sun through to shine in the windows and warm the home.

Consider these other characteristics as you choose trees for your landscape:

- Flowering and/or fruit
- Fall color
- Trunk form or character (e.g., Chinese elm, crape myrtle)
- "Trashiness" (Does it constantly drop twigs, seeds, flowers, or leaves?—very important when you have a pool.)

Refer to the following lists as you make decisions. In addition, look in your community for mature specimens of the trees you are considering, and if needed, ask a nursery professional or county extension agent for a final "thumbs up" for your choice.

Tree Purchases, Growth & Culture

Selecting trees for purchase in the nursery can be confusing. Typically, trees are described by the size of the container in which they are grown, not by tree height or trunk diameter. For example, trees are sold in 5-, 15-, 30-, and 45-gallon containers and larger 24-inch boxes (wooden). This does not tell you the tree height or trunk diameter, characteristics that are much more descriptive.

In general, perhaps the "best" size tree to purchase for homeowners is a 15-gallon tree that is approximately 8 to 10 feet tall with a trunk diameter of 1 to 1 $\frac{1}{2}$ inches. A 15-gallon tree is less expensive and can be handled by one person, and the hole that must be dug is reasonably small. Plus, this size tree will undergo much less transplant shock than larger trees and begin significant growth much sooner.

(*Note:* I have always contended that I can plant a 15-gallon tree with a 1-inch-diameter trunk and grow it to a 6-inch-trunked tree much faster than someone who plants a 45-gallon tree with a 2 $\frac{1}{2}$- to 3-inch trunk. The transplant shock experienced by larger-sized trees can be that much greater.)

Here are other guidelines for selecting the best tree to purchase:

The best size tree to purchase is one in a 15-gallon container (cedar elm [Ulmus crassifolia]).

- A single, central trunk (no multiple trunks competing to be the head "honcho")
- A trunk and major branches free of wounds or physical damage
- A uniform and balanced distribution of branches up and down the trunk
- Dense, healthy foliage free of brown leaf tips from underwatering or symptoms of disease infection and insect damage
- A healthy root system (Have the nursery staff help you knock the container off the root-ball so you can see healthy, abundant roots on all sides of the root-ball; there should be no evidence of thick circling, girdling, or kinked roots.)

The vast majority of trees grown in Texas have an episodic growth habit, meaning they grow in the spring to early summer and stop growing for the rest of the year. With this in mind it is critical to fertilize the trees prior to spring growth and during this growth phase to achieve maximum annual growth.

Many trees are labeled "slow growing" (e.g., oaks). This is generally overstated, and these trees can easily be pushed with fertilizer to become moderate to fast growing. A "spoon feeding" approach to fertilizing will generate as much growth as the tree species is genetically capable of producing. Spoon feeding describes smaller but regular applications of high-nitrogen fertilizers.

Watering newly planted trees properly will also minimize transplant shock and maximize growth. However, DO NOT overwater your newly planted trees. More trees are killed by overwatering than underwatering. You MUST also

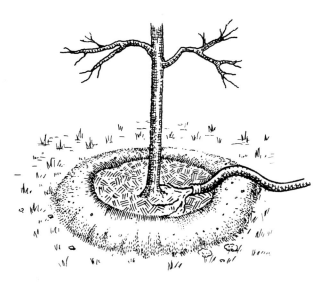

understand that spray irrigation systems do not water trees.

As a guideline for properly watering a newly planted tree, water daily for 1 week with the amount of water it took to fill the space between the soil surface and the top of the container in which the tree was growing before you planted it. For a 15-gallon tree, that would be about 1 gallon of water per day. Remember that the tree root system is growing in a very porous growing medium (soil) that holds very little water, and the tree has been watered virtually every day during the growing season.

The second week, double the amount of water, and apply it every other day depending on the soil moisture level (which you should check with your index finger). The goal is to keep the original growing medium moist and drive moisture into the surrounding soil. The root system will also follow into the surrounding soil.

The third week, water with the amount from week two every 3 days if the soil moisture level is low in the top 3 inches according to your "moisture meter" index finger. Cool to the touch indicates ample moisture; dry or warm soil indicates the time to water is at hand. Week four and beyond, water at the most weekly, and only when the soil moisture level is dry at a depth of 3 inches. Don't forget to factor in rainfall as well as the time of year. Newly planted trees require much less water during rainy periods.

Container-grown trees can be planted at any time of year, but the best time to plant trees is fall, winter, or early spring. There is less environmental stress on the trees then, and the root systems have time to become established before the heat of summer.

Tree planting is relatively simple. Dig the hole twice as wide and no deeper than the root-ball is tall. The soil you pull out of the hole is what you use to backfill around the root-ball. No soil amendments are necessary. For more details, refer to the September essay "Tree Planting Made Easy."

For training and pruning young trees, make sure you read the February essay "Pruning School." Follow the guidelines carefully to produce a structurally sound majestic shade tree.

'Little Gem' dwarf magnolia (Magnolia grandi-flora 'Little Gem')

Small Flowering Trees for Accent

TREE	FLOWERING SEASON	FLOWER COLOR
Althea	summer	multiple
Chinese fringe tree	spring	white
Crape myrtle	summer	multiple
Desert willow	summer	white, pink, rose
Dogwood	spring	white, pink, rose
Huisache	spring	yellow
Magnolia 'Little Gem'	spring/summer	white
Mexican buckeye	spring	dark pink to purple
Mexican plum	spring	white
Palo verde (retama)	summer	yellow
Panicled golden raintree	spring	yellow
Red buckeye	spring	red
Redbud	spring	white, pink, purple
Saucer magnolia	spring	pinkish white
Smoke tree	late spring	brownish red
Texas buckeye	spring	creamy white to yellow
Texas mountain laurel	spring	purple
Texas persimmon	spring	white
Wild olive	*year-round*	white

Oak Wilt–Resistant Trees

Oak wilt is a lethal fungal disease that has killed hundreds of thousands of live oaks and Texas red oaks in over 60 counties in Texas. Although the fatal disease's impact is most evident in Central Texas and the Hill Country, oak wilt is found in Abilene, College Station, Dallas, Fort Worth, Houston, Lubbock, and Midland.

Oak wilt symptoms on live oak.

Not all oaks are affected by oak wilt. White oaks are the least susceptible and recommended for planting in oak wilt–infested areas; they include bur, chinquapin, Monterrey, and post oaks. Red oaks are the most susceptible and typically die within 2 to 4 weeks of infection. Red oaks include blackjack, pin, Shumard, Spanish, and Texas. Live oak is neither a true white oak nor a red oak but lies somewhere in between. Live oaks have died from oak wilt in the greatest numbers in Texas. Death occurs over a period of a few months.

If you live in an area with oak wilt, the best strategy to combat the disease is to plant tree species that are not susceptible to the disease. If the species in communities, neighborhoods, and your yard are diversified, oak wilt will never completely denude the natural or urban forest.

The list below is a partial list of high-quality, readily available trees that are resistant to oak wilt. For more information, contact your county extension office or the Texas Forest Service, or access the Web site www.texasoakwilt.org.

American smoke tree (*Cotinus obovatus*)
Arizona cypress (*Cupressus arizonica*)
Bald cypress (*Taxodium distichum*)
Blanco crabapple (*Malus ioensis* var. *texana*)
Bur oak (*Quercus macrocarpa*)
Carolina buckthorn (*Frangula caroliniana*)
Cedar elm (*Ulmus crassifolia*)
Chinquapin oak (*Quercus muehlenbergii*)
Crape myrtle (*Lagerstroemia indica* and hybrids)
Deodar cedar (*Cedrus deodara*)
Desert willow (*Chilopsis linearis*)
Eve's necklace (*Sophora affinis*)
'Fan Tex' ash (*Fraxinus velutina* '*Fan Tex*')
Huisache (*Acacia farnesiana*)
Lacey oak (*Quercus laceyi*)
Mesquite (*Prosopis glandulosa* and hybrids)
Mexican buckeye (*Ungnadia speciosa*)
Monterrey/Mexican live oak (*Quercus polymorpha*)
Mexican plum (*Prunus mexicana*)

Montezuma cypress (*Taxodium mucronatum*)

Osage orange (bois d'arc, horse apple) (*Maclura pomifera*)

Palo verde (retama, Jerusalem thorn) (*Parkinsonia aculeata* and hybrid 'Desert Museum')

Pecan (*Carya illinoinensis*)

Plateau live oak (*Quercus fusiformis*)

Red buckeye (*Aesculus pavia*)

Redbud (Texas and Mexican) (*Cercis canadensis* var. *texensis* and *mexicana*)

Rusty blackhaw (*Viburnum rufidulum*)

Sycamore (*Platanus occidentalis*)

Texas ash (*Fraxinus texensis*)

Texas buckeye (*Aesculus glabra* var. *arguta*)

Texas hickory (*Carya texana*)

Texas mountain laurel (*Sophora secundiflora*)

Texas persimmon (*Diospyros texana*)

Texas pistache (*Pistacia mexicana*)

Texas walnut (*Juglans microcarpa*)

Evergreen Trees for Screening

American holly

Arizona cypress

Cherry laurel

Eastern red cedar

Leyland cypress

Live oak

'Nellie R. Stevens' holly

Texas mountain laurel

Wax myrtle

Yaupon holly

Select Shade Trees for Texas

(*Note:* The "select" list on page 322 includes trees that add significant value to the landscape, are available in the nursery trade, are relatively easy to grow, and are not riddled with pest problems. For example, you will not find Bradford pear [because it is overplanted and boring]; Arizona ash [because most of the tree questions I receive are about problems with this tree]; or silver maple [because it is short-lived and prone to pest problems]. This list was adapted from the publication "Landscape Water Conservation . . . Xeriscape" that William C. Welch [extension landscape horticulturist], Richard Duble [extension turfgrass specialist], and I authored for Texas Cooperative Extension. The original publication can be viewed at aggiehorticulture. tamu.edu.)

Select Shade Trees for Texas Landscapes
KEY TO AREA OF ADAPTATION

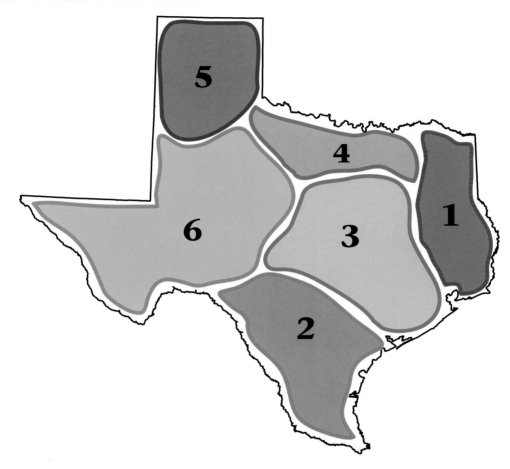

Region 1—East Texas (Beaumont, Houston, Nacogdoches, Texarkana, Tyler)

Region 2—South Texas (Brownsville, Corpus Christi, Del Rio, Laredo)

Region 3—Central Texas (Austin, College Station, San Antonio, Waco)

Region 4—North-Central Texas (Dallas, Denton, Fort Worth, Wichita Falls)

Region 5—Panhandle (Amarillo)

Region 6—West Texas (Abilene, El Paso, Lubbock, Midland, Odessa, San Angelo)

Note: Plants with an area of adaptation noted as 7 are adaptable to most areas of Texas.

Select Shade Trees for Texas Landscapes

Common name	Scientific name	Area of adaptation	Notes
Small trees (20–35 feet tall)			
American plum 🌸	*Prunus americana*	5	white blooms in spring; sour fruit good for jelly
American smoke tree F 🌸	*Cotinus obobatus*	7	round-topped small tree with profusion of pink blooms (smoke) in spring
Aristocrat pear 🌸	*Pyrus calleryana* 'Aristocrat'	1, 3, 4, 5, 6	spring flowers; fall color
Arizona cypress ⭐	*Cupressus arizonica*	7	dense, conical-shaped tree with silver-green needles
Cherry laurel ⭐ 🌸	*Prunus caroliniana*	1, 2, 3, 4, 6	small evergreen tree; screening
Chinese fringe tree 🌸	*Chionanthus retusus*	1	handsome small tree with glossy leaves and white spring blooms; cousin to less showy American fringe tree native to East Texas
Chinese pistache	*Pistacia chinensis*	7	spreading canopy; fall color
Crabapple 🌸	*Malus* sp.	1, 3, 4, 5, 6	spring-flowering tree; many varieties
Crape myrtle 🌸	*Lagerstroemia* hybrids	1, 2, 3, 4	single-trunked hybrids create small trees; summer flowers; beautiful trunks; varieties include 'Basham's Party Pink,' 'Natchez,' 'Tuscarora'
Desert willow ⭐ 🌸	*Chilopsis linearis*	2, 3, 4, 5, 6	snapdragon-like flowers in summer; willowlike foliage
Dogwood ⭐ 🌸	*Cornus florida*	1	graceful tree; large spring blooms of white and pink
Eastern or Canaert red cedar ⭐	*Juniperus virginiana*	7	evergreen for specimen or windbreak
Eldarica pine	*Pinus eldarica*	2, 3, 4, 6	best pine for alkaline soils; Christmas tree shaped

⭐ signifies Texas native plants.

🌸 signifies beautiful flowering plants.

COMMON NAME	SCIENTIFIC NAME	AREA OF ADAPTATION	NOTES
Fan d'Arc osage orange	*Maclura pomifera* 'Fan d'Arc'	7	improved fruitless selection
Honey mesquite ⭐ 🌸	*Prosopis glandulosa*	2, 3, 4, 6	lacy, spreading form
Huisache ⭐ 🌸	*Acacia farnesiana*	2, 3, 6	airy, fine-foliaged tree; intensely fragrant yellow blooms in spring
Japanese black pine	*Pinus thunbergii*	1	rounded small tree; adapted to alkaline soils
Japanese persimmon	*Diospyros kaki*	7	edible, showy fruit; glossy green foliage
Lacey oak ⭐	*Quercus laceyi*	2, 3, 6	medium-sized upright tree with bluish green foliage and lacy bark
Mexican buckeye ⭐ 🌸	*Ungnadia speciosa*	2, 3, 6	small tree or large shrub; pecan-shaped leaves; not a true buckeye; dark pink to purple spring blooms
Mexican plum ⭐ 🌸	*Prunus mexicana*	7	fragrant spring flowers; attractive trunk
Nanking cherry	*Prunus tomentosa*	5	tough, fruiting, shrubby tree
Palo verde 'Desert Museum' or retama ⭐ 🌸	*Parkinsonia* hybrid 'Desert Museum'	2, 3, 6	graceful, airy foliage on spreading tree; yellow flowers in spring
Panicled golden raintree 🌸	*Koelreuteria paniculata*	3, 4, 5, 6	showy yellow flowers and red seed pods
Pink lady euonymus	*Euonymus bungeanus*	5	alkaline tolerant; deciduous; light green foliage; showy seeds in fall
Red buckeye ⭐ 🌸	*Aesculus pavia* var. *pavia*	1, 3, 4	small tree or large shrub; five leaflets per leaf; red bloom spikes in spring
Redbud—eastern, Texas, and Mexican ⭐ 🌸	*Cercis* spp.	7	spring blooming; excellent varieties: 'Forest Pansy,' 'Oklahoma,' 'Texas White'
Slash pine ⭐	*Pinus elliottii*	1	evergreen pine
Soapberry ⭐	*Sapindus drummondii*	7	fall color

Texas buckeye ⭐	*Aesculus glabra* var. *arguta*	7	more leaflets than the red buckeye; creamy white to yellow spring flowers; leathery seed pods in fall
Texas ebony ⭐	*Pithecellobium flexicaule*	2	airy foliage and flowers
Texas mountain laurel ⭐ 🌸	*Sophora secundiflora*	2, 3, 6	treelike evergreen shrub; purple spring flowers
Wild olive ⭐ 🌸	*Corida boissieri*	2	white flowers and bold foliage
Large trees (above 35 feet tall)			
Anacua, anaqua, or manzanita ⭐	*Ehretia anacua*	2	coarse foliage; spring white, fragrant flowers; fall orange fruit; grown north to Austin
Austrian black pine	*Pinus nigra*	5	adapted to wind and cold
Bald cypress ⭐	*Taxodium distichum*	1, 2, 3, 4, 6	deciduous conifer; fine-textured foliage; fall color
Black gum ⭐	*Nyssa sylvatica*	1	adapted to heavy soils in East Texas; fabulous red fall color; fruit eaten by wildlife
Black walnut ⭐ 🌸	*Juglans nigra*	1, 5	good tree but tends to be messy
Blue spruce	*Picea pungens* 'Glauca'	5	grayish blue needles
Bur oak ⭐	*Quercus macrocarpa*	7	bold foliage; huge acorns
Cedar elm ⭐	*Ulmus crassifolia*	7	upright growth habit; good street tree
Chinquapin oak ⭐	*Quercus muhlenbergii*	1, 2, 3, 4, 6	round-topped tree; bold foliage
Deodar cedar	*Cedrus deodara*	7	bluish green conifer
'Fan Tex' ash	*Fraxinus velutina* 'Fan Tex'	1, 2, 3, 4	male selection (no seeds); medium-sized rounded tree
Ginkgo	*Ginkgo biloba*	7	slow grower; prehistoric plant; yellow fall color
Hackberry ⭐	*Celtis occidentalis*	5	variety 'Shademaster' particularly recommended for area 5
Honey locust ⭐	*Gleditsia triacanthos*	2, 3, 4, 5, 6	thornless varieties available

⭐ signifies Texas native plants.
🌸 signifies beautiful flowering plants.

Common name	Scientific name	Area of adaptation	Notes
Italian stone pine	Pinus pinea	3, 6	large pine adapted to alkaline soils
Kentucky coffee tree	*Gymnocladus dioica*	5	upright tree; fine-textured foliage
Lace bark or Chinese elm	*Ulmus parvifolia*	7	textured bark; spreading shade tree
Live oak ⭐	*Quercus virginiana*	1, 2, 3, 4, 6	evergreen shade tree
Loblolly pine ⭐	*Pinus taeda*	1	evergreen pine
Monterrey/Mexican live oak N	Quercus polymorpha	7	almost evergreen tree with bold foliage
Montezuma cypress ⭐	*Taxodium mucronatum*	1, 2, 3, 4, 6	deciduous conifer; fine-textured foliage; fall color; faster growing than bald cypress
Pecan ⭐	*Carya illinoinensis*	7	state tree; edible nuts
Ponderosa pine	*Pinus ponderosa*	5	bushy, attractive tree
River birch N	*Betula nigra*	1, 3	multitrunked; native to moist soils in East and Southeast Texas; exfoliating tan bark
Shumard oak ⭐	*Quercus shumardii*	1, 2, 3, 4, 5	fall color
Southern magnolia ⭐ 🌺	*Magnolia grandiflora*	1	bold evergreen tree; large white blooms in summer; 'Little Gem' dwarf variety is more widely adapted to alkaline, heavy soils
Southern or Texas sugar maple ⭐	*Acer barbatum*	1	only sugar maple native to Texas; thrives only in East Texas; fall color of scarlet to gold
Sweet gum ⭐	*Liquidambar styraciflua*	1	upright growth habit; fall color
Sycamore ⭐	*Platanus occidentalis*	7	huge, upright tree; bold foliage; white and gray trunk; Mexican sycamore native to South Texas

Texas ash ⭐	Fraxinus texensis	7	medium-sized, rounded tree; yellow fall color; superior to Arizona ash
Texas red oak ⭐	*Quercus texana*	7	fall color
Tulip poplar 🌺	*Lirodendron tulipifera*	1, 3, 4	unique square foliage; spring blooms; fall yellow-orange color
Water oak ⭐	*Quercus nigra*	1	holds foliage well into winter

⭐ signifies Texas native plants.

🌺 signifies beautiful flowering plants.

Top Trees for Texas Cities

County-based extension colleagues (noted) contributed their lists of top five trees recommended for their cities. (*Note:* Some of the agents simply couldn't restrict the list to just five.) With over 20 cities listed, rest assured that the trees recommended for the city nearest yours is a good place to start. Check with your local county extension agent or nursery professional to confirm your choices.

AMARILLO AND THE PANHANDLE (LEON J. CHURCH, COUNTY EXTENSION AGENT–AGRICULTURE, POTTER COUNTY)

- Austrian pine
- Cedar elm
- Chinese pistache
- Lace bark or Chinese elm
- Texas red oak

AUSTIN (ROBERT "SKIP" RICHTER, COUNTY EXTENSION AGENT–HORTICULTURE, TRAVIS COUNTY)

- Chinquapin oak (sites with decent soil depth)
- Lace bark or Chinese elm (sites with decent soil depth)
- Lacey oak (especially suited for smaller landscapes)
- Monterrey oak
- Texas red oak

BEAUMONT (MICAH MEYER, COUNTY EXTENSION AGENT–HORTICULTURE, JEFFERSON COUNTY)

- 'Aristocrat' ornamental pear
- Bald cypress
- Live oak
- Shumard oak
- Sweet gum

BRYAN AND COLLEGE STATION (DOUG WELSH, EXTENSION HORTICULTURIST, TEXAS A&M UNIVERSITY)

- Bald cypress
- Cedar elm
- Live oak
- Shumard oak
- Water oak

CORPUS CHRISTI (HELEN ORSAK, MASTER GARDENER LIAISON, NUECES COUNTY)

- Anacua
- 'Fan Tex' ash
- Texas ebony
- Texas redbud
- Texas sabal palm

DALLAS (DALE GROOM, COUNTY EXTENSION AGENT–HORTICULTURIST, DALLAS COUNTY)

- Bur oak
- Chinese pistache
- Lace bark or Chinese elm
- Live oak
- Shumard oak

EL PASO (DAPHNE LADEAN RICHARDS, COUNTY EXTENSION AGENT–HORTICULTURE, EL PASO COUNTY)
- Chinese pistache
- 'Desert Museum' palo verde or retama
- Desert willow
- Honey mesquite
- Italian stone pine

FORT WORTH (STEVE CHANEY, COUNTY EXTENSION AGENT–HORTICULTURE, TARRANT COUNTY)
- Bald cypress
- Bur oak
- Cedar elm
- Chinese pistache
- Chinquapin oak

HOUSTON (CAROL S. BROUWER, COUNTY EXTENSION AGENT–HORTICULTURE, HARRIS COUNTY)
- Bald cypress
- Chinese fringe tree
- Lace bark or Chinese elm
- Oaks—live, Monterrey/Mexican, Texas red, water
- Southern magnolia

LUBBOCK (BRANT A. BAUGH, EXTENSION AGENT–IPM, LUBBOCK COUNTY)
- Bur oak
- Cedar elm
- Chinese pistache
- Lace bark or Chinese elm
- Texas red oak

MCALLEN AND RIO GRANDE VALLEY (BARBARA A. STORZ, COUNTY EXTENSION AGENT–HORTICULTURE, HIDALGO COUNTY)
- Anacua
- Cedar elm
- Huisache
- Live oak
- Montezuma cypress

MIDLAND AND ODESSA (DEBORAH B. FROST, COUNTY EXTENSION AGENT–HORTICULTURE, ECTOR/MIDLAND COUNTIES)
- Bur oak
- Cedar elm
- Chinese pistache
- Desert willow
- Lace bark or Chinese elm

SAN ANGELO (JOHN E. BEGNAUD, COUNTY EXTENSION AGENT–HORTICULTURE, TOM GREEN COUNTY)
- Bur oak
- Cedar elm
- Chinese pistache
- Chinquapin oak
- Lacey oak
- Live oak

SAN ANTONIO (DAVID RODRIGUEZ, COUNTY EXTENSION AGENT–HORTICULTURE, BEXAR COUNTY)
- Crape myrtle (hybrids)
- Live oak
- Monterrey or Mexican live oak
- Texas red oak
- Texas redbud

TYLER (KEITH C. HANSEN, COUNTY EXTENSION AGENT–HORTICULTURE, SMITH COUNTY)
- Bald cypress
- Black gum
- Chinese pistache
- Ginkgo
- Oaks (live, Shumard, water, willow)
- Texas or southern sugar maple

VICTORIA (JOE JANAK, COUNTY EXTENSION AGENT–AGRICULTURE/NATURAL RESOURCES, VICTORIA COUNTY)
- Cedar elm
- Live oak
- Monterrey or Mexican live oak
- Pecan
- Shumard oak

WACO (DONALD W. KELM, COUNTY EXTENSION AGENT–AGRICULTURE, MCLENNAN COUNTY)
- Bur oak
- Chinese pistache
- Chinquapin oak
- Live oak
- Texas red oak

WICHITA FALLS (TARA MCKNIGHT, COUNTY EXTENSION AGENT–HORTICULTURE, WICHITA COUNTY)
- Bur oak
- Chinese pistache
- Chinquapin oak
- Live oak
- Texas red oak

Timely Tips

Flowers & Pretty Plants

- Take note again this month of which flowers are blooming. Only the toughest of the tough are still blooming. Guesses for what is blooming in your area are bougainvillea, bush morning glory, crape myrtle, firebush, hardy hibiscus, 'Knock Out' rose, lantana, mandevilla, native salvias, oleander, purslane, and Turk's cap.
- Keep watering as needed, but lay off the fertilizing this month.

Garden Design

- Evaluate the quality of your landscape this month. Look at its beauty, ability to adapt to the environment, and water needs. Late summer heat and/or drought cause a separation between those landscapes that are high quality and those that are not. Drive through any neighborhood, and you will see the differences.

Soil & Mulch

- Mulch flower and shrub beds, vegetable gardens, and areas around fruit trees to reduce soil temperatures in summer. Choose from organic mulches because they maintain soils at lower temperatures than rock mulches.

Water

- Check the performance of your irrigation system. System use has been intense, and weaknesses in the system will show up now. Run each station of the system, watching for geysers and heads that don't pop up, don't function properly, or are misaligned. Correct problems yourself, or get in line for the services of a licensed irrigator.
- Run hose-end sprinklers for at least an hour in one spot to achieve deep penetration of the water. Avoid runoff by moving the sprinkler back and forth between spots. If you drag hoses and hose-end sprinklers, you likely use less water than people with irrigation systems (research shows 40 percent less). The best hose-end sprinkler to use is the impact or pulse sprinkler. The little tractor sprinkler is surprisingly efficient. Forget the oscillating (wand-of-water-way-up-in-the-air) sprinkler—too much water lost to evaporation.
- Know that irrigation water can contain large amounts of salts

(e.g., sodium, calcium). The salts accumulate in the soil as water evaporates or transpires from the plant, and the salt is left behind. Whether in a containerized plant, flower bed, vegetable garden, or lawn, these salts can burn the plant roots and result in poor plant health. At least once a month, water twice as long (or much) in a single irrigation as normal. The heavy irrigation will dissolve the salts and flush them away from the plant roots; this is referred to as leaching. In a containerized plant, you want the water running freely out of the pot (not into a saucer). Summer rains are especially helpful in leaching these salts from the soil.

Plant Care

- Prepare your rosebushes, both modern hybrid and old-fashioned types, for a big show of blooms this fall by pruning this month. Cut back plants about 25 percent to generate new, vigorous growth for blooming. Also, pick or cut off diseased or damaged leaves and stems. Apply nitrogen fertilizer at $\frac{1}{4}$ cup of urea per plant, $\frac{1}{2}$ cup of ammonium sulfate, or 1 cup of blood meal. Repeat application again in 2 weeks if new growth is slow. Water the fertilizer in thoroughly.

- Keep pruning off old blooms on crape myrtles to generate more blossoms for the fall season. Crape myrtles are the "100-day bloomer," as long as you prune off the dead blooms.

Trees, Shrubs & Vines

- Evaluate your shade trees. Are they healthy? Are they on the downhill side of life? Do you have enough? Are they properly placed in the landscape? Plan now to plant trees this fall. Ideally, you will have several trees of different species and ages within your landscape. This protects against disastrous mass loss of trees due to disease or old age.
- Consider planting a groundcover (of vines or short plants) to replace unneeded lawn areas, particularly long, narrow strips of turf. Plant no more than 200 square feet at a time. This amount of groundcover is affordable, requires minimum effort to prepare soil and plants, and gives you a fighting chance against the weeds.

Lawns

- Realize that brown is a color, too. Maybe there are lawn areas in your landscape that you are willing to let go dormant in the summer. Okay, maybe not, but it is a worthy idea for the rough on golf courses, portions of school yards, and public parks in between the sports fields. This works only with drought-tolerant species of grass, such as Bermuda, zoysia, and buffalo, but not with St. Augustine or fescue, which will die.

- Water the lawn between 2 A.M. and 6 A.M.—it's the best time. Water pressure in town is high, evaporation levels are at their lowest, and the sun will come up and dry off the foliage. If you don't have an automated irrigation system, water before 9 A.M. or after 8 or 9 P.M. Always avoid irrigating in the middle of the day.

Vegetables, Herbs & Fruits

- Plant now. If you didn't start your fall vegetable gardening in July, then you are losing precious time. Tomatoes take about 90 days to grow and set and ripen fruit. Ninety days from August 1 is November 1. The chances of a frost are likely by then for much of the state. You may end up eating fried green tomatoes for dinner if you don't start now.
- Grow pumpkins for Halloween. For the Panhandle and West Texas, seed should be planted in early July, but for the rest of the state early August will do. (*Note:* The Panhandle is a major commercial producer of pumpkins for the nation.) Plant

moderate-sized pumpkin varieties (e.g., 'Appalachin,' 'Connecticut Field,' 'Small Sugar,' 'Triple Treat'). If you fail to produce pumpkins but produce lots of foliage, then go to the grocery store and purchase pumpkins. Place them in your pumpkin patch, and the children will never know. It's magic!

- Turn the irrigation system on every other day for 2 to 3 hours. Drip irrigation is the best way to irrigate vegetable gardens. For information on setting up a system for your garden, refer to the March essay "Saving Water Drip by Drip."
- Begin harvesting apples and pears in late August through September. Hopefully, the squirrels have left you plenty for fresh eating, baking, and preserving. If you have not grown apples or pears before, they are among the easier fruits to grow in the home landscape. The January essay "Growing Fruits and Nuts" will help you get started.
- Keep watering fruit trees to maintain healthy foliage. Next year's crop is dependent on this year's energy produced and stored by the leaves.

Butterflies, Birds & Squirrels

• Watch for the monarch butterfly migration through Texas that begins late this month as days begin to shorten. They are returning from their summer vacation resorts in the North, passing through Texas because of local hospitality, and heading on their way to overwintering sites in Mexico and Central America. Provide nourishing rest stops in your landscape by planting their favorite plant, butterfly weed (*Asclepias tuberose*).

• Notice that purple martins begin gathering in flocks late this month in preparation for their migration down to winter respites in South America. What great aerobatic insect eaters they are! If you want them to find a home in your yard next year, you will need to provide housing boxes to their specifications. Bookstores and the Internet are full of information on purple martins.

• Remember to provide water this month for all the backyard wildlife. Change out and add new water every couple of days, or you may just be creating a mosquito haven.

Notes:

September

Texas bluebonnets—white, blue, and pink
(Lupinus texensis)

COOLING OFF, MAYBE?

Fall into Gardening

Mexican bush sage (Salvia leucantha)

Who says Texas doesn't have a fall season? Maybe there is no winter season in Texas, just an extended fall (certainly the "winter Texans" from the Midwest would agree). Realistically, fall in Texas lasts from the last 90°F day until the first killing freeze. Depending on where you live, this period of time may be a couple of months or may never end before spring bursts forth. So for all practical purposes, fall in Texas is simply the period of time when you don't sweat as much.

Notice: "sweat as much." Most Texans have experienced personally or through children the dilemma of creating a Halloween costume that can be adapted readily to be comfortable regardless of the outdoor temperature. Either you are sweating and can't breathe under your gorilla mask or freezing to death in your grass skirt. Fall temperatures in Texas are widely variable and seldom land on the averages calculated by the National Weather Service.

The increased frequency of cooler temperatures and decreased day length make fall an ideal time to garden. The fall beckons you outdoors from the air-conditioned confines of Texas summers. Gardeners and yardeners alike migrate to nurseries and back home to plant flowers, vegetables, shrubs, and trees. Landscape remodeling or renovation projects abound. At a time when northern gardeners are closing up shop for the winter, Texans are beginning anew. Truly the fall may be the best season to plant, surpassing even the spring. What a wonderful time of year!

The fall months of September through December have distinct advantages for planting compared to the spring months of March to May. Fall planting follows the heat of summer and precedes cool to cold temperatures. Trees, shrubs, flowers, and vegetables planted in fall use this to good advantage.

- Plant roots grow anytime the soil temperature is 40°F or higher, which may occur throughout the winter in all areas but the Panhandle. During the fall and winter months, the root systems of fall-planted plants grow and become well established. When spring arrives, this expanded root system can support and take advantage of the full surge of spring growth.
- Fall is a perfect time to plant container-grown trees and shrubs. Restricted root systems of these plants have ample time to recover from transplanting and proliferate new roots before spring growth begins.
- Note that all bare-root plants sold in nurseries, including roses, pecans, and fruit trees, should not be planted in the fall. With such extremely reduced root systems, these plants should be planted in the winter months, when they are completely dormant and growth will occur only in the roots, not the shoots.
- The cooler days of fall reduce overall plant stress. Most newly planted shrubs, groundcovers, and perennial flowers benefit from lower fall temperatures. There are exceptions; be careful planting small plants that are marginally cold tolerant for your area. In the northern half of the state such plants may be damaged by early freezes or prolonged hard winters (e.g., best wait till spring to plant Asiatic jasmine). Check with nursery professionals to identify these plants for your area.
- Rainfall is more common in fall months, thus a reduced need for irrigation. Rainfall also helps dilute and flush salts from the soil that have accumulated during summerlong irrigation with poor-quality water (i.e., high salt content).
- For most plants, growth and flowering are induced by fall weather conditions. Roses bloom heavily, and colors are more vivid. Shrubs and perennial flowers may put forth a fall flush of growth.

- For some flowering plants, shorter days of fall are actually required for blooms to emerge or reach full bloom (e.g., candlestick plant [*Cassia alata*], chrysanthemums, Mexican bush sage, Mexican mint marigold).

- For vegetables, crops mature in the fall, as daytime and nighttime temperatures are much cooler than in summer. This results in less plant stress and higher-quality, better-tasting produce, whether it be fruits on bean, pepper, and tomato plants or edible plant parts, such as broccoli, cauliflower, leaf lettuce, and spinach.

The most important reason to garden in the fall may be a selfish one—it feels good to humans. Working in the garden is more pleasant in the fall. The heat of summer is in the past. The garden appears more vibrant and beautiful. The birds are more active. The mosquitoes and other pest populations are retreating from the cooler weather. There is exuberant life in the garden and a heightened intensity due to pending dormancy. Thank goodness in Texas that winter dormancy is of such short duration. So, "fall into gardening" once again or for the very first time!

Gardening with Perennial Flowers

A great renaissance has taken place in Texas landscapes. It has been a "back to the future" gardening phenomenon. Gardeners are rediscovering the use of perennial flowers, once a mainstay of "cottage gardens" of the late 1800s.

Annual flowers have been the focus for creating color in the landscape in recent decades with their density of bloom and in-your-face bright, almost fluorescent colors. Planting in traffic-stopping masses became a standard. By contrast, perennial flowers conjure up visions of softer flowers both in form and color. Plantings of many species grouped together to create living flower

Cottage garden filled with 'Apple-blossom' verbena, purple coneflower, and blue salvia.

arrangements and "flower borders" are becoming more common once again.

Folks often state that the major difference between annuals and perennials is that "you purchase and plant perennials once and forget them" but "annuals must be purchased and planted yearly" (and in Texas must be changed out and replanted multiple times in one year). Although there is some truth in these statements, perennials cannot just be planted and forgotten. They must be tended and are often as costly as annuals.

There should not, however, be an "either-or" mentality with annuals and perennials. The best gardens combine the strengths of both. This essay focuses on gardening with perennials:

- How to incorporate them in the landscape
- How to design and combine them in plantings and flower borders
- How to choose appropriate species for your garden
- How to plant and tend them

One of the great strengths of perennials is their multiple uses within any landscape. There are guidelines (not rigid rules) in using perennials in the landscape. The flexibility and wide range of use sometimes serve as hindrances to delving into perennials. Perennials are for every gardener and yardener. Here are a few uses culminating in the classic use, the perennial flower border.

Unifying element. To help provide unity in your landscape, one species of perennial flower can be selected and planted on different sides or points in the landscape. For example, blue plumbago could be included in plantings in the front landscape at either end of the home, repeated at the front door, and perhaps again at the mailbox.

Bed expansion. Enhance a shrub hedge or bed by expanding the planting into the lawn 3 to 4 feet and planting a row of one perennial flower species. An example would be planting a line of daylilies in front of a boring holly hedge. The late spring bloom of the daylilies will provide great beauty, and the grasslike foliage will contrast nicely with the dark green hedge.

Expand and enhance a Burford holly hedge with a front row of daylilies.

Pocket plantings. The ends, curves, or corners of a shrub planting are prime places to incorporate a small pocket planting of two, three, or four perennial flower species. One pocket planting may be just the focal point for a drab, evergreen backyard or may serve as a small source of cut flowers for use indoors. Repeat this pocket planting with the same combination of species in multiple spots in the landscape, and you produce unity in the landscape.

Container plantings. Perennial flowers are fabulous for container gardening. A single perennial flower can be planted in a container, or you can create a living flower arrangement in a pot, referred to as a "dish garden." Planting perennials in containers also allows you to grow some perennials that don't generally perform well in your garden soil conditions. Using a good potting soil containing acidifying peat moss allows gardeners to grow acid-loving plants outside East Texas. Hostas, ajuga, and violets all can be grown in containers throughout Texas. It is much easier to manipulate the soil environment in a pot than in a flower bed.

"Perannials." Jerry Parsons, extension horticulturist, coined this term to describe a perennial flower that is used as an annual. The color, appearance, and summer toughness of many perennials exceed that of many summer annuals. Try some perennial flowers in large masses or in combination with other annuals in the garden. For example, blue salvia (mealy cup sage) is a spectacular summer bloomer in huge masses as a replacement for annual salvias and periwinkle. Firebush will freeze to death each winter in the northern half of the state (so it won't be a perennial there), but it is too valuable a flowering plant not to use it as an annual.

Flower borders. The English perfected the perennial flower border hundreds of years ago. The classic 30-meter-long, 5-meter-deep flower border is seen in the finest gardens of England. The border can be downsized to fit nicely into any size landscape. There are some important design concepts and guidelines that should be followed to produce a beautiful, all-season flower border:

- Locate a flower border in front of a 4- to 6-foot-tall backdrop, such as a fence, wall, shrub hedge, or building.
- Avoid creating a straight front edge to the border, unless the garden is very formal. Curved front edges, from gentle to bold and sweeping, are essential components of flower borders. A garden hose can be used to help visualize and lay out the curves. Look at several layouts, and avoid the "too-many-small-curves, snake-look" syndrome. Generally, the bolder the curves, the better.

- Set the depth of the border at a minimum of 3 feet, and expand to 8 feet or more depending on the size of the landscape area.
- Line the border edge with steel edging, bricks, stone, or modular pavers to give a finished edge that stands out visually and can be easily trimmed. For a less formal look, don't use any edging material, and let the border blend naturally into lawns or patios.
- Plan the plantings within the border by using drifts and clumps. This is where sketching the border on paper will help you visualize the border plantings. A drift is an elongated grouping of one species that flows through a portion of the border. A clump is a circular plant or grouping. The length of drifts and the diameter of clumps, as well as heights, should vary.
- Group plants in drifts or other masses in odd numbers of three to seven.
- Place the groups of plants with the tallest perennial flowers in the back of the border and the shortest in front. Be careful not to make a simple stairstep effect. Varying the heights throughout the border with some randomness creates more interest and visual appeal.

Selecting combinations of perennial flowers for pocket plantings, containers, and borders is an art, with a few guidelines. If you are concerned about your artistic ability, use these guidelines, and you may surprise yourself and others. (If all else fails, find perennial combinations in a demonstration garden, botanical garden, nursery, perennial book, or your neighbor's yard, and copy the planting. Imitation is the highest form of flattery.)

- Foremost, concentrate your choices from perennial flowers that are locally adapted and dependable species. Refer to the perennials list at the end of this essay. In addition, check with local experts at nurseries, public gardens, and university extension offices and on the Internet. Above all, don't be afraid to try any perennial in your garden. Be a pioneer, and don't be afraid of failure. Good gardeners are always changing out plants in their perennial plantings.
- Select perennial flowers that will thrive in the sunlight conditions of the border: sun, partial sun, or shade. The best sunlight exposure in Texas seems to be morning sun and afternoon shade.
- Choose perennial flower combinations based on flower (inflorescence) type. This is also the basis of cut-flower design. Combine the four types of flowers: spike (salvia), tubular (petunia), ray (daisy), and umbel (lantana).

- Choose species based on bloom period. The goal is to have blooms ebbing and flowing through the entire growing season—newly blooming species taking over for spent bloomers. Constant blooming requires some planning. A perennial border that is bloomed out by midsummer turns into ugly fast.

- Select perennial flowers by color. It may sound counterintuitive, but flower type is much more important than color. Your color preferences and desired effect now come into consideration. Refer to "Color Concepts" later in this essay, for more guidelines on use of color in the landscape.

- Fine-tune the border by considering foliage color and texture. Consider different shades of green foliage and variegated foliage. Also, combine various foliage textures through the use of fine-textured ornamental grasses and bold-textured plants, such as cannas and gingers.

Thus far, there seems to be a plethora of guidelines for gardening with perennials. Don't let them dissuade you. They are guidelines, not rules. Try perennials, make mistakes, move plants around, and create unthought-of combinations. Fight the urge to plant perennials in rows or patterns. Learn to "smush" plants into

Four flower types: spike (salvia), tubular (petunia), ray (daisy), and umbel (lantana).

plantings. An impression of lack of organization is a strength for many perennial plantings.

The most difficult part of gardening with perennials is incorporating them into your landscape; growing them is much easier.

Care of Perennial Flowers

Plantings of perennial flowers are designed to last for years; however, unless you give them proper care, you may find yourself replanting annually and abandoning the use of these wonderful plants.

Perhaps the most important concept in tending perennial flowers is deadheading, removing old blooms. Most perennials have a limited blooming period of about 2 to 3 weeks before they stop blooming and try to set seed, thus

Deadheading is critical for a profusion of blooms on perennials.

completing their annual duties. By deadheading a perennial, you fool the plant into thinking it has not completed this life cycle, and the plant tends to bloom again. Deadheading is a regular pruning activity for perennials. There are exceptions, such as Shasta daisy and daylily, that bloom only once per year. Deadheading these plants will not induce more blooms, and they must be allowed to sit in this nonblooming stage while other perennials become the attraction in the planting.

Other pruning activities will be needed for perennials to remove freeze-damaged shoots and maintain plant vigor and health for multiple years.

Cold hardiness of perennials affects the level of pruning required, and cold hardiness is very species specific, and garden specific. Some perennials will survive Texas winters throughout the state and are thus considered "hardy." The shoots and branches of some perennials will freeze back to the ground each winter but sprout back from the roots in spring; this is considered "root hardy." Most perennials have shoots and branches frozen back to some height on the plant each year. This dead or damaged plant material should be removed each year.

"When to prune?" becomes the primary question. Ideally, you should prune after spring growth begins. Let the plant show you when and where to prune.

Simply wait until green shoots appear, and prune off the portion of the shoots or branches that do not show any new growth. If this is the entire plant and shoots emerge from the ground, the plant is root hardy. If no growth appears in spring from the ground, then the plant is d-e-a-d, dead, thus not a perennial for your garden (perhaps still valuable as an annual).

Some perennials tend to develop woody, thick branches that don't grow vigorously or bloom heavily (e.g., autumn sage and other sages, Mexican oregano, Turk's cap). These plants can be pruned back by at least a half or more every year in late winter to maintain their longevity and productivity. Some perennials should be cut within 6 inches of the ground every year or two to "re-create" a whole new, vigorous plant (e.g., esperanza, indigo spires salvia, pavonia).

Pruning perennials to keep them in bounds or nicely shaped can be done throughout the growing season. Pruning, including deadheading, is the most time-consuming task in growing perennials.

Other cultural and maintenance practices for success with perennials include the following:

- Carry out thorough soil preparation by amending the existing soil with lots of organic matter. The goal is to have about 12 inches of well-

CALLER: "Can I prune freeze-damaged, ugly stems of perennials in winter?"

ANSWER: "Yes, if you don't want to put up with ugly, then cut back the freeze-damaged shoots beginning at the tip, and keep pruning back until you find green inside the bark. I prune back the 'ugly' in the front yard and leave the ugly in the backyard. Again, letting the plant show me how much to remove helps me start the spring with the largest perennial plants possible in the garden. The bigger the plants, generally the more blooms to come."

prepared soil to maintain healthy root systems.

- Plant perennials at the appropriate time based on when they bloom. Generally, late-summer- or fall-flowering perennials are planted in spring. Spring-flowering perennials are planted in late summer or fall (for the northern half of Texas, plant large plants in the fall, or simply wait until spring to avoid heavy freeze damage).

- Properly space perennials in the planting. Refer to the plant list or plant tags for width of each species;

allow plenty of space between plants because most perennials spread quickly.

• Water perennials as needed. Many perennials are highly adapted and require less frequent irrigation than annual flowers. Determine soil moisture levels with your index finger; drip irrigation is ideally suited for perennial plantings.

• Mulch, mulch, mulch to conserve soil moisture, prevent weeds, reduce plant diseases, and provide an attractive groundcover for perennial plantings.

• Weed the plantings regularly until they are thick and well established. Few weeds, other than Bermudagrass, will invade a healthy perennial planting. Pre-emergence herbicides (which prevent seeds from germinating and growing) can be particularly useful for perennial plantings where weed pressure is intense.

• Fertilize on a limited basis. Most perennials are not heavy feeders; in fact, some (e.g., gaillardia) will grow rampantly and produce fewer blooms if fertilized too much. Once-a-year application in early spring with a lawn fertilizer should be adequate.

• Divide perennials by digging and separating masses; this is essential for many perennials for continued growth and blooming. Typical examples are daylily and iris, which will stop blooming completely when they become crowded (they bloom only on newly expanded rhizomes or roots). Dividing should be done every 2 to 4 years if the plants are not blooming well.

• Stake tall perennials that have a tendency to lodge (fall over), such as dahlia, delphinium (larkspur), and garden phlox. Specially designed metal stakes with horizontal loops are made for perennials.

• Clean up perennial plantings in the fall by removing dead plants, branches, and leaves; rake up plant debris on the mulched soil surface to tidy up the planting and reduce plant diseases and insect pests.

Color Concepts

The color range of flowers and foliage in perennials, annuals, and shrubs (e.g., roses) is enormous. Harmony, interest, and variety can be achieved in the landscape and flower beds through proper use of color. Color also evokes emotion in the garden, providing calm or excitement.

There are guidelines, not rules, for using color in the landscape. Personal preferences and experimentation are worthy components in use of color as well.

There are two types of colors, warm and cool. Red, orange, and yellow are warm colors. Blue, green, and purple are cool colors. Warm colors provide a sense of festivity or excitement. They advance to the eye (e.g., exit signs and stop signs are red for this reason). Warm colors can make a garden or landscape feel smaller or more intimate.

Conversely, cool colors create a sense of calm and tranquility. They recede from the eye and give a small garden the illusion of openness and space. In general, the smaller the landscape or garden area, the more cool colors and fewer warm colors should be used.

A note about foliage texture is appropriate because bold-textured foliage has the same effect as warm colors and fine-textured foliage has the same effect as cool colors. Use foliage texture the same way you do color in your garden.

Drama and focus occur when warm and cool colors are placed adjacent to each other (e.g., a group of purple pansies next to yellow pansies, or blue plumbago next to gold mound lantana or esperanza/yellow bells). Wild exuberance (from warm colors) or numbing calm (from cool colors) can be achieved by using the same type of color in a landscape planting or flower bed.

Perhaps the best strategy is to seek harmony and unity in landscape plantings by combining warm and cool colors, balancing the plantings so no color type dominates the other. Such an approach can result in a beautiful, ever-changing

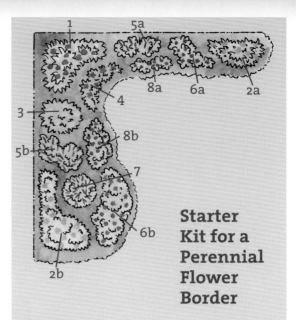

Starter Kit for a Perennial Flower Border

Similar to a starter kit for a wooden deck offered by home-improvement centers, here is a packaged design and plant list for a 100-square-foot perennial flower border. Check with local experts at nurseries or county extension offices for appropriateness of perennials listed.

PLANTING KEY

Perennial (number of plants)

1. Canna lily (3)
2a. Blue plumbago (3)
2b. Blue plumbago (4)
3. Gold star esperanza (1)
4. Purple coneflower (5)
5a. Mexican bush sage (2)
5b. Mexican bush sage (3)
6a. 'Homestead' purple verbena (3)
6b. 'Homestead' purple verbena (5)
7. 'Flare' pink hibiscus (1)
8a. Gaillardia (3)
8b. Gaillardia (5)

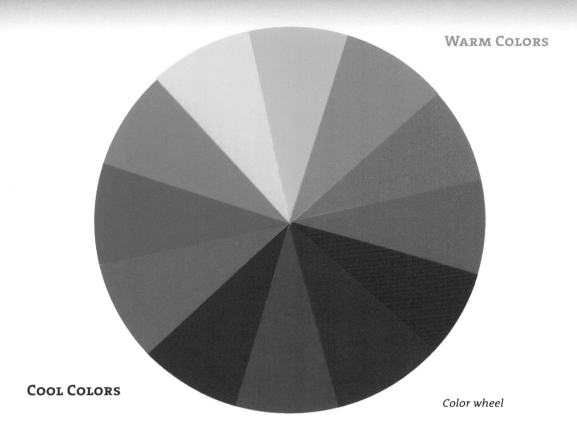

WARM COLORS

COOL COLORS

Color wheel

tapestry of color in the landscape. This strategy can also be used for incorporating texture in the landscape.

White, the absence of color, has a unique effect in the landscape. White flowers cleanly separate any color flower from another. A border of white sweet alyssum creates a clean line between a planting of red verbena and pink zinnias.

A garden planted with a variety of plants all with white flowers or white and green variegated foliage can be especially attractive. White gardens are popular near outdoor spaces (e.g., decks and patios). They are particularly visible at dawn and dusk, brightening and enhancing the landscape area.

Gray-foliaged plants (e.g., artemisia and dusty miller) can also serve to separate competing flower colors and brighten a planting. They also contrast nicely with plants that have dark green foliage.

Many gardening books showcase the use of color in the landscape using perennials, annuals, and shrubs. Look to these references for further guidance and examples as you advance your use of color in the landscape.

SELECT PERENNIAL FLOWERS FOR TEXAS LANDSCAPES

COMMON NAME	SCIENTIFIC NAME	FLOWER TYPE	FLOWER COLOR	FLOWERING SEASON	PLANT HEIGHT AND WIDTH	LOCATION (SUN TO SHADE)	NOTES
Artemisia 'Powis Castle'	*Artemisia* hybrid	n/a	n/a	n/a	2 feet by 3 feet	sun to shade	valued for its fine-textured gray foliage; 'Powis Castle' only artemisia adapted throughout Texas
'Autumn Joy' sedum	*Sedum* 'Herbst-freude'	umbel	reddish pink	late summer to fall	1 ½ feet by 1 ½ feet	sun	drought-tolerant succulent
Autumn sage	*Salvia greggii*	spike	white, red, pink, salmon	spring, summer, fall	3 feet by 3 feet	sun	native; great for butterflies and hummingbirds
Blue salvia/ mealy cup sage	*Salvia farinacea*	spike	blue, white, purple	spring, summer, fall	3 feet by 3 feet	sun	several new varieties available
Bulbine	*Bulbine frutescens*	spike	yellow, orange	spring, summer, fall	18 inches by 24 inches	sun to partial shade	valued also for succulent, upright, aloe vera–like foliage; low water requirement; perennial south of line from San Antonio to College Station
Butterfly weed	*Asclepias tuberosa*	umbel	yellow/ orange blend	summer, fall	4 feet by 3 feet	sun	monarch butterfly and caterpillar both feed on this plant
Canna	*Canna x generalis*	tubular spike	yellow, red, pink, salmon	summer	4 feet by 3 feet	sun to partial shade	many spectacular flower colors; some varieties have bronze or variegated foliage; valued source of bold texture in garden
Chrysanthemum, garden	*Chrysanthemum morifolium*	ray	many	fall	2 feet by 2 feet	sun to partial shade	choose garden mums, not florist mums, for success

COMMON NAME	SCIENTIFIC NAME	FLOWER TYPE	FLOWER COLOR	FLOWERING SEASON	PLANT HEIGHT AND WIDTH	LOCATION (SUN TO SHADE)	NOTES
Columbine, Hinckley's	*Aquilegia chrysantha hinckleyana*	tubular	yellow	spring	2 feet by 2 feet	partial shade	*A. canadensis,* close kin with red/yellow flowers
Confederate rose hibiscus	*Hibiscus mutabilis*	tubular	singles/ double white, deep pinkish red	summer, fall	6–10 feet by 6–10 feet	sun	perennial south of line from San Antonio to College Station
Coreopsis	*Coreopsis* sp.	ray	yellow	late spring, summer	2 feet by 2 feet	sun	native wildflower and hybrid varieties
Cuphea/ cigar plant/ Mexican oleander	*Cuphea micropetala*	tubular	red and yellow blend	late summer, fall	3 feet by 3 feet	sun	great for hummingbirds and butterflies
Daylily	*Hemerocallis* sp.	tubular	yellow, orange, blends of colors	spring, summer	1–3 feet by 2 feet	sun	great time-tested selections for Texas: lemon daylily (*H. flava*), tawny daylily (*H. fulva*), 'Gran Primo,' and 'Stella D' Ora' dwarf daylily
Duranta/ Brazilian sky flower	*Duranta erecta*	spike	light blue to purple	summer, fall	4–5 feet by 4–5 feet	sun to partial shade	showy golden ball fruit; perennial south of line from San Antonio to College Station
Esperanza/ yellow bells	*Tecoma stans*	tubular spikes	yellow	summer, fall	4–6 feet by 4–5 feet	sun	perennial south of line from San Antonio to College Station
Firebush	*Hamelia patens*	tubular umbel	reddish orange	summer, fall	3–5 feet by 3–5 feet	sun	perennial south of line from San Antonio to College Station
Frikarti aster	*Aster x frikartii*	ray	lavender	fall	3 feet by 3 feet	sun to partial shade	purple daisy flower for fall

COMMON NAME	SCIENTIFIC NAME	FLOWER TYPE	FLOWER COLOR	FLOWERING SEASON	PLANT HEIGHT AND WIDTH	LOCATION (SUN TO SHADE)	NOTES
Gaillardia/ Indian blanket	*Gaillardia* sp. and hybrids	ray	reddish yellow	spring, summer, fall	2 feet by 3 feet	sun	native wildflower and hybrid varieties
Garlic	*Allium* sp.	umbel	white	summer	18 inches by 12 inches	sun to shade	valued for its gray, straplike foliage
Gaura	*Gaura lindheimeri*	spike	white, deep rose	spring, summer, fall	3 feet by 2 feet	sun to partial shade	unique native flower and new hybrids
Gingers, variegated	*Alpinia zerumbet* 'Variegated'	spike	yellow with red	summer	3–5 feet by 3–5 feet	sun to partial shade	valued for bold yellow and green variegated foliage, not for the seldom-seen flowers; root-hardy perennial south of line from San Antonio to College Station
Gladiolus byzintinus	*Gladiolus byzintinus*	spike	purple-rose	late spring	2 feet by 1 foot	sun to partial shade	dwarf gladiola highly valued for blooms and foliage
Hibiscus, hardy	*Hibiscus* spp. and hybrids	tubular	red, fuchsia, pink, white, blends	summer, fall	3–5 feet by 3–5 feet	sun	'Flare' and 'Lord Baltimore' excellent varieties; hardy hibiscuses are not to be confused with cold-sensitive Chinese hibiscus
Hosta	*Hosta* spp.	spike	white, lavender	summer, fall	1–3 feet by 1–3 feet	shade	valued primarily for the foliage; blue, green, yellow, and variegated foliage varieties; adapted primarily to East Texas

COMMON NAME	SCIENTIFIC NAME	FLOWER TYPE	FLOWER COLOR	FLOWERING SEASON	PLANT HEIGHT AND WIDTH	LOCATION (SUN TO SHADE)	NOTES
Indigo spires	*Salvia* sp. hybrid	spike	purple	summer, fall	4–5 feet by 4–5 feet	sun	large shrub with loads of flowers
Iris	*Iris* spp.	tubular spike	many	spring	1–4 feet by 2–3 feet	sun to partial shade	cemetery iris (white) and Louisiana iris (many varieties) valued as much for the swordlike foliage as the blooms
Iris, butterfly or African	*Moraea* or *Dietes iridioides*	tubular spike	greenish yellow	summer	3 feet by 3 feet	sun	valued for blooms and fine, swordlike foliage; root-hardy perennial south of line from San Antonio to College Station
Lantana	*Lantana* spp.	umbel	purple, yellow, red, white, blends	late spring, summer, fall	1–4 feet by 3 feet	sun	many trailing and upright forms in a multitude of colors; trailing forms perennial only along coast and in deep South Texas
Maximilian sunflower	*Helianthus maximiliani*	ray	yellow	summer	4 feet by 3 feet	sun	native wildflower for the garden
Mexican bush sage	*Salvia leucantha*	spike	purple, purple and white	fall primarily	3–4 feet by 3–4 feet	sun	perennial in southern half of state
Mexican mint marigold	*Tagetes lucida*	ray	yellow	summer, fall	2 feet by 2 feet	sun	often referred to as Texas tarragon; wonderful, hardy herb for flavoring similar to anise or licorice
Mexican oregano	*Poliomintha longiflora*	tubular	pink/ white	summer, fall	3 feet by 3 feet	sun to partial shade	replacement for true oregano, plus blooms and is more adapted

Common name	Scientific name	Flower type	Flower color	Flowering season	Plant height and width	Location (sun to shade)	Notes
Pavonia/rock rose	*Pavonia lasiopetala*	ray	pink	spring, summer	3 feet by 3 feet	sun	very drought tolerant native
Phlox, perennial garden	*Phlox paniculata*	umbel	light pink, rosy red	summer	3 feet by 2 feet	sun	great varieties: 'John Fanick' and 'Victoria'
Pink, perennial	*Dianthus* spp.	ray	red, rose, white	spring	1 foot by 1 foot	sun to partial shade	old-fashioned, time-tested flower
Plumbago	*Plumbago auriculata*	umbel	blue, white	summer, fall	3 feet by 3 feet	sun or partial shade	perennial south of line from San Antonio to College Station; deer resistant
Purple coneflower	*Echinacea purpurea*	ray	purple	spring, summer, fall	18 inches by 24 inches	sun	a classic for every garden
Rain lily	*Zephyranthes* spp.	tubular	white, yellow, pink	following rains	12 inches by 12 inches	sun to shade	hard to find in nurseries but well worth the hunt
Rosemary	*Rosmarinus officinalis*	tubular	blue	summer	1–3 feet by 3 feet	sun to partial shade	prostrate and upright forms; valued more for the needlelike foliage and as an herb than for the flowers
Rudbeckia	*Rudbeckia* sp. hybrids	ray	yellow, orange, reddish orange	summer	2–3 feet by 3 feet	sun	native wildflower and many hybrids
Shasta daisy	*Chrysanthemum maximum*	ray	white	spring	3 feet by 2 feet	sun to partial shade	many varieties available
Shrimp plant	*Justicia brandegeana*	spike	yellow, reddish brown, red	summer, fall	3 feet by 2 feet	sun to partial shade	old-fashioned perennial with new varieties available
Skullcap, Texas	*Scutellaria suffrutescens*	tubular	pink	summer, fall	12–15 inches by 12–15 inches	sun	extreme drought tolerance

Common Name	Scientific Name	Flower Type	Flower Color	Flowering Season	Plant Height and Width	Location (sun to shade)	Notes
Society garlic	*Tulbaghia violacea*	umbel	lavender	summer	1–2 feet by 1 foot	partial shade	green and variegated foliage varieties available
Spider lily, 'Tropical Giant'	*Hymenocallis* spp.	tubular	white	summer	2–3 feet by 3 feet	sun to shade	grown primarily for the bright green, straplike foliage
Summer snapdragon	*Angelonia angustifolia*	spike	purple, rose, white, bicolor	spring, summer, fall	2 feet by 2 feet	sun to partial shade	great addition to gardens
Sweet violet	*Viola odorata*	tubular ray	purple, lavender, pink, white	winter, spring	6–10 inches by 6–10 inches	partial shade or shade	best grown in East Texas
Thrift/moss pink	*Phlox subulata*	umbel	pink	spring	8–10 inches by 12 inches	sun or partial shade	old-fashioned, time-tested plant
Turk's cap	*Malvaviscus arboreus*	spike	red	summer, fall	3–5 feet by 3–5 feet	sun to shade	deer-resistant and shade-resistant bloomer
Verbena, perennial	*Verbena* spp. and hybrids	umbel	purple, lavender, rose, pink, red, blue	spring, summer, fall	6–18 inches by 2–3 feet	sun	excellent varieties: 'Appleblossom' (pink/white), 'Blue Princess,' 'Homestead Purple,' and 'Taylortown Red'
Yarrow	*Achillea millefolium*	umbel	yellow, white, rose	spring, summer	1 foot by 1 foot	partial shade	fernlike foliage; rose color more hardy

Plant Wildflowers in Fall

Texas is blessed with over 1,000 species of wildflowers. They adorn the natural landscape, roadways, and even cultivated landscapes. By planting wildflower seed in September, you can enjoy this uniquely Texan flora in your own backyard. Below are steps to success, "select" wildflowers for Texas landscapes, and information on the state flower of Texas, the bluebonnet.

Wildflower seed becomes expensive bird seed unless you plant it properly. Follow these steps for success:

- Late August and September are the best times to plant seed.
- Purchase wildflower seed from a reliable source that has "fresh" seed (i.e., from this year's crop). Some Texas wildflowers (e.g., bluebonnets, bluebells, gaillardia, mealy cup sage)

Texas wildflowers: bluebonnet, gaillardia, Indian paintbrush, Mexican hat, Drummond phlox, and bluebell.

are available in transplants, just like petunias.

- Success the first year is more likely if you purchase a wildflower mix containing 15 to 20 species. Determine which species thrive, and enhance the area with more seed of those specific wildflowers the next fall. Not all Texas wildflowers will do well in your area or landscape. The recommended seeding rate is $\frac{1}{4}$ pound per 500 square feet (or 1 pound per 2,000 square feet) for maximum color.
- In flower beds, remove all vegetation and till the soil only 1 inch deep, or lightly till existing lawn areas of buffalograss or Bermudagrass to open the soil (St. Augustine and zoysia are not suitable for wildflower plantings).
- The most important concept in planting wildflower seed is to achieve good soil-seed contact, thus the need for tilling.
- Mix the wildflower seed mix with sand at 1 part seed to 4 parts sand. This aids in distributing the different-sized and different-weight seeds evenly over the area (e.g., gaillardia seeds are fluffy, bluebonnet like pea gravel, and Indian paintbrush like ground pepper).
- Use a hand-held whirlybird spreader to spread the seed-and-sand mixture evenly over the area.

- The seed must fall into the soil (not more than $\frac{1}{2}$ inch deep) and be tamped down with your feet (or roller) to firmly place the seed and soil together.
- Water the seeded area lightly just to settle the seed and soil. Beyond this watering, wildflowers will germinate with natural rainfall. If drought occurs in September, apply light waterings every week.
- Pull broadleaf weeds that appear through the fall and winter. Differentiating a weed seedling from a wildflower seedling can be tricky. Refer to the Wildseed Farms Web site or other reference (e.g., "Texas Wildflower Wheel," tcebookstore.org) for photos of seedlings.
- Sit back and wait until spring for your first wildflower blooms to appear. Take notes on which do well.
- If you want the flowers to set and disperse seed for next year, do not remove the dead blooms or plants until mid-June or when all the flowers die. Then you can cut the plants down and shake them over the wildflower bed or mow the lawn area. If your wildflowers were successful in the lawn area, count how many times you did not have to mow due to the beautiful wildflowers (could be six or more).

Wildflower Seed Source

Texas is lucky to have one of the largest wildflower seed companies in the nation, Wildseed Farms (located 7 miles east of Fredericksburg). John Thomas, founder of Wildseed Farms, has the unique perspective of a successful rice farmer who realized the many benefits of using wildflowers on roadways, commercial landscapes, and home gardens. He describes himself not as a wildflower lover but "a user of wildflowers" to create beauty, traffic-stopping color, and reduced mowing requirements for road crews, landscape maintenance professionals, and you, the homeowner. Wildseed Farms supplies retail nurseries and garden centers throughout Texas and has mail and online ordering services. Wildseed Farms is also a destination for thousands of visitors year-round. Contact information is Wildseed Farms, 425 Wildflower Hills, P.O. Box 3000, Fredericksburg, TX 78624; 800-848-0078; wildseedfarms.com.

Select Wildflowers for Texas Landscapes		
Common name (*Scientific name*)	Flower type	Flower color
Black-eyed Susan (*Rudbeckia hirta*)	ray	yellow with brown center
Bluebell (*Eustoma grandiflora*)	tubular	bluish purple
Bluebonnet (*Lupinus texensis*)	spike	blue, white, or pink
Drummond phlox (*Phlox drummondii*)	umbel	red
Gaillardia/Indian blanket (*Gaillardia pulchella*)	ray	yellow and red
Gayfeather (*Liatrus pycnostachya*)	spike	purple
Indian paintbrush (*Castilleja indivisa*)	spike	orange
Lemon/purple horse mint (*Monarda citriodora*)	spike	purple or gray
Maximilian sunflower (*Helianthus maximiliani*)	rays on tall spike	yellow
Mealy cup sage (*Salvia farinacea*)	spike	blue and white
Mexican hat (*Ratibida columnaris*)	ray	orange-red
Pink evening primrose (*Oenothera speciosa*)	open tubular	pink
Plains coreopsis (*Coreopsis tinctoria*)	ray	yellow
Standing cypress (*Ipomopsis rubra*)	tall spike	orange-red
Wine cup (*Callirhoe involucrata*)	open tubular	red wine

The state flower of Texas includes six bluebonnet species, including Lupinus subcarnosus, L. havardii, *and* L. texensis.

Texas Has Six State Flowers

The state flower of Texas is the bluebonnet, but there are actually six bluebonnet species native to Texas, and they are all considered the state flower.

In 1901, the Texas legislature selected the bluebonnet as the state flower (other contenders were the cotton flower and boll and cactus flower). The bluebonnet chosen was the species *Lupinus subcarnosus*. Unfortunately, this was not the species most prevalent or most attractive. *L. subcarnosus* has small blue flowers and is native to the sandy soil on rolling hills in a swath from Centerville/Madisonville southwest to Cotulla (La Salle County) and down into the Valley (McAllen).

For 70 years, Texans lobbied the legislature that a mistake was made and *L. texensis* should be the true state flower because it is more prevalent and has larger, showier blooms of blue with white tips. Finally, in 1971, the legislature addressed the concerns and made both species the state flower, plus "any other variety of bluebonnet not heretofore recorded."

Well, Texas has four other native bluebonnet species that are now considered the state flower as well; thus, these are the state flower (or flowers) of Texas:

1. *Lupinus subcarnosus*—the original state flower; adapted to sandy soil; small mono-color blue blooms
2. *L. texensis*—the most photographed and painted bluebonnet; native throughout Central Texas; blooms are robust flower spikes with popcornlike blue blooms with white tips; easiest to grow from seed and available in transplants
3. *L. havardii*—known as the Big Bend bluebonnet; tall (2 to 3 feet) bloom spikes; difficult to grow in gardens; however, has been commercially cultivated as a spectacular cut flower

4. *L. concinnus*—a small bluebonnet 2 to 7 inches tall; flowers are bluish with hints of white, rosy purple, and lavender; native to West Texas in areas along the Pecos River

5. *L. perennis*—a perennial bluebonnet; 1- to 2-foot bloom spikes; purple flowers; native from Florida to Louisiana into East Texas in sandy soils

6. *L. plattensis*—a perennial bluebonnet; 2-foot bloom spikes; native from Nebraska south to the sandy dunes of the Texas Panhandle

TIPS FOR SUCCESS IN GROWING BLUEBONNETS

- Purchase seed or transplants of *L. texensis*.
- Plant seed in September (October for San Antonio and south); plant transplants from late September to December.
- Seed germinates with rain or irrigation in fall, grows to a rosette of leaves throughout the winter (tolerates freezing temperatures), and blooms in spring; the bigger the plant grown in the winter, the more blooms produced in spring. Transplants are the same, absent the seed germination phase.
- Purchase "scarified" seeds (acid or abrasion treated) to ensure quick germination (10 days); bluebonnets are survivors and have a hard seed coat that guarantees future generations either this year or next. In the natural environment, seed coats break down slowly with heat and rain; if deterioration is sufficient and soil moisture adequate, the seed will imbibe water and sprout.
- Firm the soil and seed together by tamping the planted area with your feet, or for larger areas, use a roller; good soil-seed contact is essential to germination.
- Purchase and plant bluebonnet transplants to avoid seed germination concerns. Do not plant the plants too deep—the crown of the plant should be just above the soil surface to prevent soilborne disease.
- Plant transplants in patio containers filled with potting soil for a unique Texas display; transplants can be combined with flowering plants (e.g., dianthus, pansies, phlox) for added beauty while the bluebonnets are still in the foliage phase.
- Don't overwater bluebonnets. Natural rainfall is generally sufficient, but water lightly if drought conditions persist in fall and winter or your soil becomes dry.
- Always plant in full sun in a well-prepared garden soil or a lawn area with well-drained soil; bluebonnets need good soil drainage. Notice how well they do on slopes next to highways.

- Remove bloom spikes as they dry up to extend the blooming period; or if you want to collect seed or have the plants reseed the area, let the blooms develop seed pods. Seed is mature when the seed pod turns paper-bag brown; collect then, or let the pods pop open and throw the seed into the area.

- Don't fertilize; bluebonnets collect their own fertilizer through a natural bacterial relationship and process called nitrogen fixation.

- Watch for and control pill bugs (doodle bugs), slugs, and snails in bluebonnet plantings; these pests love bluebonnets. A slug and snail bait can be used if needed.

ALL BLUEBONNETS ARE NOT BLUE

Extension horticulturists and county extension agents in San Antonio, in conjunction with seed producers, bedding plant growers, and vegetable farmers, have made the bluebonnet available to gardeners in a variety of colors. No genetic manipulation or other artificial "gene jock" processes have been employed. This group has simply taken what nature has provided (in *L. texensis*) and segregated the colors as viable additions to blue bluebonnets.

This all began in 1982, when Texas naturalist and entrepreneur Carroll Abbott (often referred to as "Mr. Texas Bluebonnet") envisioned planting a Texas state flag made up entirely of bluebonnets for the 1986 Texas Sesquicentennial. When he succumbed to cancer, his friend and colleague Jerry Parsons, extension horticulturist, adopted this dream and focused the resources and talents of area nursery professionals, vegetable farmers, and a seed producer (Wildseed Farms). Over the past 25 years, a bluebonnet Texas flag has not been achieved (no true red has been developed); however, the result is a variety of bluebonnet colors now available through seed and transplants for all Texans to enjoy in their own landscapes.

To date, six colors of bluebonnets have been isolated and are available from nurseries and seed producers:

- Blue—obviously common, but now consistently available as seed or transplants.
- White—occurs rarely, but naturally due to a recessive gene. If white-flowered plants are isolated in farmers' fields away from blue bluebonnets, seed consistently produces white-flowered plants the next season. If blue bluebonnets and white bluebonnets are planted together in a landscape, then the seed produced will result in predominantly blue bluebonnets the next season (as is true for all color strains).
- Pink—occurs much more rarely than white, but again naturally. The same isolation technique results in seed that will produce new pink-flowered plants. The pink form was appropriately named 'Abbott Pink' as a tribute and constant reminder of where the dream started.
- Sky blue—occurs naturally and was isolated. This color strain was named 'Worthington Sky Blue' in appreciation for financial support provided by the Worthington Hotel of Fort Worth.
- Lavender blue—selection isolated from blue fields and named 'Barbara Bush Lavender' after the former first lady of the United States.
- Maroon—occurs naturally in isolated fields of pink bluebonnets. This Aggie maroon bluebonnet was named 'Alamo Fire.'

Other colors are coming for *L. texensis,* and now pink and white strains of *L. havardii* are also available and grown commercially in greenhouses for cut flowers.

Finally, three responses to common questions about bluebonnets:

- No, it is not against the law to pick bluebonnets; however, if you pick them, no one else gets to enjoy them.
- Yes, all the color strains of bluebonnets are officially included as the state flower of Texas.
- No, Texas A&M extension horticulturists have not been able to find any bluebonnet in nature that shows any hint of "burnt orange."

Spring Flowering Bulbs: The Layaway Plan

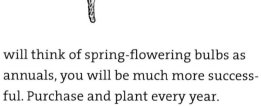

Nurseries and garden centers stock up in September (even August) with spring-flowering bulbs (e.g., daffodil, hyacinth, tulip). Mail-order catalogues for spring-flowering bulbs land in mailboxes in late spring. Don't be misled into planting these bulbs too early in Texas. Purchase your bulbs now while the selection is good, but use the layaway plan. You will hold your bulbs for a few months and plant when your soil cools off significantly—for most, in November to January.

Spring-flowering bulbs are perhaps the easiest-to-grow, biggest-bang-for-the-buck flowers you can plant. All the hard work has already been done by the commercial growers to produce high-quality bulbs.

Texas is not known for fields of daffodils, hyacinths, and tulips that naturalize and spring forth year after year. If you will think of spring-flowering bulbs as annuals, you will be much more successful. Purchase and plant every year.

The limiting factor in Texas is lack of deep-freezing weather that freezes the soil. This lack of chilling eliminates the bulbs' ability to create new flower buds each winter. Usually, the second season all you will get is foliage, not blooms. Some daffodil varieties, however, will actually naturalize and repeat-bloom in Texas (noted below).

In the nursery, select bulbs as soon as they arrive—similar to how you pick onions in the grocery store. Look for firm bulbs with no blemishes. Dried-up or moldy bulbs will reduce your chances for success.

There are many mail-order plant catalogues that offer spring-flowering bulbs. Some companies specialize in spring- and summer-flowering bulbs (e.g., Brent and Becky's Bulbs, Gloucester, Virginia, www.brentandbeckysbulbs.com; and the Southern Bulb Co., Golden, Texas, www.southernbulbs.com). The number of varieties in these catalogues is staggering but worth perusing, because only limited varieties are available in most nurseries and garden centers.

For Texans, it is best to focus on daffodils because they provide a dependable and longer bloom period, they require no special handling (no prechilling), and some will come back year after year.

Tulips and hyacinths provide early spring blooms but require refrigeration by you for about 60 days before planting. They seldom repeat-bloom, and if the spring is warm, tulip blooms may last only a couple of days. However, there is no more pleasant aroma in the spring garden than hyacinth flowers or the visual sensation provided by the varied and vibrant tulip blooms, so plant these, too.

After tulips and hyacinths bloom, simply discard the plants and purchase new bulbs each year. Select any color and form that appeal to you, and have fun with tulips and hyacinths.

Back to daffodils—there are officially 13 descriptive divisions in the *Narcissus* genus, but for simplicity here are three main categories and some recommended varieties:

- Narcissus—often called tazetta or paperwhites; bloom spikes have cluster of small blossoms; usually bloom in mid- to late winter; mostly white in color with intense (sometimes overwhelming) fragrance; paperwhites can be "forced" in containers for indoor use. Recommended varieties: 'Constantinople,' 'Erlicheer,' 'Falconet,' 'Grand Monarque,' 'Grand Primo,' 'Pearl,' and 'Silver Chimes.'

- Jonquils—bloom spikes have clusters of small, fragrant, yellow blossoms; usually bloom in late winter; when naturalized, will also spread by seed. Recommended varieties: 'Campernelle,' 'Geranium,' 'Quail,' 'Sailboat,' 'Stratosphere,' 'Sweet Love,' 'Sweetness,' and 'The Bride' (double).

- Daffodils—generally refers to all medium- and large-flowered varieties; colors range from white, yellow, gold, orange, pink, and apricot in mono-colors or blends (petals one color and trumpet another). Recommended varieties: 'Artic Gold,' 'Carlton,' 'Ceylon,' 'Dallas,' 'February Gold,' 'Fortune,' 'Ice Follies,' 'Rijnveld's Early Sensation,' 'Tahiti,' and 'Trousseau.'

Because you will likely purchase or receive spring-flowering bulbs in September, most Texas bulb experts recommend that you store all spring-flowering bulbs in the refrigerator (whether they require chilling or not). Planting will not occur until the soil cools in November to January. If planted in warm soils (above 55°F), the bulbs have a tendency to rot, not root.

With daffodils, hyacinths, and tulips, sneak into the garden when no one is looking and plant the bulbs. Your family will be surprised and ask, "Where did those flowers come from?" (My response is Santa Claus must have planted them; you know he is a great gardener.)

Spring-flowering bulbs can be planted in flower and shrub beds containing soil amended with lots of organic matter. You can plant them in containers with good potting soil and have them on the patio or bring them indoors to enjoy.

If your native soil is sandy, loamy, or well-drained clay, you can plant daffodil bulbs in natural areas or groundcover plantings that will not be mowed. Regardless of where you plant them, if you want the bulbs to have a chance of naturalizing and blooming again next spring, you must let the foliage die back on its own schedule. Resist the temptation to cut back yellowing foliage; the bulbs need all their foliage to generate energy for next year's bloom.

Prolifically growing daffodils should be divided every 3 to 4 years. Once the foliage has withered, you can divide the bulbs and spread them out or share with neighbors. Dig the entire clump of bulbs, gently separate the mass of bulbs, and replant as soon as possible.

When planting daffodil, hyacinth, or tulip bulbs, ignore the planting charts designed for northern gardeners. These charts take into consideration that the soil may freeze 6 inches to a foot deep. That doesn't happen in Texas, so plant bulbs down in the soil about two times the height of the bulb. For most bulbs, this will be approximately 6 inches.

Sunlight requirements for spring-flowering bulbs is not very important; simply avoid deep shade. Fertilizing the bulbs with a complete fertilizer (containing low nitrogen and moderate amounts of phosphorous and potassium) will help establish the roots and generate more foliage and blooms.

Other spring-flowering bulbs worth planting in Texas include anemone, Dutch iris, grape hyacinth, and ranunculus. These will be also be annuals in Texas, with the exception of grape hyacinth (sometimes).

Growing spring-flowering bulbs is a worthy exercise in delayed gratification. Plant some this winter. The happy faces of these flowers (and of your family) are well worth the wait.

Tree Planting Made Easy

Trees are a major investment in your landscape and are best planted in fall, winter, or spring. The best site for a tree is one that receives full sunlight. Dig the hole twice as wide as the root-ball (container) and no deeper than the height of the root-ball. The soil that you dig out of the hole is what you will use to backfill around the root-ball. Research documents that no soil amendments are recommended when planting a tree; no compost, peat moss, or shredded pine bark should be added to the backfill. As you backfill with your yard's soil, stomp the soil firmly into the hole to eliminate air pockets and ensure firm contact between the nursery soil and the backfill soil.

After planting the tree, build a 4-inch-tall berm (a small soil dam) around the edge of the hole. Fill the berm with mulch (e.g., shredded bark, compost). The berm makes it easier to water the tree, and the mulch reduces evaporation from the soil surface, moderates soil temperatures, and reduces weed competition.

For most newly planted trees, staking is not recommended. Staking usually results in weaker trunks. Some trees purchased at nurseries have been grown with a single stake running up the trunk of the tree. Cut the ties, and pull out the stake. If the trunk is not sturdy enough to support the top of the tree, use two stakes, each about 12 inches from either side of the tree trunk. Give the trunk support with ties woven between the two stakes and the tree for the first year only. The ties should be somewhat loose so that the trunk can sway in the wind. This creates a stronger trunk more quickly.

Right after planting, water the tree by filling the bermed basin with water. This will settle the existing soil around the root-ball. Follow these watering guidelines thereafter:

- For the first week after planting, lightly water the tree with a hose every day (about a quart to a gallon of water each day).
- The second week, water every other day with about 2 quarts to 2 gallons of water.
- During the third week, water every third day with 2 quarts to 2 gallons of water.
- For the fourth week and beyond, water once a week if needed.

No soil amendments are needed when planting trees.

The goal is to slowly wean the tree off supplemental irrigation and grow the root system large enough into the natural soil for the tree to thrive on only natural rainfall.

Remember that these are just guidelines. Use your index finger to check the soil moisture under the mulch. If the soil is cool to the touch, do not water. If it is warm and dry, then water. More plants are killed by overwatering than by underwatering. Understand, too, that irrigation systems do not water trees (unless the system is equipped with bubblers or drip irrigation specifically for the trees).

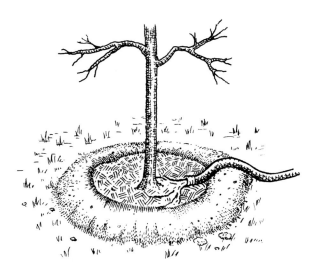

Construct a berm to hold mulch and irrigation water for a young tree.

Cold-Weather Protection for Plants

People go crazy when the first fall frost or freeze is forecast. They throw the laundry out in the yard, covering everything from tomato plants to oak trees. Tattered towels, old bed sheets, kids' pajamas all appear, strewn here and there. It looks like a strong wind blew down the clothesline. Twister!

What a waste of time and effort. Here's the rest of the story. Some plants can be damaged by freezing temperatures as well as drying wind. These are the major plants of concern:

- Warm-season vegetables (e.g., green bean, pepper, tomato)
- Warm-season annual flowers (e.g., bachelor button, impatiens, periwinkle)
- Herbaceous (green-stemmed) perennial flowers (e.g., canna, ginger, hibiscus)
- Tropical vines and shrubs (e.g., bougainvillea, mandevilla)
- Cold-sensitive palms (e.g., pygmy date, sago palm)

Woody (hard stems, branches, and trunks) trees, shrubs, and vines are generally not a concern unless temperatures dip into the teens or single digits (°F) for 2 or 3 days. Other than in the Panhandle, such temperatures are a once-in-a-decade-type event (not to say it won't happen tomorrow). The biggest threat to woody plants that carry their leaves through the winter is desiccation from drying winds. Simply irrigate these plants if the soil is dry and winter winds are persistent.

Mulching all landscape plantings and the garden in early fall is a standard cold-protection technique. Mulch helps insulate the root systems of all your plants. It also traps soil warmth built up during the growing season and preserves any soil moisture.

If you have cold-sensitive plants and a heavy freeze is predicted, there are a few plant-protection strategies that work:

- Move container-grown plants into the garage, or even indoors if needed, to protect from freeze damage.

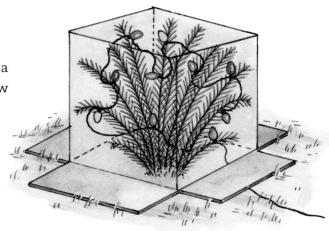

During heavy freezes, protect a sensitive plant (e.g., sago palm) with a cardboard box for insulation and Christmas lights for supplemental heat.

- Water the entire landscape and garden before a freeze—sounds counterintuitive, but a well-watered plant in the ground (or a container) is less likely to suffer freeze damage if the soil is moist. Dry soil is a poor insulator for plant roots; moisture in the soil can also be drawn through the plant to reduce desiccation of the leaves by cold winds.

- Keep the air moving. If you have electric fans, put them outdoors and let them blow; circulating the air keeps pockets of cold air from settling in your garden.

- Cover freeze-sensitive plants at dusk after the soil and plants have absorbed the sun's heat; covering the plants traps the radiating heat and can provide 2°F to 4°F more protection. Forget plastic coverings and the laundry—they don't provide enough protection. Better choices include large cardboard boxes, thick wool blankets and quilts, or bubble wrap;

make sure the covering goes all the way to the ground to trap the heat.

- Get the Christmas lights out if a heavy freeze is forecast to last more than 24 hours (this may threaten even cold-hardy plants). Use lights (e.g., Christmas, utility) to generate heat underneath the plant covers; a few-degree increase from the lights may save your valuable plants (e.g., citrus, fruit-laden tomatoes, and sago palm). Be careful when combining boxes and blankets with electrical lights and water (frost).

- Uncover plants when the temperature rises above freezing to let the plant processes resume normal function under cool temperatures.

CALLER: "My dear plants froze, so what do I do now?"

ANSWER: "If your efforts were too late or too little to protect your plants from a freeze, resist the urge to prune off the damaged plant parts. To an extent, dead leaves and stems will provide some insulation from further cold damage. The best time to cut back the plants is after they sprout out in the spring; then you can easily determine what to prune off and what to leave."

Timely Tips

occur every 2 to 4 years. Your plants will tell you when, by simply not blooming.

Flowers & Pretty Plants

• Purchase or order spring-flowering bulbs now while the selection is good. You won't plant them until later though. Read this month's essay "Spring Flowering Bulbs: The Layaway Plan" for more information on these easy-to-grow flowers.

• When night temperatures dip into the 50s, switch out unproductive, burned-out warm-season annuals with cool-season annuals, such as dianthus and petunias. Don't be too quick to plant Johnny-jump-ups, pansies, snapdragons, and violas; they prefer the consistently cooler temperatures of October.

• Wildflower seed should be planted this month to ensure fields of flowers next spring. Planting details can be found in this month's essay "Plant Wildflowers in Fall."

• Apply nitrogen fertilizer monthly to flower beds at a rate of $\frac{1}{4}$ pound of urea per 100 square feet, $\frac{1}{2}$ pound of ammonium sulfate, or 1 pound of blood meal.

• Divide spring-blooming perennials this month, such as daylily, iris, and Shasta daisy. Dividing should

Garden Design

• Plant a perennial flower border. Fall is a prime time for planting perennial flowers, as well as trees and shrubs. Transplant shock is less, and roots can prepare for spring growth. Refer to the perennial border design kit illustrated in this month's essay "Gardening with Perennial Flowers."

Soil & Mulch

• Prepare garden soils during fall planting by adding organic matter: compost, pine bark, and manure. Use individually or in combination—the more, the better.

• Till in mulch that has been sitting on top of the soil all season in flower beds and vegetable gardens to add organic matter to the soil.

Water

• Adjust your irrigation schedule; maybe even take a break from landscape watering. Hopefully, fall will bring some rain and cooler temperatures. Let the plants tell you when they need water. Tremendous amounts of water are wasted in the fall by watering on the same schedule as in summer.

Plant Care

- If your lawn has been plagued by winter weeds, apply a granular pre-emergence herbicide now to kill sprouting weed seed. Pre-emergence herbicides can also be used in the flower and shrub plantings but DO NOT use them in a vegetable garden. They will kill the vegetable seeds as they sprout.

- Be prepared for the first freeze, especially in the Panhandle. Refer to the February essay "Last and First Freeze Dates" and this month's essay "Cold-Weather Protection for Plants" for more details for your area of the state.

- Keep pruning off old blooms on roses and perennials to generate more blossoms through the fall.

Trees, Shrubs & Vines

- Plant, plant, plant. The temperature is now more comfortable for the plants and for you.

- Notice how rose bloom colors are more vibrant in the fall than spring and summer. 'La Marne,' 'Marie Pavie,' and 'Old Blush' are simply gorgeous in the fall.

- Fertilize your rosebushes to generate more growth and blooms. Apply $\frac{1}{4}$ cup of urea per plant, $\frac{1}{2}$ cup of ammonium sulfate, or 1 cup of blood meal.

- If you are planning to transplant a tree or shrub within your landscape this winter, let it know between now and November. With a shovel, cut a circle around the plant (approximately 18 to 24 inches in diameter). This will cause the plant to generate new roots within the root-ball to be dug later in the winter. For more details, read the October essay "Transplanting Shrubs and Trees."

Lawns

- If fire ant mounds are popping up in the lawn, treat with bait insecticides, since ants are foraging again after laying dormant most of the summer.

- Don't apply fall fertilizer until warm-season lawns (e.g., Bermuda, St. Augustine, zoysia) have stopped growing. Depending on where you live, this could be as soon as mid-September or as late as November. Refer to the October essay "Fall Lawn Fertilizing" for details.

- If you want a green lawn in winter (just like the soccer field and golf course), then overseed Bermudagrass with ryegrass when nighttime temperature are consistently in the low 60s. Overseeding is best done using perennial ryegrass or new, improved annual ryegrass varieties ('Pantera' or 'Axcellaz').

- Control brown patch now. If your lawn had this chronic disease of St. Augustine last fall, then prevent it this fall by applying a granular fungicide labeled for this disease. You can also take no action at all and let brown patch run its course. This fungal disease does not kill the lawn completely but does lower its quality and resistance to weed invasion significantly.

Vegetables, Herbs & Fruits

- Act quickly; you still have time to plant "quick-harvest" warm-season vegetable crops, such as green beans and radishes. You can start planting cool-season vegetables now, such as broccoli, cauliflower, leaf lettuce, and spinach. Vegetables that mature in cooler temperatures are usually higher quality. What a great time to work in the vegetable garden. Refer to the vegetable gardening essays in March and July for more inspiration and guidance.

- Plant cool-season vegetables in the flower bed as ornamentals. Cabbage, kale, leaf lettuce, and spinach are attractive additions to the landscape.

- Run out to the grocery store or produce market, and buy fresh Texas-grown sweet potatoes. East Texas grows tons of tasty sweet potatoes, high in fiber and nutrients. For a less nutritious but fabulous vegetable dish, try french-fried sweet potatoes.

- Watch your herbs flourish with cooler temperatures. Enjoy the harvest. Plant new transplants now for quick production of high-quality herbs (e.g., basil, chives, cilantro, dill, mints, oregano).

- Don't forget that herbs can be enjoyed for their flowers, too. Mexican oregano produces pink flowers from spring through fall. Rosemary, the upright form, will display a profusion of powder blue blossoms in the fall. Mexican mint marigold is strictly a fall bloomer with small, daisylike yellow flowers.

- Purchase Texas-grown pecans; harvesting begins this month. Texas is a land of the pecan. It is the state tree. If you don't have your own tree, search out Texas-grown pecans in local grocery stores and produce markets. Some of the highest-quality nuts to purchase are from the pecan varieties 'Caddo,' 'Cheyenne,' 'Desirable,' and 'Sioux.'

Houseplants

- Break the bad news gently to your houseplants that the time has come to go indoors after having spent all season enjoying the back patio. (Some houseplants are lucky—they live in deep South Texas and never have to come indoors.) Prepare your houseplants for transport back indoors by moving them to the lowest-light outdoor setting. The goal is to have them acclimatize to the indoor lower-light conditions.

When night temperatures dip to the low 50s, it is best to bring the houseplants indoors.

Butterflies, Birds & Squirrels

- With winter approaching, birds are migrating, butterflies are migrating or pupating, and squirrels are squirreling away acorns that they will never find. So feed them all; they need your help to consume energy for the winter or trip ahead. Don't forget to provide water also.

Notes:

October

*American beautyberry (*Callicarpa americana*)*

NO NEED TO STOP GARDENING

Cool-Season Annuals: Change Is a Good Thing

Alyssum, petunia, and snapdragon are cool-season annuals for fall through spring.

By now, the first cold front has taken its toll in most of Texas on warm-season annual flowers, such as penta, periwinkle, portulaca, and purslane. It is time for a change. Look to cool-season annuals to provide landscape color in fall, winter, and spring.

Except during the harsh winters of the Panhandle, most cool-season annuals will bloom nicely in the fall to midwinter. Occasional winter deep freezes will nip back blooms and foliage, but the root systems will continue to grow. When warmer weather of spring comes, your fall-planted annual flowers will burst forth with a profusion of growth and blooms.

This process is especially true for petunias. The best petunia beds in spring are ones planted in fall, believe it or not. While your flower bed is peaking, your neighbors will be rushing to the nursery to buy and plant cool-season annuals, trying in vain to reproduce your flower beds.

Plant cool-season annuals in fall, and see just how beautiful they will be when spring comes. The only disclaimer is that not every winter is mild enough for this to occur, especially in the northern half of Texas. But as is said, "Nothing ventured, nothing gained," and at a minimum you will enjoy the fall bloom of these wonderful plants.

Below is a simple list of cool-season annuals from which to choose:

Alyssum
Calendula
Dianthus
Johnny-jump-up
Kale/cabbage
Pansy
Snapdragon
Stock
Sweet pea
Viola

Berry Good Plants

American beautyberry
(Callicarpa americana)

Berries provide a special attraction to landscape shrubs that flowers and foliage simply cannot. Berries are like tiny Christmas ornaments or that extra "bling" for the landscape. Berried plants often provide food for birds, such as cardinals, cedar waxwings, and mockingbirds.

Below is a list of plants that bear attractive fruit (the berry colors are in parentheses). After choosing what berried plant(s) you want to plant, select them in the nursery when they have berries on them. Berry color and density can vary within species, so look before you buy.

Agarita (red, following yellow flowers)
American beautyberry (purple or white)
American holly (red)

Burford holly (dwarf and standard; red)
Chinese photinia (red)
Cotoneaster (red or orange)
Dogwood (a small tree but a must on this list; red)
Duranta (golden)
Foster's holly (red)
Grape (a vine but worth noting;

'Champanel,' muscadine, mustang; purple)

Indian hawthorn (blue)

Japanese barberry (red)

Mexican plum (quarter-sized purple or red)

Nandina (standard and compact forms; red)

Needlepoint holly (red)

'Nellie R. Stevens' holly (red)

Pomegranate (orange to maroon large fruit)

Possumhaw holly (berries persist after the foliage falls; red to orange)

Pyracantha/firethorn (orange)

Rusty blackhaw (reddish purple)

Sweet viburnum (blue)

Texas persimmon (quarter-sized black fruit)

Wax leaf ligustrum (blue; perhaps its only attribute)

Wax myrtle (gray)

Yaupon holly (red generally on standard, not dwarf; 'Pride of Houston' excellent variety; yellow-berried variety, 'Saratoga Gold')

Yew (blue)

Ornamental Grasses—a New Frontier for the Landscape

The most significant addition to the landscape since the reintroduction of old-fashioned roses is ornamental grasses. Spreading like wildfire across the fruited plains (how's that for a pun?), interest in ornamental grasses is growing by leaps and—no, by rhizomes, stolons, and tillers (an educational pun because this is how grasses spread naturally).

Ornamental grasses possess and provide unique qualities to any landscape:

- Fine-textured foliage
- Movement, swaying to and fro with the wind
- Variety of bloom spike (seed head) forms; different species bloom in either late spring, summer, or fall
- Earth-tone colors during the winter (even dead foliage can be beautiful)
- Low water use inherent to tall prairie grasses

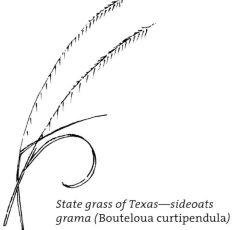

*State grass of Texas—sideoats grama (*Bouteloua curtipendula)

- Virtually pest-free plants
- Minimal maintenance
- A toughness and adaptability unsurpassed by most landscape plants

Planting and caring for ornamental grasses are simple. Provide a decent garden soil, water to establish the new plants, and watch out for grasshoppers. Like the locust plagues of the Midwest, grasshoppers will eat ornamental grasses and, in large populations, will decimate a grass planting. Use an appropriate insecticide if needed.

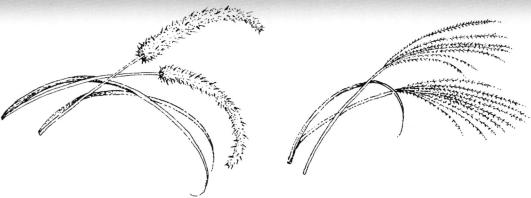

Pennisetum bloom spike (left) and miscanthus bloom spike (right).

Pruning and dividing ornamental grasses are perhaps the only necessary cultural practices to guarantee success. Each winter, the grass foliage will freeze back completely or, at a minimum, become unsightly. It is important to let spring growth begin and visually see new green grass blades emerging before pruning off old foliage. Pruning too early can severely stunt, if not kill, an ornamental grass. Let the new spring foliage reach 6 inches tall before pruning off all the old foliage back to 6 inches. Fertilizing is seldom needed with ornamental grasses.

Every 2 to 4 years, you may need to divide an ornamental grass. Grasses spread naturally away from their center point. As new growth appears at the edges of the plant, a dead center of the plant may develop. When this dead center gets about 1 foot in diameter, it is time to divide the plant. Wait until fall and dig the plant up, cut (or saw) the grass clump into fourths, and replant each section. If your planting does not have enough space to accommodate spreading these sections out, give the divisions to neighbors and friends.

Texas is blessed with many native grasses that are adapted for use in the ornamental landscape. There are also grasses from Africa to Asia that have been identified and commercially grown for use in Texas landscapes. The list presented below focuses on Texas native grasses with a few nonnative species.

Here are select ornamental grasses from which to choose for your landscape. Plant a few; you will like them.

SEED AND PLANT SOURCES
Local nurseries and garden centers
Bluestem Nursery (http://
    www.bluestemnursery.com)
Emerald Coast Growers (http://
    www.ecgrowers.com)
Madrone Nursery (http://
    home.earthlink.net/
    ~madronenursery/)
Native American Seed (http://
    www.seedsource.com)
Wildseed Farms (http://
    www.wildseedfarms.com)

CALLER: "Are nonnative grass species considered invasive species?"

ANSWER: "A worthy question considering the invasive spread of nonnative species, such as Johnson grass and bahia grass. So, a word of caution is in order for ornamental grasses not native to Texas—some have the potential to become 'invasive species' (weeds). Many nonnative species do not present a problem, but much of this depends on your local growing conditions (particularly for high-rainfall areas of Texas). Check with nursery professionals, county extension agents, or seed and plant sources to gauge concern for whether a specific grass is invasive or potentially invasive in your area."

Select Ornamental Grasses for Texas Landscapes

COMMON NAME (SCIENTIFIC NAME)	MATURE HEIGHT (FEET)	FLOWERING SEASON	NOTES
Bamboo muhly (*Muhlenbergia dumosa*) ⭐	4–6	n/a	resembles a fine-textured, small bamboo
Big bluestem (*Andropogon gerardii*) ⭐	4–6	fall	blue-green foliage; copper color in winter
Blue fescue (*Festuca glauca*)	$\frac{1}{2}$–1	n/a	gray-blue, fine-textured foliage; several varieties available; particularly adapted to drier areas of Texas
Blue grama (*Bouteloua gracilis*) ⭐	1–1$\frac{1}{2}$	summer to fall	short grass with gray-green foliage; unique, decorative seed head; tall turf alternative
Buffalograss (*Buchloe dactyloides*) ⭐	$\frac{1}{2}$	summer	turf-type grass; excellent base for wildflowers
Bushy bluestem (*Andropogon glomeratus*) ⭐	2–4	fall	similar to big bluestem but with large, cottony flower spikes
Canada wild rye (*Elymus canadensis* var. *canadensis*) ⭐	3–5	late spring	cool-season grass; wheatlike seed heads; grows in sun or shade

⭐ designates Texas native plants.

COMMON NAME (SCIENTIFIC NAME)	MATURE HEIGHT (FEET)	FLOWERING SEASON	NOTES
Carex sedges (*Carex* spp.)	1–3	n/a	many *Carex* species and varieties available in nurseries and catalogues; many adapted to Texas; work well in shade
Feather reed grass 'Karl Foerster' (*Calamagrostis* x *acutiflora* 'Karl Foerster')	3–4	summer	evergreen grass in mild climates; feathery, loose, purple-tinged flowers on stalks to 6 feet tall in summer
Gulf or coastal muhly (*Muhlenbergia capillaris*) ★	1½–2	fall	short muhly grass with pink, fuzzy seed heads
Indiangrass (*Sorghastrum nutans*) ★	3–6	late summer to early fall	golden brown winter color
Inland sea oats (*Chasmanthium latifolium*) ★	2	summer to fall	purple spring growth; bamboolike foliage; ornamental seed heads
Lemon grass (*Cymbopogon* sp.)	4–8	n/a	tropical grass used as culinary herb; also a tall ornamental green grass; perennial in South and coastal Texas
Lindheimer muhly (*Muehlenbergia lindheimeri*) ★	3	summer	fine gray-green foliage
Little bluestem (*Schizachyrium scoparium*) ★	2–4	fall	blue-green foliage; copper color in winter
Love grass, weeping (*Eragrostis curvula*)	1–1½	n/a	grows on almost any well-drained soil but prefers sandy loams; also will grow on low-fertility soils; responds well to fertilization
Maiden grass (*Miscanthus sinensis* 'Gracillimus')	6–8	fall	medium green, weeping foliage; narrow leaves with white midrib; copper-orange winter color
Mexican feather grass ★ (*Stipa tenuissima*)	2	summer	fine foliage; soft cream seed heads

Miscanthus 'Cabaret' (*Miscanthus sinensis* 'Cabaret')	6–8	late summer to fall	considered the most beautiful of the miscanthus; variegated green and white foliage; bloom spikes of pink lightening to creamy white
Nimbewill (*Muhlenbergia schreberi*) ⭐	$\frac{1}{4}-\frac{2}{3}$	n/a	true alternative to turfgrass; soft blue-green, triangular-shaped foliage; full sun to half shade; variety 'Rio Blanco'
Pampas grass (*Cortaderia selloana*)	7	summer to fall	a "monster"—must have enough space for this grass
Porcupine grass (*Miscanthus sinensis* 'Strictus')	6–9	fall	horizontally variegated leaves, green with gold bands like zebra grass; but more upright and less likely to sprawl
Purple fountain grass (*Pennisetum setaceum* 'Rubrum')	3–4	summer	burgundy-purple leaves and soft blooms; annual in northern two-thirds of Texas; may have to replace after a few years; green foliage form also available
Sideoats grama (*Bouteloua curtipendula*) ⭐	1–3	summer to fall	state grass of Texas; unique oatlike flower spike appears in summer through fall
Switchgrass (*Panicum viragatum*) ⭐	3–8	fall	tall grass with bluish foliage turning orange in fall; lacy flower spike
Texas bluegrass (*Poa arachnifera*) ⭐	2–3	spring	Texas does have a bluegrass and this is it; cool-season grass restricted to acidic soils; goes dormant (brown) in summer; fluffy silvery flowers
Zebra grass (*Miscanthus sinensis* 'Zebrinus')	5–7	fall	horizontally variegated leaves, green with gold bands

⭐ designates Texas native plants

Creating a Prairie Garden

Whether it takes up 1,000 square feet or the entire landscape, a prairie garden is a viable alternative to the mowed, high-maintenance lawn and traditional landscape plantings.

Grassland prairies once dominated the natural landscape of much of Texas. Miniature grassland prairies can be incorporated into most landscapes. In addition to the grasses, wildflowers can be used to create beauty in your personal prairie restoration.

Here are some tips on planting a prairie garden:

- Choose a site in full sun with minimal competition from tree root systems.
- Choose a site with decent soil; although grasses are adapted to a wide range of soils, you may need to amend the soil by tilling in organic matter (e.g., compost). Poor soil drainage can kill a grass planting.
- Know your city's weed ordinance. Some prairie gardens, especially in the front landscape, will violate weed ordinances (and possibly homeowner association regulations).
- Don't forget that prairie gardens can be a fire hazard; locate the garden away from the home, and have water readily available.
- Prepare the site by removing all existing vegetation, especially Bermudagrass; eliminating the existing vegetation can be achieved by repeated tilling of the area, laying black plastic sheeting over the area for at least 2 months, or using a glyphosate-type herbicide.
- Select the grass species for inclusion in the prairie garden. Refer to the list "Select Ornamental Grasses," consult with a rangeland or prairie expert, and/or mail-order prairie grass and wildflower seed catalogues. Prairie gardens include about 60 to 80 percent grasses, with the remainder planted in wildflowers.
- Choose whether to plant from seeds, plants, or both; availability of plants, size of planting, and economics may restrict the use of just plants. This is a good reason to start small, with plants for quicker establishment, and then increase the size of the garden if desired. Consult with experts on rates for seeding (e.g., common rate of $\frac{1}{2}$ pound of grass per 1,000 square feet).
- Plant the prairie garden in fall, especially when using seed. Plant seeds following guidelines in the September essay "Plant Wildflowers in Fall"; plants can be established throughout the fall to spring, as long as water is available naturally or through irrigation.

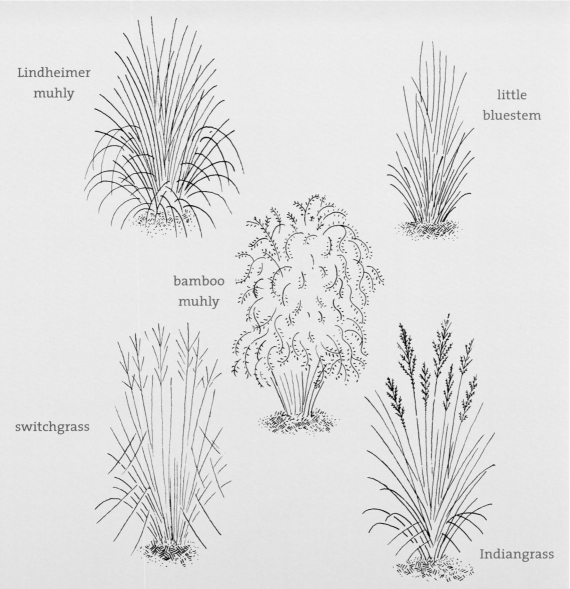

Lindheimer muhly

little bluestem

bamboo muhly

switchgrass

Indiangrass

A prairie garden can be filled with little bluestem, bamboo muhly, Lindheimer muhly, switchgrass, and Indiangrass.

● Control weeds; this will be your biggest task (another reason to start small). Pull weeds, and spot-treat with glyphosate herbicide if needed. Once-a-year trimming of the prairie garden (with a flexible-line trimmer) in spring will reduce weeds and encourage growth of the grasses.

Landscape Design—Concepts, Guidelines, and Fun Ideas

You can drive down the street of any neighborhood and easily identify homes with high-quality landscapes. What separates these home landscapes from the not-so-good? Most people think that landscape design is about what and how plants are used. Actually, design is about manipulation of people. Similar to the design (layout) of any grocery store, landscape design moves people through a space and focuses their attention on certain features or products.

In the landscape, the design and layout of beds, sidewalks, and patios highlight features of the home and move people to the home and through the garden. Plants are chosen to assist in providing scale, accent, variety, and unity within the landscape.

Designing a quality landscape is not easy. Choosing plants is easier, and this book can help, but landscape design is often best left to professionals. Some of you have the creativity and vision to create a design. (*Note:* I do not but encourage you to try.) There are many books and even computer programs that can help guide you through the design process.

Landscape design professionals fall into two categories: landscape architects and landscape designers. Landscape architects have a university degree in landscape architecture or land planning and have taken a unified examination to become licensed by the state of Texas (similar to licensing of architects and engineers). Landscape designers may or may not have a degree, are not licensed, and are often associated with nurseries or landscape contractors.

Regardless of the person's title, the quality of landscape design depends on the individual's abilities, not degrees, licenses, or associations. To choose a landscape design professional, you must see his or her past work, the "portfolio." Ask for references, and go see landscapes that were installed about 2 to 4 years ago. It is more difficult to gauge the quality of design from a newly installed landscape.

If you use a landscape architect or designer, you are paying for ideas and expertise. A landscape architect may charge a few hundred dollars to over a thousand depending on the size of the landscape and the detail of the design (e.g., plant selections, installation specifications, color-rendered design versus blueprint). Designers may charge less because you may likely purchase the plants and/or installation services from his or her company.

As with interior design, landscape design incorporates many principles and elements, plus the wishes and desires of the homeowner. Home landscape design also takes into account the existing natural environment, ranging from heavily treed landscapes to sloping land to flat "raw" land with little vegetation. Sometimes there is existing landscaping, so a renovation is called for. More frequently than perhaps desired, homeowner association or subdivision rules and regulations also come into play when designing landscapes. It seems that every home site is different, yet through the landscape design process

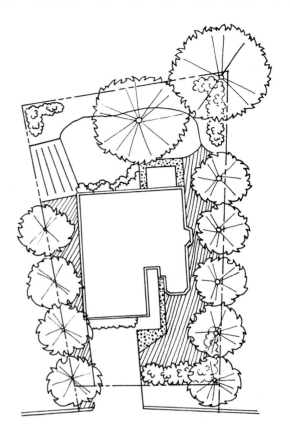

these challenges and opportunities can be addressed. All the more reason to turn to professionals for design advice.

The following guidelines will provide you with a basic knowledge for choosing plants with proper landscape design in mind:

- The front landscape is the "welcome mat" to the home. The focal point is the front door (not the gigantic garage door). You must draw the visitor's eye to the front door. A 4-foot-wide sidewalk will help welcome visitors to the front door (compare to the

CALLER: "I don't think I can afford a landscape architect or designer—any suggestions?"

ANSWER: "One economical technique worth considering is to hire a design professional for an hour-long consultation and let him or her 'design on the fly.' Have your home's 'plot plan' and sketching tissue paper ready, and then get the basic design on paper from the professional as quickly as you can. A to-scale plot plan can be found in your home's appraisal (when you purchased it) or from the blueprints for your home; or you can draw it out on graph paper. All of this will save you money and still utilize the expertise of the professional. Remember that the layout of the beds is the most critical feature in landscape design. Plant selection and placement recommendations can be obtained from the design professional, or you and/or a nursery professional can choose the plants."

near the front door help funnel the eye to the entrance. If your home has a huge, dominating garage door, you must try to balance the front landscape by placing a large planting on the opposite side of the home from the garage.

• In the absence of existing trees, tree placement and mature size are critical. Front yard trees should be placed at the ends of the home to provide a "picture frame" for the home. For one-story homes, the trees should reach a mature height of only 35 feet to avoid dwarfing the home. Two-story homes can handle larger trees, such as bald cypress, live oak, and tall pines. Do not place a tree in the middle of the front landscape. It will obscure the view of the home (an exception is for energy conservation with west-facing houses). Backyard trees can be much taller to provide a green pillow of foliage as a backdrop for the home's roofline.

• For new or old homes with existing large trees, use this setting to create a natural woodland landscape. Focus design efforts near the home with landscape plantings and people spaces (e.g., decks and patios) to take full advantage of your highly valued trees. You may even consider grouping existing trees into areas void of lawn. A coarse mulch or tree trimmings can become the ground

standard 3-foot-wide sidewalk that relegates visitors to walk single-file to the front door). Plants that are taller near the ends of the home and shorter surface, with a few woodland plants placed for interest (and for birds and butterflies). This technique is effective with pine trees in East Texas, post oaks in College Station, and groupings of live oak in Central Texas.

- In the front yard, shrubs at the ends of the home should be no taller than two-thirds the height from the ground to the eaves of the house. For one-story homes, this height is usually 5 to 6 feet. The height of an accent shrub(s) near the front door should be no taller than one-half the height of the eaves. Between the door and ends, shrubs should be no taller than one-third. Try always to keep shrub heights below the bottom of any windows. Too many homes are hidden behind shrubs that are too tall. The result is low-quality landscapes and/or the constant need for shearing plants to keep them in bounds. Dwarf shrubs are best for most of the front landscape.

- Use between five and seven plant species in the front landscape. This provides adequate variety but eliminates the "arboretum" approach to landscaping: one of this and one of that.

- Choose two or three plant species to repeat on either end of the front landscape to provide unity. For example, plant blue plumbago and dwarf yaupon at each end of the home.

- Colorful plants (flowers or foliage) add interest and quality to any landscape. Warm-season colors (red, yellow, and orange) attract the human eye (e.g., exit signs in a building are red for this reason). Warm-season colors can be used to draw attention to the front door or flower bed, as well as create a festive atmosphere. Cool-season colors (blue, purple, and green) recede from the eye and can be used both to provide dramatic contrast to warm-season colors and to provide a cooling and calming effect in the landscape (e.g., cool blue plumbago around the deck or patio).

- Try to incorporate plants with different foliage textures throughout the landscape. Most shrubs used in landscapes have medium-sized leaves (e.g., azalea, Indian hawthorn, photinia, and pittosporum). Choose bold-textured and fine-textured plants as contrast to create interest and variety. Bold-textured plants cause the same effect as warm-season colors, and fine-textured plants cause the same effect as cool-season colors.

- In the backyard, there are few guidelines on plant selection and placement. Again, the overall design and bed layout are critical. What goes in the beds is your choice and is where you can infuse personal character and themes into your landscape.

There is much fun to be had in the landscape, particularly in the backyard. Here are a few ideas:

- Flower beds and plantings are usually created to view from outside the home. Try planting a flower bed that can be viewed from inside the home. These "secret gardens" can provide great joy from indoors.

- Plant a color garden using a single color, such as white, blue, or red. White gardens containing plants with white flowers and/or variegated white and green foliage are particularly attractive at dawn and dusk. Blue gardens provide calm and serenity after a hard day's work. Red gardens are an in-your-face planting that will attract the attention of every visitor to the home.

- Theme gardens can be unique and special additions to the landscape. Biblical gardens contain plants mentioned in the Bible (e.g., coriander, fig, garlic, grapes, olive). Prehistoric gardens contain pals of the dinosaurs, such as bald cypress (substitute for dawn redwood), ferns, horsetail or equisetum unital, ginkgo, and sago palm. Children's gardens using small plants, blooming plants, and special spaces for the enjoyment of little people is a wonderful trend in today's gardens. Personal history gardens contain plants and garden accents that have meaning to you. These are some of the most endearing gardens because they include plants and features that bring back memories of events, loved ones, and friends.

- Much interest is being focused on garden art. Statuary, containers, urns, birdbaths, pillars, fencing, and water fountains are just a few examples found in nurseries and mail-order catalogues. Don't use too many, but a few well-placed items can increase landscape quality and enjoyment.

- Including whimsy in the garden is simply fun. Bottle trees, tepee structures with vines, old signs, pink flamingos, gazing balls, wind chimes, old tire planters, and even plastic plants have all been used by gardeners in the past and in the present.

- Don't forget the birds, butterflies, and other wildlife in your garden. Some can be pests, but with planning and planting you can enjoy these living, moving additions to your landscape.

Take a new look at your landscape. Think about the concepts, guidelines, and ideas presented, and strive to create a beautiful landscape to adorn your home and add quality to your outdoor living.

What to Do with Fallen Leaves?

(*Note:* In 1991, extension colleagues Vince Mannino, Robert "Skip" Richter, Sam Cotner, and I embarked on writing a publication to answer the question, "If most people are not going to have a compost pile in their backyards, then what can they do with all the fallen leaves to prevent the tons of leaves from being dumped in landfills?" The resulting publication, "Don't Bag It—Leaf Management Plan," answered the question beautifully and is available at aggiehorticulture.tamu.edu. Still believing most of you will not have a compost pile in your backyard [I don't], I have updated and gleaned from this publication information that focuses on the other options of disposing of the leaves each fall.)

Throughout Texas, trees drop tons of leaves each fall. The amount can be staggering in the eastern half of the state.

Some Texas cities have municipal composting facilities that collect the leaves from your home and combine them with sewage sludge to create a wonderful compost to amend garden soils (check with your city's solid waste department). Unfortunately, most cities do not have this service, and most will not accept your fallen leaves to throw them in landfills.

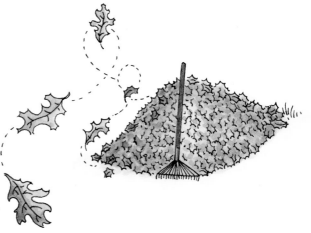

With limited landfill space throughout Texas, YOU then must decide what to do with those fallen leaves. Reducing the amount of yard waste, grass clippings, and leaves is critical to prolonging the "life span" of Texas landfills and slowing the creation of new ones.

Fallen tree leaves (including pine needles) represent a valuable natural resource, providing organic matter and nutrients for your landscape. Fallen leaves contain 50 to 80 percent of the nutrients a plant extracts from the soil and air during the growing season. Burning the leaves or bagging the leaves and throwing them in a landfill eliminates the chance for your landscape to benefit from these nutrients. In essence, you are throwing away fertilizer when you burn or toss fallen leaves.

There are four primary options (other than composting) for managing leaves and using them in your landscape and garden.

- *Mowing.* A light covering of leaves on the lawn can be mowed and simply left in place. This option is most effective when a mulching mower is used. During times of light leaf drop or if there are only a few small trees in your landscape, this option is probably the most efficient and easiest way to manage fallen leaves.
- *Mulching.* Mulching is a simple and effective way to recycle leaves and improve your landscape. Mulches carpet the soil and reduce moisture evaporation, inhibit weed growth, moderate soil temperatures, keep soils from eroding, and prevent soil compaction. As in the forest, the leaves serving as a mulch decompose slowly and release their nutrients for use by your landscape plants. Fallen leaves can be used as a mulch in vegetable gardens, in flower and shrub beds, underneath hedge rows, in natural areas, and around trees. As an option to raking up the leaves, use a lawn mower with a bagging attachment to provide a fast way to shred and collect the leaves. Fallen leaves that have been mowed or shredded decompose faster and are much more likely to remain in place than unshredded leaves. (*Note:* If I have too many fallen leaves for mulching in the landscape, then I have been known to throw them under the deck or over the neighbor's fence, at night. Anything to keep the leaves out of the landfill.)
- *Using in the vegetable garden.* In addition to mulching the garden rows, place a thick layer of leaves in the furrows between the rows to function as a mulch, an all-weather walkway, and a compost-in-place location. For the next gardening season, move the row over into the furrow. The decomposed leaves from last year can be tilled into the soil to create the new

rows. Repeating this process year after year will produce a fabulous, highly organic garden soil.

- *Tilling into the soil.* Fallen leaves can be collected and tilled directly into the soil for shrub plantings, flower beds, and vegetable gardens. It is best to collect and till the leaves into the soil during the fall. This allows sufficient time for the leaves to decompose prior to spring planting. Adding small amounts of nitrogen fertilizer or manure to the soil will speed up decomposition. A 6- to 8-inch layer of leaves turned into a heavy, clay soil will improve aeration and drainage. The same amount added to a light, sandy soil will improve water- and nutrient-holding capacity.

Transplanting Shrubs and Trees: Tell Them before You Move Them

The need to transplant a shrub or tree seems to arise more often than any of us would like. Reasons include that the plant has outgrown its space (caused by planting the wrong plant in the wrong place); the tree obscures the house or a nice view; or the plant is unhealthy due to poor growing conditions (e.g., too much or little sun, poor soil). Regardless of the reason, success in transplanting shrubs and trees starts with giving the plant some advance warning that you are going to move it.

The best time to transplant shrubs and trees is in the late winter when the plants are as dormant as possible. The chances of success decrease dramatically when transplanting shrubs and trees during the spring, summer, and fall. Also, the larger the shrub or tree is, the lower the chances of success. If the shrub is over 4 feet tall or the tree has a trunk diameter more than $\frac{3}{4}$ inch, forget trying to transplant it yourself. Hire a profes-

sional to do it, or cut the shrub or tree down, buy a new one, and plant it in the right place. The size root-ball needed to move large shrubs or trees is too big (2 to 3 feet across) and too heavy for you and a friend to handle.

Tell the plant you are going to move it by notifying it in the fall. Notification involves precutting the root-ball you will dig in late winter. Take a "sharpshooter" shovel (a long, narrow-bladed shovel), and cut a 16- to 20-inch-diameter circle in the soil around the plant. Each cut with the shovel should penetrate 12 inches deep. Space each cut one width of the shovel apart as you progress around the plant. Leaving uncut soil allows some roots to remain unaffected by this pre-transplant process. The cut roots will regenerate new roots during the fall and winter, congregating inside the circle. More roots in the soon-to-be-dug root-ball significantly increase the chances of success.

In late December or January, complete the transplanting process. Your goal is to dig a cylinder of soil (root-ball) 16 to 20 inches in diameter and 12 inches deep WITHOUT letting the cylinder fall apart. If the soil falls away from the roots (the root-ball breaks), the chance that the plant will survive transplant is reduced to much less than 50 percent.

Finish cutting the uncut portion of the circle around the plant. Create the root-ball by digging on the outside of the circle you cut, progressing around the plant to dig the soil cylinder. Once the digging is completed, wrap the cylinder of soil with burlap or an old blanket to provide support to keep the cylinder intact.

If you are going to move the plant to a new spot in your landscape, dig the new hole now before you make the final cuts to remove the plant from its current location. The new hole should be slightly larger in diameter (a couple of inches) and no deeper than the soil cylinder.

Back at the plant, make the final cuts below the soil cylinder to cut the remaining roots and free the plant. You must now pick the plant up by the soil cylinder without breaking it. Slip a blanket underneath the soil cylinder, and bring the ends of the blanket together at the base of the plant's trunk or main stems. You may want to bind the blanket corners with rope or tape. Now lift the plant by supporting the cylinder, and move it immediately to the new hole. DO NOT carry the plant by its trunk.

Place the transplant in the new hole.

Carefully remove the soil wrappings (blanket or burlap). Backfill any voids around the cylinder with the soil you dug from the hole. Water to settle the soil. Build a 4-inch-tall berm (a small soil dam) around the edge of the hole. Fill the berm with mulch (e.g., shredded bark, compost) and water.

If you don't intend to plant the newly dug shrub or tree immediately, place the soil cylinder in a container as close to the same size as the cylinder as possible. Water the plant, and keep the plant in a shaded location until spring growth begins.

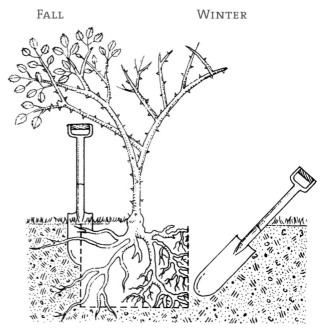

FALL   WINTER

In early fall, precut a partial circle around the plant. In late winter, complete the transplanting process: make final cuts around the plant, remove the soil outside the circle to create a soil cylinder (root-ball), wrap the cylinder with burlap or blanket, make the final cut underneath the cylinder, slip a blanket under the cylinder, and carefully move the root-ball to the new location.

Do You Need Some Shady Characters for the Landscape?

Some of you have so many trees in your yard that shade becomes a big landscape challenge. Some of you have small micro-climates where shade is a problem (e.g., north side of the house, courtyards, and fence-enclosed areas).

Some of you have tried in vain to grow shade-tolerant lawn grasses, such as St. Augustine and zoysia. If shade in your landscape is too dense for these grasses, then turn to vines and ground-covers for large areas and/or expand planting beds with more shade-tolerant plants.

When choosing plants for shade, keep in mind that few will provide interest through blooms. Focus choices on foliage texture to provide interest by contrasting textures. Also, look for foliage color and variegation—reds, yellow and green, and particularly white and green.

Turk's cap (Malvaviscus arboreus)

Here is a list of "shady characters" for your landscape (for detailed descriptions of the plants, refer to essays focused on the different plant types):

ANNUALS
Begonia
Caladium
Coleus
Elephant ear
Impatiens

VINES AND GROUNDCOVERS
Ajuga
Algerian ivy
Carex sedges
Clematis
English ivy
Liriope
Monkey grass or mondo grass
Vinca major or vinca minor

PERENNIALS, SHRUBS, AND SMALL TREES
Abelia
Acuba
American beautyberry
Aspidistra or cast-iron plant
Azalea (partial shade)
Boxwood
Cherry laurel
Coralberry
Columbine (particularly Hinckley's)
Dwarf palmetto palm
Fatsia
Ferns (holly, wood, sword)
Firespike (*Odontonema strictum*)
Ginger
Hollies (most, except yaupon holly)
Hosta
Japanese black pine (partial shade)
Japanese maple (partial shade)
Nandina (partial shade)
Plumbago
Ruellia ('Blue Shade' and 'Katie')
Sago palm
Society garlic
Split-leaf philodendron
Tropical giant spider lily
Turk's cap

Fall Lawn Fertilizing

Timing is critical for applying fall fertilizer to lawns. The turfgrass must have stopped shoot and leaf growth prior to application. The exact time of cessation of growth varies significantly depending on your geographic location as well as recent temperature conditions (e.g., cool fronts, early frost, late warm spells).

The best way to pinpoint the time to fertilize is by monitoring your mowing frequency. After a few cool nights (i.e., 50°F or below), warm-season turfgrasses, such as Bermuda, buffalo, and St. Augustine, will slow growth rapidly. Your need to mow will become less frequent. When you don't need to mow for 2 weeks, the time to fertilize is at hand. Cool-season grasses, such as bluegrass and ryegrass, need fall and winter applications of fertilizer because they actively grow in the winter months.

Fall fertilizer date	Texas region
September 1	Panhandle (Amarillo)
September 15	Southern Panhandle (Lubbock) and El Paso
October 1	North Texas (Big Bend, San Angelo, Abilene, Midland, Odessa, Dallas, Fort Worth, Waco, Texarkana)
October 15	Central Texas (Uvalde, San Antonio, Austin, Bryan, College Station, Conroe, Nacogdoches)
October 30	South and Coastal Texas (Brownsville, Harlingen, Laredo, Corpus Christi, Victoria, Galveston)

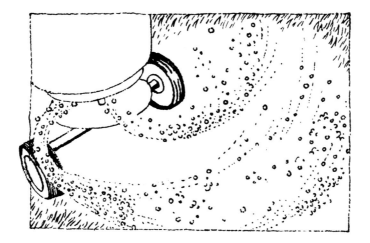

In general, fall fertilization of warm-season grasses should occur within a week either side of dates listed in the adjacent table for the regions of Texas.

Fall lawn fertilization is equally as important as spring fertilization. Fall fertilization prolongs fall color, increases winter hardiness, and promotes earlier spring green-up. It also helps maintain a dense turf that resists winter weeds.

Fertilizers used in the fall should be high in nitrogen and potassium and low in phosphorus (or no phosphrus). A 2-1-2 or 1-0-1 ratio of nutrients is preferred. The nitrogen portion of the fertilizer should be a combination of quick- and slow-release forms to encourage production of carbohydrates. These carbohydrates are then stored in the roots for use in earlier spring greening of the lawn and as an energy source for the turfgrass during winter stress.

The amount of fertilizer to apply is 1 pound of actual nitrogen per 1,000 square feet. Look on the fertilizer bag for guidance on how much area the bag will cover, turn to a nursery professional for assistance, or refer to the March essay "Lawn Fertilizing Made Simple" for a detailed explanation.

Cool-Season Vegetables in Fall

 The distinct advantage to growing cool-season vegetables in the fall is crop quality. The vegetables mature as the days get shorter and cooler; this alone creates better taste. The bitter taste of broccoli, greens, lettuce, and other cool-season vegetables does not develop as it often does in spring gardens.

In addition, insect pest pressure is less in the fall season. And perhaps best of all, it is more comfortable for you to garden in fall than late spring and summer.

Most cool-season vegetables can also be attractive additions to the landscape. Refer to the March essay "Vegetable Gardening Is for Everyone" for more details on variety selection and gardening practices. Here are cool-season crops to be planted now, whether in a dedicated vegetable garden or incorporated into your flower beds:

Beet
Broccoli
Brussels sprouts
Cabbage
Carrot
Cauliflower
Collard greens
Green bean (use fast-maturing bush types)
Lettuce (leaf, butterhead, romaine)
Kale
Mustard greens
Onion (for "green onions," not big bulbs)
Radish (fast maturing and less hot to taste)
Spinach
Sugar snap pea
Swiss chard
Turnip (for greens and/or roots)

Timely Tips

Flowers & Pretty Plants

• Enjoy the fall bloom of many ornamental grasses (e.g., bushy bluestem, gulf muhly, Indiangrass, little bluestem). Enjoy also the movement that ornamental grasses contribute to the garden. Swaying in the breeze with their green, or freeze-damaged brown, foliage, ornamental grasses should be in every landscape. Plant some this fall. Refer to this month's essay "Ornamental Grasses—a New Frontier for the Landscape."

• Enjoy the true fall-blooming perennials, such as chrysanthemum, firespike, Mexican bush sage, and Mexican mint marigold. Texans are fortunate that winter garden colors do not solely exist of brown, white, or gray (slush). Keep planting through the fall and winter season when temperatures are more pleasant for the plants and the planter.

• Plant annual flowers. You can safely plant truly cool-season annuals, including Johnny-jump-up, pansy, snapdragon, sweet pea, stock, and viola.

• Procrastinate no longer. Purchase or order spring-flowering bulbs while the selection is good. You won't plant them until December or January. Store them in the refrigerator or cool garage until planting.

Garden Design

• Engage a landscape designer or landscape architect to assist in creating a wonderful, enjoyable outdoor space. These professionals have an eye for design that most don't (including me). An economical way to get their thoughts is simply to hire a design professional for an hour or two to get on paper (or ground) how the beds, sidewalks, patios, and garden are to be laid out. Then you can take over and implement the design, using landscape contractors and this book as your guide.

Soil & Mulch

• Mulch flower and shrub plantings and vegetable gardens. Mulching now will trap soil warmth and moisture that will benefit plant roots. Mulch will also reduce winter weeds.

Water

• Turn off the irrigation system for the winter. In the absence of rain, you can turn on the system about once every 3 to 4 weeks through the late fall and winter.

Plant Care

• If you had loads of winter weeds in the lawn last year and you did not apply a granular pre-emergence herbicide last month, then do it now—last chance!

• Expect to experience the first freeze throughout most of Texas (except South and coastal Texas). It could be a light frost or heavy freeze. Move container-grown tender plants to protection when a freeze is predicted. Be prepared for more protective actions for cold-sensitive plants growing in the ground. The February essay "Last and First Freeze Dates" and the September essay "Cold-Weather Protection for Plants" will help you plan your strategy.

Trees, Shrubs & Vines

• Enjoy the ornamental shrubs that bear berries in the fall and winter—American beautyberry, dogwood, possumhaw, and yaupon. What wonderful interest and beauty they provide. If you want to plant such a plant, choose one in the nursery now while it has berries so you know what you are getting.

• Check out the fall foliage in Texas. Not exactly New England, but Texas has a few colorful fall trees, including bald cypress, cedar elm, dogwood, sycamore, sweet gum, Texas red oak, and more. For more choices, refer to the November essay "Texas Trees for Fall Color."

• Deadhead those roses, and they will bloom until the first heavy freeze.

Lawns

• Remember: Don't apply fall fertilizer until warm-season lawns (e.g., Bermuda, St. Augustine, zoysia) have stopped growing. For most of the state this occurs in October. You can tell by simply observing your mowing frequency. When you have not had to mow for 2 weeks, the time to fertilize has come.

• If you overseeded your Bermuda lawn with ryegrass, mow, trim, water, and fertilize regularly. No wonder most lawns are not overseeded. Everyone deserves some break from lawn care.

Vegetables, Herbs & Fruits

• Harvest cold-sensitive herbs, such as basil. Refer to the April essay "Herb Growing Hints for Texas" for details on preserving herbs by air-drying, oven-drying, microwaving, and freezing.

• In all but the Panhandle, continue to plant cool-season vegetables, including broccoli, cauliflower, collard greens, leaf lettuce, snow pea, and turnip.

- Don't forget to water and fertilize vegetable crops through the fall and winter, although less frequently.

- Although insect and disease management is minimal during the fall and winter, keep watch for cabbage loopers (inchworms) eating your broccoli, cabbage, cauliflower, and lettuce. Organic control using Bt is available and effective.

- If you are a fruit or nut grower, enjoy the fruits of your labor. You are among the most determined and knowledgeable of gardeners.

Houseplants

- Understand that people don't grow houseplants indoors; they simply maintain them. The simple goal is to put a new leaf on for every leaf that falls off your ficus tree or palm. If you want a big indoor palm, purchase a big one in the beginning.

- Understand, too, that light requirement is critical when choosing houseplants. Croton, ficus, and palm have high light requirements, as opposed to Chinese evergreen (aglaonema), pothos ivy, and spathiphyllum. Most houses do not have bright natural light to support houseplants that have high light requirements.

Butterflies, Birds & Squirrels

- Look outside. Most birds do not migrate and are thus your neighbors all winter long. Feed them seeds and water, and they will reward you with song.

- Because so many butterfly-attracting plants are perennials and now is prime time to plant, purchase and plant such bloomers as buddleia, butterfly weed, shrub-form lantana, purple coneflower, salvias, and verbena.

Notes:

November

*Hyacinth bean (*Dolichos lablab *or*
Lablab purpureus*)*

DOWN TIME, NOT EXACTLY

Top 10 Mistakes of Texas Gardeners

(*Note:* Almost a decade ago, I coauthored several articles with a fabulous writer and Master Gardener from San Antonio, Marsha Murray Harlow. One of those articles, "Top 10 Mistakes of Texas Gardeners," appeared in *Neil Sperry's Gardens* magazine, October 1998. Our findings then are still applicable today. Marsha passed away in 2001, so as a tribute to her, here is the article once again for your enjoyment.)

Gardening in Texas is not a one-size-fits-all experience. From West Texas to East Texas, North Texas to South Texas, growing conditions are different and nature's challenges are unique. But we all share common ground no matter where we garden: our failures. Face it; plants go belly-up from one end of this state to the other, and it's usually our fault. So, what are we doing wrong?

To answer that, we sought the experts: the men and women on the front lines of gardening in Texas, the county extension agents and horticulturists. People don't hesitate to call them when the tomato plants are puny or the turfgrass is splotchy. They are also the folks who oversee Master Gardener volunteers answering horticulture questions by phone. (Master Gardeners field more than 85,000 gardening calls annually.) In short, these county agents and horticulturists have seen and heard it all.

The six experts who contributed to an informal survey included Calvin Finch of Austin (now with the San Antonio Water System), Keith Hansen of Tyler, Jerry Parsons of San Antonio, Stacy Reese of Dallas (retired), Robert "Skip" Richter of Conroe (now Austin), and Dotty Woodson of Fort Worth.

Here is their list of the top 10 mistakes Texas gardeners make:

1. *Overwatering.* In Texas, water is precious and should be used wisely. Unfortunately, watering is one of the most confusing and misunderstood of gardening chores. Overwatering, or improper watering, encourages shallow root systems, stresses plants making them more susceptible to pests, and wastes water if runoff occurs. Roots in waterlogged soil cannot breathe, so plants wilt, turn yellow, and die. One of the worst mistakes people make in their landscapes is trying to sprinkle plants each day. Watering is best done on an infrequent, as-needed basis early in the morning when the least amount will be lost to evaporation from heat or wind. Try not to get water on plant leaves. Water so that the soil is wet several inches down, encouraging deep rooting and drought tolerance. Learn to recognize dry plants and soil, and use these signs as indications of when to water.

2. *Overfertilizing.* Proper fertilizing creates healthier plants able to resist pests and environmental stresses, but too much of a good thing causes problems for the plant as well as the gardener. Too much fertilizer can cause excessive new growth, making a plant more susceptible to disease. And that excessive growth requires more water and more mowing or pruning. Taken to an extreme, overapplication of a fertilizer can burn tender plants. Your best protection? Read labels and follow the recommended application. If chemical fertilizers are used, water in as directed to avoid burn. And pass up that weed-and-feed product in very early spring. Your real grass is still dormant, so you are only feeding the weeds.

3. *Misusing pesticides.* A wise gardener knows an insect-free landscape is impossible. The goal is to control the bad guys of the insect world and encourage the good guys. Too many chemical pesticides can upset the balance of nature and begin a vicious cycle that requires more and more pesticides. Quick action on a small problem can keep it from turning into a large one requiring heavy-duty firepower. Read up on natural insecticides and nonchemical remedies, and use chemical pesticides as a last resort. Identify the pest, and use an appropriate pesticide. Many are non-selective, so beneficial insects will be affected, too. Mix exactly according to directions, and use care in application and storage.

4. *Improperly identifying a plant problem.* Before you choose a weapon, you must know who the enemy is. Put your sleuthing skills to work to

determine if the problem is caused by an insect, disease, or environmental factor. Insects harm plants by chewing, feeding internally, or piercing and sucking. Pathogenic diseases are caused by fungi, viruses, bacteria, or nematodes. Environmental factors include too much or too little water, light, or nutrients or pollution by chemicals. Be methodical in examining the damaged plant; do some research and use common sense. Still stumped? Break off a few leaves (or representative sample), seal in a plastic bag, and take them to your county extension agent or a knowledgeable garden center. You will likely get an identification and a suggested solution.

5. *Using plants that are unproductive and/or poorly adapted to your area.* There is a reason dogwood and azaleas flourish in East Texas but not in the Hill Country. Climate, rainfall, soil types, and temperatures divide Texas into different gardening "zones," and a smart gardener learns to appreciate what grows well in his or her backyard and doesn't fight Mother Nature. Before you plant, learn what plants (trees, shrubs, perennials, vegetables, fruits) are recommended for your area. The county extension office is a good place to start, and it's free. Other sources include avid gardeners in your neighborhood, Master Gardeners, or publications written specifically for your area. Knowledgeable landscape designers and nursery professionals are another source, but steer clear of those who plant or sell mainly what customers request and not necessarily what is suited to local growing conditions.

6. *Planting the right plant in the wrong place.* Okay, you have selected a plant recommended for your area; now you need to plant it in the right location. Many folks flunk this test. Just look at oak trees planted under utility lines or close to buildings. Or at mulberry trees or others with messy habits hanging over driveways or patios. Or photinias crowded side by side along a foundation. Or a vegetable garden located in a shady part of the yard. When placing a plant, consider its mature size and its need for sunlight or shade. Try to grow vegetables in less than full sun, and you are asking for failure.

7. *Failing to prepare soil before planting.* No matter what type of soil you have, most successful gardening depends on amending the soil. Healthy soil alive with nutrients and microorganisms produces healthy plants that have few problems. Eliminating weeds, tilling the soil, adding

organic matter, and aerating compacted soil are a few important ways to prepare for planting. In some areas, building raised beds is the best solution to poor soils.

8. *Failing to use mulch.* Some experts say you can never use too much mulch. This simple layer of organic or inorganic material on top of the soil can work wonders. It helps the soil retain moisture, moderates soil temperature, keeps down weed populations, and makes the weeds that do appear easier to remove by hand. And organic mulches such as shredded bark, pine needles, and composted leaves are relatively cheap. A 2- to 4-inch layer of organic materials twice a year is recommended for most garden and landscape plants. Another benefit: When the mulch decomposes, it can be turned in the garden soil to further improve soil structure.

9. *Planting at the wrong time.* Timing is important when growing vegetables. Not only must you know which are warm-weather crops and which are cool-weather ones (don't plant broccoli in late spring) but you must consider location. Folks in South Texas plant tomatoes earlier than do those in North Texas. And vegetable varieties for Texas differ from those for northern gardens. For fall gardens of cool-weather veggies, it's important to know how long it takes the crop to mature and count backward from the first expected frost. Your local extension office is a good source of information on planting times and appropriate varieties, as are gardening publications specific to your area.

10. *Failing to think long-term.* Errors are often made when gardeners and homeowners seek short-term solutions. Need shade in a treeless yard? Do you choose a tree known for its quick growth but short life or one that grows more slowly and will outlive your children? Experts vote for more slow-growing, quality trees. Need to fill an empty flower bed? Resist the urge to pack it full, remembering that most plants grow quickly. If they are overcrowded, they will compete for food, water, and sunlight, creating stress and thus more insect and disease problems. A shrub or small tree you plant close to your home may look fine now, but in 3 years it may need constant trimming to stay manageable. Train yourself to plant with a vision of how things will look in 5 years. You will save yourself money, time, and frustration in the long run.

Snake Oil in the Garden

As gardeners or yardeners, it is important to maintain a healthy level of skepticism when choosing practices and products for use in your landscape and garden. Garden "experts" and information are literally everywhere—television, radio, newspapers, magazines, and the Internet. Advertisements for gardening products pack these venues, all claiming to have the "silver bullet" for all that ails your plants. So how do you make the right choices that are effective and safe for you, your plants, and the environment?

"Show me the data" is the best credo to abide by in making choices. Research by universities, institutes, companies, and garden organizations is conducted continually. However, many practices and products have no research to support their claims and depend on hype, slick advertising, user testimonials,

"Cures all that ails your plants and grows hair on your dog too!"

and outright pleas to sell practices or products. Testimonials can be relatively worthless, depending on the credentials of the one testifying. Stick with research data—if research on a practice or product is not readily available from the proponent, ask for it. This applies to both chemical and organic products and practices.

Research is available for all pesticides, chemical or organic, because they are regulated by the Environmental Protection Agency (EPA). Any product claiming to control pests must be registered with the EPA, and the documentation is available. Now you do have the right to believe the EPA or not, but anyone selling or recommending a product or concoction for pest control that is not registered ultimately answers to the EPA.

(*Note:* When I am asked whether an "organic" concoction that is not registered by the EPA controls a certain pest, my answer is consistent and simple: "There is no definitive research to prove that the concoction or product works or doesn't work; therefore, I will not recommend it.")

Any product claiming to provide plant nutrients, a fertilizer, is regulated by the Feed and Fertilizer Control Service in the Office of the Texas State Chemist. Fertilizers must follow the guidelines of this office and list the nutrient analysis on the bag (i.e., N-P-K percentage). Again, this applies to chemical and organic fertilizers.

No regulatory agency oversees products labeled as soil and soil amendments. For example, you can put anything in a bag and call it potting soil. Buyer beware. Soil enhancement products abound in advertisements and nurseries and garden centers. Buyer beware. "Experts" and user testimonies often tout the benefits of soil enhancers, claiming enhanced microbial activity and other somewhat mysterious properties. Simply ask the seller or manufacturer to "show me the data" to support the claims. If data are shared freely and support the claims, great. If your request is responded to by testimonials, proceed at your own (or plants') risk.

Some gardening products slip through the gauntlet of regulation by being labeled as a soil amendment or mulch and yet "quietly" claim some pesticide properties. Buyer beware.

Some products labeled for use in other household applications (e.g., powdered laundry detergents, soft drinks, alcoholic beverages, syrups) are recommended by "experts" to enhance plant growth or soil health. Buyer beware.

If you are a wary buyer and want to try some of these recommendations and/or products, then test them yourself using the "scientific method." In its simplest form, the scientific method tests a product treatment against no treatment at all (called the "control"). A conclusion as to the effect of the treatment can then be determined.

For example, if the recommended treatment is to put powdered laundry detergent on your lawn, divide your lawn in half, and apply the detergent to one half and not to the other (the control). If a positive (or negative) difference is observed in the treated half compared to the control, then it can be inferred that the effect was caused by the detergent. If no difference is observed, then you can claim that the treated area is the cleanest grass in the neighborhood.

The scientific method can be used to test any garden product or practice. You can also test similar products and practices against each other (don't forget to include a control).

A healthy level of skepticism, "show me the data," buyer beware, and when in doubt test it yourself are all worthy strategies for finding and using the best practices and products for your beloved landscape and garden.

Cloning Plants through Cuttings

Great controversy surrounds the concept of cloning animals and, most of all, humans. Cloning is an asexual propagation method to reproduce an exact genetic replica of one living organism through use of tissue from another organism. By contrast, sexual propagation incorporates combining genetic material of different organisms (generally in the same species) via sperm and egg in animals and pollen and egg in plants.

Cloning of cats, dogs, cattle, and sheep has already been achieved. The new animals (progeny) are genetically identical to the original tissue donor. Controversy heats up when considering the ethics of cloning humans. This is undoubtedly possible, but who wants another _____ (you name the person).

Plant cloning in nature has taken place for thousands of years. Gardeners have utilized cloning for nearly a thousand years to reproduce plants. The most common, and easiest, plant cloning technique is through stem cuttings.

Many types of plants, including trees, shrubs, vines, perennials, annuals, and houseplants, can be cloned through cuttings, by using this process:

- A portion of a stem is cut from the "mother" plant.
- The cutting is placed in garden or potting soil.
- New roots form on the cutting.
- New shoots grow to form a new "twin" of the mother plant.

A few easy-to-root plants are listed below. Don't stop with these; try out your cloning skills with any plants. (*Note:* Some trees, such as bald cypress, cedar elm, oak, and pecan, are virtually impossible to root.)

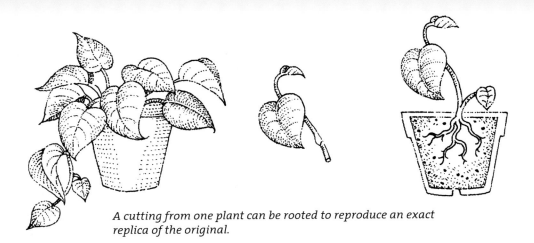

A cutting from one plant can be rooted to reproduce an exact replica of the original.

Althea
Asiatic jasmine
Basil
Bougainvillea
Boxwood
Crape myrtle
English ivy
Fig
Firebush
Geranium
Impatiens
Lantana
Photinia
Plumbago
Pothos ivy (a good beginner plant)
Rosemary
Roses
Salvias
Sweet gum
Verbena

There are two types of stem cuttings to root:

• Active, young stems from perennial and annual flowers and the youngest stems of shrubs and trees can be rooted anytime during the growing season. The goal with active stems is to keep the leaves alive and producing food as the roots form.

• Dormant, woody stems from shrubs and trees, and woody stems of perennials are best rooted during the fall and winter. The goal with dormant cuttings is to get the stems well rooted before spring to support the spring flush of growth.

The steps for rooting either type of cutting are the same with a couple of exceptions that will be noted:

• Fill containers (e.g., 6-inch to 1-gallon plastic pots) with a high-quality potting soil with good drainage. Moisten the potting soil before taking cuttings. Dormant cuttings can be placed in pots or directly into well-prepared soil in the garden.

- Take cuttings with a sharp knife or razor blade (pruning shears crush tissue). The knife or razor blade should be sterilized with alcohol to prevent bacterial or fungal disease on the cut surface. The ideal size of the cutting is pencil length and pencil diameter. Tip cuttings from the end of stems root the best. Older growth is more difficult to root during the growing season but is especially suited as dormant cuttings. Cut the end of the cutting to be stuck in the soil at a 45-degree angle. This increases the area of the stem where roots will form. (For leafless dormant cuttings, it will help you tell up from down on the cutting; cuttings will not root upside down.)

- Remove the leaves from the bottom half of the cutting. On dormant cuttings, the leaves may already have fallen off (e.g., althea, crape myrtle, fig).

- Dip the angled end of the cutting in a powdery rooting hormone (e.g., Rootone) to enhance the chances of root development. Tap off excess rooting powder from the cutting; it doesn't take much.

- Use a pencil to make a hole in the soil. Slip the cutting into the hole, careful not to wipe off the rooting hormone. Firm the soil around the cutting.

- Water the cuttings lightly. Since the cutting does not have roots, moisture will need to be drawn into the cut end (and/or the leaves). Keep the soil moist but not saturated.

- For active, young cuttings with leaves, you must maintain an environment around the leaves that has a 100 percent relative humidity. The leaves will help in absorption of water for the cutting. To increase humidity, create a miniature greenhouse from a clear plastic 2-liter soda bottle cut in half, or create a tent from a clear plastic bag with stick supports. Don't be afraid to open the bag or lift the bottle and check the soil moisture and air humidity. Condensation on the bag or bottle is all right, but water drops on the leaves indicate too much moisture. Let the pot air out some, and replace the bag or bottle.

- The best place to put the pots of cuttings is in bright light but not direct sun—under the porch, in filtered light under a tree is great, or by a bright window indoors for active, young cuttings rooted during winter.

Clear plastic soda bottles can become miniature greenhouses for rooting plant cuttings.

- Wait. It will take from 2 to 6 weeks for active, young cuttings to root, so be patient. For dormant cuttings, you will wait all winter.

- Check for root development by gently tugging on a cutting. If you feel resistance, then roots have likely developed. Stick your index finger in the soil about 2 inches from the cutting. Lift the cutting slowly to protect the fragile new roots. Transplant newly rooted cuttings into their own pot filled with potting soil. For dormant cuttings, wait until leaves have formed before transplanting.

- Newly transplanted rooted cuttings should be placed in bright but not direct sunlight. Fertilize with a water-soluble fertilizer after new shoot and leaf growth has developed.

Don't feel bad if not all the cuttings root and survive transplanting. A good strategy is to take twice as many cuttings as the number of new plants you hope to produce. A 50 percent success rate is great for most plants. Rooting cuttings is an art and a science, and there is no substitute for experience. The ability to multiply your garden plants through cuttings is a tremendous accomplishment and source of pride and enjoyment. One of the greatest feelings expressed by gardeners is to reproduce their favorite plants and give them to friends and neighbors. Try your hand at plant cloning today.

Texas Trees for Fall Color

*Bald cypress (*Taxodium distichum*)*

Texas is not renowned for its fall color; however, a few Texas trees will provide dependable fall color. The degree to which leaves turn pretty colors rather than brown depends not only on the tree species but also on weather conditions. When fall in Texas is mild and drawn out over a couple of months, colors appear more vivid. Repeated cycles of cooler temperatures followed by days of warmer temperatures through September and October seem to increase the occurrence of good fall color. Texas red oaks in the Hill Country can rival the scarlet show of sugar maples when fall is long. Regrettably, this occurs only every few years.

Tree	Fall color
Bald cypress	rust to burgundy
Black gum	deep red
Cedar elm	yellow
Chinese pistache	yellow to red
Chinquapin oak	yellow
Dogwood	red
Eastern persimmon	yellow, orange, to red-purple
'Fan Tex' ash	yellow
Flameleaf sumac	red
Ginkgo	yellow
Lacey oak	yellow
River birch	yellow
Shumard oak	red
Southern or Texas sugar maple	yellow and red
Shining sumac	red
Sweet gum	yellow
Sycamore	yellow
Texas ash	yellow
Texas red oak	red to yellow
Tulip poplar	yellow to orange

CALLER: "Why do tree leaves change color in the fall?"

ANSWER: "Leaves get their green color from the predominance of chlorophyll, a green pigment that absorbs sunlight for photosynthesis. As deciduous trees experience the shorter days and longer nights of fall, chlorophyll production slows and existing chlorophyll disintegrates. In the absence of this green pigment, three other pigments left within the leaves show through; thus, fall colors appear.

The three leaf pigments that cause fall color are red to purple anthocyanins, yellow to orange carotenoids, and yucky brown tannins. Due to these pigments, leaves of some Texas trees might turn amber, gold, red, orange, or yellow. Unfortunately, most simply fade from green to brown, as seen in many native oaks. The brown color is dead leaf tissue and dried-up sap containing tannins."

As the green pigment (chlorophyll) degrades during cool temperatures, the remaining pigments begin to shine.

Grow Vertical with Vines

The vertical plane is often forgotten in the landscape and garden. Smaller residential lots, garden homes, and condominiums are helping to revive interest in growing vertical with vines. Whether your landscape is huge or small, vines provide a unique opportunity to create beauty, color, texture, and interest to the horizontal landscape.

"The first year vines sleep, the next year they creep, and the third year they leap, perhaps right over the house!"
—anonymous, but astute, gardener

*Hyacinth bean (*Dolichos lablab *or* Lablab purpureus) *was grown by statesman and supreme gardener President Thomas Jefferson.*

The following list includes a few important considerations when choosing vines:

- Vines grow by twining, tendrils, hooks, or rootlike holdfasts; vines with holdfasts (e.g., English ivy and fig ivy) can be destructive to wooden structures and difficult to remove from masonry.
- Vines with robust growth habits should have stout structures on which

to grow; for example, grapes can destroy a flimsy structure by twisting and sheer weight.

- Vines can be perennial or annual; some annual vines can reseed themselves readily and become a weed if not kept in check (e.g., cardinal or cypress vine).

- Pruning vines will help keep them in bounds; this can be done throughout the growing season and/or in late winter.

- Cold hardiness is a concern for some vines; consider growing cold-sensitive vines in containers to be moved indoors during winter.

Select Vertical Vines for Texas Landscapes

AREA OF ADAPTATION KEY

Region 1—East Texas (Beaumont, Houston, Nacogdoches, Texarkana, Tyler)

Region 2—South Texas (Brownsville, Corpus Christi, Del Rio, Laredo)

Region 3—Central Texas (Austin, College Station, San Antonio, Waco)

Region 4—North-Central Texas (Dallas, Denton, Fort Worth, Wichita Falls)

Region 5—Panhandle (Amarillo)

Region 6—West Texas (Abilene, El Paso, Lubbock, Midland, Odessa, San Angelo)

Note—Plants with number 7 are adaptable to most areas of Texas.

Note: The "Area of Adaptation Key" was developed by William C. Welch (extension landscape horticulturist) and me for an Extension publication, "Landscape Water Conservation . . . Xeriscape," which can be found on aggiehorticulture.tamu .edu.

SELECT VERTICAL VINES FOR TEXAS LANDSCAPES

COMMON NAME (SCIENTIFIC NAME)	AREA OF ADAPTATION	SUN EXPOSURE	NOTES
Allamanda (*Alamanda cathartica*)	7	sun	tropical vine, not cold hardy; large, scented, tubular yellow blooms
Boston ivy (*Parthenocissus tricuspidata*)	7	sun to shade	deciduous; fall color; clings to walls
Bougainvillea (*Bougainvillea* spp.)	2	must have full sun to bloom properly	evergreen; many flower (bract) colors; plant outdoors in extreme South Texas; provide winter protection elsewhere
Carolina jessamine (*Gelsemium sempervirens*)	1, 2, 3, 4	sun to shade	evergreen; yellow spring flowers
Clematis (*Clematis* spp.)	5	shade	beautiful blooms; deciduous vine; sweet autumn clematis more widely adapted and a fall bloomer
Confederate jasmine (*Trachelospermum jasminoides*)	1, 2, 3	sun to shade	evergreen; fragrant white spring flowers
Coral honeysuckle ⭐ (*Lonicera sempervirens*)	7	sun	coral flower in summer; gray-green foliage
Coral vine/queen's wreath (*Antigonon leptopus*)	1, 2, 3	sun	pink clusters of flowers in late summer and fall; may freeze to the ground but returns from roots
Crossvine (*Bignonia capreolata*)	7	sun to partial shade	large snapdragon-like blooms of gold to orange-red; blooms in late winter to spring; evergreen foliage

⭐ designates Texas native plants.

Common name (Scientific name)	Area of adaptation	Sun exposure	Notes
Cypress vine/cardinal vine (*Ipomoea quamoclit*)	7	sun to partial shade	annual vine; reseeds profusely; small red tubular blooms; fine foliage
English ivy (*Hedera helix*)	7	shade	evergreen; green or variegated foliage; shade loving; Algerian ivy a larger-leaved relative but not as cold hardy
Fig ivy (*Ficus pumila repens*)	1, 2, 3	sun to shade	evergreen; clings to walls
Grape (*Vitus* spp.)	7	sun	vigorous vine that bears fruit; 'Champanel' or 'Black Spanish' great varieties
Hyacinth bean (*Dolichos lablab* or *Lablab purpureus*)	7	sun to partial shade	annual vine; purple flowers and seed pods; red and white varieties available
Lady Banksia rose (*Rosa banksia*)	1, 2, 3, 4, 6	sun	spring flowers in yellow or white; huge plant
Mandevilla (*Mandevilla* spp.)	7	sun	tropical vine, not cold hardy; large, scented, tubular blooms in pink or white
Rangoon creeper (*Quisqualis indica*)	7	sun to partial shade	tropical vine, not cold hardy; fragrant blooms that open white and mature to red
Sky flower (*Thunbergia grandiflora*)	southern portion of 1, 2, 3	sun to partial shade	blue tubular flowers; cold hardy to 25°F–30°F
Texas wisteria (*Wisteria frutescens*) ⭐	7	sun to shade	blue clusters of flowers in spring; Japanese and Chinese varieties available with larger blooms
Trumpet vine (*Camsis radicans*) ⭐	7	sun to shade	orange flowers in summer and fall; rampant grower; improved varieties available
Virginia creeper (*Parthenocissus quinquefolia*) ⭐	7	sun to shade	known for palmlike foliage; clings to walls; fall color

⭐ designates Texas native plants.

Grow Horizontal with Vines and Groundcovers

Within the horizontal plane of the land-scape, shrubs often dominate. Vines and groundcovers can tie shrub plantings together and provide unity through the landscape. Vines and groundcovers are generally low maintenance. Although more costly to establish than turfgrass, vines and groundcovers offer a lower-maintenance, lower-water-use alterna-tive to lawn areas.

*Vinca major or big leaf periwinkle (*Vinca major*).*

Select Horizontal Vines and Groundcovers for Texas Landscapes

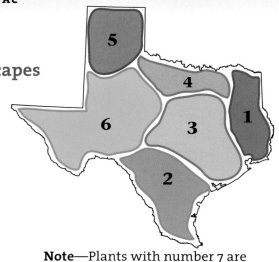

AREA OF ADAPTATION KEY

Region 1—East Texas (Beaumont, Houston, Nacogdoches, Texarkana, Tyler)

Region 2—South Texas (Brownsville, Corpus Christi, Del Rio, Laredo)

Region 3—Central Texas (Austin, College Station, San Antonio, Waco)

Region 4—North-Central Texas (Dallas, Denton, Fort Worth, Wichita Falls)

Region 5—Panhandle (Amarillo)

Region 6—West Texas (Abilene, El Paso, Lubbock, Midland, Odessa, San Angelo)

Note—Plants with number 7 are adaptable to most areas of Texas.

Note: The "Area of Adaptation Key" was developed by William C. Welch (extension landscape horticulturist) and me for an Extension publication, "Landscape Water Conservation . . . Xeriscape," which can be found on aggiehorticulture.tamu.edu.

SELECT HORIZONTAL VINES AND GROUNDCOVERS FOR TEXAS LANDSCAPES

COMMON NAME (SCIENTIFIC NAME)	AREA OF ADAPTATION	SUN EXPOSURE	NOTES
Ajuga (*Ajuga reptans*)	7	shade	variety of foliage colors; blue flowers; requires good garden soil, preferably acidic
Asiatic jasmine (*Trachelospermum asiaticum*)	1, 2, 3, 4, 6	sun to shade	evergreen foliage; variegated form available; freeze damage on foliage occurs in northern half of state
Asparagus fern (*Asparagus densiflorus* 'Sprengeri')	7	sun to partial shade	dense, fine-textured, light green foliage; annual in northern half of Texas
Confederate jasmine (*Trachelospermum jasminoides*)	1, 2, 3	sun to shade	evergreen; fragrant white spring flowers

Dalea, trailing (*Dalea greggii*)	2, 3, 6	sun	fine-textured, silvery, blue-green foliage with occasional purple flowers; very tough trailing plant adapted to alkaline soils; cold hardy south of Dallas through the Hill Country to El Paso; not adapted to East Texas
English ivy (*Hedera helix*)	7	shade	evergreen; green or variegated foliage; shade loving; Algerian ivy a larger-leaved relative but not as cold hardy
Holly fern (*Cyrtomium falcatum*)	7	partial shade to shade	bold-textured fern; ideal for deep shade; suffers foliage freeze damage in northern Texas
Juniper, trailing (*Juniperus* spp.)	2, 3, 4, 5, 6	sun	adapted best to low rainfall areas
Liriope (*Liriope muscari*)	7	sun to shade	evergreen, grasslike foliage; purple bloom spikes; varieties: standard, variegated white and green, 'Big Blue,' and 'Giganta'
Monkey grass, mondo grass (*Ophiopogon japonicus*)	7	sun to partial shade	evergreen, grasslike foliage (finer blade than liriope); dwarf and standard forms available
River or wood fern (*Thelypteris kunthii*) ⭐	1, 3, 4	partial shade to shade	fine-textured foliage; suffers foliage freeze damage in northern Texas
Rosemary, prostrate (*Rosmarinus officinalis*)	coastal areas of 1 and 3; all but northern area of 2	sun	fine-textured, gray-green, fragrant foliage; light blue flowers; culinary herb
Ruellia/Mexican petunia varieties (*Ruellia* sp.)	7	sun to shade	several heights and forms, standard upright to groundcover to vine; 'Katie,' 'Blue Shade'; blue flowers; annual in northern half of Texas
Santolina (*Santolina* spp.)	3, 4, 5, 6	sun	fine-textured, evergreen foliage of green or silver
Society garlic (*Tulbaghia violacea*)	7	sun to shade	grasslike foliage; lavender-blue blooms; green and green and white forms
Vinca (*Vinca major*)	7	partial shade to shade	blue flowers and kelly green foliage; more adapted than *V. minor*

⭐ designates Texas native plants.

Timely Tips

Flowers & Pretty Plants

• Worry some, but not much. The first heavy freeze has occurred in much of the state. This damages blooms and stems of many annual and perennial flowers. How much damage the annuals suffered will be visible after about a week of warmer weather. Either they survived or they didn't. With perennials, it is tougher to tell. Many perennials may have blooms and stems that die back, but thicker woody stems and root systems survive. Some perennials may be killed all the way to the roots but sprout back from the roots in the spring. Ask local nursery professionals, Master Gardeners, and/or extension agents for their prediction of damage before you do any pruning or removing of perennial flowers.

• Be wary of mail-order catalogues and Sunday supplements touting the latest and greatest plants, products, and elixirs for your garden. Maintain a healthy level of skepticism when considering such advertisements. Read this month's essay "Snake Oil in the Garden" for a philosophical look at garden products and recommendations.

• Fertilize and water cool-season annuals. Their ability to take the cold weather depends on energy and water to grow. Water-soluble fertilizers may be more readily available to the plant than granular products at this time of year.

• Spring-flowering bulbs should be stored until planting. Store in paper bags or vented plastic bags in the refrigerator or cool pantry or garage. Check them at least every 2 weeks to make sure none have begun to decay. If so, remove the damaged bulbs. Cooler temperatures or more ventilation is probably needed.

Garden Design

• Purchase a mixture of ornamental plants that provide variations in foliage texture for your next planting. Most shrubs have the same, mundane, medium-sized green leaves. Seek out fine-textured plants (e.g., ferns, ornamental grasses) to contrast with coarse-textured plants (e.g., cast-iron plant, fatsia, holly fern) for your new planting. You will be surprised at the dramatic effect texture provides in the landscape.

Soil & Mulch

- Send soil in for testing now before the late winter rush. Soil testing labs are available at Texas A&M University and Texas Tech University, as well as private laboratories.

- In the northern half of Texas (north of IH-20), heavily mulch perennial flowers, tender shrubs, and newly planted trees, shrubs, and roses using pine straw, pine bark, or straw or hay. Mulch helps prevent freeze damage to plant roots and crown (base of the main stem or trunk). It also moderates soil temperatures and moisture levels.

- If winter weeds are sprouting in the landscape plantings, mulch to provide the most effective and environmentally safe way to keep them in check. Hoe or pull larger weeds.

Water

- Water lawns, landscape plantings, vegetable gardens, and fruit plantings if the ground is dry and a freeze is predicted. Water at least once in November in the absence of significant rain to prevent freeze damage and desiccation or death of leaves and twigs.

Plant Care

- If winter weeds are sprouting in the lawn, mow to provide the most effective and environmentally safe way to keep them in check.

- If a hard, prolonged freeze (24 hours or more) is predicted, protect freeze-sensitive plants by covering them with cardboard boxes or blankets. Supplemental heat from a utility light or Christmas lights may also be needed. If the plants are growing in containers, simply move them indoors or, at minimum, into the garage.

- Refrain from pruning off freeze-damaged plant material; this pruning is best done in February or March.

Trees, Shrubs & Vines

- What to do with all the tree leaves that are falling? Mow them, shred them, mulch with them, compost them, or throw them over the fence; just DO NOT bag them up and send them to the landfill.

- Need a hedge to screen an unsightly view? Choose large shrubs to provide a living screen. It takes longer to screen the view than with a fence, but it costs less and looks more natural. Arrange the shrubs in a "W" or sweeping pattern, not an unnatural straight line. Great shrubs for a screen include Arizona cypress, cherry laurel, Chinese photinia, eastern red cedar, Eldarica pine, Leyland cypress, wax myrtle, and yaupon holly. Use one species or a combination in patterns.

Lawns

• You may see the fungal disease brown patch in your St. Augustine lawn; forget about it. It is too late in the season to justify a fungicide treatment. Winter damage on St. Augustine will likely hide the brown patch in all but South and coastal Texas. However, mark your calendar in February to treat the lawn area to prevent brown patch in spring.

Vegetables, Herbs & Fruits

• Even vegetable crops growing in winter will benefit from fertilizer, so apply nitrogen fertilizer at a rate of $\frac{1}{4}$ pound of urea per 100 square feet, $\frac{1}{2}$ pound of ammonium sulfate, or 1 pound of blood meal. Farm and ranch stores may be your best source for large bags of urea and ammonium sulfate.

• In the absence of rain, water the garden thoroughly.

• Maintain a thick mulch (4 to 6 inches) to preserve soil moisture,

moderate soil temperatures, retard weed growth, and reduce soilborne diseases.

• With outdoor temperatures dropping, plant a containerized herb garden for indoors. Provide the brightest natural light possible. Plant herb transplants, such as basil, chives, green onions, mint, parsley, sage, and thyme.

• For Thanksgiving, see how many Texas-grown vegetables, fruits, and nuts you can serve at the family meal. Fresh Texas-grown cabbage, carrots, onions, pecans, squash, sweet potatoes, and more are available in grocery stores and produce markets. Check the harvest time in the May essay "Texas Produce: When to Purchase?"

• Run, don't walk, to the grocery store or produce market, because fresh Texas-grown grapefruit are being harvested in the Rio Grande Valley. There is no place that produces higher-quality grapefruit than Texas. Eat all you can, and maybe send a gift box to Aunt Matilda in Oregon. The harvest lasts only about 3 months.

Houseplants

• Feel the suffering that most houseplants are enduring being indoors. Home heating systems reduce indoor humidity significantly. This dries out houseplants more rapidly than you might think. Check the soil moisture at least weekly by using your index finger. Cool to the touch means adequate moisture; warm and dry to the touch mean water is needed. Typical symptoms of houseplants suffering from low humidity and dry soil conditions are browning leaf tips and yellowing of leaves.

• Watch for insect pests that hitch-hiked indoors with the houseplants. Aphids, mealybugs, and spider mites are common. Manage these pests by washing the houseplant in the shower to remove the pest; or, if warranted,

use the least toxic, effective insecticide labeled for use on indoor plants.

Butterflies, Birds & Squirrels

• Thanksgiving is this month, so provide a feast for the birds and squirrels that share your landscape environment.

• Note that bird seed quality varies significantly. Perhaps the best indicator of quality is how much millet seed is in the bag. Millet is a "filler" seed, and most birds simply sweep it out of the feeder to get to the higher-quality seed. In general, you get what you pay for with bird seed.

Notes:

December

Amaryllis (Hippeastrum *spp.)*

DREAMING OF SPRING

Holiday Plants

The December calendar contains religious and cultural holidays, including Christmas, Hanukkah, and Kwanzaa. Indoor plants help commemorate and celebrate these holidays. Through scripture and tradition, plants have been used in symbolic teachings to remind humans of their intimate relationship with the natural world. Surround yourself with plants this holiday season. Here are a few to consider (in order of popularity), including how to select and care for them.

*Poinsettia (*Euphorbia pulcherrima*)*

Poinsettia

The most popular of holiday plants, the poinsettia is native to Central America and Mexico. Joel Robert Poinsett was the first U.S. ambassador to Mexico (1825–29) and was an avid botanist (gardener). He

is credited with bringing this plant back to his home in South Carolina, propagating the plant in his greenhouses, and sharing it with friends. The plant was assigned the name *Euphorbia pulcherrima* (meaning "the most beautiful euphorbia"), and its common name commemorates Ambassador Poinsett. The attractive plant with its colorful bracts (not flowers) in winter soon became available in northern nurseries. Today, millions are sold each December. Continuous breeding has resulted in more than just red poinsettias. There are white, pink, bicolored, red with white specks, and new "designer" colors of salmon, mauve, and purple. Miniature poinsettias are now also available, as well as painted and dyed poinsettias (even in blue).

When selecting a poinsettia, choose one that has small, tightly closed flower buds (surrounded by the colorful bracts). This helps ensure your poinsettia will last through December inside your home. Also, choose a plant that is about as wide as it is tall. Growing high-quality poinsettias is not easy, nor inexpensive. Be wary of bargain pricing. Generally, you get what you pay for with poinsettias.

Don't throw your poinsettia away after the holidays; try reblooming it. Refer to this month's essay "Poinsettia Rebloom" for guidelines.

Amaryllis

"Big bang for the buck" describes amaryllis. Bulbs are very inexpensive and often come with a pot and potting soil (peat moss), all for $10 or less. Flowers produced are huge tubular blooms with multiple flowers per tall bloom spike. Often more than one bloom spike emerges from each bulb. Flower colors range

*Amaryllis (*Hippeastrum *spp.)*

from velvety red to soft pink to white to bicolors.

This is a great holiday gift and one of those "if you can't grow it, we can't help you" plants. All you need to do is plant the bulb in a small pot with good potting soil and have the top (pointy end) of the bulb sticking up out of the soil about 1 inch. Add water and bright indoor light, and plant growth will begin. The handsome straplike foliage springs forth along with the bloom spike. You can literally watch this plant grow. Blooms will appear in about 14 days. Keep the soil moist but not saturated.

To enjoy amaryllis for months indoors, you can start growth of multiple bulbs at 1-week intervals to produce dozens of "sparkling" blooms (*amaryl-*

lis is derived from the Greek word for "sparkling"). To rebloom your amaryllis, refer to this month's essay "Amaryllis Rebloom."

Christmas Cactus

Christmas cactus is a favorite holiday plant that produces a profusion of gaudy blooms ranging from hot pink to apricot, red, purple, and white. Purchase plants with many flower buds that are just beginning to elongate and open. As with most flowering plants, don't buy the prettiest plant right now; buy the one that will be the prettiest in a few days.

Christmas cactus is not your normal cactus that lives in the desert. This plant lives in tropical jungles in the crotches of trees, so you must take care when watering it. Its soil should be moist but neither completely dry nor saturated.

*Christmas cactus (*Schlumbergera bridgesii*)*

When the top 1 inch of the soil is dry to the touch, water lightly.

Keep the blooming plant in bright indoor light. The fleshy, flattened, segmented stems will grow nicely in low light, but bright light is required for proper blooming.

Christmas cactus is another plant that should not be thrown away after it blooms. With care, you can rebloom your plant for years to come (refer to this month's essay "Christmas Cactus Rebloom").

Rosemary Topiaries

The herb rosemary is being used to produce topiaries for sale during the holiday season. Shaped as wreathes, "poodle" trees, and Christmas trees, rosemary, with its fine needlelike foliage and soothing aroma, has become a popular indoor plant during the holidays. What's next—heart-shaped topiaries for Valentine's Day or bunny-shaped rosemary plants for Easter?

*Rosemary (*Rosmarinus officinalis*) topiary*

Rosemary is a tough plant but requires the brightest light possible to survive for a month indoors. Rosemary is a very drought-tolerant plant, so overwatering it will result in collapse of the root system and damage to the foliage. Let the soil dry almost completely between waterings.

Once the holiday season is over, move the plant outdoors. It can take the cold weather and can be planted into the garden in all areas but the Panhandle. If you want to maintain the topiary shape, get your scissors out regularly and test your skill as a "hare" dresser (for Easter).

Pine Topiaries

In addition to rosemary, some pines conducive to shaping are being "topiaried" into miniature Christmas trees. Italian stone pine and Aleppo pine are both being used and produce a beautiful, dense miniature Christmas tree.

These pines do not like the indoor environment but will survive for a couple of weeks under the low light and drying heat. Get them back outdoors as soon as possible. These pines will use water rapidly under indoor conditions, so check soil moisture levels daily. Water when the soil is dry 1 inch deep.

After the holidays, you can plant these trees outdoors throughout Texas, with the exception of East and South-

east Texas. In San Antonio, Italian stone pines stand over 50 feet tall at Fort Sam Houston. Aleppo pines don't get quite as tall but are adapted to neutral and alkaline soils throughout Texas.

*Norfolk Island pine (*Araucaria heterophylla*)*

Norfolk Island Pine

If you want a "Charlie Brown"–type Christmas tree, Norfolk Island pine is your choice. Although truly more handsome with rigid and uniform branching, this pine is not densely foliaged, and the short needles and spaced branches provide a see-through look. Lightweight bows and ornaments can be used, but a heavy tree-topper may bend the tree over.

Norfolk Island pine is a Southern Hemisphere conifer native to the Norfolk Islands and Australia. In its native environment, this pine can grow to 200 feet tall. It is one of a few conifers that can tolerate low-light conditions of the indoors.

Perhaps the perfect tabletop Christmas tree, Norfolk Island pine cannot survive the outdoor temperatures in most of Texas. High temperatures (95°F to 105°F) will severely burn the needles, and low temperatures (30°F to 32°F) can kill the top growing point of the pine. Temperatures below 25°F can cause heavy freeze damage.

Cyclamen

Although not used often enough, cyclamen offers a unique flower and handsome plant for indoor flower color during the holidays. The flowers of pink, rose, white, red, or purple have reflexed (turned-backward) petals. The thick, heart-shaped foliage makes the plant resemble an African violet. Purchase plants that have a few flowers open and many just beginning to unfurl.

You can enjoy this flowering plant indoors for a month or so. Water frequently to keep the soil moist but not saturated. You can plant your cyclamen outdoors in the southern two-thirds of the state, and the plant will continue to grow and bloom. Once the temperatures heat up in late spring, the plant will stop growing and blooming. This is a plant that it is best thrown away. Cyclamens are a bit pricey because they are grown from corms (tubers), and to reproduce a new corm from an old plant is a lengthy process best left to commercial growers.

Holiday Plant Care— Dos & Don'ts

Beyond specifics noted in the essay, here are the basic dos and don'ts for holiday plant care:

DO transport your holiday plant purchase carefully. Blooms and branches can be brittle. Use a large box or roomy shopping bag to protect your plant.

DO place your plant in the brightest light possible in your home for at least 6 hours per day. Fluorescent light can supplement natural light but not replace it; however, in the absence of natural light let the plant receive twice as many hours of fluorescent light.

DO provide room temperatures between 68°F and 72°F. In Texas winters, this may require air conditioning at times. Basically, if the temperature is comfortable for you, it is right for your plant.

DO water your plant only when your index finger feels that the soil is dry 1 to 2 inches deep. Water thoroughly, and let the water drain freely from the pot into the sink. A wet-dry cycle (versus constantly moist soil) is best for most indoor plants.

DO fertilize your plant only once during the holidays, using a water-soluble fertilizer. If you have a plant that will rebloom, fertilize again after the plant finishes blooming or after the holidays, and continue to fertilize every 3 to 4 weeks.

DO check for insect pests, such as mealybug, spider mites, and white fly. If insects are present, control using an effective and safe indoor pest control strategy.

DON'T place your plant near cold drafts, in the airflow of a heat or air-conditioning register, or adjacent to a space heater or burning fireplace.

DON'T expose your plant to temperatures below 50°F. This includes during transport of the plant from the store.

DON'T overwater your plant, keep the soil saturated, or allow the plant to sit in a saucer of standing water. Remove decorative containers or wrapping before watering, and allow the water to drain completely before replacing.

DON'T neglect your holiday plants. The indoor environment is hostile to most plants. Pay attention to them, and they will reward you with great indoor beauty.

Living Christmas Trees

Artificial, "freshly" cut, or living, the choice is yours for a Christmas tree. Regardless of where you live in Texas, you can enjoy a container-grown living Christmas tree indoors and then plant it outdoors.

Living Christmas trees are a wonderful addition to the landscape. Each year, they can be decorated with traditional lights and ornaments or decorated with edible wildlife-friendly ornaments. Strings of popcorn, apple and orange cross sections, and pine cones smeared with peanut butter and rolled in bird seed all are naturally beautiful and much welcomed by your backyard wildlife.

Deodara cedar (Cedrus deodara)—enjoy indoors, and then move it outside.

Living trees can also be a unique Christmas gift to the family and commemorate the passing of another holiday season.

Here are some tips for choosing living trees for your next Christmas:

- Choose a tree adapted to your location (refer to the tree list below for area of adaptation).
- Choose a tree grown in a 3- to 15-gallon container (much larger than 15 gallons and you will need lots of help moving the tree indoors and then out to plant it).
- While it is indoors, keep the tree in the brightest natural light possible.
- Monitor the soil moisture daily; indoor central heat can suck water quickly through the plant and out of

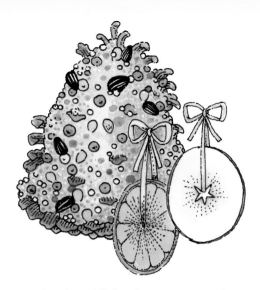

Remember the wildlife—decorate your outdoor Christmas tree with fruit slices and pine cones covered in peanut butter and bird seed.

the soil. The goal is to keep the soil moist but not saturated. Protect your indoor flooring by using a large plastic saucer under the container.

- Get the tree back outdoors as soon as possible; ideally the living tree would be indoors for only 2 to 3 weeks.

- Plant the tree into the soil right after Christmas so that the root system can expand during the rest of winter in preparation for spring growth.

- Follow the planting instructions described in the September essay "Tree Planting Made Easy."

Living Christmas Trees

COMMON NAME	AREA OF ADAPTATION
American holly	East Texas
Arizona cypress	East, Central, West, North Texas
Colorado blue spruce	Panhandle
Deodar cedar	throughout Texas
Eastern red cedar	throughout Texas
Eldarica pine	South, Central, West, North Texas
'Foster' holly	East, North Texas
Italian stone pine	Central, West Texas
Leyland cypress	Central, North Texas
'Nellie R. Stevens' holly	East, Central, and North Texas
Piñon pine	Panhandle, West Texas
Ponderosa pine	Panhandle
Virginia pine	East Texas

Note: If in doubt, check with local nursery professionals and county extension agents to confirm adaptation to your town.

Amaryllis Rebloom

Amaryllis is an inexpensive, easy-to-grow holiday plant, but don't throw it away after it blooms. You can persuade it to rebloom year after year. The plant may even multiply, developing additional bulbs that will bloom.

Here are the steps to reblooming your amaryllis:

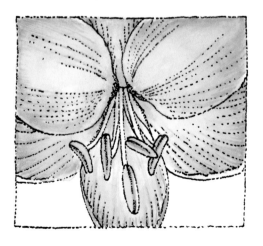

1. Provide the best indoor environment possible. Fortunately, amaryllis will survive the indoor environment of homes and offices. The key to success is providing bright natural light through a window. Fluorescent light will substitute for natural light but must shine on the plant almost night and day. Water only when the soil surface is dry to the touch, and keep the water off the portion of the bulb above the soil level. Fertilize with a water-soluble fertilizer once a month.

2. Cut the flower stalk(s). When the last flower has faded on a flower stalk, cut the flower stalk near the top of the bulb. Don't cut or damage any of the leaves. It is normal for a large amount of sap to flow out of the freshly cut flower stalk.

3. Grow leaves. Grow as many

leaves as possible to generate energy for new bulb and bud formation for next year's flowers. Increase light, water, and fertilizer. It's hard to give your amaryllis too much sunlight during winter. Move it to the sunniest location in your house, preferably a south-facing window. On mild sunny days of Texas winters (above 70°F), you can even move it outdoors to bask in the sun. Continue fertilizing monthly, and never let the soil dry out completely.

4. Move the plant out in spring. Move the amaryllis outdoors in spring when daytime temperatures are in the 70s and nights are in the upper 50s. If a late freeze is predicted, simply move the plant indoors. During the spring move out, some of the oldest leaves may die; simply trim them off. Place the plant in a sunny location (morning sun and afternoon shade are ideal). Keep watering (perhaps daily in a small pot) and fertilizing (now biweekly) to grow more leaves all summer long. By late spring your amaryllis will likely look too big for its pot. Repot into a container 4 inches larger, using good potting soil. In the southern half of the state, amaryllis can be planted directly in the garden into well-prepared soil where it may grow, multiply, and bloom naturally for years.

5. Decide when you want the amaryllis to bloom. If you want amaryllis flowers for the winter holidays, you need to let the plant go dormant by mid-August to early September. To do so, withhold water. The leaves will die back and dry up. Trim them off, and move the pot to a cool location (e.g., indoor pantry). Just forget about it for about a month.

If your amaryllis is planted in the ground, you can dig up the bulb(s) in mid-August, remove the soil and dry it out, and store the plant for a month in a cool location (or in the southern half of Texas you can leave your amaryllis in the soil; don't water in August or September; and let reblooming occur on nature's schedule, not yours).

6. Look for life. After it has spent a month in storage, take a look at the potted plant or bulb. You may see the tips of new leaves emerging from the bulb. This is a great sign. If you don't see this, wait another week or so. Even if you don't see leaves the second time, bring the potted plant out into the warm sunlight (indoors or out), and add water. Pot up individual bulbs, and add water. You want the plant to respond to this warmer, wetter environment by growing roots and shoots before you begin watering regularly. The flower stalk(s) will not be far behind emerging from the bulb.

7. Enjoy your rebloomed amaryllis. Water your amaryllis thoroughly, and allow the soil to dry 1 inch deep before watering again. Indoors, place

the plant in a warm, sunny spot to stimulate growth. Low light conditions may result in a weak flower stalk that bends or breaks under the weight of the large blooms. Even properly grown, the blooms can get so heavy that additional support may be needed by placing an 18-inch stake next to the stalk.

Once the first flower has opened, you can move the plant to a prime location indoors for all to enjoy your rebloomed amaryllis.

Christmas Cactus Rebloom

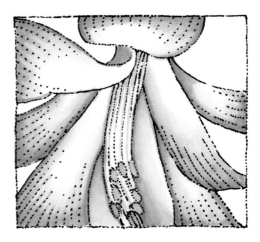

(*Note:* My mom, Julia Fowler Welsh, has had at least one Christmas cactus for as long as I can remember. Her plants always rebloom, not necessarily on Christmas day, but they bloom beautifully each year. While living in Houston, the plants were either kept outdoors or on an indoor windowsill; regardless, they bloomed. One of the common questions I receive is, "How do I get my Christmas cactus to rebloom?" I sought advice from my normally helpful mother. She said, "I don't know; they just bloom for me." She has an inherited green thumb, but that response would not suffice for my clientele. I searched further into the hallowed halls of the university to find the true answer. Here's what I found.)

Reblooming a Christmas cactus is affected by two different environmental conditions: short days/long nights and cool temperatures. Like poinsettias, these bloomers are photoperiodic, day-length sensitive. They need about 12 hours of uninterrupted darkness to initiate flower bud formation.

Flower bud formation is adversely affected by excessively high or low temperature. The preferred temperature for bloom formation is 58°F to 65°F.

There is some conflict in the literature as to whether both environmental conditions must be present for reblooming Christmas cactus; however, all agree that adequate uninterrupted darkness is a must. With this uncertainty, the best course of action is to meet both conditions.

Specific conditions that are known to halt blooming (and confuse the heck out of the plant) include these:

- Growing the plant indoors all the time with temperatures in the 70s and lights being turned on and off at night
- Growing the plant outdoors and moving it indoors just prior to the first frost into a room that is warm and has the lights turned on and off during the night
- Growing the plant outdoors all the time (in South or coastal Texas) with a security or porch light on at night

So, what are the options to rebloom your Christmas cactus?

- Grow the plant indoors on a windowsill in a room that gets natural darkness all night in the fall and winter; the microclimate created by the cold window meets the lower temperature requirements. (*Note:* My mom's plants often sat on a windowsill in the kitchen, and when dinner was over, no one went into the kitchen for a late-night snack, so darkness, and Mom, ruled.)
- Grow the plant outdoors, and let it experience cool nights and naturally

longer nights before bringing it indoors at the first prediction of frost. If natural darkness of 12 hours is not possible outdoors, place a box over the plant to eliminate all light each night (remove it during the daylight hours). Buds should already be visible by the time you bring the plant indoors; then warmer temperatures and intermittent light cannot stopped blooming at this point.

CALLER: "How do I keep the flower buds from always falling off my Christmas cactus?" ANSWER: "Having the flower buds fall off a Christmas cactus before blooming is not uncommon. Make sure you don't water too much or too little. Christmas cactus is not a true cactus from the desert—it does not like its soil to dry out completely, or it will abort buds; it does not like soggy feet, or it will drop buds. Water only when the soil is dry 1 inch deep. Also make sure your plant has enough light—the more light, the better the chances of the buds to open properly. The plant will redirect growth to stems (pads) in lower light at the expense of buds. Finally, don't jostle the plant; the buds seem to fall off with the slightest movement of the branches."

Poinsettia Rebloom

(*Note:* Ellison's Greenhouses of Brenham has ranked among the top wholesale poinsettia growers in Texas for decades. Ellen Ellison first shared with me an article on how to rebloom a poinsettia based on a schedule according to holidays. What a great idea. I have fine-tuned this concept and shared it with many gardeners and yarderers, and the results have been consistently successful.)

Poinsettias are the most popular Christmas holiday plant. Most people purchase or receive poinsettias and then struggle to maintain this native of Mexico in the inhospitable home environment. Ultimately, they are faced with the dilemma of either trashing the plants after New Year's Eve or endeavoring to keep the plants growing due to guilt in disposing of a once-beautiful plant (or gift).

With patience, dedication, knowledge, and a bit of luck, you can coax your poinsettia to rebloom next Christmas by following this schedule of activities based on holidays.

CHRISTMAS (DECEMBER 25). Two weeks prior to December 25, pick a colorful poinsettia with tightly closed clusters of yellow flower buds. Remember that the flowers are yellow; the colorful leaves surrounding the flowers are called bracts. Protect the plant from hot or cold drafts, water when the soil is dry to the touch, and place the plant in a room with bright natural light.

NEW YEAR'S DAY (JANUARY 1). Apply a water-soluble houseplant fertilizer to the plant. Continue providing bright natural light, water only when needed, and fertilize every 2 to 3 weeks. Your poinsettia should remain colorful for many weeks and lose very few lower green leaves. If the lower leaves are falling, move the plant to brighter natural light and don't water too often.

VALENTINE'S DAY (FEBRUARY 14). Do nothing unless your plant has become long, leggy, and almost leafless. If it has, prune the plant back to 8 inches from the soil. Sounds harsh, but this is now about survival.

ST. PATRICK'S DAY (MARCH 17). Put the poinsettia outdoors in morning sun and afternoon shade. Your poinsettia should begin growing rapidly. Remove any faded or dried leaves and stems from the plant. Fertilize again, and water when dry.

MEMORIAL DAY (MAY 30). Your poinsettia should be around 2 to 3 feet tall. Trim off 2 to 3 inches from the end of each branch to promote side branching. Repot into a larger container (about 4 inches larger) using a good potting soil. Move plant into direct sunlight. Poinsettias thrive in full sun. (*Note:* In South and coastal Texas—south of San Antonio and/or along the coast—poinsettias can be planted into a flower bed with well-prepared garden soil.)

INDEPENDENCE DAY (JULY 4). Trim plant back again (2 to 3 inches off each branch to create more branching). Make sure it has full sunlight. Increase the frequency of fertilizing to weekly. Water when needed.

LABOR DAY (FIRST MONDAY IN SEPTEMBER). Your poinsettia may have grown to 4 feet or more. Prepare to move the plant indoors. Avoid exposing the plant to cool night temperatures (less than 65°F). Move the plant from full sun into indirect, filtered light. Move the plant indoors when cool nights are predicted, but make sure it receives 6 hours of bright direct light through a window. Reduce fertilizer to once every 3 weeks.

FIRST DAY OF AUTUMN (SEPTEMBER 21 OR 22). Poinsettias are photoperiodic plants, meaning they set flower buds as nights lengthen in fall. Given natural light of day and night, poinsettias will bloom in December. Stray light of any kind (e.g., street lights, car lights) can halt blooming. Starting about September 21, give the plant 14 hours of uninterrupted darkness and 10 hours of bright light each day. Accomplish this by enclosing the plant in a large cardboard box or black plastic covering. You can put it in a closet, but you must bring it out into bright light every day. (Sample schedule: Put the cover on when you get home from work each day, and take it off before you go to work.) Rotate the plant each day to give all sides even light from the window. Night temperatures should be between 60°F and 70°F (so keep the thermostat low, and/or place the plant next to a window to keep it cool). Continue to water and fertilize. This regime must be carefully followed for 8 to 10 weeks. This regime can be accomplished outdoors in South and coastal Texas, but low temperatures and night lights must be avoided.

THANKSGIVING (FOURTH THURSDAY OF NOVEMBER). Discontinue day/night treatment. Keep the plant in the brightest natural light in your home. Water only when the soil surface is dry. Fertilize one last time. Your poinsettia leaves (bracts) should begin to change from green to red (or whatever color it was last year) by mid-December.

CHRISTMAS (DECEMBER 25). Enjoy your poinsettia rebloom. Congratulations!

Holiday Gifts for Gardeners and Yardeners

Do you have a gardener in the family, a yardener whose job you would like to make easier, or a child who might become a gardener? With December holidays including Christmas, Hanukkah, and Kwanzaa, you have the opportunity to shower these loved ones with gardening gifts. Here are a few to consider.

Books and Magazines

- There are literally thousands from which to choose, but try to focus on those written for Texas gardening.
- There are Texas gardening books that focus on general gardening and specific topics, such as perennials, herbs, organic gardening, antique roses, landscaping, and fruit and vegetable gardening. They are readily available in your local nursery or bookstore.
- Magazines written by Texans for Texans, such as *The Texas Gardener, Neil Sperry's Gardens,* and *Homegrown,* provide timely articles and gardening ideas.
- Garden calendars abound. Texas Master Gardener groups across the state have focused on producing gardening calendars to help educate the public. Contact your local county extension office for more information.
- For the young, and those who want to teach youth, the Junior Master Gardener program has a variety of curricula and books. Check out jmgkids.us for more information.

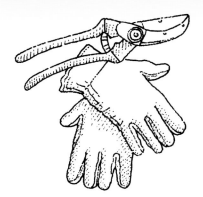

Equipment and Tools

• Lawn equipment, such as a self-propelled, walk-behind mower or riding mower, makes the task of lawn care easier and may significantly increase lawn quality.

• Gloves—you can never have enough pairs. Splurge and buy your gardener, yardener, or child a nice pair of gloves. Whether leather (cowhide, deer, or pig) or cloth and rubber combos, gloves will reduce the wear and tear on your loved one's hands.

• Pruning tools vary considerably in price, but so does quality. Gift giving provides a chance to upgrade the quality. If you want to buy the best hand pruning shears, choose Felco No. 2. They will cost over $45 but will last a lifetime. Loppers, pole pruners, hedge clippers, and folding pruning saws are all available and bring the machismo out in most any human being. (Just make sure that the gift receiver reads February's essay "Pruning School" before turning him or her loose in the landscape!)

• Planting tools, from an ergonomically designed hand shovel to a stainless-steel shovel to a hand "trake" (combo of a hand trowel and rake), can become much loved by gardeners and yardeners. Child-size planting tools, including shovels, rakes, and hoes, may provide ownership and motivation for the young gardener-to-be. Few family photos create more emotion and pride than a parent and child working side by side in the garden.

Accessories

• Virtually anything can accessorize a garden, from pottery to statuary to wind chimes to bird feeders and baths to fountains and water gardens to nostalgic signs and all-weather family heirlooms and ornaments.

• This is a chance to infuse a special theme, twist, or whimsy into a garden.

• Your gift receiver may not buy it for himself or herself, but you can. (Bet the recipient doesn't take it back.)

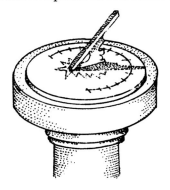

Plants

- Although difficult to wrap, plants are a great gift. They can commemorate the holiday and the individual.
- Shade trees or living Christmas trees are especially good gifts. They are more costly than many gifts but provide a lifetime of enjoyment.
- Fruit trees are welcomed by many gardeners, especially citrus. Refer to the January essay "Growing Fruits and Nuts" for a list based on difficulty of growing. Don't give a peach tree to a novice; a better choice is a pear.
- For Kwanzaa gift receivers, a green plant gift traditionally symbolizes the "oneness" between Africans and Nature.
- For the Hanukkah gift receiver, choose flowering plants or cut flowers of deep blue, silver, and white, colors that symbolize the holiday.

Garden Tours

- Perhaps in the "Neiman Marcus catalogue" class, travel tours focusing on the fine gardens of the world are inspiring, relaxing, and educational. Many tour companies specialize in gathering up gardeners and carting them across the state or around the globe in search of fine gardens and events. Simply search the Internet for garden tours, and always check references.

Gift Cards

- If none of the above gifts will do and you have drawn a blank, gift cards have made it to local nurseries and garden centers. This is one gift that one-size-fits-all.

Design a Low-Maintenance Landscape

Most homeowners are not gardeners but are "yardeners," a term coined by Jeff Ball to describe folks that have a yard and have to take care of it. Yardeners don't necessarily like yard work but know that it must be done to maintain a socially acceptable landscape. Most gardeners like to putter in the yard, but few want to be a slave to the landscape and spend endless amounts of time and money doing so.

For gardeners and yardeners, landscape maintenance can be a major chore. Take a fresh, year-end look at your landscape, focusing on reducing maintenance. Design a new or renovated landscape that requires less maintenance

Reduce landscape maintenance by expanding shrub plantings that contain properly prepared soil; adapted, attractive plants; dollar- and water-saving drip irrigation; mowing strips to reduce trimming time; and high-impact, low-tech mulch.

by incorporating any or all of the following guidelines:

- Keep the design simple—avoid the arboretum approach to landscaping: one of this and one of that.
- Have small lawn areas—lawns require the most irrigation in the

landscape and the most frequent care. If you reduce the lawn, you will reduce maintenance.

- Incorporate areas of ground-covers and/or natural pine straw, bark chips, and other mulches to reduce lawn areas.
- Pave heavily traveled areas—pavement can be concrete, concrete pavers, or gravel, rock, or wood chips with steel edging to keep them in place.
- Plant trees inside landscape plantings if at all possible to eliminate having to mow around them in the lawn.
- Construct concrete or brick mowing strips as borders for landscape planting—it is easier and faster to edge with a steel blade than maintain borders with a flexible-line trimmer.
- Utilize raised beds for plantings to increase ease of soil preparation and planting and to reduce weed infestation.

- Install an irrigation system that combines spray heads for the lawn and drip irrigation in the planting beds and gardens.
- Incorporate larger permanent shrub plantings and smaller, well-placed flower beds filled with annuals and perennials for visual impact and beauty.
- Select well-adapted, Texas-tough plants—trees, shrubs, vines, ground-covers, perennials, and annuals. Native plants to your area are particularly helpful in reducing maintenance.
- Use mulches in landscape plantings for water conservation and weed control. Place mulches around trunks of trees, or groups of trees, in the lawn to make mowing easier.
- Use herbicides, insecticides, and fungicides only if warranted. Always use them with caution, and follow label directions.

Shrubs for all Seasons

Texas mountain laurel (Sophora secundiflora)

All too often, shrubs are not thought of in terms of function or beauty but simply as obligatory plants or groupings of plants to be placed in front of a home or structure. Shrubs have become the nondescript green "meatballs" and "meatloaves" of the landscape. Shrubs have become invisible.

Shrubs should serve as the backbone or foundation of the home landscape. Within the outdoor living area of the home, trees provide the upright framework and canopy; lawns, decks, and patios provide flooring; and annual and perennial flowers provide the icing. Shrubs are workhorses serving multiple functions:

- Backdrops for other plants and structures (e.g., statuary, birdbath)
- Screens for deflecting or directing the wind
- Screens to mask an unattractive view
- Walls to separate outdoor rooms or spaces
- Design elements for scale and unity
- Beauty through season-long color from flowers and/or foliage
- Beauty through contrasting foliage texture (very important)

Through intense efforts of the nursery industry and universities, shrubs have undergone significant changes in recent years. For example, large shrub species now have dwarf forms that are more in scale with one-story homes and smaller landscapes. Native species have been identified and grown in containers and are now available for purchase and use in the home landscape. These natives are often much more adapted to the Texas climate than exotic species. There are more shrub choices today than ever before.

Choose and plant shrubs for your landscape with a purpose. Certainly don't opt out of this decision process and by default produce a "WOS" landscape plant (i.e., "what's on sale").

Choose shrubs based on their light requirements. Some shrubs can survive in surprisingly low-light situations, and some must have full sun (refer to the October essay "Do You Need Some Shady Characters for the Landscape?").

Choose shrubs based on their mature size. A wax myrtle in a gallon container looks so cute but will soon grow into a 10-foot by 10-foot monster. If you plant the wrong-size shrub in a small space, you will be relegated to pruning on a regular basis to keep the shrub in bounds.

When planting the shrubs, space them far enough apart to allow them to reach a mature width and overlap just a bit. This provides a more natural look and may totally eliminate the need for pruning. (*Note:* If your goal is to produce a formal landscape with clipped hedges and plants, then tighten up the spacing between plants considerably.)

For other unique characteristics of a shrub (e.g., winter hardiness, heat tolerance), refer to the plant's tag or check with nursery professionals, extension agents, and Master Gardeners.

Planting shrub species in attractive combinations is an art. Two guidelines for combining shrubs are grouping them by contrasting foliage textures (e.g., boxwood and cast-iron plant) or by contrasting foliage colors (e.g., dark green Burford holly and reddish nandina). Beyond these, choosing is based on what appeals to you. Look around your neighborhood and community for shrub combinations you like, or head to the nursery and start

Add texture to your landscape through foliage— fine-textured boxwood contrasting with bold-textured cast-iron plant, with the added bonus of light green leaves against dark green.

grouping shrubs together and see what you think.

Shrubs can also be chosen to accentuate the shape of a bed (e.g., informal curving beds or formal rectilinear beds). In addition, shrubs can enhance or accent contours and changing levels in a landscape.

Finally, choose a limited number of shrub species for your landscape. In the front landscape five or six shrub species should be adequate; in the backyard this number can double. Don't be overzealous and choose dozens of species, or you will be employing the "arboretum approach" to landscaping, one of this and one of that. Granted, you will achieve variety in the landscape, but absolutely no unity.

Select Shrubs for Texas Landscapes

(*Note:* This "select" list includes over 50 species of woody ornamental shrubs and shrublike plants that have significant value to the landscape, are available in the nursery trade, are dependable and relatively easy to grow, and are not riddled with pest problems. For example, you will not find ligustrum [because it is boring] and golden euonymus [because it is a "hotel for insects and disease"]. The list is not intended to be all inclusive.)

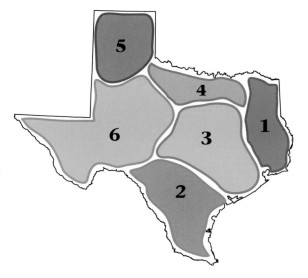

AREA OF ADAPTATION KEY

Region 1—East Texas (Beaumont, Houston, Nacogdoches, Texarkana, Tyler)

Region 2—South Texas (Brownsville, Corpus Christi, Del Rio, Laredo)

Region 3—Central Texas (Austin, College Station, San Antonio, Waco)

Region 4—North-Central Texas (Dallas, Denton, Fort Worth, Wichita Falls)

Region 5—Panhandle (Amarillo)

Region 6—West Texas (Abilene, El Paso, Lubbock, Midland, Odessa, San Angelo)

Note—Plants with number 7 are adaptable to most areas of Texas.

Note: The "Area of Adaptation Key" was developed by William C. Welch (extension landscape horticulturist) and me for an Extension publication, "Landscape Water Conservation . . . Xeriscape," which can be found on aggiehorticulture.tamu.edu.

SELECT SHRUBS FOR TEXAS LANDSCAPES

COMMON NAME (Scientific name)	MATURE SIZE (height and width in feet)	AREA OF ADAP-TATION	SUN EXPOSURE	NOTES
Dwarf shrubs (1–3 feet tall)				
Aspidistra/cast-iron plant (Aspidistra elatior)	2–3 by 1–2	7	partial shade to shade	dark green, bold-textured, donkey ear–shaped foliage; use as contrast to fine-textured shrubs (e.g., boxwood)
Dwarf yaupon holly (Ilex vomitoria nana) ⭐	3 by 3	7	sun to partial shade	dwarf form of native yaupon; fine-textured evergreen foliage; rarely sets fruit or berries; more adapted than boxwood
Holly fern (Cyrtomium falcatum)	2–3 by 3–4	7	partial shade to shade	bold-textured fern; year-round glossy green foliage; suffers some foliage damage during hard freezes; use as contrast to fine-textured plants and as groundcover
Liriope, giant (Liriope gigantea)	2–3 by 2–3	7	sun to shade	large form of liriope with fine-textured, straplike leaves; use in masses or as large groundcover
Nandina (Nandina spp.) ✿	1 by 1 to 5 by 3	7	sun to shade	varieties range from tall standard to compact to many new dwarfs; reddish, medium-textured, evergreen foliage; red berries in fall on standard and compact forms
Pittosporum, dwarf (Pittosporum tobira wheeleri)	3 by 3	southern part of 1, 2, 3	sun to shade	small, rounded evergreen of medium texture; use in masses of three to five; cold hardiness a concern
Red yucca (Hesperaloe parvifolia)	2 by 2	7	sun	upright, stiff foliage; striking red flowers on 4–5-foot-tall spikes; use in masses and for texture contrast
Rosemary (Rosmarinus officinalis) ⭐ ✿	1 by 3 and 3 by 3	1, 2, 3, 4, 6	sun to partial shade	prostrate/trailing form and upright form; fragrant herb with bluish green foliage; blue flowers; extremely heat tolerant; prostrate form much less cold tolerant
Small shrubs (3–5 feet tall)				
Abelia (Abelia grandiflora) ✿	3 by 3 and 5 by 5	7	sun to shade	dwarf and standard forms; bronze, fine-textured, evergreen foliage; dainty, bell-shaped white to pink flowers

Azalea (*Rhododendron* sp. and hybrids) ✿	3–6 by 3–6	1	partial shade	wonderful group of spring-flowering shrubs; adapted to neutral to acidic soils of East Texas; consult local experts for varieties suited to your area
Barberry, Japanese (*Berberis thunbergii*)	3–4 by 3–4	1, 3, 4, 5, 6	sun	unique purple-red, fine-textured, evergreen foliage; drought tolerant; needs well-drained soil; a few adapted varieties for Texas
Bridal wreath, spirea (*Spirea* spp.) ✿	4–5 by 4–5	7	sun to shade	sprawling; fernlike, fine-textured foliage; white spring blooms; many species and varieties; check with experts
Burford holly (*Ilex cornuta burfordii*)	5 by 4 and 8 by 6	7	sun to shade	dwarf and standard forms; glossy, medium-textured, evergreen foliage; use as hedge, backdrop, or wall/screen; needlepoint holly (a variety of *I. cornuta*) can be substituted for Burford holly
Dwarf Chinese holly (*Ilex cornuta rotunda*)	5 by 5	7	sun to shade	glossy, medium-textured, evergreen foliage; use as hedge, backdrop, or short wall/screen
Dwarf palmetto (*Sabal minor*) ★	5 by 5	1, 2, 3, 4, 6	sun to shade	bushy, trunkless native palm; extremely bold foliage; refer to July essay "Go Tropical!" for more shrublike palms
Flowering quince (*Chaenomeles japonica*) ✿	5 by 5	7	sun to partial shade	deciduous, medium-textured shrub; early spring blooms (red, pink, white or orange)
Grayleaf cotoneaster (*Cotoneaster glaucophylla*)	3–4 by 4–5	1, 3, 4, 5, 6	sun to partial shade	spreading evergreen shrub; fine-textured, dusty gray foliage; drought tolerant; contrasts in both foliage texture and color
Hydrangea (*Hydrangea* spp. and hybrids) ✿	3–6 by 3–6	1	sun to shade	wonderful group of summer-flowering shrubs; wide variety of foliage and flower types; adapted to neutral to acidic soils of East Texas; consult local experts for varieties suited to your area
Indian hawthorn (*Raphiolepis indica*) ✿	3–6 by 3–6	7	sun to partial shade	many varieties; ask for local recommendation; spring flowering; blue berries in fall; medium-textured, evergreen foliage; disease prone
Japanese aralia (*Fatsia japonica*)	3–6 by 3–6	1, 2, 3	partial sun to shade	bold-textured, palmlike foliage; use as specimen or contrast to fine-textured shrubs; check with local experts for cold tolerance in your area

★ signifies Texas native plants.

✿ signifies beautiful flowering plants.

Common name (Scientific name)	Mature size (height and width in feet)	Area of adaptation	Sun exposure	Notes
Japanese boxwood (*Buxus japonica*)	4 by 4	7	sun to shade	kelly green, medium-textured, evergreen foliage; best in acidic, well-drained soils; traditionally sheared for formal hedge
Primrose jasmine (*Jasminum mesnyi*) ❀	4–6 by 5–7	1, 2, 3	sun to partial shade	sprawling evergreen shrub; fine-textured foliage; lemon yellow blooms in late winter to spring
Rose, shrub/landscape (*Rosa* spp.) ❀	3–6 by 3–6	1, 2, 3, 4, 6	sun	wonderful group of blooming landscape roses available; refer to January essay "Roses in the Landscape"
Split-leaf philodendron (*Philodendron selloum*)	3–6 by 3–6	southern part of 1, 2, 3	partial shade to shade	bold-textured, tropical shrub; perennial along coastal areas; use for tropical effect and as contrast to fine-textured shrubs and ferns
Medium shrubs (6–9 feet tall)				
Agarita (*Mahonia trifoliate*) ★ ❀	5 by 4	2, 3, 4, 6	sun to partial shade	hollylike, blue-green, evergreen foliage; yellow spring flowers; red edible berries; drought tolerant
Althea (*Hibiscus syriacas*) ❀	9 by 6	7	sun to partial shade	old-fashioned, upright, summer-flowering shrub; deciduous, medium-textured foliage; many flower colors (white to purple) in single and double forms
Cenizo or Texas sage (*Leucophyllum* spp.) ★ ❀	5 by 4	2, 3, 4, 6	sun	new varieties available of this native shrub; dusty gray to green evergreen foliage; snapdragon-type bloom intermittent in summer
Chinese fringe flower (*Loropetalum chinensis rubrum*) ❀	5–10 by 5–10	1, 2, 3, 4, 6	partial shade to shade	green to purple-bronze, medium-textured foliage; spiderlike fuchsia blooms; spring blooming with sporadic blooming through summer; use as specimen, masses, or screen; best adapted to East Texas yet tolerant of other areas; new varieties available; check with local experts for varieties adapted to your area
Elaeagnus (*Elaeagnus pungens*)	6 by 6	7	sun to partial shade	medium-textured, gray-green, evergreen foliage

Forsythia 🌸 (*Forsythia intermedia spectabilis*)	5 by 5	1, 3, 4, 5, 6	sun to partial shade	sprawling shrub; early spring yellow flowers
'Fraser'/red tip photinia (*Photinia x fraseri*)	6–9 by 5–7	7	sun to shade	medium-textured, evergreen foliage; red new leaves; use as screen or hedge
Italian jasmine (*Jasminum humile*) 🌸	5–7 by 6–8	7	sun to partial shade	sprawling evergreen shrub; fine-textured foliage; fragrant yellow summer flowers
Juniper, 'Sea Green' (*Juniperus chinensis* 'Sea Green')	4–6 by 4–6	7	sun	fountainlike shrub with arching branches; fine-textured, mint green foliage; use as hedge or mass plantings; many other junipers available but most not as dependable
Pittosporum (*Pittosporum tobira*)	6–10 by 6–10	1, 2, 3, 4, 6	sun to shade	green, medium-textured foliage on large evergreen shrub; variegated green/white variety available
Pomegranate (*Punica granatum*) 🌸	3 by 2 and 5–8 by 4–6	1, 2, 3, 4, 6	sun	dwarf and large, upright varieties available; carnation-like orange blooms; orange to maroon edible fruit
Large shrubs (10–25 feet tall)				
American holly (*Ilex opaca*) ⭐	10–25 by 6–15	1	sun to partial shade	tree-form holly; glossy, evergreen foliage; red berries; best adapted to acidic, sandy soils of East Texas
Arizona cypress (*Cupressus arizonica*)	8–15 by 6–10	1, 3, 4, 5, 6	sun	conifer with juniper-like foliage; evergreen large shrub for screens and windbreaks
Cherry laurel (*Prunus caroliniana*) ⭐	6–10 by 4–6	1, 2, 3, 4, 6	sun to shade	glossy, medium-textured, evergreen foliage; treelike shrub; use as single specimen, cluster, or screen
Chinese photinia (*Photinia serrulata*) 🌸	15–20 by 15–20	1, 3, 4, 5, 6	sun to shade	massive, bold-textured evergreen; red spring foliage; white spring blooms; use as specimen or screen
Crape myrtle (*Lagerstroemia* spp. and hybrids) 🌸	2 by 2 to 25 by 25	7	sun	dwarf shrub to multitrunked, huge shrub; summer blooming; many varieties; refer to August essay "Crape Myrtles for Texas"
Lilac (*Syringa vulgaris*) 🌸	10–15 by 10–15	5	sun to partial shade	large, deciduous, blooming shrub; best adapted to the Panhandle
'Nellie R. Stevens' holly (*Ilex aquifolium* x *I. cornuta*)	20–30 by 10–12	7	sun to partial shade	large, upright, evergreen; glossy, medium-textured foliage; red berries; use as specimen or screen

⭐ signifies Texas native plants.

🌸 signifies beautiful flowering plants.

Common name (Scientific name)	Mature size (height and width in feet)	Area of adaptation	Sun exposure	Notes
Oleander (*Nerium oleander*) ✿	4 by 4 and 6–10 by 6–10	1, 2, 3, 4, 6	sun	dwarf and standard forms; evergreen foliage; vibrant summer blooming; many varieties available; check with local experts; use as hedge or screen
Possumhaw holly (*Ilex decidua*) ★	8–12 by 8–12	1, 2, 3, 4	sun to partial shade	similar to yaupon holly yet deciduous; red to orange berries; use as specimen or grouping
Russian olive (*Elaeagnus angustifolia*)	10–15 by 10–15	4, 5, 6	sun to partial shade	true olive; gray, fine-textured, evergreen foliage; use as windbreak or hedge
Texas mountain laurel (*Sophora secundiflora*) ★ ✿	10–15 by 10–15	2, 3, 6	sun to shade	multitrunked, treelike, evergreen shrub; fragrant purple spring flowers; use as specimen or screen
Texas persimmon (*Diospyros texana*) ★	10–15 by 10–15	2, 3, 6	sun	large shrub to small tree; deciduous foliage; light gray trunk; female and male plants; fruit edible by wildlife
Vitex (*Vitex agnus-castus*) ✿	10–15 by 10–15	7	sun	multitrunked large shrub; unique textured, palmate foliage; flowers blue or white; summer blooming; use as specimen or screen
Wax myrtle (*Myrica cerifera*) ★	10–15 by 10–15	7	sun to partial shade	olive green evergreen foliage; unique foliage aroma; use as specimen to screen; dwarf variety available
Yaupon holly (*Ilex vomitoria*) ★	10–15 by 10–15	7	sun to shade	large, upright, evergreen, fine-textured foliage; red to orange berries; great plant for wildlife

★ signifies Texas native plants.

✿ signifies beautiful flowering plants.

Top 10 New Year's Resolutions for Gardeners and Yardeners

10. I will use a pesticide only when absolutely necessary, and if I do, I will use the least toxic one. (Reference: May essays "Managing Plant Problems" and "Pesticide Safety")

9. I will continue to wage war on fire ants by using the Texas two-step method, including baits and mound treatments; and if warranted, I will use one-time-application broadcast products. (Reference: April essay "Fire Ant Management")

8. I will water the lawn only when it needs it, not by the calendar or time clock, and certainly not in the middle of the day. (Reference: March essay "When to Water, and How Long?")

7. I will not walk out of a nursery with a shrub, flowering plant, or vegetable plant purchase without buying organic matter to prepare the soil; I understand that no soil preparation is needed for tree planting. (Reference: January essay "Soils 101 for the Garden")

6. I will add one new "feature" to my garden this year, such as a new perennial flower bed, a theme garden, a bench, a statue, or an arbor. (Reference: September essay "Gardening with Perennial Flowers" and October essay "Landscape Design: Concepts, Guidelines, and Fun Ideas")

5. I will care for urban wildlife by putting up a bird feeder or planting a butterfly-friendly plant. (Reference: June essay "Attracting Birds to the Garden" and July essay "Butterfly Gardening Made Simple")

4. I will mulch all flower and shrub beds and the vegetable garden to conserve water, prevent weeds and diseases, and moderate soil temperatures. (Reference: February essay "Mulch—Low Tech, High Impact")

3. I will make my landscape edible by planting a vegetable garden or, at minimum, planting at least one vegetable or herb crop in a flower or shrub bed, such as basil, bell pepper, broccoli, cherry tomato, green bean, leaf lettuce, Mexican oregano, mint, and onion. (Reference: March essay "Vegetable Gardening Is for Everyone" and April essay "Herb-Growing Hints for Texas")

2. I will not commit "crape murder" by overpruning crape myrtles (or any other shrub or tree). (Reference: August essay "Crape Myrtles for Texas")

1. I will plant a high-quality tree for future generations. (Reference: August essay "Looking for Shade? Think Texas Trees" and September essay "Tree Planting Made Easy")

Timely Tips

Flowers & Pretty Plants

- Cool-season annuals planted in fall may not look great right now, but be patient. Most likely their root systems are still expanding and ready for brighter days to spring forth with new growth and flowers. Water at least once this month in the absence of rain.

- Refrain from pruning freeze-damaged stems of perennial flowers. They will provide some insulation for the plant through the rest of the winter. In addition, pruning now is a guessing game to determine what is dead or alive or what will be killed with future freezes.

- Spring-flowering bulbs should be planted this month, since soil temperatures have cooled. Don't plant the bulbs too deep. Texans don't have to worry about frozen soil (frozen soil explains why bulbs are planted deep in the North).

Garden Design

- Consider giving the gift of a landscape design to your loved one (or to yourself). This is not an inexpensive gift, but it is as valuable as the blueprints were to the home in which you live. A more frugal option is to purchase one of the many home landscaping books available. Look specifically for ones written for Texas or the South and Southwest.

Soil & Mulch

- Purchase the organic mulch that looks good to you and fits your pocketbook. There are dozens of different kinds of organic mulch available for purchase, from cocoa bean hulls to cypress bark to pine bark to recycled paper. Research shows no significant difference in any mulch when comparing prevention of soil moisture evaporation or moderation of soil temperatures.

- Purchase topsoil carefully. Nutgrass (nut sedge) seems to come in most dumptruck loads of topsoil. Call a couple of landscape contractors in your area, and ask where they buy their topsoil and soil mixes. Finally, inspect the load for weeds and nutgrass before it is dumped at your home.

Water

- Consider having a state-of-the-art irrigation system installed as a gift to yourself or your loved one who is the hardworking gardener or yardener. In recent years, system advancements have been considerable. Incorporate drip irrigation in the system for all the planting beds and gardens. Turn to licensed irrigators for help. You will get good value because they are much less busy now than during the spring and summer.

- Water the entire landscape at least once in December in the absence of significant rain to prevent freeze damage and desiccation or death of leaves and twigs.

Plant Care

- High-quality pruning equipment is a wonderful gift for gardeners and yardeners. Felco No. 2 hand shears are considered top of the line.
- If a hard, prolonged freeze (24 hours or more) is predicted, protect freeze-sensitive plants by covering them with cardboard boxes or blankets. Supplemental heat from a utility light or Christmas lights may also be needed. If the plants are growing in containers, simply move them indoors or, at minimum, into the garage.

Trees, Shrubs & Vines

- Purchase a living Christmas tree this year, or buy a tree as a gift. This is a special gift that will be enjoyed for decades. Refer to this month's essay "Living Christmas Trees," the August essay "Looking for Shade? Think Texas Trees," and the September essay "Tree Planting Made Easy" for guidance.
- Bare-root and container-grown roses will hit the markets this month. Consider incorporating roses in your garden. Old-fashioned roses and many new modern hybrid varieties are much less labor intensive. Refer to the January essay "Roses in the Landscape" for recommended varieties and care.

Lawns

- Mow winter weeds to keep them in check. Mow cool-season turfgrass lawns regularly. They love the cold weather. Mowing in the winter also keeps your mower from sitting idle too long.
- If your mower needs a tune-up or repair, take it now to the local small-engine repair shop. Business is slow compared to what it will be in the upcoming months.

Vegetables, Herbs & Fruits

- Water and fertilize actively growing vegetables.
- Harvest mature crops regularly to avoid freeze damage.
- In areas of the vegetable and herb gardens that are void of plants, pull winter weeds and/or plant a cover crop, such as Elbon ryegrass. Cover crops reduce weed establishment and can be tilled into the soil in February to improve soils.
- Consider giving vegetable gardeners holiday gifts, such as a drip irrigation system or a brand new shovel, pitchfork, or hoe. May not sound exciting for the nongardener, but most gardeners will be thrilled.
- Consider planting a fruit tree, vine, or pecan tree after the new year. Read the January essay "Growing Fruits and Nuts" before entering this more intense form of gardening.
- Fresh Texas-grown grapefruit are still available in the markets. Gift boxes of "No. 1 Grade" grapefruit make a great treat and can be shipped from the Rio Grande Valley to anywhere in the world. Search the Internet for sources.

Houseplants

- Check your houseplants to make sure they have adjusted to indoor conditions. If they are dropping foliage, move them to brighter light. Remember to pick off any yellow leaves. They are not going to turn green again and are not doing the plants any good.
- Use your index finger to test soil moisture on a weekly basis. Cool to the touch means adequate moisture; warm and dry to the touch mean water is needed.
- When you water, water thoroughly and let excess water drain freely from the container into the sink or bathtub. This will help reduce the salt buildup in the soil from using tap water and fertilizing.

Butterflies, Birds & Squirrels

- Give the backyard wildlife a gift this season: bird feeders of every size and shape are available; birdbaths can be functional and beautiful in the garden; and a small butterfly garden can be planted to welcome these beautiful creatures to your landscape.
- Remember to provide water for the birds and squirrels during winter, especially if you want them to stick around next season.

Notes:

Acknowledgments

I am thankful to have had great mentors (past and present) who assisted in my never-ending search for gardening answers. My Texas A&M University colleagues have graciously contributed to my knowledge and to this book. Throughout the almanac, many of these mentors and colleagues are gratefully credited.

This book would not have been possible without the opportunity provided by Charles Backus, Director of the Texas A&M University Press; the tireless efforts, guidance, and support given by Shannon Davies, Louise Lindsey Merrick Editor for the Natural Environment, the Texas A&M University Press; the fabulous artwork created by Aletha St. Romain; the beyond-the-norm book design created by Mary Ann Jacob; the patience and attention to details by project editor Jennifer Ann Hobson, and the marketing and distribution expertise of gifted professionals at the Texas A&M University Press. To each, I am indebted, humbled, and appreciative of all you have and will contribute to this project.

Finally, to my family, thank you Laura, Katherine, John, Tyler, and Elena for your constant interest, patience, and encouragement during this endeavor.

Resources

As a gardener or yardener, you will find this book to be a dependable gardening reference. If the answer to your question is not here, then there are a few other gardening resources you can consult.

The Texas A&M University System has county extension offices in all but a couple of the 254 counties in the state. County extension agents are an invaluable source for local gardening information and are a telephone call away. Look in the telephone book under your county government listings, or call the county courthouse for the phone number of the county extension office.

In over 115 counties, extension offices coordinate, train, and certify Texas Master Gardeners. This corps of over 5,000 volunteer educators multiplies the efforts of extension to meet the needs of the gardening public. Master Gardeners answer telephone inquiries, make gar-

den presentations, construct beautiful demonstration gardens, provide gardening education to youth, and much, much more. I am privileged to work with Master Gardeners throughout the state and to assist in managing this valuable source of gardening expertise. Check with your local county extension office to access Master Gardeners and find out how to get involved with the program.

The Internet is full of gardening information, but take care to learn about who is generating the information—focus on university Web sites. Aggiehorticulture. tamu.edu is the largest horticultural Web site in the world. Millions of people each year access this site for gardening information. Pull up this Web site, and plow into the information; you may never get out.

In addition, gardening information can be obtained from botanical gardens, arboreta, and nature centers throughout Texas. Horticultural and botanical expertise also resides with faculties at Sam Houston State University, Stephen F. Austin University, Tarleton State University, Texas State University, Texas Tech University, University of Texas, and other campuses of the Texas A&M University System, plus a dozen junior and community colleges and dozens of high school horticulture programs.

Finally, your local nursery is a great around-the-corner source for gardening information. The Texas Nursery and Landscape Association certifies Texas Certified Nursery Professionals and Certified Landscape Professionals. If you have a plant to be identified or a plant with a problem and want to talk to an expert face-to-face, these certified professionals are among the most knowledgeable and readily available in the state.

Index